THE NEW
AMERICAN
COMMENTARY

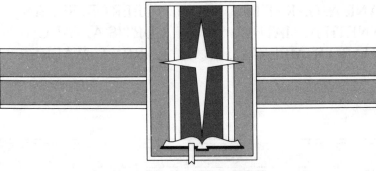

An Exegetical and Theological
Exposition of Holy Scripture

THE NEW AMERICAN COMMENTARY

Volume
34

1, 2 TIMOTHY
TITUS

Thomas D. Lea
Hayne P. Griffin, Jr.

BROADMAN PRESS
NASHVILLE, TENNESSEE

Unless indicated otherwise, Scripture quotations are from the Holy Bible, *New International Version* (NIV), copyright © 1973, 1978, 1984 by International Bible Society. Scripture quotations marked GNB are from the *Good News Bible*, the Bible in Today's English Version. Old Testament: Copyright © American Bible Society 1976; New Testament: Copyright © American Bible Society 1966, 1971, 1976. Used by permission. Scripture quotations marked NASB are from the *New American Standard Bible*. © The Lockman Foundation, 1960, 1962, 1963, 1968, 1971, 1972, 1973, 1975, 1977. Used by permission. Scripture quotations marked RSV are from the *Revised Standard Version of the Bible*, copyrighted 1946, 1952, © 1971, 1973. Scripture quotations marked NEB are from *The New English Bible*. Copyright © The Delegates of Oxford University Press and the Syndics of Cambridge University Press, 1961, 1970. Used by permission. Scripture quotations marked Phillips are reprinted with permission of Macmillan Publishing Co., Inc. from J. B. Phillips: *The New Testament in Modern English*, Revised Edition. © J. B. Phillips 1958, 1960, 1972. Scripture quotations marked Williams are from the *Williams New Testament, The New Testament in the Language of the People*, by Charles B. Williams. Copyright © 1937, 1966, 1986 by Holman Bible Publishers. Used by permission. Scripture quotations marked MLB are from *The Modern Language Bible, The New Berkeley Version*. Copyright 1945, 1959, © 1969 by Zondervan Publishing House. Used by permission. Quotations marked TCNT are from *The Twentieth Century New Testament*, copyright © 1904 Fleming H. Revell Co. Quotations marked Goodspeed are from *THE BIBLE, American Translation*, copyright © 1931 The University of Chicago Press. Quotations marked Amplified are from *THE AMPLIFIED BIBLE*, Old Testament copyright © 1965, 1987, by the Zondervan Corporation. *The Amplified New Testament* copyright © 1958, 1987 by The Lockman Foundation. Used by permission.

Library of Congress Cataloging-in-Publication Data

Lea, Thomas D.
  1, 2 Timothy, Titus / Thomas D. Lea, Hayne P. Griffin, Jr.
    p. cm. — (The New American commentary ; v. 34)
  Includes indexes.
  ISBN 0-8054-0134-2
  1. Bible. N.T. Pastoral Epistles—Commentaries. I. Griffin, Hayne P., Jr. 1947–
II. Title. III. Title: One, two Timothy, Titus. IV. Series.
BS2735.3.L39 1992
227'.8307—dc20

To *Beverly* and *Virginia*

with gratitude
for their love, support, and
encouragement

Editors' Preface

God's Word does not change. God's world, however, changes in every generation. These changes, in addition to new findings by scholars and a new variety of challenges to the gospel message, call for the church in each generation to interpret and apply God's Word for God's people. Thus, THE NEW AMERICAN COMMENTARY is introduced to bridge the twentieth and twenty-first centuries. This new series has been designed primarily to enable pastors, teachers, and students to read the Bible with clarity and proclaim it with power.

In one sense THE NEW AMERICAN COMMENTARY is not new, for it represents the continuation of a heritage rich in biblical and theological exposition. The title of this forty-volume set points to the continuity of this series with an important commentary project published at the end of the nineteenth century called AN AMERICAN COMMENTARY, edited by Alvah Hovey. The older series included, among other significant contributions, the outstanding volume on Matthew by John A. Broadus, from whom the publisher of the new series, Broadman Press, partly derives its name. The former series was authored and edited by scholars committed to the infallibility of Scripture, making it a solid foundation for the present project. In line with this heritage, all NAC authors affirm the divine inspiration, inerrancy, complete truthfulness, and full authority of the Bible. The perspective of the NAC is unapologetically confessional and rooted in the evangelical tradition.

Since a commentary is a fundamental tool for the expositor or teacher who seeks to interpret and apply Scripture in the church or classroom, the NAC focuses on communicating the theological structure and content of each biblical book. The writers seek to illuminate both the historical meaning and contemporary significance of Holy Scripture.

In its attempt to make a unique contribution to the Christian community, the NAC focuses on two concerns. First, the commentary emphasizes how each section of a book fits together so that the reader becomes aware of the theological unity of each book and of Scripture as a whole. The writers, however, remain aware of the Bible's inherently rich variety. Second, the NAC is produced with the conviction that the Bible primarily belongs to the church.

We believe that scholarship and the academy provide an indispensable foundation for biblical understanding and the service of Christ, but the editors and authors of this series have attempted to communicate the findings of their research in a manner that will build up the whole body of Christ. Thus, the commentary concentrates on theological exegesis, while providing practical, applicable exposition.

THE NEW AMERICAN COMMENTARY's theological focus enables the reader to see the parts as well as the whole of Scripture. The biblical books vary in content, context, literary type, and style. In addition to this rich variety, the editors and authors recognize that the doctrinal emphasis and use of the biblical books differs in various places, contexts, and cultures among God's people. These factors, as well as other concerns, have led the editors to give freedom to the writers to wrestle with the issues raised by the scholarly community surrounding each book and to determine the appropriate shape and length of the introductory materials. Moreover, each writer has developed the structure of the commentary in a way best suited for expounding the basic structure and the meaning of the biblical books for our day. Generally, discussions relating to contemporary scholarship and technical points of grammar and syntax appear in the footnotes and not in the text of the commentary. This format allows pastors and interested laypersons, scholars and teachers, and serious college and seminary students to profit from the commentary at various levels. This approach has been employed because we believe that all Christians have the privilege and responsibility to read and seek to understand the Bible for themselves.

Consistent with the desire to produce a readable, up-to-date commentary, the editors selected the *New International Version* as the standard translation for the commentary series. The selection was made primarily because of the NIV's faithfulness to the original languages and its beautiful and readable style. The authors, however, have been given the liberty to differ at places from the NIV as they develop their own translations from the Greek and Hebrew texts.

The NAC reflects the vision and leadership of those who provide oversight for Broadman Press, who in 1987 called for a new commentary series that would evidence a commitment to the inerrancy of Scripture and a faithfulness to the classic Christian tradition. While the commentary adopts an "American" name, it should be noted some writers represent countries outside the United States, giving the commentary an international perspective. The diverse group of writers includes scholars, teachers, and administrators from almost twenty different colleges and seminaries, as well as pastors, missionaries, and a layperson.

The editors and writers hope that THE NEW AMERICAN COMMENTARY will be helpful and instructive for pastors and teachers, scholars and students, for men and women in the churches who study and teach God's Word in various settings. We trust that for editors, authors, and readers alike, the commentary will be used to build up the church, encourage obedience, and bring renewal to God's people. Above all, we pray that the NAC will bring glory and honor to our Lord, who has graciously redeemed us and faithfully revealed himself to us in his Holy Word.

SOLI DEO GLORIA
The Editors

Authors' Preface

Preface to 1, 2 Timothy

As a pastor and staff member in four different Baptist churches, I found the teaching and instructions of the Pastoral Epistles to be helpful, insightful, and pulsing with spiritual warmth. As a teacher at Southwestern Baptist Theological Seminary, I have been able to identify with the sound teaching and practical insight which Paul has provided in the Pastorals, and I have found that students respond warmly to its message. Many a pastor and church leader would find much wisdom in reflecting again on Paul's sound advice for dealing with both older and younger men and women (1 Tim 5:1-2). Paul's appreciation of divine grace shown to him as the "worst of sinners" (1 Tim 1:16) shows a gratitude to God which no Christian must ever leave behind. The appeal to "endure hardship . . . like a good soldier of Jesus Christ" (2 Tim 2:3) constantly reminds believers of the need for stamina and staying power in the Christian life.

This commentary is written primarily for the busy pastor, staff member, or Christian leader who wants to learn better Paul's message to Timothy. The text is deliberately written so as to flow easily without extensive discussion of detailed issues of exegesis, theology, or linguistic insights. Footnotes carry on more detailed discussions of the issues touched on in the text. An effort has been made to place each paragraph in its proper context.

A brief introductory section beginning each major section of commentary tries to locate the passage in the context of Paul's argument. A primary effort has been made to bring out the theological meaning of the text. Answers to questions such as Why? and So what? appear frequently in the text.

For rendering the text more understandable I am indebted to the translations collected by Curtis Vaughan in *The New Testament from 26 Translations*. I have made reference to most recent major commentaries on the Pastorals. Those who wish additional insight can consult these. Also, I have given reference to some classic commentaries, some now out of print. Those who have access to theological libraries may wish to consult these. Many periodicals are also referenced, and most of these will be found in theological libraries.

I have ended each major section with a brief discussion of summary and application. This is a free-flowing section intended to spur the reader to apply Paul's words in personal life and in the life of a local congregation.

Many individuals deserve an expression of gratitude for their assistance. I have read so many commentaries and consumed so many of their ideas that I may overlook all those writers whose thoughts contributed seeds to my insights into the text. To all the multiple writers, I owe a debt of gratitude. The administration of Southwestern Baptist Theological Seminary under President Russell Dilday and Theology Dean Bruce Corley made available to me both time and funds for the writing and typing of this text. Two faithful secretaries, Mrs. Carol Bratton and Mrs. Linda Daugherty, gave up office, home, and personal time to help complete the typing at different stages.

This commentary was written at various stages during the period 1989-91. In the summer of 1991, when I was putting finishing touches on the work, I had the privilege of serving as interim pastor of the Village Parkway Baptist Church in San Antonio, Texas. They have prayed for my writing as I have been among them, and I am appreciative of their faithful support and encouragement.

My wife, Beverly, has seen me at work over these many months and has listened supportively to my concerns and insights. I have appreciated her encouragement, prayers, and love. My children, Lisa, Marcie, and Cliff, have been away from home during most of the time of writing; but they have shown interest with questions such as, "Dad, how is it coming?"

My hope is that this commentary on God's Word might draw each reader to our Lord and his service. May many find help from their reading and study to "Preach the Word; be prepared in season and out of season; correct, rebuke and encourage—with great patience and careful instruction" (2 Tim 4:2).

Thomas D. Lea

Preface to Titus

When I was invited to write the commentary on Paul's Letter to Titus for *The New American Commentary*, I was concerned whether I could make a legitimate contribution to the series since I had not been engaged in academic biblical studies (as a student or teacher) for quite a few years. However, the editors expressed their strong desire to have a qualified layman contribute to a series which could be used by serious Bible students, whether in a college, seminary, or local church setting. Although Titus is a brief and relatively unknown letter among many longer and more familiar Pauline letters, I was impressed by its teaching, especially in light of some issues which are timeless with regard to the church and basic Christian doctrine. As a result, I committed myself to "sharpening up some old tools" and to accept what was for me a challenge and a unique opportunity. Convinced that foundational to any correct understanding of the Bible is *to know what it actually says*, I have made every effort to clearly set forth the meaning of the biblical text. Where the meaning of the text is ambiguous, I have attempted to present legitimate alternatives suggested by various scholars.

Writing this commentary has convinced me of two other things. First, I believe that all practical teaching with regard to the church and the Christian life is only valid when based upon a correct theological understanding of who God is and what he has done for us in the person of his Son, Jesus Christ. As I hope my commentary demonstrates, the practical exhortations to Titus and to the church on Crete are based on solid theological statements contained within this letter. Second, I am convinced that understanding and applying the theological truths set forth in the letter is much easier than understanding and applying certain practical exhortations contained in the letter. I found myself "wrestling with the text" much more often with regard to practical exhortations in order to discern their meaning and application to the church today.

For as long as I can remember, I have been exposed to biblical teaching. My parents, Preston and Elsie Griffin, were committed to raising their children in the love and nurture of the Lord and through word and deed have continually encouraged me to know the Lord, both from studying Scripture and through a personal relationship with him. I shall always cherish the memory of their prayers for me and with me during important decision-making times in my life. They have always encouraged and supported my pursuit of biblical studies. The value of such a Christian heritage to me is inexpressible.

I take special delight in thanking my wife, Virginia, for all of her support and encouragement while I have worked on this project. Being a serious Bible student and teacher herself, her comments, insights, and reflections on my work have proved very valuable to me. We have discussed every issue in Titus several times over! I knew when I married her that she would be a great wife and mother but had no idea that she would be such a wonderful theological editor! Thanks are also due to my children, Hayne III and Elizabeth, for their patience and restraint from disturbing Dad. Their periodic inquiry, "Are you finished yet?" continually encouraged me to complete the work.

Considering my theological interests and education, I am often asked why I am not a pastor or theological educator. The answer is quite simple: I have not experienced God's call to serve him in either of those ways. As a boy and young man, my grandmother often expressed to me how pleased she would be if God called me into the ministry. While writing this commentary, I have often reflected upon her desire, as well as the various ways in which my contribution on Titus may be used throughout Christ's church. In a real sense, this commentary is a part of God's calling in my life to minister to his church through expounding his Word. It is therefore with a great deal of personal satisfaction that I honor the memory of Stella Griffin with this work.

Finally, I want to express my appreciation to Michael Smith and David Dockery, both of whom served as General Editor for this commentary series. Their comments and encouragement, along with those of my good friend Robert Sloan, a Consulting Editor for the New Testament, have been most helpful.

Hayne P. Griffin, Jr.

Abbreviations

Bible Books

Gen	Isa	Luke
Exod	Jer	John
Lev	Lam	Acts
Num	Ezek	Rom
Deut	Dan	1, 2 Cor
Josh	Hos	Gal
Judg	Joel	Eph
Ruth	Amos	Phil
1, 2 Sam	Obad	Col
1, 2 Kgs	Jonah	1, 2 Thess
1, 2 Chr	Mic	1, 2 Tim
Ezra	Nah	Titus
Neh	Hab	Phlm
Esth	Zeph	Heb
Job	Hag	Jas
Ps (*pl.* Pss)	Zech	1, 2 Pet
Prov	Mal	1, 2, 3 John
Eccl	Matt	Jude
Song of Songs	Mark	Rev

Commonly Used Reference Works

AB   Anchor Bible
ANF   Ante-Nicene Fathers
BAGD   W. Bauer, W. F. Arndt, F. W. Gingrich, and F. Danker, *Greek-English Lexicon of the New Testament*
BI   *Biblical Illustrator*
Bib   *Biblica*
BibSac   *Bibliotheca Sacra*

BJRL	*Bulletin of the John Rylands University Library*
BT	*The Bible Translator*
CBQ	*Catholic Biblical Quarterly*
CTR	*Criswell Theological Review*
EBC	Expositor's Bible Commentary
EGT	*Expositor's Greek Testament*
EncSB	*Encyclopedia of Southern Baptists* (1958)
EvQ	*Evangelical Quarterly*
EvBC	Everyman's Bible Commentary
ExpTim	*Expository Times*
GAGNT	*A Grammatical Analysis of the Greek New Testament*, by M. Zerwick and M. Grosvenor
GNC	Good News Commentary
GT	*Greek Testament* (H. Alford)
HBD	*Holman Bible Dictionary*
Her	*Hermeneia*
IB	*The Interpreter's Bible*
ICC	The International Critical Commentary
ISBE	*The International Standard Bible Encyclopedia*, ed. G. W. Bromiley, 1982.
JBL	*Journal of Biblical Literature*
JETS	*Journal of the Evangelical Theological Society*
JTS	*Journal of Theological Studies*
MCNT	Meyer's Commentary on the New Testament
NAC	New American Commentary
NCB	New Century Bible Commentary, W. Hendricksen
NIDNTT	*New International Dictionary of New Testament Theology*
NPNF	Nicene and Post-Nicene Fathers
NTC	New Testament Commentary
NTI	*New Testament Introduction*, D. Guthrie
NTS	*New Testament Studies*
RevExp	*Review and Expositor*
SBT	Studies in Biblical Theology
SJT	*Scottish Journal of Theology*
SWJT	*Southwestern Journal of Theology*
TDNT	*Theological Dictionary of the New Testament*
TJ	*Trinity Journal*
TNCT	Tyndale New Testament Commentaries
TS	*Theological Studies*
TynBul	*Tyndale Bulletin*
WP	Word Pictures in the New Testament, by A. T. Robertson
ZNW	*Zeitschrift für die neutestamentliche Wissenschaft*
ZPEB	*Zondervan Pictorial Encyclopedia of the Bible*

Contents

1, 2 Timothy, Titus

INTRODUCTION

In 1726 Paul Anton of Halle designated the letters of Timothy and Titus as the Pastoral Epistles, and this title has gained acceptance so that no alternate is likely to displace it. Although their title has a relatively recent history, the Pastoral Epistles have a long history of being regarded as genuine Pauline literature.

Clement of Alexandria (ca. 155–ca. 220) referred to the Pastorals when he spoke of "what is falsely called knowledge" (1 Tim 6:20) and ascribed this passage to "the apostle."[1] A glance at a textual index to Clement's works will show that there are numerous references to and quotations from the Pastorals. Origen, disciple of Clement of Alexandria, used many passages from the Pastorals, particularly in his work *Against Celsus*. He ascribed 1 Tim 1:15 to Paul in the following reference: "Moreover, Paul, who himself also at a later time became an apostle of Jesus, says in his Epistle to Timothy, 'This is a faithful saying, that Jesus Christ came into the world to save sinners, of whom I am the chief.'"[2]

The early Christian historian Eusebius (ca. 265–ca. 339) knew that the church had attributed the Pastorals to Paul. He stated, "The epistles of Paul are fourteen, all well known and beyond doubt. It should not, however, be concealed, that some have set aside the Epistle to the Hebrews."[3]

In addition to these three early leaders, who attributed the Pastorals to Paul, other sources also refer to the existence of the Pastorals in various ways. Irenaeus spoke of the widespread circulation, authority, and Pauline authorship of the Pastorals. Justin Martyr, Polycarp, and Ignatius made allusions that must stem from the Pastorals.[4] The *Muratorian Canon*, a document presenting a list of New Testament books dating from A.D. 180–200, refers to the Pastorals as Pauline.[5] Such evidence of the early attestation of Pauline authorship of the Pastorals is impressive.

The Canon of Marcion (ca. 140) omitted the Pastorals.[6] Because of this some have assumed that the Pastorals were not extant and that Marcion excluded them because he did not know of them. Marcion tended to reject those New Testament documents that did not agree with his radical distinction between Christianity and Judaism. He omitted Matthew, Mark, and John and mutilated Luke. We could easily assume that Marcion's

---

[1]Clement of Alexandria, *Stromata*, ANF 2.11.

[2]Origen, *Against Celsus*, ANF 1.63.

[3]Eusebius, *Church History*, NPNF 3.3.

[4]The most impressive collection of external attestation to the existence and Pauline authorship of the Pastorals appears in J. H. Bernard, *The Pastoral Epistles* (1899; reprint, Grand Rapids: Baker, 1980), xiii-xxi.

[5]A copy of the Muratorian Canon appears in B. Metzger, *The Canon of the New Testament* (Oxford: University Press, 1987), 305-7.

[6]Tertullian, *Against Marcion*, ANF 5.21.

omission of the Pastorals was due to his dislike of their contents or to some reason other than their nonexistence.

Additional evidence that contributes to an attitude of uncertainty about the status of the Pastoral Epistles is their apparent absence from the Chester Beatty Papyri. These papyrus manuscripts of the New Testament were purchased in 1930–31 by Sir Chester Beatty of London and are housed in the Beatty Museum in a Dublin suburb. The codex of the Pauline Epistles ($\mathfrak{P}^{46}$) dates from the mid-third century and is not completely preserved. It originally contained in the following order: Romans, Hebrews, 1 and 2 Corinthians, Ephesians, Galatians, Philippians, Colossians, and 1 Thessalonians. The manuscript lacks portions of Romans and 1 Thessalonians, and all of 2 Thessalonians is missing. The Pastoral Epistles and Philemon are also missing, and many scholars feel that the original completed codex did not contain them. They base their opinion on calculations of the amount of space in the codex which the Pastorals would require if they had been included.

Two factors make this information less than satisfactory to use in evaluating evidence about the Pastorals. First, it is possible that the copyist of the codex wrote more minutely in the latter part of the codex and actually included the Pastorals. Second, the complete Chester Beatty Papyri may not provide a true indication of the condition of the New Testament canon in Egypt, the area of its origin, in the third century. The entire Chester Beatty collection numbers three codices which contain the Gospels and Acts, the previously mentioned Pauline Epistles, and the Revelation. The General Epistles from James through Jude are not included. If we use the Beatty Papyri as evidence against the existence of the Pastorals, we could also use them for evidence against the other omitted writings.[7]

There is no evidence of widespread uncertainty about the Pauline authorship of the Pastorals until the nineteenth century. In 1807 F. Schleiermacher[8] debated the Pauline authorship of 1 Timothy on the grounds of style and language. His questions began a school of critical study that focused on philological evidence in order to determine authorship. A few years after him J. G. Eichhorn rejected the Pauline authorship of all the Pastorals on the basis of their difference in religious language from other Pauline writings.

---

[7]D. Guthrie amplifies much of this discussion in NTI, 2nd ed. (London: Tyndale, 1963), 2:200-202. Also see J. D. Quinn, "$\mathfrak{P}^{46}$—The Pauline Canon?" *CBQ* 36 (1974): 379-85, who feels that $\mathfrak{P}^{46}$ omitted the Pastorals because it did not intend to list the Pauline letters written to individuals (1 and 2 Timothy, Titus, Philemon).

[8]An excellent discussion of the modern critical history of the problem of authorship of the Pastorals appears in W. G. Kümmel, *The New Testament: The History of the Investigation of Its Problems*, trans. S. M. Gilmour and H. C. Kee (Nashville: Abingdon, 1970), 84-85, 130-33.

In 1835 F. C. Baur rejected the Pauline authorship of the Pastorals due to the similarity of the heresy mentioned in the letters to second-century Gnosticism. Baur also felt that the developed ecclesiology of the Pastorals reflected a second-century date. He viewed the Pastorals as one of several New Testament writings that attempted to overcome the division between an alleged Pauline party in the early church and Jewish Christians, who would have been considerably more committed to Jewish ways and practices.

In 1889 H. J. Holtzmann built on the work of his predecessors and marshaled the most complete argument against Pauline authorship of the Pastorals that had been produced up to that time. Holtzmann raised five objections to Pauline authorship of the Pastorals. First, he was unable to relate the historical references in the Pastorals with the narrative of Acts. Thus he dated the writings after the lifetime of Paul. Second, he noted the style and vocabulary of the Pastorals and decided that they could not have come from Paul. Third, he found connections between the heresy which the Pastorals portrayed and second-century Gnosticism. This led him to demand a second-century date for the Pastorals. Fourth, he found the theology of the Pastorals different from that of the accepted Pauline Letters. Fifth, he was convinced that the church organization presented in the Pastorals came from beyond the first century. It could not have existed during Paul's lifetime. So well did Holtzmann articulate his position that supporters of Pauline authorship of the Pastorals must still answer his five objections in their defense of a Pauline origin.[9]

Defenders of Pauline authorship of the Pastorals did not retreat into hiding during this period. In Germany, T. Zahn defended Pauline authorship and insisted that the writing of the Pastorals occurred during Paul's lifetime. In Great Britain, J. B. Lightfoot articulated a position supporting Pauline authorship of the Pastorals which was influential in the English-speaking world. Lightfoot accepted the claim of the writings to be Pauline and recognized the importance of early attestation by church leaders of the existence of the Pastorals and their authorship by Paul. He also found many Pauline characteristics in the writings.[10]

In the twentieth century, attempts to resolve the question of Pauline authorship of the Pastorals have been many and varied. Two basic positions have been defended by scholars with an astounding display of arguments. Simply put, the basic viewpoints are:

---

[9]H. J. Holtzmann, *Die Pastoralbriefe, kritisch und exegetische Behandelt* (Leipzig: W. Englemann, 1880).

[10]See J. B. Lightfoot, "The Date of the Pastoral Epistles," *Biblical Essays* (London: Macmillan, 1893), 397-410.

1. The Pastorals were written by Paul himself or under his direction by an amanuensis/secretary.

2. The Pastorals are pseudonymous and may or may not contain some genuine Pauline fragments.

Twentieth-century scholars adhering to Pauline authorship or Pauline origin of the Pastorals include W. Lock (1924), O. Roller (1933), D. Guthrie (1957), J. N. D. Kelly (1963), J. Jeremias (1963), C. F. D. Moule (1965), C. Spicq (1969), B. Reicke (1976), W. Metzger (1976), and D. E. Hiebert (1978).

Twentieth-century scholars adhering to pseudonymity in some form include P. N. Harrison (1921), M. Dibelius and H. Conzelmann (1955), F. D. Gealy (1955), C. K. Barrett (1963), N. Brox (1969), A. Strobel (1969), J. H. Houlden (1976), S. G. Wilson (1979), A. T. Hanson (1982), and J. Quinn (1990).

1. Authorship of the Pastorals

Many contemporary interpreters feel that the name "Paul" in all three Epistles is a pseudonym. Most who advocate pseudonymity feel that an admirer of Paul penned the letters at a time after Paul's death and used the name of Paul in order to secure acceptance of his ideas.

Some maintain that the writings contain genuine Pauline fragments. A Pauline admirer, it is often alleged, added some comments to provide coherence and unity for the letters. Among the passages that have been represented as fragments are 1 Tim 1:13-15; 2 Tim 1:16-18; 3:10-11; 4:6-22; and Titus 3:13-15. The passages viewed as fragments contain short biographical extracts about Paul or personal information about Timothy. The chief advocate of this theory was P. N. Harrison, whose views on the subject underwent modification over a period of several decades.[11]

---

[11]Harrison originally set out his views in *The Problem of the Pastoral Epistles* (London: Oxford University Press, 1921). He revised his estimates of the fragments in "Important Hypotheses Reconsidered: The Authorship of the Pastoral Epistles," *ExpTim* 67 (1955): 77-81. He recognized as Pauline the contents of Titus 3:12-15; 2 Tim 4:9-15,20,21a,22b; and 2 Tim 1:16-18; 3:10-11; 4:1,2a,5b-8,16-19. His views were important for popularizing the "fragment hypothesis" in Great Britain and the English-speaking world, but they had little impact in Germany. Kümmel, for example, does not even give serious consideration to the idea in his *Introduction to the New Testament*, rev. ed., trans. H. C. Kee (Nashville: Abingdon, 1975), 366-87. Scott's view of the origin of the Pastorals is best seen in his statement: "Some brief writings of Paul, addressed, most likely, to Timothy and Titus, have fallen into the hands of a later teacher. They had no value in themselves, and were mere personal notes, such as Paul must frequently have written when arranging missionary tours with his assistants. Using these fragments as a nucleus, the later writer has composed the present Epistles, which he issues in the name of Paul, since they not only give effect to Paul's teaching, but contain at least some elements of Pauline material." See E. F. Scott, *The Pastoral Epistles*, MNTC, ed. J. Moffatt (London: Hodder and Stoughton, 1936), xxii-xxiii.

Interpreters today show less interest in a fragmentary hypothesis than was true in the past.[12]

The five arguments usually advanced in support of pseudonymity are the same as those of Holtzmann. These are (1) differences in vocabulary and style between the Pastorals and other Pauline writings; (2) the nature of the false teaching that Paul opposed; (3) the ecclesiastical structure apparent in the letters; (4) conflicting circumstances; and (5) theology.

(1) Different Vocabulary and Style

The Pastoral Epistles contain many words that are rare in the New Testament.[13] The technical term used for words that appear only once in the New Testament is *hapax legomena*. Such words as "slave traders" (1 Tim 1:10; *andrapodistai*) and "integrity" (Titus 2:7; *aphthoria*) are *hapax legomena*. In addition to these unique words there are others which are rare in the other ten Pauline writings but are key terms in the Pastorals. Among these are "godliness" (1 Tim 6:11; *eusebeia*) and "to worship God" (1 Tim

---

[12]Typical of this trend are the views of D. Cook, "The Pastoral Fragments Reconsidered," *JTS* n.s. 35 (1984): 120-31, who says that the argument about the authorship of the Pastorals is reduced to a dispute between two parties, those who maintain the authenticity of the letters and those who dispute it (131).

Hanson originally advocated a "fragment hypothesis" but abandoned it in his *New Century Bible Commentary*. He explains: "The great difficulty with it consists in explaining how such small fragments of Pauline material could have survived. . . . It looks as if the 'Fragments Hypothesis' was a last desperate attempt to retain some Pauline element in the Pastorals." See A. T. Hanson, *The Pastoral Epistles*, NCB (Grand Rapids: Eerdmans, 1982), 10-11.

[13]Guthrie underscores the importance of this issue in assessing Pauline authorship of the Pastorals by his statement: "It must here be stated that the majority of those who favor the non-Pauline authorship of the Epistles are swayed more by linguistic considerations than by any of the objections mentioned above." See NTI 2:209.

This issue was a primary emphasis of Holtzmann, who included twelve pages of statistics on linguistic and stylistic information in his extensive commentary. See Holtzmann, *Die Pastoralbriefe*, 84-95.

Kümmel follows in the footsteps of Holtzmann in noting carefully the significance of the issue. He makes three comments about the language and style of the Pastorals. First, he notes that the words and stylistic features Paul used in the Pastorals differ markedly from words he used in the other ten Pauline writings. Second, he notes the absence of many shorter words and particles such as ἄν, ἄρα, διό, ἔτι, πάλιν, σύν, ὥσπερ, and ὥστε. Third, he observes that Paul used different words in the Pastorals for the same practices he elsewhere described with other words. For example, in Col 3:22; 4:1 Paul used κύριος to describe a slave owner, but in the Pastorals he used δεσπότης to describe the owner (see 1 Tim 6:1; 2 Tim 2:21; and Titus 2:9). See Kümmel, *Introduction*, 372-73.

It is interesting to observe that J. B. Lightfoot acknowledged the different language and style in the Pastorals but accepted Pauline authorship of the Pastorals. He used the statistics to argue for a later date for the Pastorals, assuming that their variant linguistic and stylistic content suggest "that some considerable period must be interposed between them and the remaining Epistles of St Paul." See Lightfoot, "Date of the Pastoral Epistles," 403.

2:10; *theosebeia*). To compound the problem, many of Paul's most significant words are missing from the Pastorals or appear with different meanings. Such a term as "righteousness" (*dikaiosynē*) is presented in the Pastorals as a virtue to be sought (1 Tim 6:11; 2 Tim 2:22), not as a gift of right-standing with God. It is also startling to find that the word "son" (*huios*) does not appear in the Pastorals as a reference to Christ. There is no mention of the cross, a key theme in most Pauline writings.

Many lexical features of the Pastorals differ markedly from Paul's undisputed writings. P. N. Harrison has collected a group of 112 particles, pronouns, and prepositions that occur in the other Pauline Epistles but which are absent from the Pastorals.[14] The style is somewhat monotonous and formal, and there is an absence of vigor and vitality in the expression of ideas.[15]

The statistics of the linguistic distinctives of the Pastorals have been summarized by E. F. Harrison, a defender of Pauline authorship of the Pastorals: (1) The total vocabulary of the Pastorals is 902 words. (2) Of these words, 306 are not found in the other ten Pauline writings. (3) Of these 306 words, 175 do not appear anywhere in the New Testament outside the Pastorals; and 131 occur in the Pastorals and some other New Testament book, but not in any other Pauline Epistle.[16]

P. N. Harrison has made additional impressive collections of statistics concerning the linguistic peculiarities of the Pastorals. He attempted to show that the variety of linguistic usage is without parallel in Paul's other writings. He also has collected statistics to suggest that the language of the Pastorals is the speech of the second century A.D. He pointed out that many of the rare words found in the Pastorals were in use in the second century.[17]

In rebuttal to Harrison, J. N. D. Kelly has pointed out that almost all of the *hapax legomena* in the Pastorals appear in use by Greek writers prior to A.D. 50. Kelly also indicates that the proportion of *hapax legomena* appearing in second-century writings is approximately the same for both the Pastorals and an undoubted Pauline Epistle such as 1 Corinthians.[18]

---

[14]P. N. Harrison, *Problem of the Pastorals*, 36-37.

[15]Contrast the forcefulness of Gal 1:8-9 with the restraint in 1 Tim 2:1-3. N. Turner (*Style*, vol. 4, *A Grammar of New Testament Greek* by J. H. Moulton [Edinburgh: T & T Clark, 1976], 105), states: "We cannot say that the Greek Style is the most elegant in the NT, but it is the least Semitic, most secular, and least exciting. It is commonplace."

[16]E. F. Harrison, *Introduction to the New Testament* (Grand Rapids: Eerdmans, 1964), 337.

[17]P. N. Harrison, *Problem of the Pastoral Epistles*, 67-86.

[18]J. N. D. Kelly, *A Commentary on the Pastoral Epistles* (1963; reprint Grand Rapids: Baker, 1981), 24. Also see F. R. M. Hitchcock, "Tests for the Pastorals," *JTS* o.s. 30 (1928): 272-79. Hitchcock, a contemporary of Harrison, demonstrates Harrison's distortion of the data with regard to *hapax legomena* (276-79).

These facts suggest that P. N. Harrison's conclusions have likely outraced the evidence.

B. Metzger has indicated that the length of the Pastorals is too brief to serve as a source of accurate information about the writing habits of the author. He says: "It seems, therefore, that a discreet reticence should replace the almost unbounded confidence with which many scholars have used this method [word statistics] in attempting to solve the problem of the authorship of the Pastorals."[19]

It is possible to attribute the change in Pauline style in the Pastorals to three different causes. First, Paul's subject matter, age, and life experiences may have led him to use a different mood and manner of expression from that which he used in his other writings. D. Guthrie, a staunch defender of Pauline authorship of the Pastorals, has expressed it this way:

> Advocates of Pauline authorship must, in any case, be prepared to accept the fact that the Paul which the Pastorals present has undergone a change, but there seems to be no psychological reason for maintaining that the character of this change is incompatible with the man we know from the earlier Epistles.[20]

We would not expect a minister to use the same words on Mothers' Day and Easter, nor would we expect a younger pastor to use the same vocabulary as a more mature cleric.

Second, the needs of Paul's readers may have prompted his omission of certain terms and theological ideas which he used in other epistles. Kelly points out that the Pastorals deal with new subjects such as church

---

[19]B. Metzger, "A Reconsideration of Certain Arguments against the Pauline Authorship of the Pastoral Epistles," *ExpTim* 70 (1958): 94. Supporting Metzger's suggestion that the length of the Pastorals is too brief to sustain a certain decision about the author's identity is the comment by the statistician G. U. Yule. Speaking as an expert in statistics and not specifically responding to Metzger's comment, Yule would discourage making fixed pronouncements about the authorship of short books such as the Pastorals on the basis of linguistic distinctives. He says: "We judged that it was best, if fairly trustworthy results were wanted, not to take a sample of much less than some 2,000 occurrences of a noun. This would imply a sample of something like 10,000 words, more or less." See G. U. Yule, *The Statistical Study of Literary Vocabulary* (n.p.: Archon, 1968), 281. See also J. J. O'Rourke, "Some Considerations about Attempts at Statistical Analysis of the Pauline Corpus," *CBQ* 35 (1973): 483-90. He concludes: "The arguments based on style are simply incorrect or to put it bluntly they are invalid" (490).

[20]D. Guthrie, *The Pastoral Epistles and the Mind of Paul* (London: Tyndale, 1956), 16. Kelly also acknowledges the stylistic differences between the Pastorals and other Pauline writing, but he warns: "While difference of authorship is clearly one possible explanation of the stylistic divergences between two sets of writings, it is by no means the only one that is possible, and the critic is only warranted in concentrating exclusively on it if much of the other evidence converges in the same direction." See Kelly, 24-25.

organization and the qualities needed in a minister. Paul faced new challenges from heretical worship practices and propaganda.[21]

Third, Paul may have used an amanuensis or secretary in writing the Pastorals and could have given him the freedom to choose some of his own words. In Rom 16:22 Paul mentioned Tertius as the framer of the words of the Epistle. In several of his Letters (1 Cor 16:21; Gal 6:11; Col 4:18; 2 Thess 3:17) Paul added a statement that he was inserting a line in his own hand. Kelly points out that it is less likely that Paul personally dictated every word of his writings and more likely that he gave a trusted amanuensis a freer hand in the composition of a letter.[22] Specifically in the instance of 2 Timothy it is likely that Paul required some secretarial assistance. If Paul were a prisoner awaiting his death (2 Tim 4:6-8), it seems highly unlikely that he could have penned the writings without some help.[23]

All of these observations indicate that it is precarious and unnecessary to reject Pauline authorship based on the stylistic contrasts between the Pastorals and the other Pauline Epistles. Too many other cogent explanations for the differences lie close at hand.

(2) The Problem of Heresy

By the second century Christianity was locked in a battle with a heretical movement known as Gnosticism. This heresy denied the resurrection of Christ, alternated ethically between moral license and rigid asceticism, and insisted that human beings could not enjoy full knowledge of God and fellowship with him.[24] Gnostics felt that the transcendent majesty of

---

[21]Kelly, *Pastoral Epistles*, 25.

[22]Ibid., 26. R. Longenecker presents an informative discussion on the role of the amanuensis in "Ancient Amanuenses and the Pauline Epistles," *New Dimensions in New Testament Study*, ed. R. N. Longenecker and M. C. Tenney (Grand Rapids: Zondervan, 1974), 281-97. He says: "Just how closely the apostle supervised his various amanuenses in each particular instance is, of course, impossible to say. . . . Paul's own practice probably varied with the circumstances of the case and with the particular companion whom he employed at the time" (294).

[23]C. F. D. Moule discusses Luke as the author or amanuensis of the Pastorals in *The Birth of the New Testament*, 3rd. ed. rev. (San Francisco: Harper & Row, 1982), 281-82. For a complete discussion of Moule's hypothesis, see his article "The Problem of the Pastoral Epistles: A Reappraisal," *BJRL* 47 (1965): 430-52.

[24]For a brief summary of Gnostic thought, see H. R. Boer, *A Short History of the Early Church* (Grand Rapids: Eerdmans, 1976), 55-60.

For a more complete discussion of Gnosticism, see R. M. Wilson, *The Gnostic Problem* (London: Mowbray, 1958). Wilson (97-98) distinguishes between a pre-Gnosticism, a full development of Gnosticism in the second century, and later developments in Manicheism and Mandeism. He feels that the false teachings mentioned in the NT are pre-Gnostic, and he makes no distinction between the heresy mentioned in Colossians and that of the Pastorals.

God so removed him from contact with mere mortals that he created a system of aeons or subordinate creatures between him and the world. Critics of Pauline authorship find some of these beliefs in the Pastorals. This has led some of them to suggest that the Pastorals are a product of the second century.

Those who seek to link the heresy addressed in the Pastorals with Gnosticism find support for their views in the reference to a Gnostic-like denial of the resurrection, a teaching Paul opposed in 2 Tim 2:17-18. The reference to Christ as the "one mediator between God and men" (1 Tim 2:5) could provide a Christian response to the systems of aeons in fully developed Gnosticism.

Others also try to link the heresy with the second-century heretic Marcion. They note that in 1 Tim 6:20 the term "opposing ideas" (*antitheseis*) is the title of a work by the heretic Marcion. They attempt to date the Pastorals in the time of Marcion.[25] Although most scholars admit that Marcion was not a true Gnostic, they recognize that his negative attitude toward the body and the physical world resembled that of the Gnostics.

Marcion also distinguished between the God of goodness and the inferior God of justice, who was the creator and God of the Jews. He viewed Christ as the messenger of the Gods, and he rejected the entire Old Testament.

The heresy Paul described in the Pastorals was characterized by an interest in Jewish law (1 Tim 1:6-7) and showed the influence of "those of the circumcision group" (Titus 1:10). It is unlikely that any of this could be said of Marcion or his followers. This makes it less likely that any reference to Marcion is intended.

Some who compare the heresy addressed in the Pastorals to Gnosticism suggest that the Pastoral errors are more advanced and developed heresies than those in Col 2:8-23. They see these more developed heresies as resembling Gnosticism. They note that Paul gave thoughtful answers to the errors in Colosse, but in the Pastorals he simply denounced his opponents and warned Timothy and Titus to avoid them (1 Tim 1:20; 6:20; Titus 3:9-11; cf. Gal 1:8-9).

Guthrie defends Pauline authorship of the Pastorals by pointing out the following features of the heresy:[26] First, Paul emphasized more the irrelevance of the heretical teaching than its falsehood. His pejorative reference to "myths" (1 Tim 1:4; Titus 1:14) and to "controversies and quarrels about words" (1 Tim 6:4; cf. Titus 1:10; 3:9) shows that "the main stock-in-trade of these teachers was empty platitudes which Paul

---

[25] Kelly, *Pastoral Epistles*, 10-12.
[26] Guthrie, NTI, 216-17.

did not even consider it worthwhile to refute."[27] Second, the error had many Jewish characteristics (1 Tim 1:7; Titus 1:10,14; 3:9). The reference to "genealogies" (1 Tim 1:4; Titus 3:9) resembles Jewish speculations centering around the genealogies of the Pentateuch. Third, Paul saw some tendencies toward asceticism (1 Tim 4:1-5; 5:23; Titus 1:15-16). The errorists abstained from certain food and practiced celibacy. The use of the future tense in 1 Tim 4:1 may indicate that the error had not arisen in the church at Ephesus, but it was already a problem in Colosse. Fourth, the only doctrinal error Paul mentioned was a denial of the resurrection (2 Tim 2:17-18). When Hymenaeus and Philetus maintained that the resurrection of believers was past, they denied the truth of the event altogether.

These facts do not seem to point to a fully developed heresy. Lightfoot observes: "Floating speculation, vague theories, coalescing gradually to a greater consistency and tending more or less in one direction—this, and not more than this, we are at liberty to assume as the date of the Pastoral Epistles."[28] Paul may have refrained from extensive discussion of the heresy because he assumed that Timothy and Titus did not need additional instruction in answering the vague speculations. They had proven themselves competent enough in discussions to respond without additional help from Paul.[29]

Kelly's examination and comparison of the teachings of the Pastorals with the Gnostic systems led him to conclude that "in general there is nothing in the sparse, vague hints we are given to indicate that the doctrine attacked had the elaboration or coherence of the great Gnostic systems."[30]

There is clearly a strain of aberrant Judaism in the heresy addressed in the Pastorals. While the errorists may not be the same as those Paul encountered in Galatia, they were ascetics who disparaged marriage and certain types of food. That Paul encountered a similar ascetic heresy (cf. Col 2:16,21-23) suggests that we do not need to search outside the first century to discover parallels to the heresy described in the Pastorals. Paul was not opposing a second-century Gnosticism; rather, he had

---

[27]Ibid., 216.

[28]Lightfoot, "Date of the Pastoral Epistles," 412.

[29]It is interesting to observe that Kümmel, no friend of Pauline authorship of the Pastorals, does not attempt to disprove Pauline authorship by linking the heresy with second-century Gnosticism. Although he feels that the descriptions given by the pseudonymous writer could apply to the false teaching in the time of the writer, he also feels "that Jewish-Christian-Gnostic false teaching which is being combated in the Pastorals is therefore thoroughly comprehensible in the life span of Paul." See Kümmel, *Introduction*, 379.

[30]Kelly, *Pastoral Epistles*, 11-12.

encountered a variant form of Judaism tinged with incipient Gnostic ideas which were not an isolated phenomenon in the first century.[31]

(3) The Ecclesiastical Structure

Ignatius served as bishop of Antioch during a part of the first half of the second century A.D.[32] He was martyred in Rome around 115. While traveling under armed guard to Rome, he wrote his Letter to the Ephesians in which he said: "We ought to receive every one whom the Master of the house sends to be over His household, as we would do Him that sent him. It is manifest, therefore, that we should look upon the bishop even as we would look upon the Lord Himself."[33]

Some have suggested that the position of the elders in the Pastorals possesses the authority Ignatius gave to the bishop (see 1 Tim 5:17). If this were true, it would be easy to date the Pastorals beyond the time of Paul and into the second century A.D.

Kümmel feels that the Pastorals come from "a community which is establishing itself in the world as Paul never knew it."[34] Hanson remarks that the attention which the Pastorals devote to ordained offices in the churches "in itself marks them as belonging to a later generation than Paul's."[35] It will be convenient to arrange the arguments made against Pauline authorship on the basis of ecclesiastical structure into five statements.[36]

First, those who oppose Pauline authorship based on this consideration often accuse Paul of having no interest in church organization. They observe, for example, the church in Corinth pictured in the Corinthian Epistles and see little discussion of church order. There the charismatic ministries are important, and they find the greater attention to organizational details of the Pastorals conspicuously lacking in the Corinthian writings.

However, references to Paul's actions in other New Testament writings clearly show that Paul always had some interest in proper organization. He and Barnabas appointed elders in the Galatian churches on the first missionary journey (Acts 14:23). In Acts 20:17 he asked the Ephesian

---

[31]For additional information on the nature of the heresy in the Pastorals, see the discussion under "Occasion and Purpose" in this introductory section.

[32]This section discusses primarily the ecclesiastical structure of the Pastorals in reference to the authorship question. For a discussion of the actual ecclesiastical structure that appears in the Pastorals, note the discussion of "Church Government" appearing under the section entitled "Theological Themes of the Pastorals."

[33]Ignatius, Letter to the Ephesians, ANF 6.

[34]Kümmel, Introduction, 382.

[35]Hanson, Pastoral Epistles, 31.

[36]Elaborations of much of this material appear in Guthrie, NTI 205-7; 213-16.

elders to meet with him and acknowledged their existence even if he had not appointed them. The Thessalonian church had in it those who stood over others in the Lord (1 Thess 5:12), and the Philippian church contained both overseers and deacons (Phil 1:1). Paul's reference to these leaders indicates his recognition of their function.

Second, it is common to see the elders in the church as bearers of traditions and as charged with the duty of passing on the teachings of the church. Kümmel leans toward this view of the roles of Timothy and Titus by saying, "The actual task of Timothy and Titus consists rather in preserving the correct teaching which they received from Paul and passing it on to their pupils."[37] Those who support this view of the function of Timothy and Titus think that the tradition was not fixed and wonder how Paul could appoint tradition-bearers at that time. Thus, they feel that the function of Timothy and Titus is too advanced for the time of the apostle.

Paul's statement in 2 Tim 2:2 urging Timothy to find "reliable" recipients of the tradition does not indicate that the main function of Timothy was to pass on tradition. It properly reflects an interest in accurate tradition guaranteed by authorized transmission. Paul's statement need only be seen as an evidence of concern that the gospel be properly understood by the succeeding generation. It is also true that Paul must have had some fixed body of doctrine to which he gave some assent. His statements in 1 Cor 15:3-8 represent a definition of the content of the gospel. In the Pastorals the apostle was showing concern that a proper understanding of this gospel be transmitted to the next generation, but he did not suggest that all Christian truth had been formulated, nor did he indicate that Timothy and Titus were mere guarantors of the truth of tradition.

Third, some who oppose Pauline authorship of the Pastorals find it strange that Paul would prohibit the appointment of a new convert to an office of leadership (1 Tim 3:6). They view the Ephesian church as newly organized and thus posit a conflict between the statements attributed to Paul and the situation of the Ephesian church. To those who oppose Pauline authorship of the Pastorals the words in 1 Tim 3:6 sound like a directive to a long-established church.

It is true that the original elders in a congregation would be novices. At the outset a church would have no other choices for positions of leadership. By the time of the writing of the Pastorals, however, the Ephesian church could have been over a decade old; and the word "novice" would describe new and untested believers in the congregation. It is interesting to note that Paul did not repeat the prohibition against novices to the Cretan church, which was presumably a more recently developed congregation than Ephesus.

---

[37]Kümmel, *Introduction*, 381.

Fourth, some who observe the positions of Titus and Timothy compare them to the monarchical bishops of the second century. In this function a bishop attained a role of authority or leadership over a surrounding area and appointed elders to serve over local congregations. Although Hanson does not use the term *monarchical*, he does feel that the authority of appointment (1 Tim 5:22; Titus 1:5) to be exercised by Timothy and Titus was not performed in Paul's lifetime.[38]

It is true that Timothy and Titus had greater authority than those whom they were appointing, but there is no indication that each church or local area had only a single bishop. Their authority certainly was not as autocratic as that of Ignatius. The unusual nature of their authority can be explained by viewing them as representatives of Paul charged with the authority to correct abuses in their church.[39]

A final objection to the Pauline authorship of the Pastorals based on the ecclesiastical organization of the church notes that the Pastorals appear to minimize the experience of endowment by the Holy Spirit. Paul's discussions concerning spiritual gifts in 1 Cor 12 and gifted leaders in Eph 4:11-16 seem to envision church leaders equipped by the Holy Spirit.

The Pastorals appear to suggest a process of election or choosing to office (Titus 1:5), and they emphasize the requirements for the office more than endowments. The Pastorals are the final writings of Paul. It should not be a surprise that Paul would focus upon the office of "overseer" or "elder" by discussing the requirements for office. The conclusion of J. N. D. Kelly seems appropriate:

> Our picture of the organization of Paul's churches is admittedly incomplete. There is nothing in it, however, which requires us to place the Pastorals outside his lifetime on the ground that the administrative arrangements they presuppose are more advanced than anything he could have known.[40]

For additional information on the ecclesiastical structure of the churches in the Pastorals, see the section entitled "Theological Themes of the Pastorals."

(4) Conflicting Circumstances

The reader of 1 Timothy and Titus gets the impression that Paul had made many travels in the eastern half of the Roman Empire. In 1 Tim 1:3 Paul had left Timothy in Ephesus to deal with false teachers, and in Titus 1:5 Paul had left Titus in Crete and headed eventually for Nicopolis

---

[38]Hanson, *Pastoral Epistles*, 33.

[39]G. Fee, *1 and 2 Timothy, Titus*, GNC, ed. W. W. Gasque (San Francisco: Harper & Row, 1984), xxiii.

[40]Kelly, *Pastoral Epistles*, 15.

(Titus 3:12), where he intended to spend a winter. In 1 Tim 3:14 Paul expressed the hope that he would return to Ephesus. When we open 2 Timothy, Paul was again in prison, clearly in Rome, and his expectation was that death was a distinct possibility (2 Tim 1:16-17; 2:9; 4:6-8,16-18). He also requested Timothy to bring him his cloak and books from Troas, informed him of Erastus's residence at Corinth, and described Trophimus's illness at Miletus as if it were a recent event (2 Tim 4:13,20).

A problem appears when we attempt to correlate these journeys with Acts. Although Paul may have briefly visited Crete on his journey to Rome (Acts 27:7-12), there is no indication in Acts that he engaged in any missionary work on Crete. We have no evidence in Acts that he visited Nicopolis. In Acts 20:4-6 Timothy accompanied Paul during his journey to Ephesus and was thus not in Ephesus to receive a letter from Paul. It is difficult to fit Paul's journeys in the Pastorals into the chronology of Acts.[41] This fact leads some to feel that a pseudonymous writer has added the above incidents to Paul's life.

The traditional answer to these observations is that Paul was released from his imprisonment of Acts 28, returned to the East, and then was later arrested and imprisoned again in Rome. Those who opposed this view would argue that Paul had intended to travel west from Rome but had not indicated a trip eastward (Rom 15:23-29). Many are also skeptical of the likelihood that Paul could be released from a Roman detention or, if released, would be arrested again.

An examination of Paul's writings will indicate the possibility that he had changed his mind about the journey westward.[42] In Phlm 22 Paul

---

[41]A creative effort to fit all of Paul's writings into the Acts narrative appears in J. A. T. Robinson, *Redating the New Testament* (Philadelphia: Westminster, 1976), 31-85. Robinson rejects the idea that linguistic or ecclesiastical arguments force a date for the Pastorals late in the first century or at the beginning of the second. In also rejecting a late dating of the Pastorals based on the nature of the false teaching, Robinson says: "With regard to doctrine too, the type of gnosticizing Judaism attacked in the Pastorals betrays no more elaboration than that refuted in Colossians . . . and certainly bears no comparison with the fully-blown gnostic system of the second century" (68).

[42]E. E. Ellis regards it as certain that Paul visited both Spain and the Aegean area after a release from his first imprisonment. Decisive evidence for him comes from the statement by Clement of Rome that Paul preached "both in the east and west" and came "to the extreme limit of the west" (*1 Clem*, ANF 5). He interprets the reference to the west as an indication that Paul preached in Spain. Ellis says: "After his release from imprisonment in Rome (and a visit to the Aegean area?), Paul completed his intended mission to Spain but, receiving grave news about his churches around the Aegean, he soon returned to Greece." See E. E. Ellis, "Traditions in the Pastoral Epistles," *Early Jewish and Christian Exegesis: Studies in Memory of William Hugh Brownlee*, ed. C. F. Evans and W. F. Stinespring (Atlanta: Scholar's, 1987), 252.

E. K. Simpson also supports a visit by Paul to Spain, indicating that the phrase "the extreme limit of the west" denotes either the whole or a specific part of the Spanish peninsula.

expressed his plans to return to Asia Minor. He also expected to be released from the first imprisonment (Phil 1:18-19,24-26; 2:24). Acts does not record all of Paul's activities, and we would not be surprised that many significant events in Paul's life occurred without a complete description in Acts (e.g., 2 Cor 11:22-33, which includes many events omitted in Acts).

Clement of Rome was a prominent Roman Christian leader who penned an epistle to the Corinthians in the late first century A.D. In his epistle Clement said, "Paul also obtained the reward of patient endurance, after being seven times thrown into captivity."[43] The accuracy of Clement's report on the total number of Paul's imprisonments may be questionable, but the report is evidence that there was a tradition that Paul had endured more than one imprisonment. Another source of support for a second Roman imprisonment comes from Eusebius, who said:

> Paul spent two whole years at Rome as a prisoner at large and preached the word of God without restraint. Thus after he had made his defense it is said that the apostle was sent again upon the ministry of preaching and that upon coming to the same city a second time he suffered martyrdom.[44]

Kümmel, who opposes Pauline authorship of the Pastorals, admits that the evidence from 1 Clement suggests the possibility that Paul was set free in Rome and later became a martyr after missionary activity in Spain. However, he finds no support in Clement for any journey to the East during which time he could have written the Pastorals. He dismisses the relevance of Eusebius's comment with the statement that it "is by no means adequately attested and must be characterized as an ungrounded construct."[45]

It is difficult to extract the order of events from the Pastoral Epistles. A possible reconstruction is that Paul went to Crete with Titus and perhaps Timothy soon after his release from Roman custody. There they evangelized many towns and encountered opposition. Paul left Titus on the island to deal with the difficulties the churches were encountering. Paul and Timothy in the meantime headed for Ephesus, where they faced difficult circumstances. False teaching similar to that in Colosse had undermined the church. Paul disciplined two leaders of the movement

---

He cites evidence in support of this identification of the phrase with Spain from both Strabo and Philostratus. See E. K. Simpson, *The Pastoral Epistles* (Grand Rapids: Eerdmans, 1954), 4.

Whether one holds to a later trip to Spain or to a cancellation of these plans will not necessarily affect the view of Pastoral authorship. Either the trip to Spain or to the East demands a release from prison during which time Paul could have penned the Pastorals.

[43]Clement of Rome, *1 Clem*, ANF 5.

[44]Eusebius, *Church History*, NPNF 2.22.

[45]Kümmel, *Introduction*, 378.

(1 Tim 1:19-20), but he pressed on for Macedonia and left Timothy behind to grapple with the situation (1 Tim 1:3). Later from Macedonia Paul wrote letters to both Timothy and Titus. At some point Paul was arrested again and returned to Rome, where he had a hearing before a Roman tribunal (2 Tim 4:16-18). He was bound over for a full trial, received a visit from Onesiphorus (2 Tim 1:16-18), and sent Tychicus to replace Timothy at Ephesus (2 Tim 4:12). Paul sent the Letter of 2 Timothy with Tychicus and urged Timothy to make his way quickly to Rome before winter made the trip impossible (2 Tim 4:21).[46]

(5) Theology

Those who reject Pauline authorship of the Pastorals emphasize that the theological content of the Pastorals varies too much from the genuine Pauline writings to be considered as Pauline. Hanson says, "He does not have any doctrine of his own, but makes use of whatever comes to him in the sources which he uses."[47] Questions concerning the theological content of the Pastorals focus around two important issues. First, many common Pauline phrases and ideas are simply not mentioned in the Pastorals. Second, the writer is seen as using a hackneyed, monotonous style to present Christian doctrine.

Those who reject Pauline authorship note the absence of discussion about the fatherhood of God and union with Christ. They see little reference to the work of the Holy Spirit, and they note the absence of discussion of the death of Christ. Why are such phrases absent? It is true that the term "father" used of God is limited to the opening greeting of each Pastoral, but the subject of God's fatherly goodness and his mercy toward sinners appears often. God is called Savior in an effort to focus on his saving action (1 Tim 1:1; 2:3; 4:10; Titus 1:3; 2:10; 3:4). God wants all men to be saved and to come to know the truth (1 Tim 2:4). God's loving-kindness is mentioned in Titus 3:4, and his grace is presented in Titus 2:11. The gracious provision of God is the theme of 1 Tim 6:17. These references do not show a God who is distant and unapproachable but near and filled with fatherly goodness.[48]

Concerning the relationship of the believer to Christ, it is true that Paul used the term "in Christ" in his other writings in reference to persons. In the Pastorals he used the phrase more in reference to qualities (2 Tim 1:1;

---

[46]Fee, xviii-xix; cf. J. B. Polhill (*Acts*, NAC [Nashville: Broadman, 1992], 518) for a discussion of sea travel in winter.

[47]Hanson, *Pastoral Epistles*, 38.

[48]Hanson notes the references in the Pastorals to Christ as God (he suggests 1 Tim 1:17 and Titus 2:13 as examples). He feels that such usage leaves the author "open to the charge of virtual Ditheism, though we may be quite sure that any such doctrine was far from his conscious mind" (ibid., 39-40).

3:12). The quality of having "life in Christ Jesus" need not be distinguished from the personal experience of being "in Christ." A person who has life in Christ is in Christ.

The Pastorals contain references to the work of the Holy Spirit (1 Tim 4:1; 2 Tim 1:14; Titus 3:5), but these are not as frequent as in some of Paul's other writings. Paul's purposes did not require that he make frequent reference to the Holy Spirit. Paul was under no obligation to declare all of his beliefs fully in each of his writings.

There is in the Pastorals a notable absence of significant references to the cross and the death of Christ.[49] However, the concept of the cross is not completely banished. The reference to the "ransom" of Christ (1 Tim 2:6) calls attention to his death. The image of redemption mentioned in Titus 2:14 performs the same function.

The second observation often raised about the theological content of the Pastorals is its stereotypical, monotonous content. Christianity has become "the faith," "the deposit," or "sound teaching." The prevalence of expressions such as "the faith" (1 Tim 3:13; Titus 1:13) and "deposit" (2 Tim 1:14) may sound like a reference to an official body of doctrine. Paul, however, used the expression "faith" in reference to Christian content in Phil 1:27; Col 2:7; and Eph 4:5. Further an emphasis on "sound teaching" (Titus 1:9; 2:1) would be perfectly normal in an environment charged with false and unsound teaching.

Some point out that the demand for ethical commitment expressed so movingly in a passage such as Eph 4:25-32 has come to be expressed in a rather bourgeois list (see 1 Tim 3:1-13).

It is correct to point out that Paul has extended appeals for moderation, self-control, and sober living (1 Tim 3:1-13; Titus 2:2-10) in the Pastorals. Paul's readers were likely surrounded by an unappreciative population who desperately needed to see a demonstration of generosity, sober action, and self-control more than to hear theoretical discussions about love and joy.[50] Paul realized that a demonstration of traditional virtues appreciated by the Ephesians would make a deep impact.

W. Kümmel thinks the writer had abandoned "a living expectation of the End."[51] Those who fault the hope of the end expressed in the Pasto-

---

[49]To Hanson this absence is "astonishing," and for him it drives one more nail in the coffin against Pauline authorship of the Pastorals (ibid., 42). It should be noted, however, that although the "cross" is central to Pauline theology (e.g., 1 Cor 1:18; Gal 6:14), the term "cross" (σταυρός) does not appear in Paul's Epistle to the Romans. This observation indicates the folly in overemphasizing vocabulary considerations with regard to authorship.

[50]Paul's appeal to the wealthy to avoid arrogance by "doing good" (1 Tim 6:18) sounds like a determined appeal to urge the Ephesian Christians to demonstrate their Christianity before watching opponents.

[51]Kümmel, Introduction, 383. He observes evidence for this in the phrasing of 1 Tim 6:14 and Titus 2:13.

rals point to the usage of the Greek term *epiphaneia*, a word used to refer to a visible manifestation of a hidden divinity.[52] Yet it is difficult to see any absence of a vivid expectation of the return of Christ in a passage such as Titus 2:11-13. The usage of the term (see "appearing" in Titus 2:13) seems fitted to express the majesty associated with Christ's appearance.

The Pastorals do contain a change in theological emphasis. Factors affecting this could be Paul's advancing age, the needs of the readers, and the subject matter to be discussed. Changes in theological vocabulary such as the reference to Christianity as "the faith" and the return of Christ as an "epiphany" may be related to the same causes.

E. E. Ellis has called attention to another phenomenon of the Pastorals which has important implications for the theological argument concerning authorship. Ellis has found evidence in the Pastorals for the presence of preformed tradition which may stem back to Paul.[53] He detects some of these traditions by observing such introductory formulas as "faithful is the Word," "know this," or "teach these things." Ellis feels that the deeply embedded Pauline features of the Pastorals come from these preformed traditions the apostle used. Ellis's argument shows the complexity of the process of authorship. It also provides a warning against presuming that an unknown author attempted merely to imitate Paul's style or theology. Ellis suggests that the likenesses of the Pastorals to Paul come because Paul used in all of his writings preformed tradition which he fashioned to his own needs. The presence of such tradition in the Pastorals is an additional indicator of Pauline authorship. For additional discussion on the theological content of the Pastorals, see the section in the Introduction dealing with "Theological Themes of the Pastorals."

(6) The Question of Pseudonymous Writings

Pseudonymous literature has appeared in writings from many cultures. In America, Samuel Langhorne Clemens entertained millions using his better-known pen name of Mark Twain. During the intertestamental period and portions of the first Christian century, Jewish writers used

---

[52]Kümmel describes the word as "Hellenistic terminology which is totally foreign to Paul for describing the redemptive event." See Kümmel, *Introduction*, 382. The term appears in 1 Tim 6:14; 2 Tim 1:10; 4:1,8; Titus 2:13.

[53]Ellis's use of the term refers to oral or written material such as doxologies (1 Tim 1:17), lists of vices (1 Tim 1:9-10), congregational regulations (1 Tim 3:2-13), prophecies (1 Tim 4:1-5), confessions (Titus 3:3-7), and admonitions (2 Tim 2:11-13). He feels that Paul found them at hand and incorporated them in his letters. Ellis provides criteria for detecting them and suggests that recognizing their presence brings into question the use of internal criteria such as style, idiom, and theological expressions in rejecting Pauline authorship of the Pastorals. See Ellis, "Traditions in the Pastoral Epistles," 237-53.

pseudonymity in producing such literature as 1 and 2 Enoch and the Testament of Job. The most important question for our investigation concerns whether or not the church would have admitted a work of known pseudonymous origin into the New Testament canon.

In 2 Thess 2:2 Paul apparently warned against the acceptance of a pseudonymous writing attributed to him. His insistence in Gal 6:11 that he had written "large letters" in his own hand may indicate that the letter had indeed come from him and not from an imposter.

Tertullian was a North African theologian who lived in the late second and the early third centuries. In *On Baptism* he described what happened when an elder of a church in Asia wrote pseudonymously in the name of Paul:

> But if the writings which wrongly go under Paul's name claim Thecla's example as a license for women's teaching and baptizing, let them know that, in Asia, the presbyter who composed that writing, as if he were augmenting Paul's fame from his own store, after being convicted, and confessing that he had done it from love of Paul, was removed from his office.[54]

Such statements as those of Tertullian and Paul indicate the rejection by the early church of pseudonymous writings. In addition to this issue the advocate of pseudonymous writing in the New Testament must face the ethical issue posed by a writer who would write falsely in the name of another when such proscriptions as Eph 4:15,25 had been previously given by Paul. The practice of pseudonymity cannot be easily correlated with the high appeals for truthfulness and honesty among the early Christians.[55]

Those who advocate the idea of pseudonymous authorship for the Pastorals do not normally insist on a willful imposter who deliberately attempted to mislead a gullible readership into thinking that he was actually Paul. P. N. Harrison has expressed his own ideas about the identity of the pseudonymous writer in the following words:

> He was, in my view, a devout, sincere and earnest Paulinist who set out to express in this familiar form what he and his readers really believed the Apostle would have said had he been still alive. The mistaken idea that Paul himself wrote these Epistles arose later in the century, when their author was no longer there to correct it.[56]

---

[54]Tertullian, *On Baptism*, ANF 17.

[55]A recent author favorable to the practice of pseudonymity is D. G. Meade, who has written *Pseudonymity and Canon* (Grand Rapids: Eerdmans, 1987). For a brief statement of the opposite viewpoint, see T. D. Lea, "The Early Christian View of Pseudepigraphic Writings," *JETS* 27 (1984): 65-75. See also Guthrie, NTI 282-94.

[56]P. N. Harrison, "Important Hypotheses Reconsidered: The Authorship of the Pastoral Epistles," *ExpTim* 67 (1955): 77.

Still another defender of pseudonymity for the Pastorals is A. T. Hanson, who feels that they are "wholly pseudonymous, and were composed by a writer subsequent to Paul's day who wished to claim Paul's authority for his material."[57] He finds that the Pastorals contain no authentically Pauline elements, but he admits that those advocating pseudonymity have a wide variety of options in stating their views.

In the face of the known practice of the early church and Paul's opposition to a pseudonymous letter, it seems unlikely that the church would have knowingly accepted a pseudonymous writing into the New Testament. It would present an ethical problem if a writer, knowing the opposition of the church, persisted in writing a pseudonymous epistle. Pauline authorship seems to be the more viable option.

(7) The Picture of Paul in the Pastorals

The Pastoral Epistles provide us with much information about Paul. Paul's initial verses in 1 and 2 Timothy identify him as an apostle. The initial verses of Titus identify him as both a servant and as an apostle.

Paul described himself as formerly a blasphemer and a persecutor (1 Tim 1:12-17). This identical picture of Paul appears in Acts 8:3; 9:1; and in 1 Cor 15:9. After conversion Paul received a divine appointment to be a preacher and apostle (1 Tim 1:11; 2:7; 2 Tim 1:11). This same picture of Paul can be found in Acts 9:15 and in Gal 1:1. In the proclamation and defense of the truth, Paul suffered much (2 Tim 1:12; 3:10-11). Acts 13–14 narrates Paul's sufferings in Antioch, Iconium, and Lystra.

The structure of the Pastorals is the same as that of the other ten Epistles of Paul. They begin with a salutation that mentions the writer, the recipients, and a greeting. They present a body of material that concludes frequently with a salutation and a benediction.

The Pastoral Epistles indicate a relationship between the writer and the addressees of a spiritual "father" speaking to spiritual "children" (1 Tim 1:2; Titus 1:4). The tone of the writing conveys both authority and affection. The relationship between Paul and his two young friends in the Pastorals is identical to that suggested in 1 Cor 4:17; Phil 2:19-23; and 2 Cor 2:13; 7:6,13.

The similar personal background and the similar portrait of the helpers Timothy and Titus seem to indicate that the same author penned these three writings and Paul's other ten writings. It appears less likely that a clever copier included these correct bits of information in order to give the impression that the apostle Paul was the writer.

---

[57]Hanson, *Pastoral Epistles*, 11.

It is interesting also to note that some themes of the Pastoral Epistles are similar to those which appear in Paul's other ten writings. Paul's appeal to Timothy to "fight the good fight" (1 Tim 1:18) is similar in tone to the athletic metaphors in 1 Cor 9:26-27 and Phil 3:12-14. The command that Timothy stir up the Holy Spirit of God and endure affliction (2 Tim 1:6-8) bears resemblance to the discussion about life in the Spirit and the cosuffering with Christ mentioned in Rom 8:12-17. The statements about Scripture in 2 Tim 3:16-17 and Rom 15:4-6 both assert that the Scriptures are a source of instruction and encouragement to the faithful Christian. The repetition of such similar themes provides evidence of common authorship.

Two Pauline traits that link the Pastorals with other Pauline material are noteworthy. First, Paul quoted a pagan Cretan poet (Epimenides) in Titus 1:12. Paul also quoted pagan sources in Acts 17:28 and in 1 Cor 15:33 (Menander). Second, Paul occasionally referred to individuals by their name and profession. In Titus 3:13, Paul referred to Zenas, "the lawyer." Such professional descriptions are also found in Rom 16:23 (Erastus, "the city's director of public works"); Col 4:14 ("Luke, the doctor"); and 2 Tim 4:14 ("Alexander, the metalworker").

(8) Conclusion of Arguments Concerning Authorship

The arguments against Pauline authorship of the Pastorals are unconvincing. The internal evidence from the Epistles indicates that Paul was the author of the writings. The external evidence from the orthodox church indicates a uniform tradition ascribing the Pastorals to Paul. The Pastorals appear by name in the earliest lists of New Testament writings. During the period A.D. 90–180 there is clear evidence that the Pastorals were in existence, held in high esteem, and were frequently quoted. Many of these early witnesses do not mention the author by name, but such a method of referring to these books is not unusual. The fact that the Pastorals had many witnesses to their existence indicates that they must have had a wide circulation and that their date of origin must go back to the period of earlier years. The best evidence suggests that Paul wrote these Epistles in the closing years of his ministry.

2. A Chronology for the Pastorals

Assuming Pauline authorship, we must place the composition of the letters in the shadowy period between Paul's release from his first Roman imprisonment and his execution. An exact chronology of Paul's life is impossible to ascertain. Some conclude that Paul arrived in Rome in the spring of 59, and others opt for a later date of 61. Depending upon the date for the beginning of Paul's imprisonment, we would judge Paul's release date from prison to be either 61 or 63 (Acts 28:30). The only certain information concerning the time of Paul's death is that it took place during the reign of Nero (54–68), most likely between 64 and 67.

Paul's exact movements during this period are uncertain. It is likely that 1 Timothy was written in Macedonia (1 Tim 1:3). In 2 Timothy, Paul is represented as a captive, perhaps for the second time, and apparently was in Rome anticipating death (2 Tim 4:6-8,13-18). The Epistle of Titus pictures Paul as having carried out an extensive missionary tour of Crete (cf. 1:5). When he wrote the Letter, he was planning to spend the winter at Nicopolis (3:12).

We do not know whether Paul ever went to Spain (Rom 15:24) or if he headed straight to Asia Minor after release from an initial imprisonment. Since 1 Timothy and Titus cover similar subjects, it is possible to suggest that they were written close together. The last of the Letters must have been 2 Timothy. A suggested chronology (with wide possibility for variation) is:

A.D. 61–63. Paul's first imprisonment. Writing of the Prison Epistles of Ephesians, Philippians, Colossians, and Philemon.

A.D. 63–65/66. Paul freed for additional mission work. Writing of 1 Timothy and Titus.

A.D. 65/66. Paul arrested again. This was followed by the writing of 2 Timothy, second Roman imprisonment, and martyrdom.

3. Occasion and Purpose

Identifying the occasion and purpose for writing any document is usually important for fully understanding the content and meaning of the message conveyed. Commentators on the Pastoral Epistles who maintain that these Letters are pseudonymous must find such an occasion and purpose other than that which is stated in the letters themselves. A. T. Hanson, an advocate of pseudonymity for the Pastorals, suggests that the unknown writer had three purposes in writing these letters: (1) to provide a handbook for church leaders, thus strengthening the authority of ordained ministers; (2) to alert church leaders to the need for opposing growing heresy; and (3) to assert a Pauline tradition among the churches of the Aegean area.[58] Hanson also asserts that "there is no great significance in this order of writing [1 Timothy, 2 Timothy, Titus]. All three may have been composed and published at the same time."[59] It is noteworthy, however, that J. Quinn, also a proponent of pseudonymity and

---

[58]Ibid., 23.
[59]Ibid., 28.

sympathetic with Hanson's views, proposes a hypothesis that the Pastorals constitute the third portion of an intended Lukan trilogy (i.e., the Gospel of Luke, the Acts, and the Pastorals) in the form of an "Epistolary Appendix." In this hypothesis, Luke would be the pseudonymous writer of the Pastorals. Central to Quinn's hypothesis is ordering the Letters as follows: Titus; 1 Timothy; 2 Timothy.[60] Such a hypothesis has ingenious features, but its arguments are unconvincing.

However, it is important to provide a plausible explanation of both the occasion and purpose for the writing of the Pastorals. If possible, we should relate the content of the Pastorals to a specific occasion in Paul's life and also with developments in the New Testament world of the day.[61]

Paul had likely left Titus in Crete to finish the task of organizing and instructing the churches there. He proceeded with Timothy to Ephesus and found a church in spiritual shambles. Leaving Timothy in Ephesus, he proceeded to Macedonia. There he wrote 1 Timothy back to Timothy to give additional instructions and to emphasize his initial oral statements. As he wrote 1 Timothy, he probably also reflected on the needs of Titus in Crete. He penned this Epistle at approximately the same time with a view to clarifying and adding to earlier oral instructions.

(1) 1 Timothy

In 1 Timothy Paul stated two purposes for writing. First, he directed Timothy to give vigorous personal opposition to the false doctrine developing in Ephesus (1:3). Second, he instructed Timothy about the kind of behavior that should characterize Ephesian believers as members of "God's household" (3:15). Nothing in Paul's statement in this verse implies that 1 Timothy is a manual for church organization. The presence and rapid development of the false teachers provided both the occasion and purpose for Paul's statement in 1:3. The need for presenting a committed Christian life-style in contrast with the corrupt, self-seeking practices of the false teachers provided the occasion and purpose for the statement of 3:15. The Epistle of 1 Timothy provides us information on the identity of the false teachers and the characteristics of their error. Understanding these facts will provide an explanation of the reason for Paul's writing.

First, Paul's statements in 1 Timothy show us the identity of the false teachers. Paul had warned the Ephesian elders in Acts 20:30 that false

---

[60]J. D. Quinn, "The Last Volume of Luke: The Relation of Luke-Acts to the Pastoral Epistles," in *Perspectives on Luke-Acts*, ed. C. Talbert (Macon, Ga.: Mercer University Press, 1978), 62-75. See also his recent commentary, *The Letter to Titus*, AB 35 (New York: Doubleday, 1990), 17-22.

[61]Many of the ideas in this section are derived from the seminal discussion in Fee, *1 and 2 Timothy, Titus*, xx-xxvi.

teachers would arise from within their own body. In 1 Tim 1:18-20 Paul urged the excommunication of Hymeneas and Alexander, who were apparently influential leaders of the Ephesian church. His emphasis on the personal qualifications of church leaders in 3:1-13 and in 5:17-25 leaves us the hint that spiritually unqualified leaders had posed a severe threat in the church. Paul's statements also indicate that the heretics had found a ready response among certain gullible women in Ephesus (2:9-15; 5:3-16; 2 Tim 3:6-9). Probably the church situation in Ephesus consisted of multiple house churches that were falling under the sway of the erring teachers. Paul's words to Timothy provided guidelines on meeting the challenge that these double-dealing charlatans provided.

It is interesting to contrast the problems in Ephesus with those earlier encountered in Galatia and in Corinth. In those two locations outside troublemakers appeared on the scene (Gal 2:4; 2 Cor 11:4). In Ephesus the problem was homegrown.

Second, Paul's statements in 1 Timothy provide information on the nature of the false teaching and false teachers. The problem makers, were Jewish in background, claimed an interest in the law (1:7-8), and observed dietary restrictions (4:3). The teachers claimed access to a superior knowledge (6:20-21) and expended their energies in word-battles (6:4), fables, and genealogies (1:4). Apparently a strain of Greek influence caused the false teachers to disparage the body and prohibit marriage (4:3). The character of the false teachers was utterly corrupted and deceitful (4:2; 6:5).[62]

With such perverse, strategically placed opponents Paul found it necessary to write this letter in order to establish Timothy before the church as his personal representative. The letter exposed the false teaching Timothy was to oppose. It also provided a strong warning to the church to avoid trifling with such a doctrinal monstrosity. Paul urged Timothy to emphasize "sound doctrine" (1:10) in order to counter the vicious, pernicious doctrine of the heretics. As a longtime friend and companion of Paul, Timothy already knew this truth. It was Timothy's responsibility to pass it on clearly to the gullible, defenseless believers in Ephesus.

(2) Titus

The content of Titus is similar to but much briefer than that of 1 Timothy. Two sections in contrast to 1 Timothy appear in Titus 2:11-14 and

---

[62]Much of this is Lightfoot's summary of the heresy. Lightfoot links the Pastoral heresy with the teaching of the Ophites or Naasenes mentioned in Hippolytus's *The Refutation of All Heresies*. See J. B. Lightfoot, "The Date of the Pastoral Epistles: Additional Note on the Heresy Combated in the Pastoral Epistles," *Biblical Essays* (London: Macmillan, 1893), 411-18.

3:3-7. In 2:11-14 Paul reflected upon the theological meaning of the historical work of Christ as it applies to the believer's behavior in this present life and his hope for complete redemption at Christ's second coming. In 3:3-7 Paul clearly set forth the Christian's motivation for good works, i.e., simply that God has saved us, renewed us with the Holy Spirit, and has given us the hope of eternal life. Similar statements to these are absent from 1 Timothy.

The occasion for writing Titus appears in 1:5. Paul had left Titus behind in order to appoint elders in a church younger and less organized than the Ephesian church. There are evidences of false teaching in the background, but the threat is less urgent and menacing than that in 1 Timothy. Paul described the errorists and their false teaching in 1:10-16 and in 3:9-11. Paul's purpose in writing was to instruct Titus to appoint and train the newly appointed elders of the Cretan church to reprove the heretics of their error (1:9), but Titus was also to rebuke the false teachers himself (1:13). The less menacing nature of the false teaching is evident in that this letter lacks the urgent appeals that appeared in 1 Timothy, such as "fight the good fight" (6:12) and "what has been entrusted to your care" (6:20), which appeared in 1 Timothy.

One antidote to the spread of the heresy in Crete was the demonstration of a godly life-style by the believers (2:2-10; 3:1,2,14). Paul's words to Titus place a heavy emphasis on this feature (3:1,8,14). He reminded Titus that the aim of Christ's death was to produce a "people that are his very own, eager to do what is good" (2:14).

(3) 2 Timothy

Paul's mood in 2 Timothy is utterly different from that in the other two Pastorals. Paul had apparently been arrested again and had passed through a preliminary hearing (4:16-18). He expected to die soon (4:6-8). He had been treated unevenly by Christian friends. Some had sacrificed greatly to minister to him (1:16-18). Others, perhaps "false brothers," had abused and deserted him (4:14-16). He was lonely, for most of his close friends had left on specific ministries (4:10-12).

The problem in the church at Ephesus had worsened. There was widespread defection from commitment to Christ (1:15). The deceitful, meddlesome Hymeneus, excommunicated in 1 Tim 1:20, continued to spread his insidious teaching among the faithful like a disease (2 Tim 2:17-18). Paul, however, was not preoccupied by the heresy.

Paul focused his interest on Timothy. This is a personal word to a beloved follower. He reminded Timothy of their longtime acquaintance (3:10-11) and appealed to his loyalty to Pauline teaching (1:6-14; 2:1-13; 3:10–4:5). To Paul this was also loyalty to Christ (see 1 Cor 11:1). False teachers still hovered in the background, but Timothy was not to focus merely on defeating them (2:24-26). He was to focus on proper teaching and was to pass on the gospel truths to faithful, committed followers of Christ gathered around him (2:1-2). Paul appealed for Timothy to come to his side (4:9). No doubt the memory of Timothy's warm affection and sharing of difficulty gave warmth to the lonely, weary heart of the apostle.

Despite his imprisonment and the likelihood of death Paul was not discouraged. He asserted that "God's word is not chained" (2:9), and he reminded Timothy of the faithfulness of God (2:11-13). He stood confident that the foundation of God for his people was secure (2:19). Paul was preparing Timothy to carry on the work of Christ even after he was gone. His reminders of divine faithfulness would provide that incentive to the younger friend of the apostle.

4. Theological Themes of the Pastorals

A brief discussion of the objections to Pauline authorship of the Pastorals on the basis of theological argument has already appeared in this introduction. It will be helpful for us to have an understanding of the chief theological statements Paul made in the Pastorals. We will consider six issues: (1) the Trinity; (2) the gospel; (3) the Christian life; (4) eschatology, (5) church government, and (6) salvation.

(1) The Trinity

Paul described God the Father by reference both to his attributes and his actions. He portrayed God as living (1 Tim 4:10) and as observing the moral actions of his creatures (1 Tim 5:21). Paul referred to God as eternal, immortal, invisible, and as the only God (1 Tim 1:17). He reflected monotheism by his reference to God as one (1 Tim 2:5). Two of the Pastorals refer to the Father as Savior (1 Tim 1:1; 2:3; Titus 1:3; 2:10), and all three speak of the grace of God (1 Tim 1:2; 2 Tim 1:2; Titus 1:4; 2:11). The majesty of God is such that he is unapproachable (1 Tim 6:16), and he is deserving of blessing and thanksgiving from his creatures (2 Tim 1:3). The tenderness of describing God as Father prevents any tendency to view God as distant and remote from his people (1 Tim 1:2; 2 Tim 1:2). God is also faithful and truthful in his promises (Titus 1:2), merciful in salvation (Titus 3:5), and generous in giving the Holy Spirit (Titus 3:6).

Paul described the action of God as Creator (1 Tim 4:3) and the bestower of life (1 Tim 6:13). He is the sovereign ruler who has condescended to reveal himself in Scripture (1 Tim 4:13; 5:18; 2 Tim 3:15-17). The course of all history is in his hands.

Paul pictured Jesus Christ as gracious (1 Tim 1:14,16; 2 Tim 1:2), faithful (2 Tim 2:13; 4:17) and as a descendant of David (2 Tim 2:8). He is both Lord (1 Tim 1:2,12; 6:3,14; 2 Tim 1:2) and Savior (2 Tim 1:10; Titus 1:4; 2:13). In Titus 2:13, Jesus Christ is clearly referred to as "God" in the phrase "our great God and Savior, Jesus Christ." Jesus appears as the object of all hope (1 Tim 1:1) and as the source of life (2 Tim 1:1). He became incarnate (1 Tim 3:16) for the purpose of saving sinners (1 Tim 1:15). He will serve as the righteous judge of the living and the dead (2 Tim 4:1,8).

Paul made reference to such events as Christ's death (Titus 2:14), resurrection (2 Tim 2:8), ascension (1 Tim 3:16), and return (1 Tim 6:14; Titus 2:13). He portrayed Christ's death as a ransom (1 Tim 2:6; Titus 2:14) and Christ himself as a mediator (1 Tim 2:5).

As previously mentioned, references to the Holy Spirit are infrequent in the Pastorals. In 1 Tim 4:1 Paul described the teaching work of the Spirit, and he mentioned the concept of spiritual gifts without referring to the Spirit personally (1 Tim 4:14). In 2 Tim 1:14 the Holy Spirit is seen as a guardian of the truth of the gospel. In Titus 3:5-6 Paul pictured the Spirit as the author of renewal and as generously given to believers.

The descriptions of the Triune God in the Pastorals are both similar to and different from those descriptions in the other Pauline Epistles. In the Pastorals we find references to the great saving events in the life of Christ. There is less obvious discussion of the significance of Christ's death, but the purpose of his death is affirmed. The unity, faithfulness, and mercy of God are emphasized in the Pastorals as in other Pauline writings. Unique to the Pastorals are the descriptions of God as immortal and unapproachable. The references to the Holy Spirit are less numerous, but the descriptions of the Spirit that do appear have teaching similar to the other Pauline writings. A unique emphasis of the Spirit's work in the Pastorals is the presentation of the Spirit as one who aids in guarding the truth of the gospel. It is noteworthy that in Titus 3:4-7 ("a trustworthy saying") each person of the Trinity is specifically identified in relation to salvation. Paul underscored the unity of the Godhead by referring to both the Father and the Son as Savior. Indeed, it is not immediately apparent in several passages whether the Father or the Son is in view (e.g., Titus 2:13; see the discussion at this point in the commentary).

(2) The Gospel

In all three Pastorals a concern for the truth of the gospel is a powerful influence (1 Tim 1:9-11; 2 Tim 1:13-14; Titus 1:9).[63] Paul used both the courtroom image of justification (Titus 3:7) and the social image of

---

[63]The discussion in Fee (*1 and 2 Timothy, Titus,* xxvii-xxiv) contains much material that will amplify this section.

redemption (Titus 2:14) to describe the results of responding to the gospel. Paul presented faith as the proper response to the gospel (1 Tim 1:16; 3:16; 2 Tim 3:15) and emphasized that godly living must be a result of this faith response (2 Tim 1:9). Paul's own example showed the importance of spreading the gospel (2 Tim 4:17), and he warned that those who taught an erroneous gospel must be avoided or silenced (Titus 1:11; 3:10).

The terms that Paul used in describing the gospel in the Pastorals are not common in his other writings, but they are not unique to the Pastorals. He referred to the gospel as "the faith" (1 Tim 3:9; 2 Tim 4:7; Titus 1:13), but he also used this term as a reference to the gospel in Phil 1:27 and in Eph 4:5,13. He described the gospel as "the truth" (1 Tim 4:3; 2 Tim 2:25; Titus 1:1), and he used this term in reference to the gospel in Gal 5:7 and in Col 1:5. Paul made unique references to the gospel as a deposit to be guarded in 1 Tim 6:20 and in 2 Tim 1:14. He also described the gospel as sound or healthy teaching in 1 Tim 1:10; 2 Tim 1:13; 4:3; and in Titus 1:9; 2:1, a use unparalleled in any other New Testament writings. A final term that Paul used in reference to the gospel was godliness or sound religion in 1 Tim 3:16; 6:3; and Titus 1:1. No other Pauline writing refers to the gospel in this way.

Many find fault with these terms as non-Pauline because the final pair of terms ("sound teaching"; "godliness") appear to be borrowed from the Greek religious vocabulary. Also the various terms used seem to change the gospel from a dynamic message to a fixed body of doctrine that must be believed.

Paul may have used these terms because they represent the phrases used by his opponents. As he used them, however, he renovated them for his purposes by attaching a new meaning to them (see commentary at 1 Tim 1:10-16; 2 Tim 1:9-13; Titus 2:11-14; 3:3-7). Paul also may have used terms that refer more to an objective content for the gospel because his recipients Timothy and Titus knew well the content of the gospel. He did not need to give lengthy definitions for the content of the truth because the responsibility of Timothy and Titus was to deal with the waywardness of the professing believers in Ephesus and Crete. Paul wanted them to use the truth of the gospel to correct the errant actions of these believers.

Even though an explanation of the gospel is not a primary emphasis of the Pastorals, we can find statements of its content scattered within the writings. In 1 Tim 1:12-16; 2 Tim 1:9-10; Titus 2:11-14; and 3:3-7, Paul gave a modicum of definition to the content of the gospel.

For Paul the gospel was a fixed body of knowledge, and it presented a message about Jesus that had led him to an abundant experience of grace and righteous living. Paul's representatives, Timothy and Titus, were to use this gospel to call wavering followers of Christ away from false teaching and back to true obedience.

(3) The Christian Life

In all of the Pastorals, Paul emphasized the importance of a response of holiness to God's act of salvation (1 Tim 2:15; 4:12; 5:10; 2 Tim 1:9; Titus 2:12). Holiness called for behavior that was both positive in emphasis (Titus 3:8) and also negative (2 Tim 2:19). The practice of holiness would affect the manner of dress (1 Tim 2:9-10), speech (1 Tim 5:13), choice of companions (2 Tim 3:5), and personal piety (1 Tim 2:1-3,8). Paul also singled out special groups to receive an appeal for holiness. Among these were the wealthy (1 Tim 6:17-19), widows (1 Tim 5:14), and slaves (Titus 2:9-10).

Some who observe the traits for which Paul made an appeal find them to be bourgeois and mediocre. They fault Paul for omitting references to the great Christian traits of love, joy, and forgiveness. How can we respond to this criticism?

Two facts may help us understand that the writer was not making merely paltry demands of his readers. First, Paul's chief concern was the reputation of the church before unbelievers outside the church. The qualifications that he demanded in overseers and deacons, for example, in 1 Tim 3:1-7 and Titus 1:6-9 focus particularly on easily observable public behavior. Paul wanted his readers to convince their closely watching critics that their Christian faith was genuine. Honesty, decency, self-control, generosity, and caring for a family would give credibility to the Christian profession of the readers. Second, many of the distinctive Christian traits that Paul elsewhere demanded in his converts are also emphasized here. The lists of moral demands in 1 Tim 4:12; 2 Tim 3:10-11; and Titus 2:2-10 are similar to Paul's list of virtues in Gal 5:22-23. A distinctive Pauline Christian ethic is clearly observable throughout the Pastorals.

(4) Eschatology

Many find fault with the theology of the Pastorals because the author, it is said, changed his eschatological perspective. Critics fault two chief eschatological features. First, they call attention to Paul's expectation of death before the return of the Lord (see 2 Tim 4:8) as a change to "make adjustments for a prolonged stay in the world."[64]

Second, the Greek word Paul used to express the return of Christ (*epiphaneia*) in 1 Tim 6:14; 2 Tim 1:10; and Titus 2:13 is "language similar to that found in Hellenistic religion."[65] The more common word

---

[64]M. Dibelius and H. Conzelmann, *The Pastoral Epistles, Her*, trans. P. Buttolph and A. Yarbro (Philadelphia: Fortress, 1972), 8.

[65]Fee, *1 and 2 Timothy, Titus*, xxxi.

(*parousia*) does not appear in the Pastorals. It is possible to find clear outlines of Pauline eschatology in the Pastorals that accord with statements outside them. For example, Paul viewed the apostasy of the present time as a harbinger of the end (cf. 1 Tim 4:1; 2 Tim 3:1; 2 Thess 2:3,7). Also Paul expected suffering to be the present lot of believers as they waited the return of Christ (cf. 1 Tim 6:12-14; 2 Tim 1:8,12; Rom 8:18-25; 2 Cor 4:16-18). Further, both the Pastorals and other Pauline writings emphasize that salvation has both present and future aspects (cf. 1 Tim 4:8; 2 Tim 1:9-10,12; 2:11-13; Titus 2:12-14; Phil 2:2-13; 1 Thess 5:4-11).

Even in 2 Timothy, in which Paul expressed his anticipation of death, he clearly kept a future hope of Christ's return as a bolstering, encouraging force. The nearness of the "day of Christ" pushed Paul and his readers toward fresh commitment (2 Tim 1:12; 4:1-5,8). Paul felt that the return of the Lord would bring a crown for committed believers (2 Tim 2:5-8). Such words do not seem to suggest the mentality of a man who is preparing the church to remain a long time in the world destitute of a hope of the impending return of Christ.

(5) Church Government

Paul pictured the church in the Pastorals as a united family ministering to its constituency and organized for service. The church is the family of God (1 Tim 3:5,15), and believers are brothers and sisters (1 Tim 4:6; 5:1-2; 6:2; 2 Tim 4:21). Paul charged the church with a responsibility to minister to the poor (1 Tim 5:16) and to serve as a foundation of doctrinal and ethical truth (1 Tim 3:15). Leaders of the church were known as overseers or elders (1 Tim 3:1-7; 5:17-19; Titus 1:5-9), and they were assisted by deacons (1 Tim 3:8-13). Women also filled a special position of service in the church (1 Tim 3:11; 5:9-10).

Most of the discussion on church and church order appears in 1 Timothy and Titus. Paul was unusually silent about issues of church order in 2 Timothy. He did urge that Timothy fulfill his work as an evangelist (2 Tim 4:5), and he urged that Timothy pass the Christian message on to those believers who were reliable and qualified to teach others (2 Tim 2:1-2).

Critics of the Pauline authorship of the Pastorals compare the roles of Timothy and Titus to that of Ignatius, at least fifty years later. Hanson, who supports this view, says, "Both Timothy and Titus seem to be free to choose whom they like as church officers."[66] Some who follow Hanson's reasoning see Timothy and Titus vested with primary authority in the

---

[66]Hanson, *Pastoral Epistles*, 33.

local church with other leaders beneath them. They also find evidence of
an order of women deacons and widows by reference to 1 Tim 3:11; 5:9.
They see the Pastorals as a type of ministers' manual for church leaders.
Fee exposes a shortcoming in this view when he says:

> The weakness of this view is perhaps also demonstrated by the fact that the
> entire spectrum of church government, from the hierarchical episcopacy of
> Roman Catholicism, through the mediating expression of Presbyterianism,
> to the extreme congregationalism of the Plymouth Brethren, all find support
> for their polity in these letters. If the Pastor intended with these letters to
> set the church in order, he seems not to have altogether succeeded.[67]

These writings are not a church manual but an *ad hoc* statement
intended to provide Timothy and Titus with directions to correct doctrinal
and life-style variations in the church of their day. Paul provided them
full authority, but they were his delegates on a special assignment. They
were not permanently resident pastors.

Paul used the terms "elder" and "overseer" interchangeably in the Pastorals (Titus 1:5-7), and in this usage he followed the rest of the New
Testament (Acts 20:17,28). Paul gave Titus the responsibility to appoint
elders in Crete, but apparently in Ephesus the elders had already been
appointed, perhaps by Paul himself.

In the earliest writings of the New Testament the leaders were simply
called those "who are over you" (1 Thess 5:12; cf. Rom 12:8—*hoi
proïstamenoi*). This same term appears in the Pastorals (1 Tim 5:17). In
the Pastorals, however, the more common term for the leaders is "overseer" (1 Tim 3:1-2), or "elder" (Titus 1:5,7). Each congregation seems to
have had a plurality of these elders, and their chief responsibilities were in
teaching, church leadership, and care of the church (1 Tim 3:5; 5:17). The
extent of their authority and responsibility is not clear from the Pastorals.

It is possible that each elder or overseer presided over a single house
church and that the complete body of elders for an entire city such as
Ephesus was viewed as the elders in that area. Apparently the deacons
also had a responsibility for service or ministry, perhaps working with the
elders or overseers. Their exact responsibilities are not clearly stated in
the Pastorals.

The exact duties of the women mentioned in 1 Tim 3:11; 5:9,11 is also
unclear. Like Phoebe (Rom 16:1-2), they served the church in some
capacity, but their functions are unclear.

The offices of elder or overseer and deacon did not originate in Paul's
writing of the Pastorals. The mention of these offices in Phil 1:1 suggests
that the offices were also used in other churches at an earlier time. Likely

---

[67]Fee, *1 and 2 Timothy, Titus,* xxxii.

the nature of church organization was undergoing changes throughout this early period. Paul's aim in church organization seems to have been to devise a workable, efficient organization that functioned well in the specific circumstances in Ephesus and in Crete. The lack of clear discussion about the duties of these leaders is a likely indication that he did not intend for later churches to feel bound to duplicate every feature of his organization in Ephesus or Crete.

(6) Salvation

The Pastorals recognize the universal problem of sin (1 Tim 1:15; 5:24; 6:16; 2 Tim 3:2-5; 3:13; Titus 1:11-16; 3:3) and God's desire to redeem humanity from sin's power and penalty (1 Tim 2:4; Titus 3:4-7). Both God and Jesus Christ are referred to as "Savior" throughout the Pastorals (1 Tim 1:1; 2:3; 4:10; Titus 1:3,4; 2:10; 3:4,6; and 2 Tim 1:10). Indeed, Paul boldly asserted that "Christ Jesus came into the world to save sinners" (1 Tim 1:15). Salvation is God's work alone, promised by God before the beginning of time (Titus 1:2), and historically realized at his "appointed season" (Titus 1:3). Believers are referred to as God's elect (2 Tim 2:10; Titus 1:1), as redeemed through Christ's self-sacrifice (Titus 2:14), and can be described as "saved," "reborn," "renewed," and "justified" (Titus 3:5-7).

Just as Paul argued in his Epistles to the Romans, the Galatians, and the Ephesians, so also in the Pastorals he unequivocally maintained that salvation is not in any way based on works but rather on God's grace and mercy alone (1 Tim 1:16; 2 Tim 1:9; Titus 3:5). Any attempts by false teachers to compromise this doctrine of salvation by the addition of required religious works is to be vigorously exposed, confronted, and corrected (Titus 1:10-16).

5. Timothy and Titus

Timothy was a younger colleague of Paul whom the apostle probably met on his first missionary journey in Acts 13:4–14:27. Paul's frequent reference to him as his son (Phil 2:22; 1 Tim 1:2,18; 2 Tim 1:2; 2:1) may indicate that he was a Pauline convert, but the evidence is not clear. Paul may have used the expression "son" to refer to Timothy as his "son in the ministry," one whom he had trained and encouraged greatly in his Christian development. The fact that Timothy was already converted when he was first mentioned with Paul (Acts 16:1) indicates that most likely he was not a convert of Paul. After the contact with Timothy mentioned in Acts 16:1, Paul had him circumcised and took him along as a younger associate. Since Timothy's father was a Greek, Timothy had not previously been circumcised. Paul's practice of circumcision reflected his policy of "becoming all things to all men" (1 Cor 9:19-23).

From the time of joining Paul, Timothy seems to have been almost inseparable from the apostle. Paul referred to him as beloved and "faithful" (1 Cor 4:17) and as a "fellow-worker" with God (1 Thess 3:2). He lavished special recognition on him when he declared to the Philippians, "I have no one else like him, who takes a genuine interest in your welfare" (Phil 2:20). Because of his close relationship with Paul, Timothy was able to articulate his concerns (1 Thess 3:2-3) and understand his viewpoint (2 Tim 3:10-11).

Paul sent Timothy on several important assignments in ministry. The assignment mentioned in 1 Thess 3:1-10 was an effort to encourage a congregation that faced serious persecution. Following this assignment, Paul sent him to Corinth to remind the believers there of Paul's teachings (1 Cor 4:17; 16:10-11). He later sent him to an unspecified ministry in Macedonia (Acts 19:22) and to a special visit to Philippi (Phil 2:19-24). At the time of the writing of 1 Timothy, Timothy was still on assignment in Ephesus (1 Tim 1:3), and he was apparently still at the same tasks in 2 Timothy. The mention of Timothy's name in Heb 13:23 may suggest a release from imprisonment, but it is not certain that the "Timothy" mentioned there was Paul's companion.

Timothy received much spiritual encouragement and teaching from his mother and grandmother (2 Tim 1:5; 3:14-15). He apparently suffered some type of stomach trouble (1 Tim 5:23). The view that Timothy was timid and diffident derives from Paul's advice to him in 2 Tim 1:6-8. It is unlikely that anyone who had already accomplished the assignments previously mentioned lacked courage or forcefulness. Timothy's youthfulness (1 Tim 4:12) may have caused some of the intense opponents whom he encountered to attempt to take advantage of him. Paul's warnings may be related more to his youth and the fierce opposition he faced in Ephesus.

Our lack of information about Titus stands in contrast with the reasonably full picture of Timothy. Titus is not mentioned in the Book of Acts and is mentioned most prominently in 2 Corinthians along with other references in Galatians, 2 Timothy, and Titus. Paul's designation of Titus as a "true son" (Titus 1:4; gnēsiō) may suggest Titus was one of Paul's converts. The word "son" is the same word used in connection with Timothy, but the appending of the adjective "true" seems to suggest that Titus may have been a genuine Pauline convert.

Titus was of Gentile background, and Paul refused to have him circumcised despite a remonstrance by Jewish loyalists against his uncircumcised condition (Gal 2:2-5). Titus may have been considerably younger than Paul but perhaps older than Timothy. Paul's failure to describe him as a "youth" in Titus 2:15 (cf. 1 Tim 4:12) may suggest that he was older than Timothy. Titus is called "brother" (2 Cor 2:13) and "partner" (2 Cor 8:23) as well as "son."

Most of the assignments Paul gave to Titus revolved around troubles at Corinth. Paul entrusted Titus with the delivery of a delicate message to Corinth (2 Cor 2:3-4,13; 7:6-16). Titus apparently successfully delivered the writing and persuaded the Corinthians to respond positively to Paul. Later Paul sent him to administer the Corinthian church's contribution to the collection for the Jerusalem believers (2 Cor 8:16-24). In the Epistle to Titus, Paul had left him at Crete to appoint elders, refute false teaching, and instruct the church (Titus 1:5,13; 2:15). He was later to be replaced by Artemas and would join Paul at Nicopolis (Titus 3:12). In 2 Tim 4:10 Paul indicated that Titus was on another mission into Dalmatia.

Paul seems to have used Titus as an effective troubleshooter in delicate situations. His performance under such pressure appears to have been superlative.

Despite the positive evidences of his usefulness in Christian service, Titus remains a lesser-known character in the New Testament. If, as some charge, the name Titus is a pseudonym in the Letter to Titus, it is difficult to imagine the motive of a writer in selecting a less-prominent New Testament personality as a recipient. This fact in itself suggests that the Epistle to Titus is a genuine Pauline product.

6. Significance of the Pastorals

The Pastorals provide insight for dealing with contemporary problems of heresy, divisiveness, and leadership difficulties. They are not a collection of rigid rules for church organization, but they are guidelines providing direction for facing problems and church needs.

The Pastorals are realistic. They present the churches Paul founded with all their needs, weaknesses, and shortcomings (1 Tim 4:1-3). However, they also present the mighty power of God as a prescription to human failure (1 Tim 1:17), and they show this divine power at work in the lives of people (1 Tim 1:12-17).

The Pastorals provide encouragement. Despite the likelihood that Paul was facing death as he wrote 2 Timothy, he remained steadfastly optimistic (2 Tim 4:6-8). He was lonely (2 Tim 4:9-11), but he was vigilant (2 Tim 4:16), irrepressibly a preacher (2 Tim 3:14-17), and confident in the Lord (2 Tim 4:18). The Pastorals provide a picture of the early church as it faced error (1 Tim 1:3-7; Titus 1:10-16), greed (1 Tim 6:9; Titus 1:11), and moral turpitude (1 Tim 5:24-25; Titus 3:3). Despite these shortcomings there is a clear sign of anticipated victory and hopeful moral restitution (1 Tim 6:11-16; Titus 2:14). Churches today need a heavy dose of such realism and encouragement.

One additional feature of significance in the Pastorals is their influence on hymnody. Some of the better-known hymns based on the Pastorals include "Immortal, Invisible, God Only Wise" (1 Tim 1:17), "Fight the Good Fight" (1 Tim 6:12), and "I Know Whom I Have Believed" (2 Tim 1:12).

7. Content of the Pastorals

(1) 1 Timothy

The letter begins with a salutation identifying Paul as the author and Timothy as the recipient. Paul wished grace, mercy, and peace to his younger follower (1:1-2).

In 1:3-20 Paul explained a threefold task to Timothy. First, he charged Timothy to prevent the spread of false teaching in Ephesus (1:3-11). Second, he expressed gratitude to God for the grace shown in his salvation and labeled his experience a pattern of divine mercy to all sinners (1:12-17). It was this gospel Timothy was to impress again upon the Ephesians. Third, he charged Timothy to fight the battle of the Christian life and to avoid the destructive examples of Hymeneus and Alexander (1:18-20).

In the remainder of 1 Timothy the apostle suggested emphases and practices that would accomplish the task of chap. 1. These emphases included prayer, an appeal for righteous living, a correct application of Christian truth, a warning against falsehood, and an appointment of godly church leaders.

In 2:1-7 Paul urged Timothy and the Ephesians to widen their prayers to include all people in the light of the universal intent of Jesus' atonement. In 2:8-15 he urged both men and women to practice a godly lifestyle which would leave heretics no room to make accusations against believers.

Paul emphasized the importance of the selection of committed servants to serve as overseers, deacons, and women helpers in the Ephesian church (3:1-13). This emphasis indicates that some of the doctrinal difficulty may have originated among clever, manipulative church leaders. In 3:14-16 Paul indicated that he had written to change the behavior of the Ephesians. He also made a brief reference to the doctrinal content of Christianity (3:16).

In 4:1-5 Paul described some of the doctrinal and practical errors of the false teachers. To oppose these falsehoods, Timothy was to remind the Ephesians of Christian truth and to live before them as a credible example of Christian commitment (4:6-16).

In chap. 5 Paul singled out groups within the church in need of special instruction. He urged Timothy to give proper and wise treatment to all ages and sexes within the church (5:1-2). He gave special instructions concerning the widows (5:3-16). He also urged great care in the appointment and recognition of elders (5:17-25).

In 6:1-10 Paul made a special appeal to slaves and added a closing indictment of the false teachers (6:3-10). He concluded with a series of special instructions, not only for Timothy personally, but also for those who were "rich in this present world" (6:11-21).

(2) 2 Timothy

Paul included a salutation that identifies him as the author and Timothy as the recipient. Paul wished grace, mercy, and peace to Timothy (1:1-2).

After making an expression of gratitude for Timothy's faithfulness in gospel ministry (1:3-5), he began an appeal for spiritual stamina in Timothy. He discussed qualities needed in ministry such as courage, a willingness to suffer, faithful imitation of righteous examples, and faithfulness in service (1:6-18). He used the metaphors of a teacher, a soldier, an athlete, and a farmer to show effectiveness in ministry (2:1-7). He explained truth that promoted effectiveness in Christian service such as a proper understanding of Christ, the development of stamina, and the certainty of spiritual reward (2:8-13).

He also appealed for soundness in both doctrinal belief and spiritual performance. He reminded them of the pernicious doctrines of the heretics and appealed for his readers to follow the path of righteousness (2:14-26). He described the stubborn character and deeds of human beings (3:1-9). He presented his own example and the encouragement of Scripture as sources of strength for Timothy (3:10-17). He appealed for Timothy to show consistent behavior despite the stubbornness of his opposition (4:1-5). He expressed his own hope of reward for self-sacrifice (4:6-8).

Paul presented Timothy with a number of personal appeals (4:9-18). He wanted him to come to him quickly. He asked him to bring along some of Paul's personal possessions such as a cloak and some scrolls. He warned him against adversaries whom he might meet. He reminded him of the power of God in protecting his people from harm.

In conclusion (4:19-22) he sent greetings to friends and supplied information about mutual friends. He delivered a personal appeal and benediction to Timothy.

(3) Titus

The opening salutation of the Letter to Titus is essentialy the same as that for its companion Letters, 1 and 2 Timothy. Paul identified himself as the writer and Titus as the recipient. However, unlike 1 and 2 Timothy, Titus's salutation contains theologically rich phrases and statements indicating the scope and nature of God's redemptive plan, as well as Paul's own personal role in promoting the gospel (1:1-4).

In 1:5-16, Paul addressed the matter of church leadership on Crete. Paul's reason for leaving Titus on Crete temporarily was to appoint qualified leaders (1:5-9). Qualified church leaders were especially necessary for promoting correct Christian doctrine and refuting false doctrine (1:9). Paul indicated the nature both of the false teachers and their false teachings (1:10-16).

In chap. 2, Titus was urged to remind the Cretan believers that their everyday conduct must be appropriate to the Christian doctrines which they profess. Paul offered specific exhortations for specific groups within the Cretan churches (i.e., older men, older women, young women, young men, and slaves; 2:2-10). Their everyday behavior should not reflect adversely upon the gospel message (2:5b) but rather make the gospel message attractive (2:10).

In 2:11-15, Paul indicated that the only true motivation for Christian behavior prescribed in 2:2-10 is theologically based in all that God has done for us in Christ. Paul's linking of this outstanding theological statement in 2:11-15 with the behavioral exhortations of 2:2-10 clearly establishes the true rationale and motivation for Christian behavior. Believers do not behave in certain ways in order to obtain God's grace and favor. Rather, it is precisely the other way around: because believers have experienced God's grace in salvation, they have the reason and the motivation to behave in ways pleasing to God.

In 3:1-2 Paul addressed the matter of the Christian's relation to the state and to pagan society in general. Believers were reminded that before their conversion, they had thought and acted like unbelievers (3:3). Once again, in 3:4-8 Paul included profound theological statements concerning God's grace in initiating and securing salvation through Jesus Christ and the work of the Holy Spirit. Because of God's work in their lives, Christians are to do good works that will benefit society (3:8).

In 3:9-11, Paul returned to the matter of false teachings and false teachers. Foolish false teaching is to be avoided. Divisive persons within the church are to be warned with the hope of rehabilitation but rejected by the church if unrepentant.

Paul concluded the letter (3:12-15) with comments concerning his fellow workers, his future travel plans, and encouragements for hospitality and help on behalf of other Christian missionaries.

─────────────── *OUTLINE OF THE BOOKS* ───────────────

1 Timothy
I.   Salutation (1:1-2)
     1. Author (1:1)
     2. Recipient (1:2a)
     3. Greeting (1:2b)
II. The Explanation of the Task to Timothy (1:3-20)
     1. To Prevent the Spread of False Teaching (1:3-11)
        (1) Content of the Warning (1:3-4)
        (2) Goal of the Warning (1:5-7)
        (3) Reason for the Warning (1:8-11)
     2. To Preach the Gospel (1:12-17)
        (1) Thanksgiving to God (1:12-14)
        (2) Statement of the Gospel (1:15)
        (3) Purpose of the Divine Mercy (1:16)
        (4) Doxology (1:17)
     3. To Prevent a Decline of Commitment (1:18-20)
III. The Emphases That Will Accomplish the Task (2:1–6:21)
     1. Prayer for All People (2:1-7)
        (1) Objects and Content of Prayer (2:1-2)
        (2) The Goal of Prayer (2:3-4)
        (3) The Goodness of the Goal of Prayer (2:5-7)
     2. Holy Living by Men and Women (2:8-15)
        (1) An Appeal to Men (2:8)
        (2) An Appeal to Women (2:9-15)
     3. Church Leadership by Committed Servants (3:1-13)
        (1) Qualifications of Overseers (3:1-7)
        (2) Qualifications of Deacons (3:8-10,12-13)
        (3) Women Helpers (3:11)
     4. Correct Application of Christian Truth (3:14-16)
        (1) Plans for a Visit (3:14)
        (2) Purpose for Writing (3:15)
        (3) A Hymn for Believers (3:16)
     5. Understanding False Practice (4:1-5)
        (1) A Warning against Apostasy (4:1-3)
        (2) An Argument against Asceticism (4:4)
        (3) An Argument for Blessing Food (4:5)
     6. Timothy's Performance of His Task (4:6-16)
        (1) Facing Falsehood (4:6-10)
        (2) Demonstrating Christian Behavior (4:11-16)

2. Stubborn Character of Human Beings (3:1-9)
    (1) What They Are (3:1-5)
    (2) What They Do (3:6-9)
3. Sources of Strength for Endurance (3:10-17)
    (1) The Example of Paul (3:10-13)
    (2) The Enrichment of Scripture (3:14-17)
4. Charge for Consistent Behavior (4:1-5)
    (1) Basis of the Charge (4:1)
    (2) Timothy's Charge to Ministry (4:2)
    (3) Reason for the Charge (4:3-4)
    (4) Timothy's Personal Charge (4:5)
5. Reward for Self-sacrifice (4:6-8)
    (1) The Sacrifice of Life (4:6)
    (2) The Service of Ministry (4:7)
    (3) The Reward for Obedience (4:8)
V. Personal Appeals from Paul to Timothy (4:9-18)
    1. A Few Requests and Warnings (4:9-15)
    2. A Reminder of God's Delivering Power (4:16-18)
VI. Conclusion (4:19-22)
    1. Greetings to Friends (4:19)
    2. Information about Mutual Friends (4:20)
    3. Final Request and Greetings to Timothy (4:21)
    4. Benediction (4:22)

Titus
I. Salutation (1:1-4)
    1. Author (1:1-3)
    2. Recipient (1:4a)
    3. Greeting (1:4b)
II. Instructions for Establishing Church Leadership (1:5-16)
    1. The Charge to Appoint Elders on Crete (1:5)
    2. The Qualifications for Elders on Crete (1:6-9)
        (1) Marriage and Family Qualifications (1:6)
        (2) Personality and Character Qualifications (1:7-8)
        (3) Devotion to Sound Doctrine (1:9)
    3. The Need for Qualified Church Leadership (1:10-16)
III. Instructions for Exhorting Various Groups (2:1-15)
    1. Exhortations for Right Behavior (2:1-10)
        (1) Behavior in Accord with Sound Doctrine (2:1)
        (2) Exhortations for Older Men (2:2)
        (3) Exhortations for Older Women (2:3)
        (4) Exhortations for Younger Women (2:4-5)
        (5) Exhortations for Younger Men (2:6-8)

1 Timothy

—————— **I. SALUTATION (1:1-2)** ——————

Letters, secular or Christian, written during the New Testament era typically followed the salutation formula: *A* to *B*. Greeting. *A* represented the author, and *B* represented the recipient. The greeting contained a gracious wish for the reader. Christian writers often included appropriate Christian expressions in their salutations. Non-Christian writings contained either an expansive greeting wishing good health or success for the reader or a brief statement worded simply "Greetings" (cf. Acts 23:26). The ancient method carries more logic than the modern practice, which compels the recipient to turn to the signature to determine the sender.[1]

1. Author (1:1)

[1]**Paul, an apostle of Christ Jesus by the command of God our Savior and of Christ Jesus our hope,**

"Paul" was the Gentile name of the great missionary statesman and was used to designate the writer in each of the thirteen Pauline Epistles.

---

[1]The normal form of greeting in a personal letter of this period would have been: Παῦλος Τιμοθέῳ χαίρειν. Paul wrote his epistles with a specific religious purpose and added more specifically spiritual greetings in his salutation. Instead of merely giving the expression χαίρειν ("Greetings"), he included "grace" and "peace" in eleven of his writings and "grace, mercy, and peace" in 1 and 2 Timothy. Only James among NT epistles has a one-word greeting.

Paul also wrote as one conscious of his authority, and he designated himself an "apostle." He used this reference in nine of his writings (excluding only 1 and 2 Thessalonians, Philippians, and Philemon). In most instances his use of the term "apostle" indicated an assertion of authority in the face of a likely challenge. For additional examples of salutations from papyrus letters of the NT period, see F. X. J. Exler, *The Form of the Ancient Greek Letter of the Epistolary Papyri* (Chicago: Ares, 1976), 24-68.

In first-century literature the name was usually a cognomen (i.e., a surname) and not a praenomen or nomen (cf. "Sergius Paulus" in Acts 13:7). Initially the apostle was designated in Scripture by the Jewish name Saul, but he came to be known by the Greco-Roman name Paul (Acts 9:4; 13:9, 13,16). He was the son of a Jewish father who was also a Roman citizen (Phil 3:5; Acts 22:28), and he may have received both names at birth. The name Saul was commonly used so long as his life was linked with the Jews, but when his work expanded into the world of the Gentiles, he used the Gentile or Christian name.

The term "apostle" is used in the New Testament in at least two senses. It can refer to a messenger (*apostolos*) or a representative of a church (Phil 2:25), or it can describe God's chosen ambassador who is commanded to testify concerning the resurrection and to herald abroad the gospel (1 Cor 9:1-2). In the Pastorals Paul used it in the latter sense. He may have attempted to counter his Ephesian opponents with the authoritative nature of his commission from the Lord.

In order also to stress the legitimate nature of his apostleship, Paul mentioned that he had been appointed to the office by God's command. The term "command" is used of royal directives to be obeyed without equivocation. Paul viewed himself as under orders. He also saw his appointment to the apostleship as God's will (Col 1:1). His use of "command" does not suggest that God tugged him into the office against his own will. It stresses the divine source of his appointment in order to gain support from the church for the directives he was giving to Timothy.

Most Christians will refer to Christ as their "Savior" (Phil 3:20) and God the Father as their object of hope (Rom 15:13). In the Pastorals Paul reversed this normal designation and designated the Father as "Savior" and Christ Jesus as our object of hope. Although this usage appears only occasionally outside the Pastorals (cf. Col 1:27; Luke 1:47), it is a common way of referring to Father and Son in these writings (cf. Titus 2:13; 1 Tim 2:3).

"Savior" was commonly used in reference to the emperor in the Roman emperor cult and was applied to the infamous Nero. Paul may have intended an impressive contrast by calling God "our Savior." In Christian usage the term portrays God as a powerful deliverer. It was a common method of referring to God's activity in Old Testament piety (Pss 25:5; 27:9).

Outside of the Pastorals Paul never used the term "Savior" (*sōtēr*) as a reference to God the Father. In Phil 3:20 Paul referred to Jesus as our Savior, and in Eph 5:23 he described Jesus as the Savior of the body. In the Pastorals Paul used the term "Savior" to refer both to God the Father (1 Tim 1:1; 2:3; 4:10; Titus 1:3; 2:10; 3:4) and Jesus Christ the Son (2 Tim 1:10; Titus 1:4; 2:13; 3:6). Although Paul did not use the appellation "Savior" in reference to the Father outside the Pastorals, he clearly accepted the saving activity of the Father. He pictured God the Father as the actor or subject in the idea of salvation (see 1 Cor 1:21; 1 Thess 5:9).

Paul's use of the term probably reflects two features. First, it is a natural development of his vocabulary in other writings to designate God as the Savior. Paul had always considered God as the ultimate subject of saving action, and he simply expressed the logical consequence of that thought. Second, since the term "savior" was used commonly in Hellenistic mystery cults, it is likely that Paul may have employed the term as an acknowledgment of usage by many Ephesians. Fee adds, "It is just as likely that Paul's use of it in these letters reflects the emphasis of the errorists."[2]

"Hope" has primarily an eschatological reference. In Jesus, God had begun a process of redemption which he would consummate at the last day. Christ has become our hope since we have made him the object of our trust and look with expectancy for his unveiling at the end of time. Unlike our common English usage of "hope," which implies a desire with only some expectancy of accomplishment, the biblical usage of "hope" suggests a desire with an absolute certainty of accomplishment. Our hope in Jesus will become a reality.

2. Recipient (1:2a)

[2]To Timothy my true son in the faith:

The first New Testament reference to Timothy appears in Acts 16:1-3 near the beginning of Paul's second missionary journey. The mention of Lystra twice in Acts 16:1-2 suggests that this was Timothy's hometown. Timothy made a good impression on Paul and accompanied him on the second and third missionary journeys. His father was a Greek (Acts 16:1); and his mother, Eunice, and grandmother, Lois, reared him in Christian faithfulness (2 Tim 1:5). Paul paid a high compliment to Timothy's compassionate service in Phil 2:19-24. The biblical portrait of Timothy (cf. 2 Tim 1:6-8) is that of a young man, somewhat retiring and perhaps shy. Paul urged him to stand firm for the gospel against menacing opponents and circumstances.

The term "true" (*gnēsios*) is used in other writings to describe a "legitimate" child or to refer to "genuine" writings. Paul used it to describe the genuineness and sincerity of Timothy's Christianity. Timothy may not have been Paul's convert, for he appears to have been a Christian when

---

[2]G. Fee, *1 and 2 Timothy, Titus*, GNC, ed. W. W. Gasque (San Francisco: Harper & Row, 1984), 3.

Paul met him (Acts 16:1-3). Paul could legitimately view him as a spiritual child or a "son" in the ministry.

The term "the faith" is anarthrous[3] in Greek. In the Pastorals the articular usage of faith often describes the content or belief-system of Christianity (cf. 1 Tim 1:19; 3:9). The usage here is either an instrumental idea (Timothy became a son by faith) or a reference to the sphere in which Paul and Timothy had a relationship. Probably Paul had the latter idea in mind. He meant that he and Timothy related to one another in the sphere of faith (cf. Phil 2:22).

3. Greeting (1:2b)

Grace, mercy and peace from God the Father and Christ Jesus our Lord.

1:2b Outside of this letter among Paul's writings only 2 Tim 1:2 employs a threefold greeting of "grace, mercy, and peace." As Paul's special representative in a difficult situation, Timothy had great need for an abundant supply of all three qualities. The term "grace" is a noun form of the normal Greek word for "Greetings." It describes the gracious goodness which God offers to undeserving sinners. Grace removes the guilt of previous sin and relieves the offender of punishment that is truly deserved. "Mercy" is God's help offered to the discouraged and stumbling (Heb 4:16). Paul's use of the word may have reminded Timothy of the sustaining mercy he needed in the face of intense opposition and difficulty. Every new deliverance out of trouble was a new experience of divine mercy.

"Peace" is a Greek expression identical with the Hebrew greeting *shalom*. It describes a state of salvation which results from the grace and mercy of God. Its meaning is not primarily personal and psychological in the sense of inner peace. It refers to a condition of wholeness and harmony existing between a person and God. It is the condition of wholeness which provides a foundation for stability in all of life.

The fact that both Father and Son are the cosources of these three graces indicates that they are put on the same level. It implies the coequal deity of Father and Son.

---

[3]The term "anarthrous" means that a noun lacks the Greek definite "the." Normally the presence of the article makes a noun specific, and its absence makes it general in its reference. In the Pastorals it is common for an anarthrous reference to "faith" to describe the personal faith of an individual (see 1 Tim 1:5; 6:11; 2 Tim 1:5; 2:22) or to a Christian virtue such as trustworthiness (see Titus 2:10).

The presence of the Greek definite article with a noun is called "articular." In the Pastorals the articular usage "faith" often refers to the belief system of Christianity (see 1 Tim 4:1; 2 Tim 3:8; Titus 1:13). Paul also had this same usage outside the Pastorals (e.g., Phil 1:27), but its frequency in the Pastorals is unusual.

──────── **II. THE EXPLANATION OF THE TASK** ────────
TO TIMOTHY (1:3-20)

Paul wasted no time in explaining the aim and purpose of his letter. He directed Timothy to remain in Ephesus so that he could warn false teachers not to involve themselves in the spread of false belief and practice (1:3-11). The false teachers had given themselves to spreading fanciful tales and unscriptural myths. Instead of dabbling in this false teaching, Paul ordered Timothy to proclaim the same gospel that had so changed Paul (1:12-17). Paul charged Timothy to maintain his commitment and obedience to the Lord so as to avoid the decline of commitment that had overtaken Hymenaeus and Alexander (1:18-20).

1. Prevent the Spread of False Teaching (1:3-11)

Paul outlined the content of the warning Timothy was to give false teachers in Ephesus (1:3-4). Timothy was to order certain men in Ephesus to cease spreading speculative ideas that promoted controversy rather than the work of God. The goal of warning these false teachers was to turn them to the production of love based on a committed conscience (1:5-7). The reason for this warning was to prevent a misuse of the law (1:8-11).

(1) Content of the Warning (1:3-4)

[3] As I urged you when I went into Macedonia, stay there in Ephesus so that you may command certain men not to teach false doctrines any longer [4] nor to devote themselves to myths and endless genealogies. These promote controversies rather than God's work—which is by faith.

It is unusual for Paul to have begun his message to Timothy without any expression of gratitude. Galatians, like 1 Timothy, moves from salutation to body without an expression of thanks. What was happening in the church at Ephesus left Paul no basis for gratitude. For additional information on Ephesus, see the excursus at the end of the chapter.

Paul had previously warned the Ephesian Christians that some of their own group would draw them away (Acts 20:29-30). Later in this chapter he mentioned two of the offenders by name (1 Tim 1:20). The heresy in Ephesus had arisen from within the church, and Paul was urging Timothy to act on Paul's behalf to thwart the advance of mischievous falsehood.

The NIV translation of vv. 3-4 conceals the fact that the Greek text contains an awkward, difficult expression. A literal paraphrase of vv. 3-4 is: "As I urged you to stay in Ephesus . . . to command certain men not to teach falsehood nor to involve themselves with myths and unending genealogies." Paul never drew a conclusion from the "as" clause even though the KJV inserts "so do." Lenski regards this expression as an ellipsis,[1] and Huther suggests that Paul may have failed to express a conclusion because of the thoughts cascading through his mind.[2]

1:3 Paul had traveled into Macedonia, but he urged Timothy to remain in Ephesus. The word "command" (*parangellō*) is a strong word calling for stern orders. It was used to describe Jesus' orders to the Twelve in Matt 10:5; Mark 6:8 and the orders of the Sanhedrin prohibiting apostolic preaching in Acts 4:18. The term "urged" (*parakaleō*) may indicate that Timothy was reluctant to stay in Ephesus, but the word may have served equally well to give Timothy authorization before the Ephesian congregation. It is best to see this as Paul's reaffirmation of his appointment of Timothy to serve as his personal representative before the church. He charged him with full responsibility to carry out his task. The "certain men" whom Timothy was to charge may have included Hymenaeus and Alexander as the most egregious offenders, but it also included others who had not been as stubbornly in error as those two. The charge against teaching "false doctrines" prohibits spreading speculative ideas that contradicted Paul's explanation of the truth. There was an accepted standard of apostolic teaching Paul wanted Timothy to follow. The descriptions of life in Ephesus in Acts 19:1-40; 20:17-38; and Rev 2:1-7 portray a church tempted by the occult, enticed into error by savage heretics, and finally abandoning its first love of commitment to Christ.

---

[1] R. C. H. Lenski, *The Interpretation of St. Paul's Epistles to the Colossians, to the Thessalonians, to Timothy, to Titus and to Philemon* (Columbus, Ohio: Wartburg, 1946), 495.

[2] J. E. Huther, "Critical and Exegetical Handbook to the Epistles to Timothy and Titus," *Meyer's Commentary on the New Testament*, trans. D. Hunter (1884; reprint, Peabody, Mass.: Hendrickson, 1983), 63.

1:4 Paul warned against "myths and endless genealogies." Interpreters see these stories as either fictitious Jewish distortions of the Old Testament or Gnostic myths about creation.[3] The false teaching mentioned in 1 Tim 4:3 is Jewish in origin, and this fact leads many interpreters to label the false teaching here as Jewish myths. This appears to be the best option for interpretation. The terms used by Paul regularly appear in Hellenistic and Hellenistic-Jewish sources to refer to traditions about peoples' origins. The term "myths" is used in a pejorative sense to contrast the legendary character of many of these stories to historical truth.

The Jewish Book of Jubilees, an apocryphal work from the second century B.C., has a number of legendary accretions to the Old Testament which may resemble what Paul had in mind.[4] These stories are patriotic legends that are similar to such American traditions as the story of George Washington and the cherry tree.

The term for "myths" also appears in 1 Tim 4:7, where Paul described them as "old wives' tales" ("godless legends which were not worth telling," author's paraphrase). In 2 Tim 4:4 Paul pictured them as enticing and attractive because they snared the attention of the listeners away from the truth and toward the fables. In Titus 1:14 Paul referred to them as "Jewish legends." The term "genealogies" appears in Titus 3:9, where the results of reflecting on the genealogies were "unprofitable and useless." The damage of these "myths" came from their empty content (not worth telling), their attractiveness (snaring the attention of listeners), and their general uselessness. They clearly seem to have reflected Jewish interests in legends with a tinge of Hellenistic influence but no full-blown Gnosticism.

Paul opposed the myths because of what they produced and what they caused Christians to ignore. The false teaching promoted questions or controversies. The false teachers paid close attention to what did not need to be a focus. This led to fruitless discussions and strife. The result of the irrelevant teaching contrasted the true edification that sprang from godly instruction.

Paul indicated that the false teachings failed to further "God's work" (*oikonomia*).[5] The word is used in Greek to denote the management of

---

[3]For further discussion see F. J. A. Hort, *Judaistic Christianity* (Grand Rapids: Baker, 1980), 130-46. Hort supports the idea that the stories reflect Jewish interests in legendary ancestor stories. Spicq agrees that they are Jewish apocryphal legends that "are stories dealing with the patriarchs, heroes, and illustrious individuals [translation mine]." See C. Spicq, *Saint Paul: Les Epitres Pastorales* (Paris: Gabalda, 1947), 21. Hanson sees the terms "myths and genealogies" as a form of Jewish Gnosticism and a reference "to the accounts of the movements and couplings of the various aeons as described in this or that Gnostic system" (A. T. Hanson, *The Pastoral Epistles*, NCB [Grand Rapids: Eerdmans, 1982], 57).

[4]Note the embellishments to the history of Abraham in Jubilees 11.18-24.

[5]The translation of the KJV ("edifying") is based on a variant reading rejected in most modern English translations.

another's household. It has that usage in Luke 16:2 ("management"), but in Paul's Epistles it frequently referred to God's plan of redemption (Eph 3:2,9). The work of God that Paul was discussing here was the arrangement God had made for people's redemption. This work is furthered by an attitude of faith or commitment. Paul feared that the Ephesians might spend so much time in fruitless discussion of novel doctrines that they would not carry out God's plan of bringing people to a place of obedience and faith before Jesus. No petty project or cause should usurp the place of promoting the gospel as a part of God's plan.

(2) Goal of the Warning (1:5-7)

[5]The goal of this command is love, which comes from a pure heart and a good conscience and a sincere faith. [6]Some have wandered away from these and turned to meaningless talk. [7]They want to be teachers of the law, but they do not know what they are talking about or what they so confidently affirm.

Paul outlined two goals he wanted his warning of vv. 3-4 to accomplish. First, he wanted the Ephesians to develop a genuine love (v. 5). Paul did not specify the object of love, but he likely included both God and other persons as recipients. Hendriksen calls the love "a personal delight in God, a grateful outgoing of the entire personality to him, a deep yearning for the prosperity of his redeemed, and an earnest desire for the temporal and eternal welfare of his creatures."[6] Second, Paul wanted to prevent the Ephesians from dabbling with teachings that were only empty talk (vv. 6-7).

1:5 The term "command" here is the noun form of the verb "command" in v. 3. It refers to the directives Timothy was to deliver to the Ephesian heretics. The goal of issuing this warning was to lead the false teachers to develop genuine love. This love was to spring from a pure heart, a good conscience, and genuine faith.

In biblical thought the heart is the seat of the mind, the emotions, and the will. Ward portrays it as the seat of religious experience from which moral conduct springs.[7] Any person who lacks a pure heart cannot radiate Christian love. The term "pure heart" is a Hebrew concept and is a rough equivalent of the Greek term "good conscience."

Conscience refers to an individual's inner awareness of the moral quality of personal actions. In Rom 13:5 and 1 Cor 8:10 conscience serves as a guide to life, but Paul recognized that a conscience can be scarred by receiving imperfect information (1 Tim 4:2; Titus 1:15). In order to

---

[6]W. Hendriksen, *I-II Timothy and Titus*, NTC (Grand Rapids: Baker, 1957), 61.
[7]R. A. Ward, *Commentary on 1 & 2 Timothy & Titus* (Waco: Word, 1974), 31.

develop a good conscience, individuals must fill their minds with God's message and render obedience to it (1 Cor 8:7-12; 1 Pet 3:15-16).

"Sincere faith" is a trust in God that Paul believed Timothy possessed (2 Tim 1:5). Lock characterizes such faith as having simplicity of aim, which is always ready to listen to truth, and a constant desire to do right.[8] Faith is "sincere" only when it is not mere talk but is genuine trust and confidence in God.

1:6 The "some" who had wandered away were the same as the "certain men" of v. 3 who had taught false doctrines. "Wandered away" comes from a verb (*astocheō*) that means *to be wide of the mark* or *to shoot past the goal*. The false teachers had wandered away from a pure heart, good conscience, and sincere faith and had turned to aimless talk which did not lead to the goal of godliness. They had missed the mark with regard to the faith.

The word for "meaningless talk" (*mataiologia*) contains a prefix (*mataios*) that means *empty, useless*, or *fruitless*. The talk leads nowhere. There is content in what the false teachers propagate, but it does not lead anyone to holy living.

1:7 By describing them as "teachers of the law," Paul pictured the false teachers as aspiring to be like Jewish rabbis and spinning out sterile interpretations of Old Testament stories and regulations. They pretended to be wise sages, but they were really pontificating on truths they did not begin to fathom.

The false teachers in Ephesus had Jewish roots just as did the Judaizers with whom Paul had wrestled in Galatians. The false teachers were not primarily butchering grace by adding law to it, but they were an ignorant group of idle tale-tellers. They weaned the minds of their listeners away from the simplicity of the gospel, and in doing this they missed both the truths of the Old Testament and the teaching of Christ.

An early fictitious collection of stories about Jesus is gathered in The Infancy Gospels, dating from the second century. In 18:1-3 the writer narrated the following incident about Jesus:

> [1]In the month Adar Jesus gathered together the boys, and ranked them as though he had been a king. [2]For they spread their garments on the ground for him to sit on; and having made a crown of flowers, put it upon his head, and stood on his right and left as the guards of a king. [3]And if any one happened to pass by, they took him by force, and said, Come hither, and worship the king, that you may have a prosperous journey.[9]

---

[8]W. Lock, *The Pastoral Epistles*, ICC (Edinburgh: T & T Clark, 1924), 10.
[9]*The Lost Books of the Bible and the Forgotten Books of Eden* (New York: World, 1971), 55.

This interesting legend probably resembled the Old Testament stories in which the Ephesian false teachers combined imagination and history. Doubtless their frivolous methods attracted attention from the listeners, but they contained distorted perversions that stimulated idle talk and arguments rather than Christian growth.

(3) Reason for the Warning (1:8-11)

[8]**We know that the law is good if one uses it properly.** [9]**We also know that law is made not for the righteous but for lawbreakers and rebels, the ungodly and sinful, the unholy and irreligious; for those who kill their fathers or mothers, for murderers,** [10]**for adulterers and perverts, for slave traders and liars and perjurers—and for whatever else is contrary to the sound doctrine** [11]**that conforms to the glorious gospel of the blessed God, which he entrusted to me.**

1:8 Paul's reason for warning against the false teachers in Ephesus was that they had misunderstood the intent and use of God's law. In speaking of the law, Paul was not merely referring to the Ten Commandments or to the law of Moses. He was speaking of the principle of making legal demands, and he argued that legal demands are good if a person knows rightly how to make those demands. The law itself is intrinsically noble and honorable, but its teachers must use it according to its spirit and intention.

What is the right use of the law? Theologians have summarized three uses of the law. First, the Bible resembles a locked door to restrain individuals from trespassing onto the wrong territory (Rom 7:7; Ps 19:13). Second, the law resembles a mirror to reveal sin and lead us to Christ (Rom 3:19-20; Gal 3:24). Third, the law serves as a rule and guide to point out the works that please God (Rom 13:8-10). The errorists whom Paul was addressing did not know they needed restraint, a mirror for their sins, or a guide in life. They used the law as a launchpad to turn out spellbinding tales about ancestors and thereby robbed the law of its convicting power. If these teachers had used the law as a means of leading their hearers to Jesus, that would have been fine with Paul.[10] In saying that the

---

[10]A similar view of expressing the right use of the law, but stated in different words, appears in H. A. Virkler, *Hermeneutics: Principles and Processes of Biblical Interpretation* (Grand Rapids: Baker, 1981), 143. Virkler outlines four uses of the law that include showing human beings the difference between right and wrong, restraining evil, bringing individuals to Christ, and providing a guideline for godly living.

E. P. Sanders in *Paul and Palestinian Judaism: A Comparison of Patterns of Religion* (Philadelphia: Fortress, 1977) began a revolution in Pauline studies by denying that Paul held a legalistic perception of Judaism. According to Sanders, it is incorrect to picture first-century Judaism as encouraging a works-type of righteousness. Rather, according to Sanders, both Judaism and Paul felt that obedience to the law was not required to enter into God's covenant but was necessary for maintaining participation in the covenant. Aware of Sanders's

law was not made for "the righteous," Paul was describing believers as the righteous. Committed believers do not need the law to propel them to holy living. They have pleasure in God's law and have entered the sphere in which the promptings of the Holy Spirit spur them to obedience (Gal 5:22-24).

1:9-10 Paul presented a list of vices that begins with three pairs of adjectives and then follows the order of the Ten Commandments. The three pairs of adjectives refer respectively to moral vagabonds who willfully break the law and refuse to obey its authority ("lawbreakers and rebels"), the outwardly disobedient who wantonly disregard God's will in their lives ("ungodly and sinful"), and the inward scoffers who irreverently trample on God's name ("unholy and irreligious"). The latter group treated nothing as sacred.

Those who kill their parents (v. 9) had lost all natural affection and violated the Fifth and Sixth Commandments. "Murderers" violated the Sixth Commandment, and "adulterers and perverts"[11] violated the Seventh Commandment. "Slave traders" disregarded the Eighth Commandment, and "liars and perjurers" sinned against the Ninth Commandment. Paul's list spotlighted easily recognizable external sins. He made no specific mention of the Tenth Commandment prohibiting covetousness.

There is implied reference to the Tenth Commandment and all other violations in Paul's mention of "whatever else is contrary to the sound doctrine." The word "sound" (*hygiainousē*) is a medical metaphor that contrasts healthy doctrine with the sickly, unhealthy teaching of the heretics. "Doctrine" (*didaskalia*) can refer either to proper belief (1 Tim 6:1)—the content of doctrine—or to proper behavior (Titus 2:1)—the result of right belief. In v. 10 the emphasis is on right behavior stemming from correct moral teaching. Kelly points out that Paul's metaphor expressed his conviction that a morally disordered life is diseased and

---

emphases, R. Sloan has said that the law cannot save because it "now operates within the power sphere of sin and death and, thus weakened, has not the power to save" ("Paul and the Law: Why the Law Cannot Save," *NT* 33, no. 1 [1991]: 54). Sloan feels that both in the Jews and in the unconverted, Paul felt the power of evil operated through their devotion to keeping the law so that they were incapable of actually seeing Jesus as the Messiah. Sloan's views reflect an understanding of Sanders's insights but also show an appreciation for consistency in Paul's thinking.

[11] The term "perverts" is used only once additionally in the NT (1 Cor 6:9). In each instance Paul was warning against male coital homosexuality. In 1 Cor 6:9 the term is translated "homosexual offenders," and it is paired with a related term "male prostitutes," which referred to a man or boy who allowed himself to be abused homosexually. The term "homosexual offenders" ("Sodomites" [translation mine]) describes the initiators of a homosexual encounter. The term "male prostitutes" ("Catamites," [translation mine]) described the recipients of active homosexual behavior. Paul used the term in 1 Tim 1:10 to warn against an active homosexual life-style.

stands in need of treatment by the law. A life based on the teaching of the gospel is clean and healthy.

1:11 Paul presented three facts about the gospel. First, the gospel concerns the glory of the blessed God. The content of the gospel is to set forth and proclaim the glory of God. Second, this gospel comes from "the blessed God." The term "blessed" pictures God as the source and fountain of all blessedness. Blessedness rests in and proceeds from God. Third, this gospel had been entrusted to Paul. The malicious perversions of truth Paul cited in vv. 9-10 did not proceed from the God of glory, and Paul wanted such heretical teaching to cease.

Paul's chief concern was that the life-style and testimony of a Christian aid in the spread of the gospel concerning Jesus. The false teachers in Ephesus had given their energies to many enticing replacements for the gospel. That trend had to stop! No program, aim, or emphasis in our lives can be allowed to hinder our full involvement in sharing the gospel of Jesus' saving power.

2. To Preach the Gospel (1:12-17)

In this section Paul explained the unlimited power of the gospel to which he had referred in v. 11. After elaborating on this gospel, he returned to discuss the subject of heresy and heretics in vv. 18-20.

In vv. 12-14 Paul expressed gratitude to God for having saved him despite his previous opposition to the truth. In v. 15 he gave a brief outline of the gospel in the form of a personal testimony, and in v. 16 he explained the positive purpose of God's mercy to him. These reflections evoke an outburst of praise in the doxology of v. 17.

(1) Thanksgiving to God (1:12-14)

[12]I thank Christ Jesus our Lord, who has given me strength, that he considered me faithful, appointing me to his service. [13]Even though I was once a blasphemer and a persecutor and a violent man, I was shown mercy because I acted in ignorance and unbelief. [14]The grace of our Lord was poured out on me abundantly, along with the faith and love that are in Christ Jesus.

1:12 Paul marveled that God would take a man who had been a blasphemous, prideful opponent of Christianity and put him into ministry. His expression of thanksgiving (*charin echō*) differed from his normal method of showing thanks and expresses continuing gratitude along the line of "I am having gratitude."[12] The verb "has given ... strength," a Greek aorist, is the same word rendered "gives ... strength," a Greek

---

[12]Williams best renders the sense of Paul's expression with his translation, "I am always thanking Christ Jesus our Lord."

present, in Phil 4:13.[13] The "strength" God had shared with Paul was seen in his conversion and call, not merely in the strength he received for suffering or the enabling power to perform miracles. Christ's strength enabled Paul to share the gospel that had been committed to him (v. 11).

Paul provided a statement and illustration of this gospel-sharing strength in 2 Cor 4:7-12. There he said that God had committed the treasure of the gospel to apostles whose frailty resembled cheap, earthenware lamps. Paul gave illustrations of his vulnerability and the divine power in 4:8-9 and then asserted in 4:10-11 that despite being constantly subjected to forces that led to death, he was continually upheld, sustained, and led in triumph by the life of the risen Lord.

Most versions (e.g., KJV, NASB, Williams) regard the "that" clause of v. 12 as expressing a reason for Paul's thanksgiving rather than expressing its content as the NIV relates. The reason for Paul's thanksgiving was that Christ had shown confidence in his worth by putting him into ministry. Spicq provides an appropriate quote from Augustine: "God does not choose a person who is worthy, but by the act of choosing him he makes him worthy [translation mine]."[14]

The term "faithful" is actually a reference to Paul's worth in God's sight. Paul was not suggesting he had received the appointment to ministry because God thought so well of him. He was amazed that a man from his background would ever be entrusted with the gospel at all. He was overjoyed at God's demonstration of confidence in him by placing him, a man of violence and a threat to Christians, in a place of service for God's kingdom.

1:13 Paul mentioned three liabilities God could have held against him in considering his call to service. As a "blasphemer" Paul had denied Christ by word and deed and attempted to force others to do the same (Acts 26:11). As a persecutor Paul hunted down Christians like wild animals (Acts 22:4,7). As a "violent man" Paul acted like a "bully."

Paul's explanation of the reason for his receipt of mercy suggests a negative cause of the divine mercy. God demonstrated mercy to Paul because Paul was ignorant of the true nature of Jesus as Lord and Savior. Paul's explanation was not intended to diminish his guilt but to put his sin into the category of a sin of ignorance rather than a "presumptuous" or "defiant" sin (cf. Num 15:22-31). Paul did not sin against better knowledge and commit a willful sin (Heb 10:26). His unbelief contained a form

---

[13]The presence of a present tense "gives . . . strength" instead of an aorist "has given . . . strength" in some manuscripts is probably inspired by the present tense in Phil 4:13 and is not from Paul's hand.

[14]Spicq, *Saint Paul*, 40. Note Paul's statement in 1 Cor 4:2 that the chief requirement for God's stewards is that they be found faithful or trustworthy.

of ignorance, an ignorance that brought Jesus to the cross (Acts 3:17). Paul's conversion was a fulfillment of Jesus' prayer in Luke 23:34. God can bring to salvation willful sinners as well as "ignorant" sinners, but both groups need to come to God in faith and repentance. The more willful the persons, the less likely is their repentance.

1:14 From a positive standpoint Paul stated that God's grace, the undeserved favor shown in Paul's conversion, had come into the apostle's life as an utterly transforming power. It is in accord with God's gracious nature to show such grace, and that gracious nature was a positive cause of mercy. Dabbling with "myths and endless genealogies" (v. 4) could not transform a life as divine grace had changed Paul. The verb for "poured out . . . abundantly" is a hapax legomenon intensified by adding the prefix *over* (*hyper*) to a verb that of itself signified *to abound* or *to increase*. Paul was saying that God's grace superabounded toward him.[15]

The result of the gushing forth of divine grace was an experience of faith and love for Paul. Faith came as a response to God's grace, and love was a combination of forgiveness and compassion which only committed believers can possess.[16]

(2) Statement of the Gospel (1:15)

[15]Here is a trustworthy saying that deserves full acceptance: Christ Jesus came into the world to save sinners—of whom I am the worst.

1:15 In this verse Paul elaborated facts about Jesus and about himself. Concerning Jesus, Paul referred to the incarnation and made an implied reference to Jesus' redeeming activity. Jesus' statements in Matt 18:11 and Luke 19:10 may have been a source for Paul's statement.

Concerning himself Paul indicated that he stood foremost in the ranks of sinners. His use of the term "worst" (*prōtos*), literally *first*, does not merely suggest the idea of first in order but the concept of the most prominent or leading. Paul sincerely saw himself as the leading sinner among candidates for the dubious honor. Guthrie points out that a man who could rank himself as "less than the least of all God's people" (Eph 3:8) was not speaking morbidly but expressing sincere humility.[17] Paul had

---

[15]Paul made frequent use of verbs intensified by the addition of the Greek preposition ηυπερ in such passages as Rom 5:20 (ὑπερεπερίσσευσεν); 2 Cor 7:4 (ὑπερπερισσεύομαι); Phil 2:9 (ὑπερύψωσεν); 2 Thess 1:3 (ὑπεραυξάνει).

[16]G. Fee (*1 and 2 Timothy, Titus*, GNC, ed. W. W. Gasque [San Francisco: Harper & Row, 1984], 20) points out the play on words for faith (πίστις) and its cognates used by Paul in vv. 11-14. In v. 11 Paul was "entrusted" (ἐπιστεύθην) with the gospel, and in v. 12 Christ considered Paul "faithful." In v. 13 Paul was in "unbelief" (ἀπιστίᾳ) and in v. 14 he received "faith" from his union with Christ Jesus.

[17]D. Guthrie, *The Pastoral Epistles*, TNTC (London: Tyndale, 1957), 66.

fought so stubbornly against the truth and light of Jesus that he now saw himself in the forefront of those whose sins cried out for God's mercy. Paul added superlative humility to his description by indicating that he still functioned as "chief" among sinners ("I am" and not merely "I was").

This passage introduces the first of five sections in the Pastorals that contain the term "trustworthy" saying.[18] The passages in which the formula appears are 1 Tim 1:15; 3:1; 4:9; 2 Tim 2:11; Titus 3:8. All five of the passages contain the statement "Here is a trustworthy saying." Two passages (here and in 1 Tim 4:9) contain also an added phrase that says the statement "deserves full acceptance."

Three issues surface concerning this formula each time it appears. First, does the formula follow or precede the trustworthy saying? In 1:15 the formula clearly precedes the saying, and in 4:9 the formula follows the saying. Scholars debate whether the faithful saying in 3:1 follows or precedes the formula.[19] Second, which verse or verses contain the formula? In 1:15 the entire trustworthy saying appears in the verse. In Titus 3:8 the trustworthy saying is generally regarded as appearing in the preceding verses, but the identification of those verses is not unanimous.[20] Third, what is the meaning of the formula? The formula clearly marks the saying as an article of belief worthy of acceptance and deeply cherished by all believers. Dibelius and Conzelmann affirm that each saying contains an application to the present of some aspect or feature of salvation.[21]

E. Ellis points out that the phrase appears in Jewish and Greco-Roman writings, but it identifies a report as credible without serving as a formula. He also calls attention to the saying of the angel at Rev 22:6 which contains the statement "These words are trustworthy and true." Ellis locates the origin of the formula in prophets from the Qumran community and feels that Paul and his coworkers began to use it during his Caesarean or first Roman imprisonment. He feels that both Caesarea and Rome had a group of teachers with connections to Jerusalem and that the Jerusalem church had contact with and converts from the Qumran community. He feels that Paul may have formulated many of the sayings, but he believes

---

[18]For a complete discussion of the interpretation of these sayings, see G. W. Knight II, *The Faithful Sayings in the Pastoral Letters* (Grand Rapids: Baker, 1979).

[19]Fee (*1 and 2 Timothy, Titus*, 42) feels that the actual saying follows the formula in 3:1a, and M. Dibelius and H. Conzelmann (*The Pastoral Epistles* [Philadelphia: Fortress, 1972], 28-29) locate the saying in the preceding verses.

[20]Fee (*1 and 2 Timothy, Titus*, 159) feels that the saying appears in 3:4-7, but Kelly (*A Commentary on the Pastoral Epistles* [London: A & C Black, 1963], 254), while preferring to see 5b-6 as the saying, adds, "It is perhaps hazardous . . . to try to identify the trustworthy saying exactly."

[21]Dibelius and Conzelmann, *Pastoral Epistles*, 29.

that Titus 3 includes a midrash (a running commentary on Scripture) based on Joel 2:28f., understood as fulfilled at Pentecost.[22]

The idea that Jesus "came" into the world frequently appears in John's Gospel. Such passages as John 3:19; 9:39; 12:46; 16:28; and 18:37 interpret Jesus' coming.

Paul's statement here and in 1 Cor 6:9-11 indicates that early Christians came from backgrounds of extensive wickedness, but they all shared the life-transforming power of Jesus Christ. Such passages as these led Celsus, an early opponent of Christianity, to criticize the apostles as "infamous" and "wicked" men.[23] Wickedness was in their past, and previous moral bankruptcy had been replaced by a purity that attracted the barbed attention of their non-Christian neighbors. Paul's desire was to serve as an example of God's gracious ability to transform sinners into saints.

(3) Purpose of the Divine Mercy (1:16)

[16]But for that very reason I was shown mercy so that in me, the worst of sinners, Christ Jesus might display his unlimited patience as an example for those who would believe on him and receive eternal life.

1:16 Here Paul elaborated a further positive purpose (cf. 1:14) for God's mercy. The phrase "for that very reason" (*dia touto*) introduces Paul's explanation. Paul's explanation begins with "so that" in the middle section of the verse. God wanted to make a public display of his grace to a notable sinner such as Paul so that other despairing sinners might also find mercy.

"Mercy" is a verbal form of the noun in 1:2 and refers to God's pity for the miserable and distressed. The identical word is used in v. 13 ("I was shown mercy"). Both verbs mean literally *I was mercied*.

The NIV reads "in me, the worst of sinners" and reflects a correct interpretation of the Greek text, which literally says "in me first" (*prōtos*).[24]

Christ's "unlimited patience" is an attitude of moral restraint that holds out under provocation. This longsuffering held back overdue judgment and offered pardon and forgiveness instead of separation and lostness.

---

[22]E. E. Ellis, "Traditions in the Pastoral Epistles," *Early Jewish and Christian Exegesis: Studies in Memory of William Hugh Brownlee*, ed. C. Stevens and W. F. Stinespring [Atlanta: Scholars, 1987], 239-42.

[23]See Origen, *Against Celsus*, 1.63.

[24]The KJV rather inconsistently translates the πρῶτός of v. 15 as "chief" and that of v. 16 as "first." Modern translations (NIV, NASB, Williams) see both references as a description of Paul as the "worst" or "foremost" of sinners.

The word translated "example" (*hypotypōsis*) suggests that Paul is a prototype. Paul's experience provides an outline of the sort of pity that a greatly patient God will provide for all sinners. Paul saw himself as a standard example for all who would be saved in the future. The verb "would believe" suggests simple futurity (i.e., "going to believe") and provides no indication of determinism.

Despite the abundance of divine mercy, some successfully choose to go their own way and receive judgment instead of mercy. The most significant New Testament example of such resistance appears in Judas, who persisted in following his own way to ruin despite the abundant offer of divine mercy (Acts 1:15-26).

The "eternal life" Paul mentioned is frequently discussed in John's Gospel (John 3:16; 5:24; cf. 10:10). This life is the blessed life of the world to come of which believers can claim a foretaste on earth. The earthly life of a believer is fuller and richer, while heavenly life is unending.

(4) Doxology (1:17)

[17]Now to the King eternal, immortal, invisible, the only God, be honor and glory for ever and ever. Amen.

1:17 What Paul had begun as a thanksgiving now concludes with a doxology of divine praise. Such Pauline doxologies appear also in Rom 11:36; 16:27; Gal 1:5; Phil 4:20; and Eph 3:21. The Lord's gift of mercy and Paul's experience of need caused his heart to swell with praise. Paul ascribed four characteristics to God and then offered him honor and glory.

First, Paul designated God as "the King eternal," a phrase that picks up on the theme of eternal life in v. 16. The term denotes God as the ruler of all ages from creation and pictures him as literally the *King of the ages*. Second, he described God as "immortal" or immune from decay and corruption. Third, he described God as "invisible," but believers can view the splendid glory of God residing in the person of Jesus (2 Cor 4:6; John 1:14). Finally, he presented God as the "only" God, an adjective which insists that God has no competitors. God is unique, incomparable, and glorious. The term "wise" (KJV) is absent from the best Greek texts and most modern translations and is likely due to the influence of Rom 16:27.

The "honor" Paul gave to God involves esteem and reverence due to God because of his personal qualities of excellence. The term "glory" is an acknowledgment of God's majesty and power. Paul's "Amen" is an emphatic word which affirms that the preceding truths are justified and correct. Before the advent of printing made copies of Bibles accessible, a lector read the message to a congregation. When early congregations heard the reader intone "Amen," they responded in like manner.

EXCURSUS 1: THE HISTORICAL, SOCIAL, AND RELIGIOUS BACKGROUND OF EPHESUS. Josephus designated Ephesus as "the metropolis of Asia,"[25] and in the first century the city was one of the four great metropolises of the Roman world after Rome, Alexandria, and Antioch.[26] Scholars estimate its population at a quarter of a million. The city was located at the mouth of the Cayster River at the Aegean coast between Smyrna and Miletus. The rapidly flowing Cayster deposited silt at its mouth. The lack of tides in the Mediterranean created a problem with sediment in the Ephesian harbor. Evidence of this difficulty appears throughout the history of the city.[27]

The Lydian King Croesus conquered the city around 560 B.C. Greeks in the area had linked the traits of the Greek Artemis with an Oriental goddess native to the area. Croesus erected a temple in her honor. The building and rebuilding of this temple after battles and fires took place frequently over the centuries. Croesus was eventually defeated by Cyrus and the Persians; and Ephesus belonged progressively to the Macedonians, the Ptolemies, the Seleucids, and the city of Pergamum. After 133 B.C. Ephesus became a part of the Roman province of Asia with Pergamum as the capital. Ephesus, however, was the more prominent city.

The location of Ephesus on the Aegean Sea made it of commercial importance in the buying, selling, and transporting of goods. In addition several land routes of commerce passed through Ephesus. Lavish buildings including baths, gymnasia (large sports plazas), and theaters have been excavated in the city. A prominent site that has been excavated is a theater to which Claudius and Nero made additions. Here "twenty-four thousand screaming Ephesians gathered to protest Paul's ministry" (Acts 19:23-41).[28] Other findings have included evidence of the existence of a lecture hall or an auditorium in which discussions such as Paul gave could have taken place (Acts 19:9). A brothel, a library, and a commercial agora (gathering place, especially a marketplace) also have been unearthed.

The most magnificent structure at Ephesus was the Temple of Artemis (Roman Diana). Yamauchi says that "the rebuilt temple was the largest structure in the Hellenistic world and the first of such monumental proportions to be built entirely of marble."[29] The goddess Artemis appeared

---

[25]Josephus, *Antiquities*, 14.10.11.

[26]Useful sources of information about the historical, social, and religious background of Ephesus include G. Borchert, "Ephesus," *ISBE* (1982); S. H. Gritz, *Paul, Women Teachers, and the Mother Goddess at Ephesus* (Lanham, Md.: University Press of America, 1991); and E. M. Yamauchi, *New Testament Cities in Western Asia Minor* (Grand Rapids: Baker, 1980).

[27]Yamauchi, *New Testament Cities*, 79-81.

[28]Ibid., 94.

[29]Ibid., 103.

with many rows of bulbous objects on her chest. These are frequently interpreted as breasts. Some scholars have suggested that the bulbous objects were ostrich eggs, symbols of fertility; others have viewed them as astrological symbols. The cult linked with Artemis was extremely popular among pagan women, and "this religion allowed them greater freedom than anything experienced previously."[30]

The temple also functioned as a bank and a sanctuary. The temple itself generated much wealth due to the traffic in Ephesus of pilgrims wanting to visit it. Money was deposited in the temple in its function as treasury or bank. One indication of the wealth of Ephesus may come from the refusal by the city to accept funds from Alexander the Great for rebuilding the temple.

Criminals had the right of sanctuary within the environs of the temple. In the time of Alexander the right of sanctuary extended outward a distance of about two hundred meters, but it was later enlarged. The extension attracted so many criminal types in the temple vicinity that Augustus revoked plans for an enlargement of the sanctuary area.[31]

Ephesus was also a center of worship for the Roman emperor. The term "guardian of the temple" (*neōkoros*) in Acts 19:35 came to be used of cities that had temples used for emperor worship. Yamauchi feels that the "officials of the province" in Acts 19:31 were wealthy, influential Roman citizens who presided over the cult of emperor worship.[32]

Ephesus was a magnet that drew wealthy businessmen, religious enthusiasts, criminals, and tourists to live and to visit. Citizens of the city could follow the routes of materialism, flagrant immorality, pagan religion, or pleasure in their quest for satisfaction. Such a cafeteria of choices in this very open city affected the atmosphere of the Christian church growing in its midst.

Paul spent nearly three years of ministry in Ephesus (Acts 20:31). In an address to the elders of the church (Acts 20:17-35), he advised them to beware of false teachers who would attack the flock of the Ephesian church like predatory wolves (Acts 20:29). These false leaders would rise up from within the church itself. He called the elders to a watchful lifestyle, ministry to one another, and commitment in ministry.

Some Ephesian women had come from pagan backgrounds and had perhaps been influenced by Artemis worship. Gritz points out that Paul would naturally have wanted to curtail or circumscribe any practices among these Christian women that might confuse them with the devotees of Artemis and their emotional excesses. He would have wanted the

---

[30]Gritz, *Paul, Women Teachers*, 43.
[31]Yamauchi, *New Testament Cities*, 108.
[32]Ibid., 109.

pagan converts to comprehend that neither ascetic continence, sacred intercourse, nor any other cultic activity could provide them with salvation or eternal life.[33]

Paul would also have been concerned for those Jewish women in Ephesus who had come to Christ. He would want them to "relax in the equality before God that faith in Jesus Christ offered. They too could study, learn, and serve in the Christian community."[34]

3. To Prevent a Decline of Commitment (1:18-20)

[18]Timothy, my son, I give you this instruction in keeping with the prophecies once made about you, so that by following them you may fight the good fight, [19]holding on to faith and a good conscience. Some have rejected these and so have shipwrecked their faith. [20]Among them are Hymenaeus and Alexander, whom I have handed over to Satan to be taught not to blaspheme.

Paul had begun his charge to Timothy in 1:3-4 by urging him to warn the false teachers in Ephesus to stop devoting themselves to useless "myths" that promoted controversy rather than commitment. In 1:12-17 he digressed from this warning in order to explain the nature of the gospel on which Timothy was to focus. Now he urged Timothy to renew a moral appeal to the Ephesian congregation. As incentives to obey, he reminded Timothy of earlier expressions about his potential for service and of the spiritual failure of two Ephesian leaders who had dabbled with the unprofitable myths.

1:18 The "instruction" (*parangelia*) of v. 18 is the same word as that translated "command" in v. 5 (same root word as the verb "command" in v. 3). Paul was not merely dropping hints to Timothy but was reminding him that he must act in a specified manner. In giving this directive, Paul used a term for "give" that is also used in 2 Tim 2:2 to describe passing on Christian traditions from one generation to another. Paul was passing to Timothy insights that would help him in his struggle against the false teachers of Ephesus. The "prophecies" probably represent promising comments concerning Timothy's spiritual usefulness spoken at earlier occasions in his ministry. The events of Acts 13:1-3 provide a helpful parallel to guide our understanding of how the prophecies may have come.[35]

Inspired by these prophecies, Timothy could successfully fight against the errors of Ephesus. The military term "fight the good fight" suggests

---

[33]Gritz, 43.

[34]Ibid.

[35]The plural "prophecies" suggests that they were spoken more than once, perhaps on such occasions as Timothy's initial contact with Paul (Acts 16:1-3) and his setting aside for ministry (1 Tim 4:14).

that Timothy faced a grueling spiritual battle and not a pleasant rural retreat.[36] By remembering and responding to these earlier prophecies about him, Timothy could recapture the spiritual excitement of using his spiritual gifts so that he could wage a successful battle on difficult turf.

1:19 Paul united "faith" and a "good conscience" (cf. 1:5; 3:9). The term "faith" refers to a personal commitment to Jesus Christ, a personal faith in him. The earlier discussion in 1:5 concerning conscience suggests that only an obedient Christian can enjoy a good conscience. Paul's use of the terms in tandem links religion and morality inseparably together. Most religious error is born of moral rebellion rather than intellectual denial.

The term "reject" (*apōtheō*) normally describes (in the New Testament) a violent, willful rejection. In Acts 7:39 it describes the rejection of the authority of Moses by those Jews who begged Aaron to make a golden calf for them to worship. In Acts 13:46 it showed the rejection of the gospel by the Jews of Pisidian Antioch, an event that occasioned Paul's turning to the Gentiles. In Rom 11:1-2 Paul denied that God had "rejected" Israel, his own people. In 1 Tim 1:19 Paul suggested that Hymenaeus and Alexander (v. 20) had virulently rejected commitment to Christ and the obedient life-style that would come from that. The result of such rejection is the spiritual shipwreck of the individual.[37]

Paul's appeal in v. 19 reminds us that correct belief alone does not guarantee a useful Christian life. Each Christian must combine a right understanding of Christ with a proper response to that understanding. Our faith must produce good works, not pious platitudes (Jas 2:14-26).

1:20 The names of Hymenaeus and Alexander appear in other New Testament passages, but we are not sure that all passages describe the same persons (cf. 2 Tim 2:17; 4:14-15; Acts 19:33).[38] To "hand over to Satan" has at least two possible interpretations. First, it may refer to some illness or physical disability Satan is allowed to inflict on evildoers (see Job 2:6). Kelly insists that we "must infer that illness, paralysis, or some other physical disability was in the Apostle's mind."[39] Second, it may be used as a semitechnical phrase that regards life in the church as the sphere of the Spirit and life outside the church as the sphere of Satan. Paul may have been saying that he had removed the offenders from the fellowship of the church and placed them in Satan's realm, where they would experience his malice. This seems the more likely interpretation.

---

[36]Paul again used the same military imagery to describe our spiritual battle in 2 Tim 2:3-4.

[37]Paul was well qualified to describe shipwrecks, for at the time of his writing he had been shipwrecked at least four times (2 Cor 11:25; Acts 27:3,9-44).

[38]Many commentators link Hymenaeus with the same person in 2 Tim 2:17 and Alexander with the troublesome coppersmith in 2 Tim 4:14-15.

[39]Kelly, *Pastoral Epistles*, 59.

Lock implies that both ideas are involved and indicates that the term is "at least illustrated by, the contemporary Pagan 'execration-tablets' by which a person who has been wronged handed over the wrong-doer to the gods below, who inflicted bodily suffering upon him."[40]

The purpose of handing them over to Satan was not merely punitive but chiefly corrective or formative in purpose. By excluding them from the fellowship of God's people, Paul hoped that Satan's affliction of the troublemakers would teach them not to insult the Lord by their words and deeds.[41] It is instructive to study the context of 1 Cor 5:5 in which Paul also spoke of handing a sinner over to Satan. There the transgressor had committed incest, and Paul wanted to "hand him over to Satan" so that he could learn to grow weary of following the sinful urgings of the flesh. In 1 Corinthians Paul urged the church to decide upon the action of discipline, but in 1 Timothy he had already determined the course of action on his own, with or without the church.[42]

Summary. Paul's words in this section are helpful at three points of application. First, in vv. 3-11 Paul warned against the false doctrine permeating Ephesus. His statements were blunt and incisive. He accused the heretics of not properly understanding and using the law, and he gave a brief theological statement on the proper use of the law. He understood theologically the purpose of the law and tried to communicate that insight to his readers. His words show the importance of having a theological understanding of the gospel. With a theme as majestic as the gospel, we can wax eloquent with moving platitudes about God's love and divine grace but can omit a discussion of sin and repentance. We can face the danger of "saying nothing well." Paul's forceful discussion of the purpose of the law reminds us that we must communicate the divine message with sound theology and not merely with a sublime but glib tongue.

Second, in 1:12-17 Paul refreshingly recounted his conversion experience. He never got beyond a response of wonder and gratitude to God's act of saving him "warts and all." We must never move beyond the excitement and joy our conversion generates in us.

Third, in 1:18-20 Paul was reminding Timothy of truths Timothy had previously heard. Much Christian communication consists not of bringing new ideas forward but of recounting tested, tried principles which we often forget or neglect.

---

[40]Lock, *Pastoral Epistles*, 19.

[41]The activity of the "beast from the sea" in Rev 13:1-6 shows what blasphemy involves.

[42]In a chapter entitled "Christian Discipline and a Regenerate Church Membership," F. B. Edge discusses the need for discipline in Baptist churches. He mentions that historically Baptists have practiced three levels of church discipline in the increasing order of seriousness: rebuke, suspension from the Lord's table, and excommunication, or exclusion from the church. See Edge, *A Quest for Vitality in Religion* (Nashville: Broadman, 1963), 223-39.

Overview. In 1:3-20 Paul explained the task that lay ahead of Timothy. The job involved preventing the spread of false teaching (1:3-11), declaring the gospel of God's saving grace for all sinners (1:12-17), and preventing a decline of commitment among leaders and members of the Ephesian congregation (1:18-20). How would Timothy carry out this task? What emphases would accomplish the job? Paul devoted the remainder of 1 Timothy to listing those teachings that would complete the job he outlined for Timothy.

First, Paul counseled that prayer be made for the conversion of all people and not merely for an elitist group (2:1-7). He also pointed out the need for holy behavior by both men and women in the church (2:8-15). Turning to the problem of leadership, Paul outlined the traits competent leaders must demonstrate (3:1-13), and he indicated that his purpose was to develop believers who would function as holy members of God's family (3:14-16). Paul also warned again concerning the false teachers (4:1-5), and he gave specific instructions for action to Timothy (4:6-16). In 5:1-2 Paul provided directions for dealing with different age groups within the church, and then he dealt consecutively with widows (5:3-16), elders (5:17-25), and slaves (6:1-2a). He presented a final warning against false teachers in 6:2b-10 and offered a closing exhortation to Timothy in 6:11-16. He urged generosity by wealthy believers in 6:17-19. A caution to Timothy appears in 6:20-21.

We have just concluded in this chapter an examination of the task Paul assigned to Timothy in dealing with the problem of false teaching at Ephesus. Now we will examine the emphases Paul outlined for Timothy in 2:1–6:19. The emphases cited above will function in most instances as the subject of a chapter. Paul began his presentation with a discussion of the urgency of offering prayers for all people so that they might come to know spiritual deliverance through faith in Christ.

──────────── *SECTION OUTLINE* ────────────

III. THE EMPHASES THAT WILL ACCOMPLISH THE TASK (2:1–6:21)
   1. Prayer for All People (2:1-7)
     (1) The Objects and Content of Prayer (2:1-2)
     (2) The Goal of Prayer (2:3-4)
     (3) The Goodness of the Goal of Prayer (2:5-7)
   2. Holy Living by Men and Women (2:8-15)
     (1) An Appeal to Men (2:8)
     (2) An Appeal to Women (2:9-15)
        Moral Behavior of the Women (2:9-10)
        Church Activity of the Women (2:11-12)
        An Explanation of Paul's Appeal (2:13-14)
        A Promise for Obedient Women (2:15)
        Excursus 2: Women in Ministry
   3. Church Leadership by Committed Servants (3:1-13)
     (1) Qualifications of Overseers (3:1-7)
     (2) Qualifications of Deacons (3:8-10,12-13)
     (3) Qualifications of Women Helpers (3:11)
   4. Correct Application of Christian Truth (3:14-16)
     (1) Plans for a Visit (3:14)
     (2) Purpose for Writing (3:15)
     (3) A Hymn for Believers (3:16)
   5. Understanding False Practice (4:1-5)
     (1) A Warning against Apostasy (4:1-3)
     (2) An Argument against Asceticism (4:4)
     (3) An Argument for Blessing Food (4:5)
   6. Timothy's Performance of His Task (4:6-16)
     (1) Facing Falsehood (4:6-10)
     (2) Demonstrating Christian Behavior (4:11-16)
   7. Responsibilities toward Church Groups (5:1-16)
     (1) Proper Treatment for All Ages (5:1-2)
     (2) The Care of True Widows (5:3-8)
     (3) Warning to Younger Widows (5:9-16)
   8. Proper Handling of Leaders (5:17-25)
     (1) Recognition and Discipline of Leaders (5:17-20)
     (2) Special Directions to Timothy (5:21-25)
   9. A Warning to Slaves and Sinners (6:1-10)
     (1) The Responsibility of Christian Slaves (6:1-2a)
     (2) An Indictment of the False Teachers (6:2b-5)
     (3) The Greed of the False Teachers (6:6-10)

10. Instructions to Timothy and the Wealthy (6:11-21)
(1) A Program for Godliness (6:11-16)
(2) A Promise for the Prosperous (6:17-19)
(3) A Concluding Caution (6:20-21)

─────── III. THE EMPHASES THAT WILL ACCOMPLISH ───────
THE TASK (2:1–6:21)

In chap. 1 Paul explained that Timothy's task involved preventing the spread of false teaching (1:3-11), sharing a gospel that could save sinners (1:12-17), and preventing a decline of commitment among church leaders (1:18-20). How would Timothy accomplish this task?

Paul's first emphasis was that Timothy lead his hearers to pray for the salvation of all people. Apparently the false teachers in Ephesus promoted an attitude that presented Christianity as a religion for an elite group. Paul demolished this exclusivist idea and suggested that the object of Christian prayer must be as wide as the object of Christ's death—for all people.

The Greek text[1] has periods at the conclusion of verses 2,4,6,7. This punctuation suggests the view that Paul presented the objects and content of prayer in vv. 1-2 and the goal of prayer in vv. 3-4. In vv. 5-7 he put forth three features that prove the goal of prayer is acceptable with God.

1. Prayer for All People (2:1-7)

(1) The Objects and Content of Prayer (2:1-2)

[1]**I urge, then, first of all, that requests, prayers, intercession and thanksgiving be made for everyone—**[2]**for kings and all those in authority, that we may live peaceful and quiet lives in all godliness and holiness.**

2:1 The "then" with which v. 1 begins may either refer to what precedes or serve as a transition to something new. If we accept that the purpose of the book is stated in 1:3, it seems best to see Paul providing instructions for Timothy to use in carrying out the purposes he had already mentioned.

Because of the stubbornness of the Ephesian heretics, Paul felt it necessary to give Timothy some specific guidance for combating their challenge. He attempted to correct abuses that flowed from the teachings of the errorists. It would be wrong to see Paul beginning an outline on how to organize a church. He was not outlining church organization, but he was confronting errors and heresies already underway.

─────────────────────

[1]UBS, 1983.

The words "first of all" are not so much the introduction of the initial item on a list as a reference to the primary importance of what Paul was about to discuss. Prayer for all kinds of people (including those of 2:2) is an item of great significance.

Paul listed four words for prayer in v. 1. "Requests" are petitions to God based on a sense of deep spiritual need (see the same word translated "prayer" in Jas 5:16). The term "prayers" is the most general word for prayer in the New Testament (see "prayers" in 1 Pet 3:7). It is used of all types of prayers to God including general requests or specific petitions. The verbal form of "intercession" is used of Christ's prayers for believers in Heb 7:25. Huther indicates that the initial prayer term distinguishes the element of insufficiency by the requester, the second highlights devotion by the seeker, and the third underscores the childlike confidence of the petitioner. [2]

The fourth word, "thanksgiving," adds gratitude as a motivation for asking. Whereas the initial three words express various ways of making requests of God, the final word describes the expression of gratitude to God. Paul probably did not intend any sharp distinction between the words but was collecting synonyms that effectively communicate the importance of prayer.

Paul was concerned that Ephesian believers pray for everyone. He would emphasize in v. 4 that God wants "all men to be saved" and in v. 6 that Christ died "for all men." This shows the breadth of his concern. The false teachers among the Ephesians may have limited their concerns to a certain elite group. Kelly says that "Paul makes it plain that narrowness of this kind offends against the gospel of Christ."[3]

2:2 The object of these prayers is "everyone," but Paul reminded his readers that kings and other leaders are the special objects of prayer. To pray for "everyone" does not suggest that we must mention each human being by name but that our prayers should include all groups of human beings. All needy sinners—without distinction of race, nationality, or social position—must receive our prayers.

The terms "kings and all those in authority" refer to the authorities of the state including emperors, governors, and other local authorities. Persecuted Christians could easily omit prayers for their persecuting rulers. Such prayers for leaders had a long history in Judaism (Ezra 7:27-28; 9:6-9).

---

[2] J. E. Huther, *Critical and Exegetical Handbook to the Epistles to Timothy and Titus,* MNTC, trans. D. Hunter (1884; reprint, Peabody, Mass.: Hendrickson, 1983), 94.

[3] J. N. D. Kelly, *A Commentary on the Pastoral Epistles* (1963; reprint, Grand Rapids: Baker, 1981), 60.

The final clause of v. 2 designates the content of the prayer. First, Paul's words imply that Christians must pray that their leaders will have the knowledge needed to guide them in their duties. Freedom from anarchy, persecution, and economic hardship can facilitate the spread of the gospel. Wise rulers can provide sound, solid leadership to accomplish these goals. Paul was not merely requesting that Christians pray for the conversion of their leaders, although this was at least a part of the prayer. The prayers include thanksgivings for those decisions that facilitate the spread of Christianity and requests for wisdom in making important decisions.

Second, Paul desired that believers live "peaceful and quiet lives." He may not have intended that this "quiet" life be free of all conflict and persecution. Such an interpretation is unlikely in view of Paul's realistic expectations of persecution in 2 Tim 1:8; 3:12. Vigorous Christianity has spread rapidly even under conditions of severe opposition and persecution.

In 1 Thess 4:11-12 Paul urged the Thessalonian believers to live a quiet life in such a way as to win the respect of unbelievers. Perhaps strife and discord in the church caused outsiders to scoff at the religion of the Ephesian Christians. Paul wanted his readers to live an orderly life free of strife and discord so as to convince unbelievers that Christianity was worthy of their attention.[4]

An added reason for referring "quiet" to the godly conduct of the Ephesians is that the terms "godliness and holiness" appear to refer to behavior. Godliness involves a proper respect for God, and holiness demands a serious and earnest life-style before observers, even those who are hostile.

In Rom 13:1-7 Paul counseled that believers owed obedience to and respect for officials and payment of taxes to the government. His words here are in keeping with that perspective. Paul's attitude is the more remarkable when we realize that the fiendish Nero likely was the emperor during these times.

(2) The Goal of Prayer (2:3-4)

[3]This is good, and pleases God our Savior, [4]who wants all men to be saved and to come to a knowledge of the truth.

2:3 The antecedent of "this" is the reference to prayer for all people in v. 1. Paul stated that God is pleased to see believers earnestly concerned for the salvation of all humankind and not simply for an elitist group. The knowledge that such prayer pleases God provides a throbbing

---

[4]The Greek term for "quiet" in 1 Tim 2:2 is ἡσύχιον, an adjective. The verb of 1 Thess 4:11, ἡσυχάζειν, comes from the same word family. Paul explained the purpose of living this orderly life in 1 Thess 4:12. He wanted them to win the respect of outsiders.

incentive to pray. Paul described God as "our Savior" because he was dealing with the concept of salvation in the verses that follow. Paul's use of the phrase shows that God is the author of salvation (1 Thess 5:9) and that Paul and his readers had experienced it.

2:4 The relative clause of v. 4 provides the basis for the assertion in v. 3 that prayer for all people is pleasing to God. The goal of the prayers Paul urged is that all people be saved. Intercession for all people pleases the God who desires all to be saved.

The term "all" in v. 4 must refer to the same group as the reference to "everyone" in v. 1. The petitions of v. 1 are to include all human beings, and the objects of Christ's death must include the same group. It would certainly include all persons without distinctions of race or social standing, but it also refers to all persons individually. The difficulty of praying for every single inhabitant on the earth should not hide us from the fact that God's "will to save is as wide as His will to create and protect."[5] In suggesting a broad extent for the death of Christ, Paul was taking issue with the idea that only the spiritually elite are the beneficiaries of Christ's death.

The term for "wants" (*thelō*) should not be taken to support a universalistic idea. The fact that God desires the salvation of all does not guarantee that all will be saved.[6] God will not override the reluctance or opposition of individuals bent upon pursuing their own way in defiance of God. Passages such as Matt 6:10; 7:21; 12:50 suggest that what God delights in may not always be done by disobedient human beings. The will of God does not function as a ruthless bulldozer crushing and forcing into obedience any who resist it. God urges us to repentance with his goodness rather than coercing us toward the truth by the application of naked power (Rom 2:4).[7]

The use of the term "truth" is a reference to the gospel (cf. Gal 2:5, 14), and it suggests that salvation has a cognitive side. The absence of a reference to faith is no disparagement of the volitional aspect of conversion. To come to the knowledge of the truth is a synonym for conversion.

---

[5]W. Lock, *The Pastoral Epistles*, ICC (Edinburgh: T & T Clark, 1924), 27.

[6]The proper meaning of "wants" is the subject of much discussion. The term can mean *to take pleasure in* as in Matt 9:13, where "desire" is a translation of θέλω. However, the term can also be used with the force of a purpose or resolve by God to do something. In 1 Cor 12:18 θέλω is used to describe the resolve or purpose of God. The same emphasis appears in Rom 9:18; 1 Cor 4:19; 15:38. It is best to see θέλω in 1 Tim 2:4 as expressing the genuine resolve by God that all be saved. The fact that all are not saved can be attributed to the stubbornness of the human will rather than to the weakness of the divine intent.

[7]Kelly suggests two purposes behind Paul's mention of the universal scope of God's plan. First, he feels that Paul opposed the Jewish belief that God willed the destruction of sinners. Second, he feels that Paul opposed the Gnostic idea that salvation belonged only to a group of the spiritually elite (see Kelly, *Pastoral Epistles*, 63).

In the Pastorals, Paul frequently used "truth" as a reference to the gospel message (1 Tim 3:15; 4:3; 6:5; 2 Tim 2:15; 3:7-8; Titus 1:1).

(3) The Goodness of the Goal of Prayer (2:5-7)

[5]For there is one God and one mediator between God and men, the man Christ Jesus, [6]who gave himself as a ransom for all men—the testimony given in its proper time. [7]And for this purpose I was appointed a herald and an apostle—I am telling the truth, I am not lying—and a teacher of the true faith to the Gentiles.

How could Paul affirm that God wants all to be saved? Paul responded to this question by presenting three facts concerning God and Christ (2:5-6).[8] He concluded his emphasis with a brief explanation of his role in heralding the message of salvation (2:7).

2:5 First, Paul declared that there is one God. He did not intend that this be a prideful claim by an exclusivist Jew but rather an affirmation that the one God is to receive worship from all people. Paul was countering the idea that human beings face a plethora of angel-like deities to whom they must answer. There is only one God, and Paul wanted all to know him. The knowledge that God has the single purpose of causing all to know him follows from God's unity. If there were different aims for different individuals to know different beings, the Godhead could be divided in nature.

Second, there is a single mediator between God and humankind. As a mediator Christ removed the separation caused by sin and reconciled humankind with God. As the God-Man, Christ is uniquely qualified to serve as a go-between who can bring sinful people into God's family. The reference to Jesus as the one mediator between God and humanity rules out any understanding that angels (Dan 6:22; Gal 3:19) served as mediators. It also excludes the Gnostic idea that intermediary deities stand between God and humanity. Paul stated what Christ did to accomplish this mediation in v. 6.

The term "mediator" links Jesus with the concept of covenant (see Heb 8:6; 9:15; 12:24). It pictures Jesus as a "negotiator," who brings in a new arrangement between God and human beings. The term also emphasizes that God has acted uniquely through him to fulfill his purpose. There is the additional reminder that only through him can human beings reach the goal intended by God. Only through Christ can sinful human beings come to God. Part of the offense of the cross consists in accepting this fact (see John 14:6).

---

[8]Paul's statement in vv. 5-6 is almost surely a confession or statement of faith with which Paul and his readers were familiar. The statements in the verses form four compact, balanced, and rhythmical assertions. E. Ellis ("Traditions in the Pastoral Epistles," *Early Jewish and Christian Exegesis: Studies in Memory of William Hugh Brownlee*, ed. C. A. Evans and W. F. Stinespring [Atlanta: Scholars, 1987], 246) calls it a hymnic-type confession.

In referring to Christ as "the man Christ Jesus," Paul summarized the conception of Christ as the second Adam, the author of a redeemed humanity.[9] Christ is thus the head of a new race of people who profess allegiance and likeness to him rather than to Adam (cf. Rom 5:12-21; 1 Cor 15:21-22,45-49).

2:6 Third, Paul described Christ's death as a "ransom." This is the sole instance in the New Testament of the use of this word (*antilytron*), but a related word appears in Mark 10:45. The concept of paying a ransom was a commercial idea. The concept was used outside the New Testament to describe the setting free of captives taken in war or the liberation of slaves from their owners. The sum of money paid for setting free was known as the "ransom."

In the passage Paul plainly stated that Jesus' death is the price paid for the release of humankind from captivity to sin. The term attests to the substitutionary nature of Christ's death.[10] The term also suggests that Christ's purpose in giving himself as a ransom is to provide deliverance from sin.

The expression "gave himself" shows the voluntary nature of Christ's death. Other passages that emphasize this self-surrender of Christ include Gal 1:4; 2:20; Titus 2:14. The emphasis on self-surrender spotlights the commitment of Christ to do the Father's will.

The objects of Christ's death are as wide as the objects of prayer in 2:1, "all." The death of Christ is potentially in behalf of all people, but its saving effects are limited to those who respond in faith. Kelly states: "It is the fact that Christ died for all men, without any kind of favoritism, that makes it obligatory for Christians to pray for them all without distinction."[11]

The death of Christ is an act of divine love, but it must be proclaimed to the world in order to be understood. The closing words of v. 6 refer to this act of proclamation.

The words "the testimony given in its proper time" are difficult because their connection with the previous words is unclear. The word

---

[9]Kelly, *Pastoral Epistles*, 63.

[10]For additional discussion of the significance of the passage, see L. Morris, *The Atonement* (Downers Grove, Ill.: InterVarsity Press, 1983), 106-31; idem., *The Apostolic Preaching of the Cross* (Grand Rapids: Eerdmans, 1956), 9-59. In the latter work Morris wisely warns that the NT writers "did not intend ransom to be taken as a full and sufficient statement of what the atonement was and did, but as far as it goes it gives a picture of one aspect of that great work. It is a metaphor which involves the payment of a price which is plainly stated in several places and understood in others to be the death of Christ" (49). For a more cautious statement see the comments by D. Hill, *Greek Words and Hebrew Meanings* (London: Cambridge University Press, 1967), 49-81. For a lexical defense of the idea of substitution, see A. T. Robertson, *A Grammar of the Greek New Testament in the Light of Historical Research* (Nashville: Broadman, 1934), 572-74.

[11]Kelly, *Pastoral Epistles*, 64.

"testimony" stands in a loose apposition to the content of vv. 5-6a. "What Paul is saying is that, by dying for all mankind in accordance with the divine plan, Christ has borne overwhelmingly convincing witness to God's desire for the salvation of all men."[12] The phrase "in its proper time" suggests that in the development of the divine plan of salvation the time for demonstrating God's mercy to all humankind has now come. The work of Jesus inaugurated the gospel era. Unstated but implied is the fact that believers are to proclaim the words of this "testimony" to all the world.

2:7   Paul outlined the special nature of his own ministry in order to prove the validity of praying for all people. Paul had received these offices in order to proclaim the testimony about Jesus to the world. Paul described his appointment as involving the work of a "herald," "an apostle," and "a teacher."[13] Paul made the same assertion of his appointment in 2 Tim 1:11 (cf. Eph 3:7). As a "herald" Paul proclaimed the truth to needy hearers. The term denotes someone with important news to bring such as an announcer at an athletic event, religious festival, or even a political messenger in a royal court. As an apostle Paul operated with a divine commission (Gal 1:11-17). Paul preceded the introduction of his final office with an emotional outburst, insisting that he was telling the truth. This emphatic parenthesis applies to the work of Paul as teacher of the Gentiles. That was his distinctive appointment beyond that which the twelve apostles received. As a herald and an apostle Paul was essentially a teacher of the Gentiles. As a "teacher" Paul operated in the realm of faith, the subjective response to the gospel, and truth, the objective appropriation of the gospel.[14]

Paul's impassioned remonstrance was intended to teach the troubled Ephesian church that the gospel reaches out for all people, even the Gentiles. It also certified Timothy as Paul's representative and gave him standing before a difficult, cantankerous congregation.

Although Christ's death has potential effect for all people, it is effective only with those who come to Christ in faith and repentance. God used Paul's magnificent efforts to bring many wandering Gentiles to faith

---

[12]Ibid.

[13]The presence of the pronoun "I" (ἐγώ) in v. 7 in connection with "appointed" suggests that the appointment Paul had in mind was one unique to him. There were other apostles; but only Paul was a herald, apostle, and teacher of the Gentiles.

[14]The NIV translation speaks of the "true faith." This translation makes a single concept out of two Greek words, "faith" and "truth." Both the NIV translation and the interpretation followed in this commentary interpret the terms in reference to the response by the hearers, both subjectively and objectively. An alternative interpretation is to see the two nouns "faith" and "truth" refer to the faithfulness and truthfulness with which Paul delivered the gospel. Most modern translations have not chosen to follow this possible rendering.

in Jesus as their Messiah. His example becomes an appeal to us to reach out in a bold thrust to a world cut off from the life that is only in Christ.

Paul's words challenge our prayer life in at least three ways. First, we are to pray for all people. It is easy to limit the sphere of our concern merely to family, friends, and even a few foes. Our prayers ought to include requests, thanksgivings, and entreaties for friend and foe, committed and uncommitted, prominent and insignificant. Second, the goal of all our prayers is that people come to a personal knowledge of God's saving power. As we intercede for the sick, needy, confused, and suffering, we must not forget that our ultimate aim is that they experience divine saving power. Third, as we pray, we have the confidence that Christ's death has provided the ransom for sin. Christ's death has a potential effect that is worldwide. Our prayers for others can break out of their narrow limits because Christ's death represented God's effort to reach all sinners.

2. Holy Living by Men and Women (2:8-15)

Among the men in the Ephesian church were some who loved controversy (1:3-4), denied the future resurrection (2 Tim 2:17-18), promoted strife (1 Tim 6:3-5), and took advantage of gullible women (2 Tim 3:6-7). No church could carry out God's Great Commission with members such as these!

The women[15] in Ephesus were equally culpable in that some became gadabouts flitting in idleness from house to house and ignoring domestic

---

[15]The literature on the role of women in the church appears to increase almost exponentially annually. Among the useful books on this topic are J. B. Hurley, *Man and Woman in Biblical Perspective* (Grand Rapids: Zondervan, 1981) from a more traditional perspective and *Women, Authority and the Bible*, ed. A. Mickelsen (Downers Grove, Ill.: InterVarsity Press, 1986) with articles by C. Kroeger, D. M. Scholer, S. N. Gundry, and W. W. Gasque from a more egalitarian perspective.

Useful articles from a more traditional perspective include: D. J. Moo, "1 Timothy 2:11-15: Meaning and Significance," *TJ* n.s. 1 (1980): 62-83; G. W. Knight III, "The New Testament Teaching on the Role Relationship of Male and Female with Special Reference to the Teaching/Ruling Functions in the Church," *JETS* 18 (1975): 81-91; P. W. Barnett, "Wives and Women's Ministry (1 Tim 2:11-15)," *EQ* 61 (1989): 225-38. More egalitarian in viewpoint are P. B. Payne's "Libertarian Women in Ephesus: A Response to Douglas J. Moo's Article; 1 Timothy 2:11-15: Meaning and Significance," *TJ* n.s. 2 (1981): 169-97; K. A. van der Jagt, "Women Are Saved through Bearing Children (1 Timothy 2:11-15)," *BT* 39 (1988): 201-8, and G. D. Fee, "Issues in Evangelical Hermeneutics, Part III: The Great Watershed Intentionality and Particularity/Eternity: 1 Timothy 2:8-15 as a Test Case," *Crux* 26 (1990): 31-37. The September 1983 issue of *Crux* contains several articles reflecting a diversity of viewpoints by W. W. Gasque, B. Waltke, J. Nolland, and M. Adeney. The October 3, 1986, issue of *Christianity Today* features a symposium on "Women in Leadership" with insights from W. Kaiser, B. Waltke, R. Hestenes, and others. The Winter 1986 issue of *RevExp* treats the role of women in ministry with articles written by faculty members of the Southern Baptist Theological Seminary and guest writers.

duties (1 Tim 5:11-14). Some were also prone to sexual misconduct. They chased aimlessly from one doctrinal novelty to another (2 Tim 3:6-7).

Two features of this section deserve comment at the outset. First, the context for Paul's appeal was not the world or the home front but the worship life of the church. Paul was providing instructions for praying and teaching within the confines of the local congregation. Second, Paul's advice was generally for men and women, but the responsibilities of wives and mothers were also in Paul's mind. It is recognized that the women in 2:15 must be wives, but the references in 2:8-9 are for men and women.[16]

In 2:8-15 Paul appealed both to men and women to show behavior that was holy, teachable, and peaceable. In 2:8 he appealed to the men. In 2:9-15 he appealed to the women. In vv. 9-10 he described the moral behavior of the women, and in vv. 11-12 he outlined their proper church activity. He gave a reason for his appeal in vv. 13-14, and he delivered a promise to obedient women in v. 15.

In 2:1-7 Paul had urged Timothy to lead his hearers to pray for the salvation of all people. Now in 2:8-15 Paul described the attitude and actions of the men and women who would do the praying. Instead of living in dissension, controversy, and selfishness, Paul directed both the men and women of Ephesus to practice holiness.

One feature of Ephesus that may have spawned the trouble Paul addressed was the presence of the Temple of Artemis. The temple was one of the ancient world's Seven Wonders. The cult connected with it used women in sensuous, orgiastic practices. The prominence of women in the cult may have affected even Christian women, but its relationship to the church troubles at Ephesus is a moot point.[17]

(1) An Appeal to the Men (2:8)

⁸ I want men everywhere to lift up holy hands in prayer, without anger or disputing.

2:8 Since Paul had just discussed the subject of prayer, it was proper for him further to discuss the role of men in praying. The expression beginning "I want" (*boulomai*) indicates what he intended for the men to carry out. Fee points out that Paul's instruction is not that *only* men

---

[16]The word for "men" in v. 8 is articular and probably reflects a generic reference to males. The anarthrous "women" in v. 9 is not a reference to wives but to females. Although the word "men" (ἀνήρ) can signify a husband and the word "women" (γυνή) can describe a wife (Matt 5:31), both Paul and Peter used "your" (ἴδιος) in Eph 5:22 and 1 Pet 3:1 to indicate that the husband-wife relationship and not the generic male-female relationship was in view. The absence of similar indicators in vv. 8-9 suggests that Paul used the generic reference.

[17]S. H. Gritz, *Paul, Women Teachers, and the Mother Goddess at Ephesus* (Lanham, Md.: University Press of America, 1991), 116, concludes that the context of Paul's discussion is a gnosticizing form of Jewish Christianity that reflects affinities with the Artemis cult.

should pray (cf. 1 Cor 11:5), nor that men *should* pray, nor that they should do it with raised hands, but that they should do it with holiness and without anger or controversy.[18]

The "everywhere" in which the men pray is wherever believers gathered together in Ephesus. Probably this is a reference to local house-churches. The types of prayer to which Paul called the men are those indicated by the terms for prayer in 2:1.

In calling for men to "lift up holy hands," Paul was not prescribing a universal posture for prayer but was alluding to the mode of prayer normally practiced by Jews and many early Christians. Standing with uplifted hands was seen among both Jews and Christians in the first century (Pss 134:2; 141:2).[19]

Paul's primary emphasis was the attitude that the men were to bring to prayer. The term "holy hands" describes hands that are morally pure. This calls for a devout life-style that seeks passionately to please God (John 4:34). The "anger" Paul denounced is a settled attitude of indignation against another. The word "disputing" refers to a spirit of controversy that was the special hallmark of the Ephesian false teachers (1 Tim 6:3-5). Controversy and contempt would vitiate the effectiveness of prayers. Men defiled by these attitudes were in Ephesus, and Paul knew that no good could come from their prayers. Paul's description of the manner in which the men should pray has universal application although local circumstances had stimulated the earnestness of his appeal.

(2) An Appeal to Women (2:9-15)

⁹I also want women to dress modestly, with decency and propriety, not with braided hair or gold or pearls or expensive clothes, ¹⁰but with good deeds, appropriate for women who profess to worship God.

¹¹A woman should learn in quietness and full submission. ¹²I do not permit a woman to teach or to have authority over a man; she must be silent. ¹³For Adam was formed first, then Eve. ¹⁴And Adam was not the one deceived; it was the woman who was deceived and became a sinner. ¹⁵But women will be saved through childbearing—if they continue in faith, love and holiness with propriety.

Paul, as observed earlier, was generally addressing women and not merely wives. He also was prescribing for the church and not the home, although the directives about dress (vv. 9-10) can apply in both. The general tenor of the passage is more appropriate when applied to women in worship.

---

[18]Fee, *1 and 2 Timothy, Titus*, 34.

[19]Standing with raised hands was not an unusual sign of earnestness but was the common prayer posture also for NT believers. The NT petitioner showed great seriousness whenever kneeling was the practice (Eph 3:14).

MORAL BEHAVIOR OF THE WOMEN (2:9-10).   **2:9**   The NIV obscures the
link of v. 9 with v. 8 brought out by "in like manner" (KJV; *hōsautōs*).
This expression shows that vv. 9-10 are still dependent on the "I want" of
v. 8 and that Paul was discussing the dress and deportment of women in
times of public prayer.[20]

Although Paul discussed dress, his true emphasis was not merely that
women should dress modestly but that genuine ornamentation is not
external at all and consists of an attitude of commitment to good works.[21]
To dress "modestly" demands that the women dress tastefully and not
provocatively. The term "dress" (*katastolē*) describes the outward deportment of the women as expressed in the clothes they wear. To practice
"decency and propriety" demands that the women not flaunt their wealth
or their beauty. The former word shows reserve in matters of sex, and the
latter word indicates a mastery of the appetites, particularly in matters of
sex. The two terms refer to inner virtues.

The prohibition against "braided hair" or expensive jewelry or clothing
prohibits a gaudy, showy display, not normal attention to neatness and
good taste. Paul perhaps referred to a style in which "women . . . wore
their hair in enormously elaborate arrangements with braids and curls
interwoven or piled high like towers and decorated with gems and/or gold
and/or pearls."[22] At best such a style demonstrates pride and self-
centeredness and should not be the concern of Christian women (cf. 1 Pet
3:3). The fact that some Christian women could afford gold or pearls indicates that the Ephesian church had some members of substantial wealth
(cf. 1 Cor 1:26-28). Acceptable standards of modesty will vary with place
and generation, but Paul wanted the women to cultivate the fear of God
rather than vanity.

2:10   Paul urged the women to produce good works instead of devoting attention to mere physical appearance. Some women in Ephesus had a
desire to fulfill their sexual urges in any manner (2 Tim 3:6) and probably
expressed this in their dress. Paul warned against indulging these drives
and appealed for good works. This is healthy teaching for godly women.

---

[20]Kelly suggests that what Paul had in mind was that it would be improper for women to
exploit their physical charms on such occasions, for this would be a deterrent to prayer (*Pastoral Epistles*, 66). However, Huther (*Epistles to Timothy and Titus*, 102) disagrees, feeling
that the infinitive "to dress" expresses what Paul wanted for the women. Under this interpretation Paul was not discussing public prayer for the women but how they were to dress on
occasions of public worship. Kelly's arguments seem more compelling.

[21]M. Dibelius and H. Conzelmann, *The Pastoral Epistles* (Philadelphia: Fortress, 1972),
46.

[22]J. B. Hurley, *Man and Woman in Biblical Perspective* (Grand Rapids: Zondervan,
1981), 199.

Paul later would explain that the good works he had in mind must first appear in the home (1 Tim 2:15; 5:9-10,14). Ward aptly says that the women are to show their religion not by "barefaced dazzle but character and conduct."[23] The "good works" Paul demanded represent more than a performance of general benevolence, for they include an appeal to a reverent godliness (2 Tim 3:5) which begins in the home.

The Ephesian women in these passages doubtless were wealthy. Their costly clothing, ornate hairstyles, and expensive jewelry suggest luxuries only the wealthy could afford. There is evidence from outside these passages that wealthy, prominent women were among those converted under the preaching of Paul (Acts 16:15; 17:4,12). Peter's description of the women in the churches of Pontus, Galatia, Cappadocia, Asia, and Bithynia (1 Pet 3:3) also suggests that some of the women were wealthy. Barnett points out that the leading women of Roman imperial society were wealthy, politically powerful, patronesses of the arts, and educated; and he feels that it is likely these wealthy women in the Ephesian congregation had the same characteristics.[24] The probability is that the presence in the church of prominent, powerful women called for comment by Paul on their dress, adornment, and behavior. Barnett says:

> This does not mean, however, that the teaching in these Petrine/Pauline passages is thereby limited in application to wealthy/educated women. The presence of wealthy women in church was a historical catalyst which raised the more general question. Problems posed by women from this socioeducational background created the need to address these questions in broader ways, as relating not merely to wealthy women, but to women and wives in general. This Paul does in the passage under discussion.[25]

CHURCH ACTIVITY OF THE WOMEN (2:11-12). The church life that this section presupposes allows more congregational involvement than most twentieth-century churches practice. Probably varied speakers arose to teach, exhort, and prophesy; and in this situation Paul commanded that the women learn. Women may have rudely interrupted speakers, and Paul found it necessary to confront this insubordination as well as the previously mentioned immodesty.

2:11 Paul's words here spotlight a role women are to play in church meetings. They are to learn spiritual truth. Lenski suggests that the use of

---

[23]R. W. Ward, *Commentary on 1 & 2 Timothy & Titus* (Waco: Word, 1974), 51.

[24]See P. W. Barnett, "Wives and Women's Ministry," *EvQ* 61 (1989): 226-28. Barnett also points out that it is questionable to suggest that the ban on elegant appearances was linked to the practice of cultic prostitution in the Artemis temple in Ephesus. Peter's statement in 1 Pet 3:3 has words similar to those of Paul here, and it is obvious that Peter's words are for a general readership and are not linked with a pagan religious background.

[25]Ibid., 228.

the singular "woman" indicates that the issue concerns all women and not merely wives.[26] Paul's command that the women "learn" reflects Christian practice which differed from the customs of Judaism. Judaism would enforce physical silence on women without concern for their growth in knowledge. At this point Paul was not borrowing from his Jewish heritage but was reflecting as a Christian a greater appreciation for the role of women in spreading the gospel. Paul's commands encourage the women to give attention to God's message in order to learn the essentials for Christian growth and development.

Paul specified two features about a woman's attitude in learning. First, she was to learn in "quietness." The word *hēsychia* emphasized the attitude or spirit with which the woman was to learn and prohibited her dashing about as a busybody (5:13).[27] Paul was not demanding physical silence but a teachable spirit. Second, she was to learn in "full submission." Paul was not specifying to whom the submission was due, but it at least included the leaders of the congregation, who were responsible for giving instruction in doctrine. The submission did not demand a surrender of the mind or conscience or the abandonment of the duty of private judgment. It was a warning against abusing the leadership of the congregation by disrespectful, boisterous actions.[28]

2:12 Paul referred to activities in the public meetings of the congregation, and he continued to speak of females in a primarily generic sense.[29] The role of these women as wives and mothers, however, was not far from Paul's mind. His comments call for three observations.

First, Paul did not permit a woman to teach. He used the Greek present tense for "I do not permit" (*epitrepō*). This tense indicates that Paul was delivering authoritative instructions for the situation he encountered at Ephesus, but it is tenuous to decide for or against the permanence of Paul's injunctions based on the evidence of tense alone.[30]

---

[26]R. C. H. Lenski, *The Interpretation of St. Paul's Epistles to the Colossians, to the Thessalonians, to Timothy, to Titus, and to Philemon* (Columbus, Oh.: Wartburg, 1946), 562.

[27]The adjective "quiet" in 1 Pet 3:4 and the noun "quietness" (KJV) in 2 Thess 3:12 reflect the same root. Both verses appeal for orderly, teachable behavior more than for physical silence. The NASB gives well the sense of 2:11: "Let a woman quietly receive instruction with entire submissiveness."

[28]R. Earle, "1, 2 Timothy," *EBC*, ed. F. E. Gaebelein (Grand Rapids: Zondervan, 1978), 11:361.

[29]The Williams translation uses the term "married woman" in vv. 11-12.

[30]Assessments of the significance of the tense vary widely. C. Rogers suggests that the present tense points to an abiding attitude (*A Linguistic Key to the Greek New Testament* [Grand Rapids: Zondervan, 1976], 621), and Payne ("Libertarian Women," 170-73) concludes that the tense signifies nothing timeless but refers to the particular situation in Ephesus. Scholer limits the application of the passage but refuses to use the tense as a support for

Teaching involved official doctrinal instruction in the Scriptures (1 Tim 5:17) and was a task delegated to the pastor-teacher (Eph 4:11). The heavy emphasis in the Pastorals on proper doctrine (1 Tim 1:10; 4:6,13, 16; 6:1,3; *didaskalia*) implies the need for a trusted source of doctrine. The fact that Paul next discussed the elder/overseer (3:1-7) who needed to be "able to teach" may have indicated that he viewed the occupant of the position as the official declarer of doctrine.[31] Doubtless, the immediate occasion for Paul's prohibition against teaching by the Ephesian women was due to their gullibility and instability (1 Tim 5:11-13; 2 Tim 3:6-7). However, Paul consistently refrained from appointing a woman to a place of authoritative teaching responsibility in a congregation. [32]

Second, Paul did not permit a woman to "have authority over" a man. This rare word (*authenteō*) occurs here only in the New Testament, and its meaning is greatly disputed.[33] The best evidence suggests that it refers to the authority a teacher has over those who are learning.

Why would it have concerned Paul if the teacher were a woman? Two reasons may have been in his mind. The first stems from the likelihood that the women would have authority over any other elder/overseer in the congregation. If the elder/overseer were under the authority of the woman teacher in the church, it could hinder his ability to manage his household in private; and hence it could hinder his ability to manage the church of God (1 Tim 3:4-5). Barnett points out that the submission of the elder/overseer to the woman teacher would limit his ability to serve as a role model to other married men in the church and could prove to be a liability.[34]

A second reason may be related to Paul's concerns about marriage and the raising of children. There is evidence in 1 Timothy that some women were neglecting their roles as wives and mothers (1 Tim 5:11-15). Paul may have feared that a combination of personal ambition and the demands of the office of elder/overseer would prevent the women from

---

his position ("1 Timothy 2:9-15 and the Place of Woman in the Church's Ministry," *Women, Authority and the Bible*, 203, n. 28).

[31]For support of this emphasis see W. Grudem, "Prophecy—Yes, But Teaching No: Paul's Consistent Advocacy of Women's Participation without Governing Authority," *JETS* 30 (1987): 11-23, and C. L. Blomberg, "Not Beyond What Is Written: A Review of Aida Spencer's *Beyond the Curse: Women Called to Ministry*," *CTR* 2 (1988): 403-21.

[32]There is no intent by Paul to ban all teaching by all women at all times. In Corinth women prophesied (1 Cor 11:5) and provided some teaching (Acts 18:24-26). The teaching Paul commended for women is more informal and less "official" (2 Tim 1:5; Titus 2:3-4).

[33]G. W. Knight III, "ΑΥΘΕΝΤΕΩ in Reference to Women in 1 Tim 2:12," *NTS* 30 (1984): 143-57, concludes that the word means *to have authority* and prohibits a woman from assuming this position over a man by teaching him. Scholer, "1 Timothy 2:9-15," 205, disagrees and insists that the term carries the negative sense of *domineer* or *usurp authority*.

[34]Barnett, "Wives and Women's Ministry (1 Timothy 2:11-15)," 233. He provides an extended discussion of the reason of Paul's use of αὐθεντέω given above.

serving effectively as wives and mothers. He was perhaps taking steps to prevent this situation from developing further. Nothing in Paul's words need be seen as a suggestion that women were incompetent to serve in the office of elder/overseer. His concern was for marriages in the church and the mothering role.

Third, Paul wanted the women to "be silent" (lit. "to be in silence"). The word for "silence" is identical to "quietness" in v. 11 and calls for the women to demonstrate a teachable spirit. Most modern translations suggest Paul intended that the women show their teachable attitude by remaining physically quiet (cf. "she must keep quiet," Williams). It is more likely that Paul was banning disruptive behavior rather than enforcing complete silence on women in worship settings. (See 1 Cor 11:5, where Corinthian women prayed and/or prophesied.)

The role of the teacher mentioned in this passage is most closely linked with the office of the pastor or senior pastor in contemporary churches. The normative principle behind Paul's directive is that the woman should not carry out the role of senior pastor. This does not amount to a prohibition against a woman's teaching or against her ministry to men. The New Testament has examples of significant teaching roles by women (Acts 18:26—both Priscilla and Aquilla were involved; Titus 2:3-4; 2 Tim 1:5; 3:15—women teach the faith to other women and children; 1 Cor 11:4-5—women prayed and prophesied). Paul was not suggesting that the woman is incompetent to occupy the role of pastor/teacher. His concern related to the effect the woman's position would have on marriages in the church and on the value of the mothering role. Paul would assert the value of the role of motherhood in v. 15. For additional discussion on the normative principles of this passage, see Excursus 2: Women in Ministry.

AN EXPLANATION OF PAUL'S APPEAL (2:13-14).   Paul elaborated on the reasons for his appeal to allow the woman to learn in submission but not to teach.

2:13 Using the biblical history of creation from Gen 2, Paul argued that Adam was chronologically prior to Eve. The fact of the chronological priority of Adam was established before the fall of humankind and the subsequent entrance of sin. The fall of humankind would not alter Adam's chronological priority. The chronological priority of Adam becomes the support of Paul's command that the women were to show a spirit of attentiveness to learning and were to avoid an attempt at domineering men.[35] In 1 Cor 11:8 Paul had inferred the dependence of Eve from the chrono-

---

[35]Paul's use of γὰρ in v. 13 appears to be illative in that it introduces a reason for Paul's injunction of v. 12. Obviously a reason does provide an explanation for Paul's prohibition of female teaching in v. 12.

logical priority of Adam. Paul apparently felt that the spiritual privileges of men and women in Christ (Gal 3:28) do not negate differences due to creation. The designation of Adam as "formed first" reflects the Jewish practice of primogeniture, where the firstborn male inherited a double portion of the inheritance and the responsibility of leadership in the home and in worship (Deut 21:15-17).[36] Paul's point was that Adam's status as the oldest carried with it the leadership role suitable for the firstborn son. Paul transferred this quality of leadership role in the congregation to the male.

What Paul seems to have suggested is that a woman's assumption of the role of teacher would make her an overseer and would overturn the principle of headship in marriage (1 Cor 11:1-8), jeopardizing the God-ordained foundation of husband-wife relationships in marriage.[37] Paul did not want the practices of the church to weaken marriages in any way.

2:14 Paul's additional explanation for his prohibition concerning women's teaching in v. 12 relates to the history of the fall in Gen 3. Paul saw Eve as the representative woman who broke God's law due to Satan's deception. In describing Adam, Paul denied that he was deceived. In describing Eve, the apostle used an intensive form of the same verb employed in reference to Adam. Williams translates it as "utterly deceived." Paul saw Eve as thoroughly duped by the serpent. His use of the Greek perfect tense for "became" suggests that Eve passed into a state of sin and remained a sinner. What was Paul declaring about Adam and Eve?

Paul's favorable comments on women as teachers (2 Tim 1:5; Titus 2:4) seem to rule out the likelihood that his intent was to characterize all women as naive and gullible. The Ephesian women may have been credulous pawns in the hands of false teachers, but Paul knew most women were not. Nor was Paul commending Adam while disparaging Eve. Paul had made clear his view of Adam's guilt in Rom 5:12-21. Eve listened to Satan and fell for the vanity of his promises. Eve let herself be betrayed by the serpent and fell into the condition of a sinner (cf. 2 Cor 11:3). Adam listened to her and sinned with his eyes open. Paul's point was that men, including those in Ephesus, are more susceptible to mistake and error when they carelessly surrender leadership to the woman.[38]

---

[36]Hurley, *Man and Woman*, 207.

[37]Barnett, "Wives and Women's Ministry," 234.

[38]"It is not because Eve had a greater guilt than Adam that women were subjected to men in the way outlined by Paul, but rather because *both* male and female were more vulnerable when the female was allowed to take the lead. It is for the protection of both, and not the glory of one over the other, that Paul's commands are given in the way they are" (G. L. Bray, "The Fall Is a Human Reality," *Evangelical Review of Theology* 9 [1985]: 338.

A PROMISE FOR OBEDIENT WOMEN (2:15). **2:15** Paul expressed a promise for those women who showed obedience, but few verses have caused such vexing problems for interpreters.

To arrive at the proper understanding, it is important to observe that Paul used the Greek word for "saved" in the spiritual sense of obtaining the forgiveness of sins.[39] The NIV translation obscures the fact that Paul made a subtle shift from Eve to "the women" in Ephesus in v. 15. Paul used the feminine singular "she" or perhaps "a woman" instead of the plural "women" in the first part of v. 15. His shift back to the plural "they" at the conclusion of the verse applies the words to all the Ephesian women. Paul employed the term "childbirth" as a synecdoche[40] for that part of the woman's work that describes the whole. Paul's words are a reminder that a woman's deepest satisfaction comes from her accomplishments in a Christian home. Paul was teaching that women prove the reality of their salvation when they become model wives and mothers whose good deeds include marriage and raising children (1 Tim 5:11,14). His words contain an implicit warning that the wealthy women in Ephesus were not to aspire selfishly to the office of teacher or overseer. Paul may also have been aiming a blow at the false teachers who had disparaging views about sex (1 Tim 4:3). His comments assume (cf. Gen 3:16) that motherhood is a divinely appointed role.

Four other possibilities for interpretation appear. No serious interpreter accepts the first alternative that Paul promised women salvation by their having children. A second interpretation is suggested by the translation of the 1978 edition of the NIV:[41] "Women will be kept safe through childbirth." The fact that even Christian mothers sometimes die in childbirth would nullify this as a viable interpretation. A third view sees a reference to the birth of the Messiah in the verse. The word "childbirth" follows an article in the Greek so that an acceptable reading of the phrase may be "the childbirth," Mary's giving birth to Jesus in the virgin birth. However, Paul located the salvation event in Jesus' death (2:6), not in his birth. Also the noun "childbirth" refers to the act of bearing children, not to a single birth of a child. Fourth, Paul may have meant that women would avoid the errors of vv. 11-12 by childbearing, but giving birth to a child does not necessarily affect a woman's theology (other than increasing her understanding of suffering and may also awaken awe at God's gift of life and her sharing in it [cf. Gen 4:1]).

---

[39]Observe the Williams translation, which reads, "Women will be saved" or Knox, who says, "Woman will find her salvation." See 1 Tim 1:15; 2:4 for the same usage of "saved."

[40]A synecdoche is a figure of speech in which a part is put for the whole, a whole is used for a part, or the species is used for the genus. The KJV translators use a synecdoche when they refer to the passengers aboard the ship as "276 souls" (Acts 27:37) instead of 276 persons.

[41]The NIV (1978) reads as above, but the 1984 revision says, "Women will be saved through childbearing."

Fulfillment of motherhood alone does not assure the woman salvation, for she must continue in faith, love, and holiness combined with good judgment.[42] It is assumed that such a woman has the faith that will activate her love and holiness so that her salvation does not spring from works alone. Paul's words spotlight the importance of the domestic role for the woman. They do not preclude the possibility that a woman can serve as a model wife and mother while also adding to the family income. No wife (and no husband) should permit career opportunities to precede domestic commitments.[43]

Summary. Paul faced a problem in Ephesus because some church leaders had lost any semblance of godliness. They were apparently influencing women to follow them in their practice of contentious, self-seeking rebellion. The women in Ephesus had neglected home responsibilities and had selfishly tried to claw their way to a position of dominance in the local church. Paul wanted to see the practice of serious Christianity make a return to Ephesus.

The need for saints has scarcely ever been more evident than it is today. In a world that alternates between viewing Christianity with a sneer and a yawn, only saintly (godly, unselfish, consistent, sacrificial, courageous) living can make an impact on our society. Both men and women must assume places of responsibility in the home. Further, both must respond to one another with mutual respect and love and must demonstrate the behavior of servants of Christ rather than that of contenders for ecclesiastical office.

EXCURSUS 2: WOMEN IN MINISTRY. Is there a place for a woman in ministry? If we define ministry as the service that all Christians are urged to render (Eph 4:12), it seems ludicrous even to ask the question. In a Christian church that has seen accomplishments by Susanna Wesley, Selina Countess of Huntingdon, and Lottie Moon, it is flawed to overlook the marvelous contributions women have made to the forward progress of Christianity.

Do Paul's words provide any direction for interpreting the role of women in ministry in the twentieth century? Do they provide any limitation to the female role? Do they make any contribution to decide the issue

---

[42]D. E. Hiebert, *First Timothy*, EvBC (Chicago: Moody, 1957), 62-63.

[43]Hurley (*Man and Woman*, 223) says: "The selfishness of our twentieth century, which does not want its enjoyment of pleasures undercut by the financial and personal obligations entailed in raising a family, was not common in the first century. In his day the bearing of children which Paul selected as a part to represent the whole of the high calling of women was a valued activity which women embraced with joy and with pride and for which they were deeply respected." Although we may question the suggestion by Hurley that selfishness was not common in the first century, it seems likely that the role of motherhood was more esteemed at that time than in modern America.

of the ordination of women that nags at the unity of many denominations today? The first two questions deserve a yes response, and the final question should receive a more hesitant not necessarily.

First, Paul's words make little specific contribution to the question of female ordination. The issue of ordination surfaces in 1 Tim 4:14; 5:22; 2 Tim 1:6, where the practice of "laying on hands" is mentioned. There is no detailed discussion of ordination in the Pastorals, and there is no confrontation with the question of female ordination. The practice of ordination in most churches today has roots more in tradition than in biblical teaching. It is difficult to find in the Bible any clear information concerning the practice of the ordination of females. In fact, there is so little information in the Bible on ordination even of men that acrid debates about it seem strangely out of place for churches that use the Bible as a pattern for church organization. For further discussion of the practice of ordination, see Excursus 3: Ordination in the New Testament.

Second, the Pastoral Epistles and the entire New Testament envision a broad role for women in ministry. The New Testament presents women who prophesied (Acts 21:9; 1 Cor 11:5) and some who served undefined roles as helpers (1 Tim 3:11). Paul commended two women as his fellow workers (Phil 4:1-3) and explained that Phoebe was a "servant" (*diakonos*) of the church in Cenchrea (Rom 16:1) and a "help" (*prostatis*) to many, including Paul himself. Paul presented women as teachers in 2 Tim 1:5 and Titus 2:3, and Luke presented Priscilla in a teaching role (Acts 18:26). The teaching mentioned in these passages seems to be less formal and structured than that in 1 Tim 2:12, from which Paul excluded females.

Third, the teaching of 1 Tim 2:12 appears to limit the role of women in ministry. Paul prohibited women from teaching in an authoritative position in 2:12 and supported the prohibition with the reasons of vv. 13-14. It is difficult to support the view which holds that Paul's reasons for limiting female involvement in ministry applied only to his own day. In v. 13 Paul suggested that as God gave Adam certain leadership functions with respect to Eve, he has given men certain leadership roles in the church. In v. 14 Paul warned that Adam fell into trouble when he heeded Eve's advice. He implied that men would fall into difficulty by submitting to a woman as an authoritative teacher. The position taken in this commentary is that the difficulty comes because the actions in the church might "overturn, deny or detract from the roles and relationships of men as husbands and fathers and women as wives and mothers."[44] The position of an authoritative teacher relates most closely to the modern office of the pastor in Protestant churches. Paul's advice would limit that office to men.

---

[44]Barnett, "Wives and Women's Ministry," 237.

Some evangelicals will respond differently to the data of this passage. G. Osborne says that the normative principle from 1 Tim 2:8-15 is the idea of submissiveness by the women.[45] He avers that at the time of Paul's writing a woman who taught a group of men would be "lording" it over them. He feels that Western society today does not accord the same position of authority to the teacher as was true in the New Testament era. Thus, according to Osborne, a woman serving in the position of a teacher would not violate the attitude of submissiveness Paul demanded. He cautions women not to demand their rights or force the issue, suggesting that proclaiming the gospel is the chief concern. He suggests that women in ministry may need to work within the confines of today's culture to alter entrenched attitudes against women in ministry.

Even Barnett, who opposes women's serving in the role of teacher/ overseer, suggests that the prohibition against their serving in the teaching role is more applicable in a family church. He adds that there is no reason why women "should be prevented from the whole range of pastoral, didactic or sacramental ministry under the leadership of the senior teacher in a team or in their own right in specialist, single sex congregations."[46]

3. Church Leadership by Committed Servants (3:1-13)

Paul had experienced problems with some strong-minded leaders of the Ephesian church (1 Tim 1:19-20; 2 Tim 3:5-7). His instructions here were not merely a manual for church organization, but they were an effort to guarantee that new leaders in the church would have commitment to Christ and would encourage godliness and unity.[47] In this section Paul discussed the qualifications of three groups of church leaders. In 3:1-7 he discussed overseers or bishops. In 3:8-10,12-13 he discussed the requirements for deacons or church helpers. In 3:11 he presented requirements for women helpers.

Paul's discussions majored on qualifications for office and not on duties. Aside from a reference that the overseer be "able to teach," Paul did not mention the function of the overseer. The requirements given for the deacons and the women helpers also provide no clear sign of the role these church leaders were to play. Some of the duties of the leaders are

---

[45]G. Osborne, "Hermeneutics and Women in the Church," *JETS* 20 (1977): 337-52.

[46]Barnett, "Wives and Women's Ministry," 237.

[47]Fee (*1 and 2 Timothy, Titus*, 32) suggests that the weakness of the "church manual" view of the Pastorals is evident from the attempt by representatives of the entire spectrum of church government such as Roman Catholics, Presbyterians, and Plymouth Brethren to support their polity from these letters. Christian groups with such varied forms of church government could not legitimately use Paul's directives in the Pastorals to support their practices.

evident from the qualifications Paul asked. Additional help in discovering duties is available from parallel passages in the Pastorals (cf. 1 Tim 5:17).

The traits demanded of the church leaders stood in sharp contrast with the character of the false teachers (1 Tim 1:6-7; 6:3-10; 2 Tim 3:1-4; Titus 1:10-16). Although Paul had suggested elsewhere (cf. Acts 20:28; Eph 4:7-11) that leadership depended upon endowments from the Holy Spirit, we need not feel that the idea of an office for ministry conflicts with the idea of a spiritual gift for performing that office.[48] The qualifications mentioned in 3:1-13 are not as distinctively Christian as the requirements of 1 Tim 4:12 and 6:11. Paul mentioned those traits that would commend Christians to their pagan observers (3:7). He also demanded sensible traits that would aid in job performance (3:8).

Although the word "overseer" (v. 1) is singular, leadership in the church apparently was plural ("elders," 5:17). Knowing exactly what type of situation this plural reference described is difficult. It is possible that each elder presided individually over a local congregation that resembled a house-church. These house-church leaders collectively became the leaders of Christianity in that city. Huther takes another view when he says that "in the N.T. the presbyters are always named as the superintendents of one congregation, and there is nowhere any hint that each house-congregation had its special superintendent."[49] The leadership position of the overseer is most similar to the pastor in today's churches. The pastor leads the church, teaches God's Word, and wins the hearts of the people by service to the flock (1 Pet 5:1-4).

(1) Qualifications of Overseers (3:1-7)

[1]Here is a trustworthy saying: If anyone sets his heart on being an overseer, he desires a noble task. [2]Now the overseer must be above reproach, the husband of but one wife, temperate, self-controlled, respectable, hospitable, able to teach, [3]not given to drunkenness, not violent but gentle, not quarrelsome, not a lover of money. [4]He must manage his own family well and see that his children obey him with proper respect. [5](If anyone does not know how to manage his own family, how can he take care of God's church?) [6]He must not be a recent convert, or he may become conceited and fall under the

---

[48]R. Y. K. Fung refers to E. Käsemann's conviction that the presence of an institutionalized office in the Pastorals is the antithesis of the Pauline doctrine of spiritual gifts. Fung finds references to church offices in passages outside of the Pastorals (Phil 1:1; Acts 14:23; Col 4:17; 1 Thess 5:12) and sees this as an indication that the Pauline "doctrine of charisma is not incompatible with the existence of an organized ministry." See Fung's "Charismatic versus Organized Ministry? An Examination of an Alleged Antithesis," *EvQ* 52 (1980): 203. For an additional supportive view see M. A. G. Haykin, "The Fading Vision? The Spirit and Freedom in the Pastoral Epistles," *EvQ* 57 (1985): 291-305.

[49]Huther, *Epistles to Timothy and Titus*, 116.

same judgment as the devil. ⁷He must also have a good reputation with out-
siders, so that he will not fall into disgrace and into the devil's trap.

A COMMENDATION (3:1) **3:1** The word "overseer" receives such
translations as "bishop" (KJV, ASV), "Presiding-Officer" (TCNT),
"superintendent" (Goodspeed), or "pastor" (Williams). In such passages
as Acts 20:17,28 and Titus 1:5,7 the terms "elders" and "overseers"
appear together to suggest that the positions are partially, if not fully,
interchangeable.

In discussing the office of an overseer, Paul was not requesting that
Timothy begin a new office in the church. Men were already functioning
in the position (Acts 14:23; 20:17,28). What Paul stipulated was that
those appointed to the office were to possess qualifications of commitment. Four general statements summarize the qualifications Paul listed in
3:2-7. First, the overseer was to be obedient in observable behavior (3:2-
3). Both Christians and non-Christians needed to see commitment in his
life-style. Second, the overseer was to lead his own family well (3:4-5).
Paul viewed leadership in the family as a proving ground for leadership in
the church. Third, the overseer needed experience in his Christian walk
(3:6). A neophyte believer appointed to a place of leadership could be
blinded by a cloud of pride. Finally, the leader needed the respect of outsiders (3:7). These outsiders might not prefer his doctrines and morals,
but they had to respect his integrity and commitment.

Paul opened his discussion of qualifications for the office of overseer
with a commendation of the position. The term "sets his heart on" can
refer to a desire coming from self-centered ambition, but it may also be a
desire that springs from genuine love and commitment (cf. Heb 11:16,
where "longing" is the same Greek word). The word "desire" (*oregomai*)
signifies to "stretch oneself out."[50] In a figurative sense it describes aspi-
ration or desire. Paul did not suggest that longing for the office was
blameworthy in itself; in fact, he suggested it is a "fine work he desires to
do" (NASB).

The "trustworthy saying" can be a reference backwards to 2:15, or it
can refer to the latter part of v. 1.[51] The obscurity of the saying in 2:15
does not make it a serious candidate for a "trustworthy saying," which
represented a belief widely accepted as important. Paul was more likely
suggesting the common knowledge that the office of a church leader was

---

[50]*BAGD*, "ὀρέγω."

[51]A few Greek manuscripts contain the statement "It is a human [i.e., "a popular"] saying" instead of "Here is a trustworthy saying." The reading would suggest that the desirabil-
ity of the office of overseer was commonly known and widespread in its appeal. However,
the manuscripts supporting this reading are not impressive, and the most reliable sources
suggest that the reference is to a "faithful saying."

an important, significant work. Despite the fact that some leaders in Ephesus had performed poorly, the office of overseer was a noble and highly desirable task. This is the second time we meet the "trustworthy saying" formula. For additional discussion see the initial presentation on this subject at 1:15.

We must not confuse the office of overseer or bishop mentioned here with the ecclesiastical office of bishop that developed later. In later times a bishop was a superintendent over a diocese. This office did not appear in a fully developed sense until the second century. Paul was not discussing a hierarchical office, but he was presenting someone who directed the affairs of the church (1 Tim 5:17). This was a noble, important task; and Paul commended it as desirable. Paul's object in commending the office was to add force to the following request for church leaders to have the highest qualifications.

Probably the first early leaders of Paul's churches were apostles, prophets, and teachers inspired by God's Spirit. Many of these leaders were itinerants who traveled widely and had a formative influence on many local congregations. During their travels between congregations, local leaders must have arisen to carry out practical roles of leadership. This local role would have involved pastoring and teaching, and initially some of these leaders may have been volunteers who had little official recognition (see 1 Cor 16:15, where the members of Stephanas's household probably functioned in this way). Gradually by faithfully performing their tasks, these local leaders became recognized for their activities. Paul's words reflected a concern that these leaders would receive the proper respect and would reflect the requisite character.[52]

AN APPEAL FOR OBEDIENT BEHAVIOR (3:2-3). Paul mentioned qualifications mostly of an outward, observable nature for those who desired to serve as leaders. The qualifications mentioned in v. 2 are largely positive in their statement. The first requirements in v. 2 are personal in nature, and the final two requirements ("hospitable"; "able to teach") deal with relationships to others. The demands of v. 3 are negative in their statement.

Some have criticized Paul's list as containing nothing specifically Christian and as being rather elementary in its demands. Three comments are in order. First, the requirements Paul listed do relate to the function of an overseer. Stability, a model family life, experience, and a reputation for integrity are not to be called commonplace or trite. Second, Paul may have assumed the presence of more avowedly Christian traits (e.g., Eph 5:18b-21) without specifically calling for them. Here he may have emphasized particularly those traits that were highly valued by the pagan world. The absence of these traits would affect the witness of an overseer in

---

[52]For additional discussion on this development, see Kelly, 71-72.

work with inquiring pagans. Third, lists of virtues and vices demanded in different callings (such as rulers, military leaders, doctors) were common in the Hellenistic world. Some of Paul's demands for the home in Col 3:18–4:1 and in Eph 5:22–6:9 reflect a similarity to these lists. Paul may have allowed his content to be influenced by these lists. We should realize that enlightened pagans would have emphasized the need for certain traits that even Christians would have admired. Paul may have been echoing the traits both Christians and pagans respected.

3:2 Paul's use of the singular for "overseer" does not suggest that he was advocating a monepiscopacy (single person serving as pastor). The singular is generic in meaning just as is the "woman" in 2:11-12. A reference to overseers or elders in the plural appears in 1 Tim 5:17. Also the phrase "if anyone" in v. 1 suggests a group larger than one. Probably the overseer served over a single house-church with the group of overseers from within a city constituting "the overseers."

To be "above reproach" demanded that the overseer be a man of blameless character. The same word (*anepilēmpton*) is used of widows in 5:7 and of Timothy in 6:14. It may serve as a general, covering term for the following list of virtues that should distinguish a church leader. The etymology of the word suggests the meaning *not to be taken hold of.* It describes a person of such character that no one can properly bring against him a charge of unfitness.[53]

The NIV translation that the overseer be "the husband of but one wife" implies that Paul was prohibiting polygamy among the overseers. Such a practice would be so palpably unacceptable among Christians that it would hardly seem necessary to prohibit it. It is best not to see Paul as writing primarily in opposition to polygamy. Some have felt that Paul was demanding that the overseer be a married man. However, Paul's own singleness (1 Cor 7:7-8) and his positive commendation of the single state (1 Cor 7:1,32-35) would seem to allow a single man to serve as a church leader. Others have felt that the passage rules out remarriage if a first wife dies, but Paul clearly permitted second marriages in other passages (1 Tim 5:14; Rom 7:2-3; 1 Cor 7:39). His statements here should not contradict the permission for remarriage he gave in other passages. Another interpretation is to understand Paul to have prohibited a divorced man from serving as a church leader. While this can be Paul's meaning, the language is too general in its statement to make this interpretation certain. Some evangelical New Testament scholars suggest that there are New Testament passages that appear to permit divorce (Matt 19:9; 1 Cor 7:15).

It is better to see Paul having demanded that the church leader be faithful to his one wife. The Greek describes the overseer literally as a

---

[53]Lenski, *St. Paul's Epistles,* 579.

"one-woman kind of man" (cf. "faithful to his one wife," NEB). Lenski suggests that the term describes a man "who cannot be taken hold of on the score of sexual promiscuity or laxity."[54] Glasscock uses Lenski's understanding to support his view that a divorced man can serve as a church leader if he is thoroughly devoted to the wife whom he has married.[55] His application prohibits a monogamous man known to be flirtatious from serving in a place of leadership. Glasscock does not seek to encourage either divorce or the presence of divorced men in the ministry. He suggests that we must not hold a man's preconversion sins against him (Col 2:13). Had Paul clearly meant to prohibit divorce, he could have said it unmistakably by using the Greek word for divorce (*apolyō*, cf. Matt 1:19).

To be "temperate" shows that the church leader had to be free from rash actions. The word describes self-control with regard to use of intoxicants, but it can also be used to describe a mental self-control that rules out all forms of excess. Paul dealt with the use of alcohol in 3:3. He was not covering this same subject here. Paul's term here referred to someone who was sober and balanced in spirit.

To be "self-controlled" pictures the leader as a sensible person. The adjective describes a person who is trustworthy and balanced in judgment, not flighty or unstable. This would be an essential trait in the character of an overseer.

To be "respectable" demands dignity and orderliness in behavior. It is not merely a demand for good breeding or flawless manners, but it describes a person whose orderly outward life is a reflection of inner stability.[56] The trait related especially to the external actions of the overseer.

These last two terms are not uniquely Christian ideals. They do represent traits that could have commended Christianity to thoughtful pagans who would have ignored a religion whose followers lacked these attributes.

In relation to other believers Christians needed to be "hospitable." Traveling Christian groups (3 John 5-8) would be dependent upon the kindness of local Christians as they passed through communities while spreading the gospel. The task of caring for Christians and other "strangers" was highly respected in both Christian and Greek culture (Rom 12:13; 1 Tim 5:10; 1 Pet 4:9).

---

[54]Ibid., 580.

[55]E. Glasscock, "'The Husband of One Wife' Requirement in 1 Timothy 3:2," *BibSac* 140 (1983): 255. For a rejection of the view that the phrase "husband of but one wife" prohibited remarriage after the death of a first wife, see P. Fairbairn, "On the Meaning of the Expression 'Husband of One Wife,' in 1 Tim III. 2, 12, Tit I.6," *The Pastoral Epistles* (1874; reprint, Minneapolis: Klock & Klock, 1980), 416-32.

[56]Ward, *1 & 2 Timothy & Titus*, 55-56.

The appeal to be "able to teach" demands competence and skill in communicating Christian truth. The trait requires intellectual and didactic ability. One who can teach others needs also a willingness to accept teaching. The presence of this requirement shows that an overseer needed the ability both to explain Christian doctrine and to refute or oppose error. He would use this skill in giving instruction to converts, building up the church, and in correcting error.

3:3 The first negative qualification demands that a church leader control his thirst for alcohol. The word describes one who is addicted to wine.[57] It does not prohibit medicinal use of alcohol (1 Tim 5:23). In our American society satiated with a thirst for alcohol, the practice of total abstinence by Christians could curb the destructive effects alcoholism has brought to us.

A second negative qualification sought by Paul was that the leader not practice browbeating people with threats of violence. The term "violent" pictures a quick-tempered individual who would prefer to use his fists rather than a reasoning tongue. Such a leader uses the threats of a bully to bludgeon people into conformity. The violence Paul described here could have been an outgrowth of drunkenness.

In contrast to practicing violence, the Christian leader is to be "gentle" or forbearing in his relationships to troublemakers. The "gentle" man uses elasticity in supervision and is flexible rather than rigid. Synonyms for "gentle" include yielding, kind, forbearing, and considerate.

A "quarrelsome" man is a verbal (perhaps also a physical) fighter. He is contentious, grasping, and pugnacious. What Paul demanded in the church leader was a peaceable attitude that rejects all forms of threatening and fighting.

Christian leaders who possessed these outward traits gave evidence that they had inner control and commitment to Christ. Such traits would be mandatory in meeting, opposing, and defeating the rampant, controversial false teaching of Ephesus. When Paul demanded that the overseer not be "a lover of money," he hinted that a responsibility of the overseer lay in the area of handling congregational finances. A lover of money would be stingy and grasping. He would have get-rich-quick schemes rather than the souls of his people on his mind. Such greed was a distinguishing feature of the false teachers in Ephesus (1 Tim 6:5-10). For a Christian leader to have the same spiritual disease would be a fatal sickness for spreading the truth.

---

[57]It may seem strange that Paul should find it necessary to prohibit drunkenness among church leaders. It is helpful to remember that church leaders had been converted out of a society that knew little moral restraint. A warning about drunkenness could always be timely. Believers in Corinth had become drunk in the observance of the Lord's Supper (see 1 Cor 11:21).

LEADERSHIP OF THE FAMILY (3:4-5). **3:4** Paul demanded that the church leader be exemplary in controlling his own family. He was to raise children known for their obedience and morally upright behavior. The verb for "manage" carries the idea of governing, leading, and giving direction to the family. The same Greek word appears in 1 Thess 5:12 ("are over you") and 1 Tim 5:17 ("direct") and also in v. 5 ("manage"). The term demands an effective exercise of authority bolstered by a character of integrity and sensitive compassion. Its use in v. 5 with the verb "take care of" defines the quality of leadership as related more to showing mercy than to delivering ultimatums.

For the father to see "that his children obey him" does not demand excessive force or sternness. It demands primarily a character and manner of discipline that develop a natural respect. "Either the children show respect for their father or the meaning is that his character and demeanor call it forth. . . . This is not the martinet's paradise but is the Christian home, in which the husband exercises love, as the context in Ephesians shows."[58]

The NIV translation takes the phrase "with proper respect" as a description of the manner of the children's obedience. It is better to translate the term for "respect" with the word "seriousness" and use it as a description of the overseer's manner in the discipline of his children. The Williams translation brings out the idea "managing his own house well, with perfect seriousness keeping his children under control." The passage assumes that the leader is married but does not require it. It does not demand that the married leader have children. If he does, they must be obedient children who reflect a skillful blend of authority and compassion in their training.

3:5 Paul indicated that the experience the leader gained in the home would develop sensitive compassion ("take care of") for his role in the church. The verb "manage" appeared in v. 4. The development of proper leadership skills in the home was a prerequisite for using them in the church. Paul's reference to the church as "God's household" (1 Tim 3:15) underscores the close relationship between church and home. Paul intended that the church leader exhort his people to obedience not by ruling them with a heavy hand but by showing the care and compassion of a servant-leader (1 Pet 5:1-4). The overseer's duty is to so "conduct himself that the members of the church may be obedient to him, not as servants to a master, but as children to a father, that they may show him obedience in love."[59] The skillful pastor will give to the church the type of leadership that will encourage his people to follow him.

[58]Ward, *1 & 2 Timothy & Titus*, 57.
[59]Huther, *Epistles to Timothy and Titus*, 121.

An Experienced Leader (3:6). **3:6** The term "recent convert" means literally to be "newly planted," hence recently converted. The condition of being a novice has more to do with spiritual than with chronological age. Churches could not carry out the prohibition against using a recent convert in their first few years of existence. Only the first converts could assume office where the gospel had recently appeared (Acts 14:23). Eventually it would be important to select leaders with enough maturity to avoid the pitfalls of pride. The danger of appointing a recent convert to a place of leadership is that he may become a victim of conceit that comes with his important new position. To be "conceited" (*typhoō*) means *to be blinded.*[60] The pride in a prominent position produces a blindness that blunts spiritual alertness.

The reference to falling "under the same judgment as the devil" is literally translated from the Greek as "the judgment of the devil." That literal phrase is capable of two different interpretations. It can refer either to the judgment the devil receives or the judgment the devil causes.[61] The translation of the NIV suggests that the former interpretation is preferable. The translation of the NEB ("a judgment contrived by the devil") reflects the latter interpretations. Fee follows the former interpretation, suggesting that the judgment is that given to the devil by Christ's death and resurrection (cf. Rev 12:7-17; 20:7-10). However, Kelly points out that this interpretation does not prepare us for the devil's role in setting a trap in v. 7. In that verse Paul described Satan as setting a trap for the unwary overseer. It seems best to take the references in both v. 6 and v. 7 as condemnations or spiritual traps Satan causes.[62] Proud people will become blind to Satan's working and will fall into defeat, trouble, and ruin (cf. 1 Tim 6:9, where Paul described the progression of falling, entanglement, and drowning). This is a condemnation Satan can inflict on spiritually insensitive leaders. Although Peter's denial of Christ was not due to pride, it displayed an arrogance and conceit that came from blindness to Satan's working (Matt 26:30-35).

Respected by Unbelievers (3:7). **3:7** An effective church leader needs the respect of even the unsaved world. If the behavior of the leader

---

[60]The similarity of the word used here (τυφόω) to the Greek τύφω ("give off smoke," "smolder") leads some to suggest that Paul's thought contains a warning against being wrapped in the smoke of pride (see Lenski, *St. Paul's Epistles*, 588). Hanson points out that the correct meaning is "blinded" or "beclouded" (*Pastoral Epistles*, 76). The idea is that pride leads to a conceit that produces blindness. Pride can produce moral blindness as a defective retina can cause physical blindness.

[61]In the Greek the interpretive question revolved around whether the genitive should be seen as objective or subjective. If it is objective, then the term refers to a judgment Satan receives. If it is subjective, then the term refers to a judgment or a condemnation Satan brings about. The most likely interpretation sees the genitive as a subjective genitive.

[62]Fee, *1 and 2 Timothy, Titus*, 45-47. Kelly, *Pastoral Epistles*, 79.

does not present a creditable witness, the devil can entrap the church by making outsiders wary of believing the gospel.

The "good reputation" is literally a "good witness." This is an appeal that the church leader have a good name and standing in the wider community. The mention of the leader's name should not cause derision among the opponents of the gospel. The behavior of the leader should provide an example of integrity and commitment to the gospel he professes.

The outsiders are those who have not believed the gospel. The moral instincts of enlightened outsiders are sound and worthy of respect. Christians ought not ignore such opinions in assessing the character of a potential leader.[63]

The "disgrace" may be that reproach which outsiders bring on professing Christians who dishonor Christianity by disobedience. Satan uses such disgraces to trap his victims.

If the overseer has an unsavory reputation with the unsaved world, he and the entire church will fall into disgrace. Paul stated that such disgrace is a trap set by the devil. When church leaders live in such a way that unsaved outsiders refuse to listen to their message, the devil has clearly lured believers into a trap. Christians must realize that unbelievers scrutinize their actions with a searchlight of fault-finding investigation. Paul's implied appeal is that church leaders give no opportunity for unbelievers genuinely to find fault. Perhaps the discouragement that comes from learning of a disgraceful reputation among unbelievers might induce an unwary Christian to turn to further disobedience. In this verse Paul presented Satan as a hunter who lays out traps into which the careless, shortsighted Christian can fall. This trap is clearly one set by the agency of Satan. This leads Zerwick and Grosvenor to view the uses of "devil" in both vv. 6 and 7 as subjective so that Satan is causing both the judgment and the trap.[64]

(2) Qualifications of Deacons (3:8-10,12-13)

[8]Deacons, likewise, are to be men worthy of respect, sincere, not indulging in much wine, and not pursuing dishonest gain. [9]They must keep hold of the deep truths of the faith with a clear conscience. [10]They must first be tested; and then if there is nothing against them, let them serve as deacons. . . .

[12]A deacon must be the husband of but one wife and must manage his children and his household well. [13]Those who have served well gain an excellent standing and great assurance in their faith in Christ Jesus.

---

[63]N. J. D. White, "The First and Second Epistles to Timothy and the Epistle to Titus," *EGT*, ed. W. R. Nicoll (New York: George H. Doran, n.d.), 4:114.

[64]M. Zerwick and M. Grosvenor, *GAGNT*, 2 vols. (Rome: Biblical Institute, 1979), 2:630.

The qualifications demanded of the deacons are similar to those required of the overseers. In 3:8-9 Paul demanded that the deacons be sincere, maintain a clear conscience, and manifest obedient life-styles. In 3:10 he required that the deacon be tested or proven. This stipulation is similar to the requirements that the overseer not be a "recent convert" (3:6). In 3:13 Paul expressed a promise to the faithful deacon. There is no specific request that the deacon have a good relationship with outsiders. We would assume that one who has the requirements Paul prescribed will earn the respect of even the most grudging unbeliever.

The term "deacon" refers literally to someone who serves. Some modern versions have used the term "church helper" (GNB) or "Assistant-Officer" (TCNT) in v. 8. Bible scholars view the overseer as providing administrative leadership for the church. They see the deacon as helping the overseer in the ministries or work of the church. The distinction between a bishop and a deacon became more sharply defined as centuries passed.[65] Sometimes the Bible uses the term "deacon" to refer to a person who functions as a helper or a servant (Matt 20:26). At other times the term refers to a position (see Phil 1:1, where "deacon" is the translation of *diakonos*). In 1 Timothy 3 the term "deacon" refers to a position.

Several traditions and various denominations commonly view the seven men mentioned in Acts 6:5-6 as deacons, but the Scripture uses no specific term to describe their office. Since the "seven" ministered in a manner similar to deacons, it is perhaps best to regard these men as forerunners in performing a task the deacons later assumed.[66]

---

[65]Concerning the duties of the deacon we can infer from the list of qualifications, J. M. Ross has said: "All that can be said is that while the deacons were expected, like the bishop, to govern, to visit, and to handle money, they were not expected, as the bishop was, to give hospitality or to teach or preach" ("A Reconsideration of the Diaconate," *SJT* 12 [1959]: 152).

[66]The term "deacon" is clearly used in the NT to refer to a church office only in two passages (see Phil 1:1; 1 Tim 3:8-13). The term is used in Rom 16:1 in reference to Pheobe (translated as "servant"), but it is debatable whether the reference was to a church office or to Phoebe's function as a servant. Paul's use of the same word in reference to himself (see "servant" in Col 1:23) is a reference to his function and not to his office. The probability is that the reference to Phoebe is made in the same way.

The office of deacon in the early church likely developed from a need within the church. There is no evidence that the office was borrowed from the Jewish synagogue structure.

The lack of information on the formation and function of deacons has led to significant differences in usage among denominations. In Catholicism deacons represent a lower grade of ecclessiastical office. In Presbyterian and Congregational churches deacons are usually administrators of benevolent work and financial affairs.

In most Baptist churches deacons are elected by the local congregation and work with the pastor in serving the church. Baptist polity permits a wide range of form and practice, but

ANOTHER APPEAL FOR OBEDIENCE (3:8-9). **3:8** Paul listed four
requirements for the position of deacon. The first serves as a cover term
for his description of deacon qualifications. The remaining three requirements of the verse are negative in that they prohibit certain attitudes in
the deacon.[67] Requirements were needed for the office of deacon as well
as that of overseer.

"Worthy of respect" suggests that deacons are to be serious minded
men whose character merits respect. The term combines such ideas as
dignity, earnestness of purpose, and winsome attractiveness. A cognate
noun ("proper respect") is used in 3:4 to describe the manner of the overseer in the discipline of his children.

The deacon would be a frequent visitor in homes, and he needed to be
consistent in what he reported to others. The NIV's metaphorical translation "sincere" obscures the fact that the Pauline phrase (*dilogos*) has the
meaning of *not double-tongued* and refers primarily to controlling speech
(i.e., "not indulging in double talk," NEB). The deacon is not to spread
rumors to different groups of listeners.

The prohibition against indulging "in much wine" forbids the love of
alcohol. The requirements resemble the demand of 3:3 for the overseer.
Total abstinence today from alcohol would guard the deacon from the
clutches of intoxicants. It would provide a credible witness to a society
that needs help in combating alcoholism.

The deacon is to avoid the temptations of materialism by "not pursuing
dishonest gain" (not given "to questionable money-making," TCNT).
Any deacon would face the temptation of using his spiritual office for
financial gain. He is not to develop a questionable integrity by currying

---

the common practice is for the deacon to render an administrative and officiating function.

Paul's emphasis in 1 Tim 3:8-13 focuses clearly on the personal and spiritual requirements
for office. Deacons likely served in an undefined way to assist the overseer, but they may not
have been deeply involved in church financial affairs.

Although most denominations seek to support their use of deacons as a scriptural practice,
it is difficult to prove that every facet of the modern function of the deacons is proved from
Scripture. Historically the function of deacons has developed over the centuries to meet the
need which the church foresaw. Likely it was Paul's intention in this passage to prescribe a
general personal and spiritual requirement for the office but to avoid a binding statement
about the function of the deacon. That function could change in accordance with the varying
needs of the churches. For information about the office of deacon, especially in Southern
Baptist churches, see J. B. McMinn, "Deacon," *Encyclopedia of Southern Baptists* 1958.

[67] The term "likewise" ties the description of the deacons to that of the overseers.
Lenski (*St. Paul's Epistles*, 594) connects the statements in v. 8 with "must be" ($\delta \epsilon \tilde{\iota} \ldots$
$\epsilon \tilde{\iota} \nu \alpha \iota$) of 3:2. He sees vv. 2-7 as a unit describing the qualifications of the overseer and v. 8
as the beginning of another unit. The requirements Paul would mention are necessitated by
the nature of the diaconic office.

favors for mercenary ends. The quest for gain becomes base or dishonest whenever one makes personal gain rather than God's glory the prime object of life. The use of this term does not merely prohibit the quest for gain in a dishonest manner. That would obviously be blatantly wrong. What Paul prohibited was the use of a spiritual office for material benefit, even if no dishonesty or illegality was present. The deacon is not to be perceived as greedy. In Titus 1:7 Paul used this same word (*aischrokerdēs*) as a requirement for overseers. Compare this with the appeal to the overseer in 3:3 that he not be "a lover of money."

3:9 Christian leaders are to exhibit a proper doctrinal and moral response to Christ's message. Paul's demands here turned positive. The "deep truths" of the faith are teachings once hidden but now revealed (cf. "the open secret of faith," Williams). The "faith" is the content of the Christian religion. It is objective Christian truth.

"Conscience" is a frequent emphasis of the Pastorals (1 Tim 1:5,19; 4:2; 2 Tim 1:3; Titus 1:15). Paul used the term in 1:5,19 to describe that inner guide to life which demonstrates obedience to God. To have a "clear conscience," a Christian leader must give continual obedience to God's truth as revealed in Scripture (cf. 1 John 1:7). The false teachers Paul had described (1:5-6,19) lacked a clear conscience. Paul placed more emphasis on the clear conscience with which the deacons held the faith than on their merely holding to the faith.

OF PROVEN WORTH (3:10). **3:10** The demand for "testing" raises two questions. First, what is the nature of the testing? Paul did not clarify whether the examination of the candidate concerned doctrinal beliefs, moral practices, or a combination of both. The emphasis of 3:9 suggests that both doctrine and practice are important in Christianity. The use of the present tense for "be tested" implies testing over a period (i.e., "let them continue to be tested"). The testing may not be so much a period of probation as a continual testing so that when deacons are later needed they may come from the available worthy group.

A second question concerns who did the testing. Again there is no specific statement from Paul. Acts 6:5 implies that the "Seven" were chosen by the entire congregation, but Titus 1:5 highlights the role of Titus in selecting leaders for the church on Crete. Perhaps a more mature congregation would act as a body in selecting its leaders, but a fledgling flock might rely on the wise insight of its founding pastor. The examination may have been informal, but the deacon-candidate needed to convince the church of his genuine Christian faith.

After the experience of testing, those who had "nothing against them" served as deacons. The word translated "nothing against them" (*anengklētos*) is a synonym for "above reproach" of 3:2 and signifies someone against whom no specific charge of wrongdoing can be laid.[68] Paul's requirements assure that the deacon would not normally be a recent convert. Following this demand would prevent the premature acceptance of unworthy men (see 1 Tim 5:22).

Paul did not specifically mention a process of testing for the office of overseer. Such action is implied by Paul's general description of the qualifications to be sought in the overseer. Although he did not mention any formal act of testing, it is implied that some process similar to that of v. 10 probably took place also in regard to the office of overseer.[69]

EXCELLING AT HOME (3:12). **3:12** The exact nature of Paul's meaning here is dependent on our understanding of "wives" in 3:11. If Paul referred to deacon's wives, then v. 12 is a return to the subject of deacons because of what Paul had just spoken about the wives. If he was thinking of "women helpers," then his return to the deacons is a supplement in which Paul stated, "Let me say a few more words about the deacons."[70]

A PROMISE FOR PERFORMANCE (3:13). **3:13** The use of the related verb "served" (*diakoneō*) so close to the noun for deacon in 3:12 suggests that Paul's words here are primarily spoken in reference to deacons. However, the truth of the verse would apply also to overseers (3:1-7) and women helpers (3:11).

In the verse Paul explained a promise for the deacon who serves well. The present-tense verb "gain" states what the committed deacon can normally expect to get for his service.[71] Paul outlined two promises. First, the servant will receive an "excellent standing" for his effective service. This standing is not an advance in ecclesiastical rank, a concern that was foreign to Paul's mind. Nor is it likely that Paul was promising a good standing in heaven, namely heavenly rewards. The standing likely was an assurance of a good reputation or good respect from the church for a job

---

[68]"In one sense, then, all Christians are blameless; in another sense all are unworthy; but in the mercy of God some men, though they feel their own unworthiness, are adjudged fit by their experienced fellow believers. God uses men before they are completely sanctified, and the church perforce must do likewise. But in that same mercy, some men have progressed far enough in discipleship to hold office in the church" (Ward, *1 & 2 Timothy & Titus*, 60).

[69]Justification for this statement comes from the appearance of "also" (καὶ; not translated in the NIV) in the Greek. A literal translation of the opening statement of v. 10 is, "And let these *also* first be tested." The "also" implies that the call for testing renews a practice being carried out with the overseers.

[70]The phrase "husband of but one wife" is the same in meaning as the phrase in 3:2. The verb "manage" is the same verb used in vv. 4-5 and calls for the deacon to show an effective authority in his home.

[71]This is an example of the "customary" present that describes what may be reasonably expected to occur. The temporal element is remote because the promise is seen as true in the past or future, as well as the present. See H. E. Dana and J. R. Mantey, *A Manual Grammar of the Greek New Testament* (New York: Macmillan, 1942), 183.

well done, although it could also refer to a good standing with God. Second, the faithful servant receives "great assurance" (*parrēsia*), a term used frequently to describe access to God (see Eph 3:12; Heb 10:19). However, New Testament use of this term also refers to boldness before others (e.g., 2 Cor 3:12). It is possible that the term "assurance" could refer to an exercise of confidence both before God and those who hear the gospel. However, the prepositional phrase modifying "faith" clearly refers the noun to personal faith in Jesus. The absence of the article before "faith" in the Greek text is further support for identifying this faith as a personal response to Christ.[72] It is best to see the "assurance" as a confidence before God produced in the sphere of a mature faith in Christ.

(3) Qualifications of Women Helpers (3:11)

[11]In the same way, their wives are to be women worthy of respect, not malicious talkers but temperate and trustworthy in everything.

3:11 The word "wives" (*gynē*) is the same word translated "women" in 2:9-10 or "woman" in 2:11-12. The context will usually show whether the word refers to a married woman ("wife") or is a reference to the female gender ("women"). Was Paul discussing the wives of the deacons, or was he presenting a special order of female helpers in Christian work?

In favor of viewing these as "wives" of the deacons is the fact that deacons are addressed on each side of the verse. Huther, who adopts this view, thinks the work of the deacon is of such a nature that the wives had a special role to play. Support for the view that Paul spoke of a special order of women helpers comes from a comparison of the structure of this verse to that of v. 8. The "likewise" (*hōsautōs*) of 3:8 appears to begin the enumeration of requirements for an office by reference to the previous requirements of 3:1-7. The same Greek word appears in v. 11 (translated "in the same way") and seems to introduce qualifications for another office as v. 8 does. The statements of v. 8 and v. 11 are both logically dependent on "must be" of 3:2, and this further implies the presence of three categories of positions.

New Testament Greek did not have a special word for "deaconess," but it used the same word with masculine endings to refer to both male and female helpers (see Rom 16:1, where Phoebe is described as a

---

[72]In the Pastorals Paul frequently placed the Greek article with "faith" when he intended to designate the content of the Christian faith (1 Tim 3:9; 4:1; 5:8), and he omitted the article when he referred to the personal experiential faith of the believer (1 Tim 1:5; 6:11; 2 Tim 1:13). The presence or the absence of the article in English is not always a safe indicator of Paul's usage (see 1 Tim 1:2, which has the article in English, lacks it in Greek, but probably describes the sphere in which Paul and Timothy were related).

diakonos). Perhaps Paul's failure to use a more specific title for these women was due to the fact that there was not one in use at that time. Paul's use of the term "wives" or "women" implied that these were women who helped the church in some manner.

The early church did have women whose special responsibility was to work with women and children (see Titus 2:4 for an indication of the beginning of this task). They performed pastoral work with the sick and the poor and helped at baptism.[73] The godly women Paul mentioned here stand in stark contrast with the gullible, immature women in 2 Tim 3:6. At 1 Tim 3:11 modern translations divide over the advisability of the translation "wives" (KJV, NIV, Phillips) or "women" (ASV, NASB, Amplified). Several versions use the term "deaconesses" (Williams, NIV margin, Montgomery). The GNB uses "wives" with a marginal alternative of "women helpers." The term "women helpers" refers to a special order of women who had a responsibility for ministry within the congregation. Phoebe (Rom 16:1-2) may have served in this kind of role, and perhaps Euodia and Syntyche (Phil 4:2-3) held the same position.

Paul outlined four requirements for a woman helper. First, she was to be "worthy of respect," a term used also of the deacons in v. 8. In prohibiting "malicious talking," Paul used a word normally employed to designate the devil (*diabolos*, see 1 Pet 5:8). The literal meaning of the term is "slanderer," or "accuser," and in this sense it becomes an apt designation for Satan (Rev 12:9-10). In 2 Tim 3:3 and Titus 2:3 the word refers to people who slander or misrepresent others. Paul was prohibiting gossip and insulting usage of the tongue as he did for the deacons in 3:8 (see in 3:8 the term "sincere," literally "not speaking a double-word" or "not being "double-tongued").

The women are to be "temperate" by showing control or moderation in all their behavior. Paul had used the same word in 3:2 to refer to the

---

[73]Ross, "A Reconsideration of the Diaconate," indicates that from the earliest times deaconesses visited the sick, acted as doorkeepers at the women's entrance for the church, kept order among church women, assisted in baptism for women, taught females in preparation for baptism, and acted as sponsors for exposed children (153). An insightful presentation of the role of women in the early church (including both heretics and heroines) appears in *Christian History* 7:17 (1988).

The early Christian writing known as the *Apostolic Constitutions* presents a picture of church life near the end of the third century. It outlines the work of a woman helper or deaconess as follows: "Ordain also a deaconess who is faithful and holy, for the ministrations towards women. For sometimes he cannot send a deacon, who is a man, to the women, on account of unbelievers. Thou shalt therefore send a women, a deaconess, on account of the imagination of the bad. For we stand in need of a woman, a deaconess, for many necessities; and first in the baptism of women, the deacon shall anoint only their forehead with the holy oil, and after him the deaconess shall anoint them: for there is no necessity that the women should be seen by the men" (*Apostolic Constitutions* 3.15).

overseer. The demand that the women be "trustworthy in everything" was an insistence on absolute reliability and faithfulness. Their trustworthiness could not be limited to a single sphere but had to be a part of all they did.

Whoever these women were, their qualifications stand in contrast to those of the women in 5:11-15 and 2 Tim 3:6-7. These women leaders were to have qualifications greatly contrasting with those who were duped by the false teachers.

Churches today that give women special places of responsibility rarely limit their work to women and children. A woman can certainly be as effective in handling finances as a man and often can be much more effective in maintaining church property. In light of the susceptibility of male leaders to moral failure in their working with women, it is sensible to look freshly at the pattern of the early church of using women to work with other women and children. The New Testament gives evidence that women who work with other women, the poor, and with children can render an important service for the cause of Christ. In taking advantage of the marvelous talents of highly trained, twentieth-century Christian women, we must be careful not to ignore special areas of natural competence in which women have long ministered effectively.

Summary. Paul's appeals to the men and women leaders called for visible, mature, righteous living that commended Christianity to its observers. God desires that the righteousness of spiritual leaders shine forth for his glory (Matt 5:16) so that the transforming power of Christianity might be evident for all to see (e.g., 1 Tim 3:7). He also wants spiritual leaders to show a maturity that has been proven by obedience and endurance under trials and testing even though they themselves have been examined in addition by human scrutiny.

4. Correct Application of Christian Truth (3:14-16)

These verses serve as a bridge between the guidelines Paul had given in 2:1–3:13 and the warnings about false teaching that follow. In 1:18-20 Paul concluded his explanation of the task facing Timothy with personal words of encouragement. Following his instructions about prayer, the behavior of men and women, and committed church leaders, Paul penned another personal word. The "instructions" of 3:14 probably include both what Paul had said in 2:1–3:13 and the new emphases he would make beginning with 4:1. In these verses Paul expressed his hope for making a visit to see Timothy (v. 14). He also stated his purpose for writing the Epistle (v. 15). In v. 16 Paul outlined a hymnic expression of Christian truth to prepare Timothy for a censure of false teaching in 4:1-5.

(1) Plans for a Visit (3:14)

14 Although I hope to come to you soon, I am writing you these instructions so that,

3:14 Paul had written these words with the full intent of making a personal visit to Timothy in Ephesus. However, his travel plans were always subject to the will of God. Paul never knew where a new day would take him. His actual hope was that he might come "soon" and personally give the instructions, but the possibility of interruption led him to put them in writing. Paul's words in this section serve as a bridge between his directives about prayer and ministry and his more practical advice in chaps. 4–6.

His writing was not due to his previous forgetfulness to mention these words to Timothy. Nor was Timothy so incompetent that Paul jotted off this note to prevent him from acting carelessly. The letter could serve as a confirmation of advice already given to Timothy on Paul's departure earlier from Ephesus. It would buttress Timothy's authority before a testy congregation. A critic of Timothy in Ephesus could argue that Timothy had misunderstood what Paul had directed him to do. No one could easily argue with a written word from the apostle.

Did Paul make his anticipated visit to Ephesus? We do not know. At about the time of the writing of 1 Timothy, Paul also told Titus to meet him in Nicopolis, where he intended to spend the winter (Titus 3:12). Probably Paul hoped to visit Timothy in Ephesus before going to Nicopolis, but nothing in any of the Pastorals confirms that he made the journey.

(2) Purpose for Writing (3:15)

15 if I am delayed, you will know how people ought to conduct themselves in God's household, which is the church of the living God, the pillar and foundation of the truth.

3:15 Paul's expression in v. 15 is somewhat elliptical, but its intent is expressed by the NASB's insertion of "write" into its translation: "In case I am delayed, I *write* so that you may know how one ought to conduct himself in the household of God." Paul's statements also omit any subject for the infinitive "conduct." The meaning will be much the same with either a "you" (a reference to Timothy himself) or a "one" (a reference to the behavior of any Christian). Since Paul here viewed the church as God's family, it is more likely that he applied these statements to the entire Ephesian church and not merely to Timothy.

Paul's statement of purpose in the clause "you will know . . . in God's household" calls for *two* comments. First, the translation "house of God" in the KJV brings to mind images of a church building (the church as the house of God). That translation gives the impression that Paul was providing a church manual for organizing activity in the "church house." It is better to understand that Paul was viewing the "house of God" as God's family or household.[74] Both NASB and NIV bring out this idea. This metaphor develops naturally with the realization that God is the Father, and believers are brothers and sisters.

Second, the "conduct" Paul was prescribing is not merely the official conduct of a leader in supervising the church or in arranging church organization. Paul's directive "includes the conduct of individual Christians, the qualifications required in ministers, and sound doctrine in contrast to the doctrine of false teachers."[75] Paul viewed the church as God's family, not merely as a building in which people meet. He was not describing behavior suitable for the church building but the type of conduct fitting for one who is a member of God's family.

The relative clause "which is the church of the living God" expresses a reason for proper conduct by the readers. The family of God Paul addressed is God's living church. Other gods that enticed Ephesian citizens into pagan practice were dead, but the God of the church is alive! Christian behavior must throb with the vitality of divine power.

The last phrase of v. 15 describes the church as "the pillar and foundation of the truth." A building would have many pillars, and they would support the roof. The pillars would themselves rest on the foundation. Paul saw the church as a temple and indicated that it is the very foundation that supports the truth of the Christian faith. Paul selected a robust figure to express the task of the church in the world. He was not thinking of propping up a building about to collapse but of a vigorous, triumphant church commending the gospel to the world by the united commitment of its members.[76] Paul's emphasis on "truth" relates well to his previous call for "knowing the truth" (2:4), but it also forms a transitional bridge to his statement of the content of truth in 3:16.

Some have felt that the description of the church in 3:15 gives greater prominence to the church than to the truth. Paul's intention, however, was not to exalt the institutional church but to call its members to active, united witness. "Each local Church has it in its power to support and strengthen the truth by its witness to the faith and by the lives of its members."[77]

---

[74]In Eph 2:19-22 Paul referred to the church as a family or household and then moved to view it as a "holy temple." He made a similar progression in 1 Tim 3:15. Other passages in the NT that present the church as the family of God are Gal 6:10; 1 Pet 4:17; 1 Tim 3:4-5.

[75]Ward, *1 & 2 Timothy & Titus*, 62.

[76]Ibid., 62-63.

[77]Lock, *Pastoral Epistles*, 44.

(3) A Hymn for Believers (3:16)

[16]Beyond all question, the mystery of godliness is great:
He appeared in a body,
   was vindicated by the Spirit,
was seen by angels,
   was preached among the nations,
was believed on in the world,
   was taken up in glory.

3:16 Paul's phrase "Beyond all question" introduces an outline of Christian truth that had the unanimous consent of Christians. The clause "the mystery of godliness is great" has a triumphant ring to it, much like the cry of the Ephesians in Acts 19:28. The term "mystery" also appears in 3:9 (translated "deep truths") and refers to truth that is now revealed. The word "godliness" (*eusebeia*) has the article in Greek and in this context means *the godliness.* This structure causes translators to see the term as a synonym for the Christian religion (Fee; Moffatt; Williams). The mystery of the Christian religion to which Paul pointed refers to God's redemptive plan which had been kept secret but was now revealed. Paul was extolling God's powerful actions that form the basis of the gospel and the transforming results that derive from accepting it.

Paul's outline of the Christian religion is representative but not exhaustive. For example, it does not mention the return of Christ. It is presented in the form of an early hymn.[78] The mere recitation of a creed could be cold and lifeless, but a hymn would pulsate with warmth and vigorous emotion. For example, the hymns of Martin Luther ("A Mighty Fortress Is Our God") and Charles Wesley ("O Sacred Head Now Wounded") spearheaded great spiritual revolutions. Paul probably did not compose this hymn but found it current in the life of the church.

The hymn contains six distinct statements with Christ as the understood subject of each line. Experts differ on the arrangement of the statements. Lenski agrees with the KJV in rendering it as a single stanza with six consecutive lines. Kelly agrees with the NIV in calling for three verses of two lines each. Fee agrees with the GNB in calling for two verses of three lines each.[79] The widespread disagreement even among experts makes one cau-

---

[78]Evidence for this comes from the parallelism of each line of the hymn. Each line begins with a verb in the Greek aorist passive tense followed by a prepositional phrase introduced by "in," "by," or "to." There is a deliberate assonance in Greek marked by the sound *th* from the aorist passive verbs. Reading the passage aloud in the Greek shows the presence of rhythm in the diction. For a similar hymn see 2 Tim 2:11-13. Some scholars think that a creed would lack the deliberate parallelism or assonance of a hymn.

[79]For discussion of the arrangement of the hymn see Lenski, *St. Paul's Epistles,* 607-9; Kelly, *Pastoral Epistles,* 88-93; and Fee, *1 and 2 Timothy, Titus,* 54-58.

tious in dogmatically following any set rendering. Fee's suggestions will serve as the basis for arranging this hymn, and we will analyze six distinct statements of the hymn.

The quotation of the hymn in this verse is only a sentence fragment, for it begins with a relative pronoun literally translated "who" (*hos*). The NIV's translation "he" disguises the fact that the Greek lacks a main clause. The absence of a principal clause led some early exegetes to alter the text. Some inserted the neuter relative pronoun "which" (*ho*) in order to link the clause with the term "mystery" so that the text spoke of a "mystery . . . which appeared in a body." Others placed the word "God" (*theos*) in the text to create a complete sentence that read, "God appeared in a body." The best manuscripts contain the reading "who," from which it is easy to trace the development of the other readings.

There is agreement that the first line, "He appeared in a body," is a reference to Jesus' incarnation. The term "body" (literally "flesh"; *sarx*) is a reference to all that belongs to our human nature (except sin; cf. Rom 8:3). Paul was asserting that in Christ, God himself had appeared in a human body.

There is similar agreement about the content of lines four and five. Line 4, "preached among the nations," refers to the proclamation of the gospel among the nations of the known world by early Christians. Line 5, "believed on in the world," describes a response to the previous proclamation. Christians preached the gospel throughout the nations of the world, and commitment to Christ was the result.

This interpretation of the content of lines 1, 4, and 5 suggests that the hymn is a story of salvation, somewhat along the line of J. Wilbur Chapman's gospel song "One Day." If this is correct, then we can understand the more difficult lines by relating them to the story of salvation.

Line 2 speaks of Christ's "vindication by the Spirit." The idea of vindication or the demonstration of Christ recalls statements about the resurrection in Rom 1:4 and 1 Pet 3:18. There is disagreement among some interpreters over whether "Spirit" is a reference to the Holy Spirit (NIV; NASB) or Christ's spiritual nature. Lenski takes "spirit" to be a reference to the vindication of Christ's spirit of holy obedience even to the death of the cross.[80] Since the first line of this hymn refers to being manifest in the realm of the flesh, it seems that the parallel in line 2 is suggesting that Christ was vindicated or declared righteous in the sphere of his spiritual

---

[80]Lenski, *St. Paul's Epistles*, 612. The presence or absence of the article before the word is not always a clear indicator of the referent of the word "spirit." Sometimes a reference to the Holy Spirit is anarthrous (e.g., 2 Cor 3:3), and sometimes it is articular (e.g., 1 Cor 2:12). Sometimes a reference to the human spirit of an individual is anarthrous (e.g., 2 Cor 7:1), and at other times it is articular (e.g., 1 Cor 2:11). The fact that "spirit" in the Greek text of v. 16 is anarthrous does not settle the issue of interpretation.

nature. The resurrection becomes the means of publicly declaring this vindication. What Paul was saying is that just as Christ was manifested in human flesh, so he was proved to be what he claimed to be in the spiritual realm. The resurrection of Christ declared that he was God's Son.[81]

Line 3, "was seen by angels," lacks the Greek preposition *en* and instead has a Greek dative case used with angels (literally "to angels").[82] The verb "was seen" is used in the New Testament to describe Jesus' post-resurrection appearances (1 Cor 15:5-8). The angels who worshiped Christ may have been either fallen (Col 2:15) or unfallen (Heb 1:6; 1 Pet 1:12). The expression of Paul is likely a reference to the worship given by angels to the ascended Christ.[83] If this interpretation is correct, then the first three lines of the hymn express Jesus' incarnation, resurrection, and glorification. The first stanza of three lines extols the glory of Christ in his early ministry and concludes with a word of triumph and victory.

The next two lines (4 and 5) also offer expressions of Christ's victory, but they sing about the developing ministry of Christ in his church. The sixth line of the song, "was taken up in glory," uses a verb that elsewhere in the New Testament describes the ascension (Acts 1:2,11,22). Since the ascension preceded the preaching of the gospel, we might think that it is out of order to mention it at this point. However, Jesus ordered the preaching of the gospel (Matt 28:19-20) before the act of the ascension, and it is this order that the hymn follows. "Glory" is a reference to the

---

[81] J. H. Bernard explains the meaning of the phrase to be that "as Christ was manifested in human flesh, so in His spiritual activities, words and works, He was proved to be what He claimed to be, Son of God no less than Son of man; His personal claims were vindicated" (*The Pastoral Epistles* [1899; reprint, Grand Rapids: Baker, 1980], 63).

[82] In form the expression could read either "was seen by angels" or "appeared to angels." The former translation would have "angels" in the instrumental case, showing agency. The latter translation would have "angels" in the dative case, indicating to whom the appearance was made. Guidance in deciding between these options can come by observing usage elsewhere.

In Acts 9:17 Luke used the same verb, and the NIV translates it "appeared to you." In 1 Cor 15:5-8 the same verb is again translated "appeared," and the persons to whom the appearances occurred ("Peter, the Twelve, five-hundred brothers, James, all the apostles, Paul") are again preceded in the NIV by the preposition "to." These translations take the case usages in these verses as dative, showing the person(s) to whom the appearances were made. Since these passages use the dative in translation, it seems wisest to continue that usage here. No serious issue is at stake in choosing the dative over the instrumental. To say that Jesus "was seen by angels" does not differ greatly in meaning from the statement that he "appeared to angels."

[83] The term translated "angels" can also mean *messengers*, and it can refer to those who reported Christ's resurrection. However, Paul was attempting to show the worship given to the glorified Christ by angelic powers, and a reference to messengers on earth during Jesus' incarnate life would be out of place here.

brightness and majesty of God's presence in Jesus, not merely a reference
to the ascension. The emphasis may relate to the glory Christ received as
he was declared and accepted.

This approach to the hymn finds two stanzas of three lines each. The
first stanza praises the earthly ministry of Christ and concludes with a
statement of triumph. The second stanza extols Christ's ongoing ministry
and concludes with a note of victory.

Paul used this hymn as an example of the mystery of godliness the
church proclaimed. This mystery relates to the incarnation and resurrection of Christ and the church's proclamation of him. Paul probably had
two purposes in mind in placing the hymn at this point. First, his emphasis on the past humiliation and present triumph of Christ probably stood
in contrast with the deficient Christology of the false teachers. They
apparently spiritualized the resurrection (2 Tim 2:18) and drank in other
Hellenistic ideas that could corrode Christian truth. Paul's statement
served as a corrective. Second, Paul was about to return to an attack
against the false teachers. His statement of the truth here prepared for the
attack by providing a broad expression of glorious truth in contrast to
their demonic errors.[84]

Summary. Two characteristics of believers stand out in the statements of Paul in vv. 15-16. First, he wrote to point out how Christians
should conduct themselves as members of God's family. Christians are to
distinguish themselves by a life-style of holiness. The mere mouthing of a
creed without transformation of life does not denote a believer. Believers
are those whose behavior designates them as God's children and demonstrates the reality of their faith. Second, Christians are those who do have
certain fixed beliefs about Christ. The incarnation, resurrection, and exaltation of Christ appear in the hymn Paul quoted. There is an appeal for
belief. Christians are not merely those who think nice thoughts about a
benevolent Jesus. They are those who have committed themselves to the
incarnate Son of God and risen Lord. We must affirm fixed truths about
Jesus.

5. Understanding False Practice (4:1-5)

Paul elaborated on the nature of the errors in Ephesus (4:1-5) and on
Timothy's role in opposing them (4:6-16). In describing the nature of the
false teaching, Paul was giving new information. However, it is not unre-
lated to what he had written before. In 1:3-7 he had warned of the

---

[84]For further discussion of the question of why Paul placed the hymn at this point, see
Fee, *1 and 2 Timothy, Titus*, xxii-xxiii, and 57.

"myths" and legalistic demands of the false teachers in Ephesus. He now gave an example of such errors.

In 4:1-3 Paul warned against adopting ascetic practices that would prohibit marriage and also against abstinence from certain foods. In 4:4 he argued that all of God's creation is good. The expression of gratitude in a prayer of thanksgiving sanctifies everything which God has made (4:5).

(1) A Warning against Apostasy (4:1-3)

[1] The Spirit clearly says that in later times some will abandon the faith and follow deceiving spirits and things taught by demons. [2] Such teachings come through hypocritical liars, whose consciences have been seared as with a hot iron. [3] They forbid people to marry and order them to abstain from certain foods, which God created to be received with thanksgiving by those who believe and who know the truth.

4:1 Christians saw themselves as living in the last days. These final days began with Jesus' ministry and will conclude with his return. Paul's expression for "in later times" is not the same as the related expression "in the last days" (2 Tim 3:1). However, the two expressions are to be viewed as the same in meaning. Paul saw evidence for the arrival of the last days in the persons of the false teachers in Ephesus with their emphasis on asceticism and abstinence from foods.[85] He later characterized the period in which he was living as "the last days" (2 Tim 3:1-8). Paul's refutation of the false teaching in 4:3-5 showed the present danger of the heresy.

The "Spirit" is the Holy Spirit, who is the source of prophecy. The word which the Spirit spoke does not appear in any passage of Scripture. It may have been a truth God had revealed to Paul (cf. Acts 20:29). Paul could also have referred to the general teaching of a passage such as Mark 13:22. The word may have come through a Christian prophet in the context of worship (see Acts 11:27-28).

The "some" who were to depart from the faith were professing Christians in Ephesus. They would turn from the doctrinal content of Christian-

---

[85] In 2 Thess 2:3-12 Paul had stated that the "last days" would be accompanied by apostasy, deceit, and a decline in love for the truth. He would make the same emphasis in 2 Tim 3:1. His words here harmonize with these statements in other locations and serve as clear evidence for Paul that he was living in the time of the end.

Doubtless, Christians had a concept of imminence along with their emphasis on the last days, but they also saw the last days as a new period in the divine plan. The culmination of the work of Christ (see particularly Heb 1:2) inaugurated the last days, and the coming of the Holy Spirit provided strength for living through those days. Christians saw themselves as living the life of the future in the present time (see the emphasis on living in "the heavenly realms" in Eph 2:6), and they anticipated that Christ would consummate his work in the future.

ity they had earlier accepted. A mere profession of faith does not guarantee the actual possession of eternal life. The emptiness of mere profession would become clear by the departure from Christianity of some of the Ephesians (see 1 John 2:19 for the same idea).

The "deceiving spirits" may be supernatural evil spirits who work through individuals, but against this view is the fact that Paul later described these false teachers in Ephesus as "deceiving and being deceived" (2 Tim 3:13). It is best to view the term "deceiving spirits" as a reference to the false teachers themselves. Deception was a leading trait of the errorists.

Paul's concluding statement of v. 1 located the source of the deceitful teachings in demonic influence. Satan's ability to enlist Judas to do his will shows his competence to influence belief and behavior (Luke 22:3).

4:2 Paul described the false teachers who practiced misleading the Ephesians. It was these false teachers whom the demons were using to carry out their bidding. First, Paul pictured their treachery by denouncing them as hypocrites. They presented themselves as pious followers of Christ, but they were in reality glib tools of the devil. They presented an air of devotion, but it was only a deceitful mask. Second, he described them as "liars." They used lies to conceal their own arrogance. Sadly they had apparently come to believe their own lies. Third, their consciences were cauterized. Two possible emphases may come from this statement. So insensitive had their consciences become that they had lost the power of moral decision making (cf. Eph 4:19). Grieving the Spirit had led to resistance, and resistance had led to quenching (Eph 4:30; 1 Thess 5:19). Paul may also have been suggesting that their consciences carried the brand of Satan.[86] By teaching what was actually false, they had been branded by Satan as his possession and therefore did his will. This shade of meaning emphasizes that the false teachers were willing tools of Satan. Since the context had already emphasized demonic involvement in spreading error, this likely was Paul's chief emphasis.

4:3 Paul called attention to two features that characterized the teaching of the heretics. First, some false teachers forbade marriage. Paul's warning in 1 Tim 5:11-15 indicates that younger widows in Ephesus may have been influenced by these prohibitions. The heretics who supported these views probably felt that abstinence from marriage was the means to

---

[86]The translation of the NIV emphasizes the insensitivity that results from the searing of the conscience. The NEB emphasizes that the searing is a mark of Satan's ownership with its translation of "branded with the devil's sign." Either emphasis is possible in rendering the translation, but the context suggests that ownership by Satan is likely the more dominant teaching of the word.

a higher degree of holiness. They placed the celibate life on a higher spiritual level than the married life.[87]

Second, the false teachers demanded abstinence from certain foods.[88] This error likely reflected the Mosaic distinction between clean and unclean foods. This same error is also apparent in Col 2:16,21-23. To Paul the proper response to the question of eating foods was to eat after having expressed thanksgiving through prayer.[89]

Paul's statement at the end of v. 3 ("those who believe . . . the truth") does not suggest that only believers are to eat. Those who know the truth of the gospel are especially able to offer the thanksgiving that sanctifies the food. Believers have made far better preparation than unbelievers to receive the food in the manner God intended.

Paul's comments about eating call for three observations. First, Paul normally regarded what a person eats as an indifferent matter so long as the practice does not cause spiritual harm to another believer (1 Cor 8:8-9). Second, partial asceticism may be a helpful experience for some, but it should not be enforced as a means of salvation (Col 2:20-23). Third, Paul was resisting a theologically based asceticism. He would not necessarily oppose an asceticism whose goal was to give physical strength to the body.

(2) An Argument against Asceticism (4:4)

[4] For everything God created is good, and nothing is to be rejected if it is received with thanksgiving,

---

[87] In 1 Cor 7:1-9 Paul had encountered Greeks who questioned and opposed marriage. Their opposition to marriage was probably based on a Greek concept which emphasized that the human body was evil and that marriage and sex were discouraged. This later became an emphasis of Gnosticism.

Although the false teachers in Ephesus discouraged marriage, they were probably not as negative in their emphases as those whom Paul encountered in Corinth. The heresy Paul encountered in Ephesus had a Jewish emphasis, and Judaism had no inherent opposition to marriage and sex. We think that the Essenes disparaged marriage, but Judaism did not generally have this emphasis. The error about marriage in Ephesus was not a fully developed Gnostic view but a tendency in that direction likely caused by converted Jews who were living in a pluralistic religious setting (see Kelly, *Pastoral Epistles*, 95 for further discussion).

[88] The word "order" is absent from the Greek text but is a legitimate inference of Paul's meaning so as to make sense of the context. Some interpreters see this as an instance of *zeugma*, and others believe Paul was using ellipsis by omitting the word "order." *Zeugma* is a figure of speech in which a single word governs two or more words but makes better sense with only one (e.g., "He is eating bread and water").

[89] Jesus' statements in Mark 7:14-19 abolish the Jewish distinction between clean and unclean foods. It is likely that such statements as these influenced Paul's opposition to an enforced asceticism.

4:4 Paul presented two reasons in support of his opposition to a theologically based asceticism.[90] First, he affirmed that God's creation is good. There is no dualism in creation. God had made only that which was good (see Rom 14:14). This fact of God's benevolent creation implies that we can eat all that God has made. Lenski aptly says, "He created them, and in consequence, because of this, every one of them is excellent (Gen 1:31)."[91]

Second, we must eat with thanksgiving what God has created. Paul did not refer to a general spirit of gratitude but to the expression of that gratitude in table blessings (notice this practice in Jesus' life [Mark 6:41; 8:6]). His words suggest that a thankless heart can transform even good food into unacceptable food.

We must not apply Paul's words to an approval of gluttony or drunkenness if thanksgiving precedes it. Paul would ban such undisciplined action under all circumstances (1 Cor 6:9-12; 11:21-22).

(3) An Argument for Blessing Food (4:5)

[5]**because it is consecrated by the word of God and prayer.**

4:5 The combination of "word of God" and "prayer" can be interpreted in at least three ways. First, it may be a reference to God's word of "good" pronounced over all creation (Gen 1:31). The idea would be that God's pronouncement of "good" consecrates all food for human consumption. The presence of the Greek verb for "consecrate" in a present rather than a perfect tense works against this interpretation. Had Paul intended to refer to the completed action of Gen 1:31, the perfect tense would have been more appropriate.

Second, the terms may refer to the act of blessing food, perhaps incorporating the use of some biblical expressions.[92] It is a prayer involving Scripture and in harmony with God's truth. Because God's word has a cleansing effect (John 15:3), prayer could remove any unacceptable features of the food.

Third, the terms may refer to the act of blessing food, but the term "word of God" may refer to the gospel message rather than to the Old Testament as Scripture. In the Pastoral Epistles the expression "word [of

---

[90]Paul's discussions in vv. 4-5 treat only the question of abstinence from certain foods. He did not elaborate about dealing with those who "forbid people to marry." Perhaps he omitted this because he had already spoken clearly and positively about marriage and child rearing (2:15; 3:4,12).

[91]Lenski, *St. Paul's Epistles*, 624.

[92]White, *Epistles to Timothy* (122), calls the combination of "word of God" and "prayer" a hendiadys. Together the terms form elements in thanksgiving. Thus thanksgiving (4:4) includes the use of a passage of Scripture in praying to God. Note Paul's use of Ps 24:1 in 1 Cor 10:26.

God]" is generally a reference to the gospel message (cf. 2 Tim 4:2; Titus
1:3; 2:5). Paul was probably following that usage here and was suggesting that in responding to the gospel the believers in Ephesus had learned
that there are no food laws. The gospel had brought them to a proper
understanding of food, and they acknowledged by prayer that it was a gift
from God. Although there is no theological problem with the other
options, this view provides the best understanding in this context.[93]

This act of blessing the food makes it special or consecrated before
God. A prayer of thanksgiving recognizes God's prior creative actions
and is a conscious appropriation of God's work into the life of the wor-
shiper. Blessing the food does not add an additional sanctity over and
above what it already has. It sets the food in its true perspective so that
believers can see its sacredness.

Although Paul denounced both asceticism in marriage and enforced
abstinence from certain foods, he would not oppose singleness and vegetarianism. He viewed the single state as quite acceptable (1 Cor 7:33-35),
but he saw marriage as the norm (1 Cor 7:2). Paul did not specifically
commend vegetarianism as superior,[94] but he seemed to feel that eating
any food that would promote good health is acceptable (1 Tim 5:23).

Summary.   Paul described a destructive legalism in this section. First,
legalism prevents a clear grasp of the freedom and power of the Holy
Spirit. People involved in avoiding marriage, food, and other God-
sanctioned privileges would never be able to seek divine power and
experience spiritual liberty. Second, legalism destroys gratitude toward
God. Legalists show such concern for practicing the negative that they
fail to appreciate God's positive provisions. Legalism cannot endure long
in the presence of an attitude of thanksgiving to God for his created gifts
and marvelous institutions.

6. Timothy's Performance of His Task (4:6-16)

Paul outlined some of the errors among the false teachers in Ephesus
(4:1-5). He now focused on Timothy's role in the face of these errors.
First, he told Timothy what to do as he met the ungodly ways of the false
teachers (4:6-10). The command to Timothy was: Develop godliness.
Second, Paul outlined the specific action Timothy was to take in providing a model for others to follow (4:11-16). The command was: Persevere
in teaching and preaching the truths of Scripture.

---

[93]For further elaboration of this viewpoint, see Fee's discussion of the meaning of "Word
of God" in the Pastorals, *1 and 2 Timothy, Titus,* 62-63.

[94]His reference in Rom 14:2 to vegetarianism admits the practice but does not prescribe
it as the norm.

Following the false faith of the heretics had led some in Ephesus to abandon obedience and faith (1 Tim 1:19-20). In 4:7-8 Paul used the word "godly" or "godliness" (*eusebeia*) to call Timothy back to the proper practice. As Timothy faced falsehood, he was to major on the development of godliness.

In 4:11-16 Paul emphasized that Timothy was to persevere in what he had begun. Timothy had begun well by obeying God's commands. Paul desired that he continue on the path of obedience to provide an example for other believers.

(1) Facing Falsehood (4:6-10)

[6] If you point these things out to the brothers, you will be a good minister of Christ Jesus, brought up in the truths of the faith and of the good teaching that you have followed. [7] Have nothing to do with godless myths and old wives' tales; rather, train yourself to be godly. [8] For physical training is of some value, but godliness has value for all things, holding promise for both the present life and the life to come.

[9] This is a trustworthy saying that deserves full acceptance [10] (and for this we labor and strive), that we have put our hope in the living God, who is the Savior of all men, and especially of those who believe.

What should be our strategy when we live in a world inundated with false teaching? First, we must expose the errors we oppose. Second, we must also develop personal holiness to assure continuation in integrity. The combination of exposing error and practicing truth is a powerful antidote to heresy. Paul proposed this strategy for Timothy.

4:6 Paul urged Timothy to make a positive presentation of the truth. His expression "point . . . out" ("continue to put . . . before," Williams) implies a suggestion, not an order. Timothy was to use a gentle reminder rather than verbal harangue. The "things" of which he was to remind the Ephesian Christians could refer either to the full content of 2:1–4:5 or specifically to the warnings of 4:1-5. The nearness of the latter passage to 4:6 makes it more likely that Paul wanted Timothy to warn the Ephesians against an enforced celibacy and asceticism.

In describing Timothy as a "minister," Paul used the word translated "deacon" in 3:8 (*diakonos*). Paul was not suggesting that Timothy held the office of a deacon. He pictured Timothy as having the function of a servant.

The phrase "brought up in the truths . . . good teaching" pictures the manner by which Timothy could become an excellent minister.[95] He had

---

[95]The participle "brought up" (ἐντρεφόμενος) is better translated "nourishing yourself." The verb is a metaphor referring to raising children. As a present middle participle, the word

to continue to nourish himself on the truths and teaching of Christianity he had always followed (2 Tim 3:14-16). This was how Timothy was to act at all times in order to be a good minister of Jesus Christ.

Paul commended Timothy by suggesting that he had faithfully "followed" this teaching. As a disciple of Christ he had made a past commitment to Christian obedience and had been consistent in his practice. A Christian can receive no higher compliment.

Much Christian teaching involves reminding ourselves and others of beliefs and practices we know but ignore or forget. Paul commended Timothy's obedience and implied that he was to continue more of the same.

4:7 Paul appealed for Timothy to reject the empty ideas of the heretics. He described the teaching of the Ephesian heretics as "godless" and as "old wives' tales."[96] The former term suggests something that is religiously bankrupt. The latter term describes an idea that is frivolous and not worthy of serious attention. Hiebert uses the adjective to picture the "myths" as "nothing but silly fictions, fit only for senile, childish old crones to chatter about."[97] The word "myths" is the same word used in 1:4. The command "Have nothing to do with" suggests a strong rejection (see 2 Tim 2:23, where "Don't have anything to do" is the same word). Paul did not want Timothy even to occupy his time with answering such profane chatter. Some false teaching is best ignored rather than discussed.

In contrast to following the vapid vagaries of the false teachers, Timothy was to seek after God. Paul borrowed a metaphor from the sphere of athletics to describe the pursuit of godliness (cf. 1 Cor 9:24-27). Paul urged Timothy to concentrate his energy on vigorous training for genuine godliness. For Paul genuine godliness involved both right belief and obedient action. Godly habits would not appear without determined human purpose and effort. Timothy was to persist in that Christian discipline which would prepare him for God's highest purposes.

4:8 Paul introduced an explanation of his command that Timothy should train in godliness. His statement in the first half of the verse is not a disparagement of bodily exercise but asserts that it is of some value. Interpreters take two views of the meaning of "physical training." Some feel Paul was using an illustration from the physical realm to

---

clearly emphasizes that Timothy was to feed himself continually on the truths of the gospel that would sustain his faith, commitment, and spiritual vigor. It is not a reference to the training he received as a child but to his present situation.

[96] The translation of the NIV disguises the fact that in the Greek both "godless" and "old wives' tales" are adjectives with both words modifying "myths." Phillips colorfully describes them as "stupid Godless fictions."

[97] Hiebert, *First Timothy*, 81.

suggest that godliness is superior to mere gymnastics or athletic train-ing.[98] Against this interpretation is the fact that Paul was not really dis-cussing athletic training in this passage. He used the term only because of the metaphor "train" in v. 7. Others more properly feel that the term refers to asceticism, "the mortification of the body for religious purposes, as in the abstinence from marriage and meats."[99] This latter view appears to be more in harmony within a context in which Paul had denounced enforced abstinence from marriage and meats (1 Tim 4:3). Paul renounced extreme forms of bodily discipline, but he admitted that there is some profit in seeking to control the body. He did on occasion use this practice (1 Cor 9:27; 2 Cor 11:27—"I . . . have often gone with-out food"). He recognized that we must use spiritual weapons to control the body (2 Cor 10:4-6). Kelly says, "True Christianity consists rather in ever renewed submission to the control of the Spirit, with the cheerful acceptance of toil and suffering . . . and the practice of those virtues which are the fruit of the Spirit."[100]

Paul reasoned that godliness shows its superiority over mere ascetic discipline because it offers advantages in two realms. Asceticism repre-sents an effort to control the appetites in this life. Godliness represents an effort to practice self-control in this life and to reap benefits in eternity. A thinking Christian could see that godliness represented a higher priority than mere physical training. Godliness has the potential of impacting all actions, experiences, and relationships for good.

4:9 What is the "trustworthy saying" to which Paul referred? Guthrie agrees with the NIV translation and suggests that the weighty subject matter of v. 10 makes it a more likely candidate to be the saying.[101] Most other interpreters (Fee, Ward, White) feel that the saying is a reference to the content of v. 8. Fee clarifies the issues when he indicates that the nature of the saying of v. 8 is more epigrammatic, while the statement of v. 10 is actually a reflection on the latter part of v. 8.[102] He locates the "saying" as the latter part of v. 8. This is the better option. For additional discussion on "trustworthy sayings," see the initial presentation at 1:15.

4:10 Paul concluded v. 8 with a statement that the practice of godli-ness held a promise for both the present and the future. In v. 9 he desig-nated this as a "trustworthy saying." In v. 10 Paul provided a reason for

---

[98]The translation of the NIV appears to interpret the training as a reference to physical exercise. Phillips's "bodily fitness" supports this view. Other versions (RSV, NASB) use a term such as "bodily training" or "bodily discipline," which could support either of the two interpretative options presented.

[99]Hiebert, *First Timothy*, 82.

[100]Kelly, *Pastoral Epistles*, 101.

[101]Guthrie, *Pastoral Epistles*, 96.

[102]Fee, *1 and 2 Timothy, Titus*, 66-67.

his statement that godliness is profitable for all things. The NIV translation "and for" reflects the Greek conjunction *gar*. The statement of the NIV provides an explanation that the practice of labor and striving shows that godliness is useful for all things, but the relationship is not explicitly stated. Because the Ephesians had hoped upon the promise of the gospel, their lives were filled with a vigorous effort and activity that prove the present and future usefulness of the gospel.

The verb for "labor" (*kopiaō*) suggests a strenuous toil that saps energy. Godliness demands energy! Hiebert notes that the word for "strive" presents "the picture of the athlete putting the last ounce of his energy into the race in order victoriously to reach the goal."[103] The use of a Greek present tense for both verbs suggests a continual outpouring of this energy. White says: "A consciousness that we are in a harmonious personal relation with the living God lifts us into a sphere in which labor and striving have no power to distress us."[104]

The "that" of the NIV is a translation of the Greek *hoti*, better translated "because" (so translated in NEB, ASV, Moffatt). With the translation "because," the clause explains why Christians go through the difficulty of laboring and striving. The perfect tense for "have put our hope" suggests a settled confidence in God. Paul designated God as living because he fulfills his promises to believers. Paul further designated this living God as the "Savior of all men."

Paul called God "the Savior of all men" in that he genuinely wants all human beings to experience salvation. The fact that more are not saved is not due to the weakness or impotence of the divine intent but to the stubborn opposition of the human will (see Matt 23:37). Some might see in the statement an evidence for universalism, but Hanson has well said, "The author is not committed to Universalism in the modern sense."[105] Guthrie suggests that the designation of God as Savior of all means that he is the Preserver of all (Matt 5:45).[106] However, in light of 1 Tim 2:6 (cf. 1 John 2:2) his universal saviorhood appears in that Christ is potentially a ransom for the sins of all. In those believers who have trusted him, he is Savior in a far deeper and more profound sense. The term "especially" introduces the explanation that assurance of salvation belongs to those who have received Christ. His purpose in stressing this assurance for believers was to remind them that their hope in God would not be in vain.

---

[103]Hiebert, *First Timothy*, 83. Some Greek manuscripts read "suffer reproach" (ὀνειδίζομαι), and this translation is reflected in the KJV. Most modern translations (NEB, Williams, Phillips) follow the reading "strive" (ἀγωνίζομαι). The latter reading has better attestation from manuscripts and seems to suit the context better.

[104]White, *Epistles to Timothy*, 125.

[105]Hanson, *Pastoral Epistles*, 92.

[106]Guthrie, *Pastoral Epistles*, 96.

Paul's statement that God is the Savior of all people is no endorsement of universalism. Nothing in these statements supports the idea that Christ's death provides any benefit for those who reject him as Savior and Lord.

(2) Demonstrating Christian Behavior (4:11-16)

[11] **Command and teach these things.** [12] **Don't let anyone look down on you because you are young, but set an example for the believers in speech, in life, in love, in faith and in purity.** [13] **Until I come, devote yourself to the public reading of Scripture, to preaching and to teaching.** [14] **Do not neglect your gift, which was given you through a prophetic message when the body of elders laid their hands on you.**

[15] **Be diligent in these matters; give yourself wholly to them, so that everyone may see your progress.** [16] **Watch your life and doctrine closely. Persevere in them, because if you do, you will save both yourself and your hearers.**

In 4:11-16 Paul emphasized that Timothy was to persevere or continue in what he had begun. Timothy had begun well in obeying God's commands. Paul desired that he continue in the path he had started so as to provide an example for other believers.

4:11 Timothy was possibly a diffident, timid young man. His timidity could hinder a bold assertion of Christian truth. Paul used the term "command" in v. 11 to indicate the authoritative transmission of a message. He wanted Timothy to speak with authority. In teaching, Timothy was to urge his words onto the thinking of the listeners in order to make obedience easy. In the Pastorals, Paul frequently pressed this charge of teaching and exhorting on both Timothy and Titus (1 Tim 6:2; 2 Tim 2:2; Titus 2:15).

What were the things Timothy was to "command and teach"? They included primarily the words of 4:6-10 which urge warnings against "old wives' tales" and put stress on the importance of genuine godliness.

4:12 Paul expressed some of the emphases that were to characterize Timothy's ministry in 4:12-16. First, Timothy was to live as a spiritual example of what a believer truly can be. His practice of godliness and the demonstration of Christian character could compensate for the lack of calendar years. The term "example" signifies a pattern or a model. Paul desired that people in Ephesus develop godliness by modeling Timothy. These words produced encouragement in Timothy himself, but they could also set in order some dissident, fault-finding elements of the congregations. After all, Paul was bestowing his full blessing on Timothy, and he wanted the Ephesians to learn from what the young disciple did.

We need not take Paul's description of Timothy as "young" to picture him as a teenager or a young adult in his early twenties. Acceptable estimates of Timothy's age could easily place him between thirty and thirty-five years old.[107] Some Christians in Ephesus could chafe at receiving instructions from a man even this young.

The traits listed by Paul ("spirit" is absent from most modern translations) divide into two groups. The terms "speech" and "life" are outwardly observable or public traits. "Speech" refers to all types of verbal expression, and "life" describes general behavior. Paul wanted Timothy to be known for wise words rather than for rash, impetuous drivel. The second group, consisting of "love," "faith," and "purity," refers to inner traits. Paul desired a love that demonstrates itself for both God and others. The term "faith" is anarthrous in the Greek and likely represents an attitude of faithfulness or trustworthiness rather than right belief. The call for "purity" demands both sexual purity and integrity of heart.

4:13 A second emphasis Paul wanted Timothy to make involves proclaiming God's message. Until Paul arrived back on the scene, Timothy was to apply himself to reading, preaching, and teaching. The very brevity of these instructions indicates their genuineness. If these words had come from the second century, the list would have been longer and would have included some reference to the ordinances. Some interpreters see these instructions as a model for public worship patterned after the synagogue. Fee points out that public worship also included prayers (2:1-7), singing (cf. the hymn in 1 Tim 3:16), words of testimony (1 Cor 14:26), and the Lord's Supper (1 Cor 11:17-34).[108] Public worship was much more than reading, praying, and teaching. These instructions are not merely a pattern for worship, but they present a positive method of opposing false teaching.

"Reading" refers to the public reading of Scripture. Scripture included at least the Old Testament, but it may have referred also to the rapidly growing collection of New Testament writings (see 2 Pet 3:16). The command to read would presuppose a wise selection of passages for reading and an alertness to guard against the reading of suspicious or erroneous words. At a time when believers lacked personal copies of God's Word, such a practice was essential to promote knowledge of the divine message. "Preaching" includes moral instruction that appeals to the will (e.g., Acts 13:15). "Teaching" makes an appeal to the intellect and informs listeners about the truths of the Christian faith. (See Rom 12:7-8, where Paul mentioned teaching and encouraging together.)

---

[107]Fee suggests that Timothy's age was thirty to thirty-five and defends it by suggesting 49-50 as a date for his joining Paul and 62-64 as the date for writing 1 Timothy. Irenaeus (*Against Heresies* 2.22.5) says, "The first stage of life embraces thirty years, and that this extends onwards to the fortieth year, everyone will admit."

[108]Fee, *1 and 2 Timothy, Titus*, 69.

4:14 A third directive Paul gave Timothy was that he not neglect the spiritual gift he had received. The construction of the Greek text suggests he should stop neglecting this gift. The "gift" likely represented an aptitude for teaching and preaching together with an ability to understand the gospel and discern error.

Several problems of interpretation appear in the passage. First, what was the "prophetic message"? It referred to some prophetic indication affirming Timothy's call. It could have taken the form of a promise, an exhortation, or a prayer. The incident of Acts 13:1-3 provides illustration of such a message. There the Holy Spirit directed that Paul and Barnabas be set aside for special service. The church instantly responded with obedience. Perhaps a similar statement about Timothy's potential usefulness had been spoken about him.

Interpreters have also wondered when this event took place. It may have taken place as Paul left Ephesus and appointed Timothy to deal with the heresy. It also could have occurred during Paul's second visit to Lystra in Acts 16:1-5. Pinpointing the time of occurrence is an impossibility.

Questions have arisen from comparing 1 Tim 4:14 with 2 Tim 1:6. Here the "body of elders" laid on hands, but there Paul mentioned the imposition of his hands alone. The different information could show that two separate times were involved. If the laying on of hands in the two passages refers to the same incident, the present passage could reflect a corporate response to the prophecy concerning Timothy's usefulness. It is more probable that Paul was referring to the same occasion in both 1 Tim 4:14 and in 2 Tim 1:6. In the former passage he emphasized the role of the elders, and in the latter he focused on his role alone.

Is it proper to call this event an ordination service? Fee says that it is somewhat of an anachronism to label this "ordination," but the incident does show the response of the Ephesian church to Timothy's ministry.[109] Paul's language in v. 14 is more an apt description of a special service that recognized and affirmed Timothy's gift. Paul's statements in 2 Tim 1:6-7,14 made clear that the Holy Spirit, not merely a group of elders, was the source of his gift. The affirmation Timothy received through "laying on hands" allowed him the freedom to minister with greater effectiveness among the Ephesians.[110] Paul's point in mentioning this incident was not to insist that Timothy had been ordained as an elder but to remind him and the Ephesian congregation that Timothy had spiritual gifts that had been confirmed by the prophetic message. For further discussion of the

---

[109]Ibid., 70.

[110]For additional information on the background of ordination and on the significance of this event in Timothy's life, see M. Warkentin, *Ordination* (Grand Rapids: Eerdmans, 1982), 16-28, 136-52.

practice of ordination, see Excursus 3: Ordination: Biblical Evidence and Baptist Practice (following commentary on v. 16).

Mention should be made of one difficulty in the translation of the term "body of elders." The term has normally been taken to refer to a body of elders in a Christian congregation. If this is its usage, this is its only New Testament reference to a body of Christian elders. (In Luke 22:66 and Acts 22:5 the term refers to the Jewish body in Jerusalem, as indicated by the translation "council." A related terms occurs in 1 Tim 5:17; Jas 5:14). Some have suggested that the phrase is the translation of a technical Jewish term meaning *your ordination as an elder.* However, the use of the term in Judaism to describe the installation of teachers or judges did not become current until the second or third century A.D., and it would be inappropriate to apply this usage to the first century. Also, there would be nothing improper about the transfer of a term for body of Jewish elders to a body of Christian elders. It is best to see the expression as a reference to an affirmation of Timothy's spiritual gifts by a body of elders of the Ephesian congregation.[111]

4:15 A fourth appeal Paul made to Timothy was for consistent spiritual growth. This emphasis appears in vv. 15-16. The phrase to "be diligent" comes from a verb that implies either meditation or practice. Timothy could either think hard about Paul's directives or zealously do them. Perhaps Paul's idea was that Timothy ponder his directives in vv. 12-14 and eagerly put them into operation. To give himself "wholly to them" called for Timothy to immerse himself in both the teaching and the doing of the demands. Paul used the noun for "progress" to describe the advance of the gospel (Phil 1:12). The verbal form was used in Luke 2:52 to picture Jesus' development intellectually, physically, spiritually, and socially.

In 2 Tim 2:16 and 3:9 Paul used the verbal form of "progress" to describe progression in ungodliness. The Ephesian false teachers may have suggested that following their teaching would lead to progress, but Paul suggested that the only progress was in the area of ungodliness. Here he suggested that true progress is seen by development in the teachings of godliness that accord with the gospel.

Paul's purpose in the appeal was for Timothy to make a powerful demonstration of the spiritual advance since his earlier years. If Timothy obeyed Paul's advice, his friends in Ephesus would not see him as an inexperienced youth but as a growing man of God. Church members will follow someone whom they respect when the mere authority of the office makes them react or resist.

---

[111]For an extensive discussion of the entire issue, see J. P. Meier, "*Presbyteros* in the Pastoral Epistles," *CBQ* 35 (1973): 323-45.

4:16 Paul commanded Timothy to "watch [his] . . . life and doctrine closely." Timothy was to scrutinize both his behavior and his theology. Moral and doctrinal rectitude are the inseparable twins of the Christian life.

Paul's final statement in v. 16 has important application for the doctrine of eternal security. First, Paul indicated that believers must endure to obtain the benefits of salvation. If Timothy persevered, his salvation would be evident to him as well as others. Both holy living and sound teaching are the inevitable fruits of saving faith.

It is not that Timothy's endurance would merit salvation but that a stamina that produced holiness and doctrinal orthodoxy gave incontrovertible evidence of heading for salvation. Second, Paul suggested that the obedient perseverance of the preacher is an important factor in the endurance of the hearers. The preacher's model of perseverance builds the same trait in his flock. The stumbles and fumbles of a wandering spiritual leader will infect a congregation with a variety of spiritual sicknesses.

Summary. The best antidote for error is a positive presentation of the truth. Paul urged Timothy to follow this method in dealing with opponents and false teaching in Ephesus (v. 6). It is also mandatory for the teacher of truth to accredit the presentation with personal supportive evidence. Paul mentioned two types of personal supportive evidence. First, he appealed to Timothy to demonstrate godliness (v. 7). A reverence for God offers promise in this life and hope for the life to come (v. 8). Second, Paul directed Timothy to persevere (v. 16). To overcome error and misunderstanding, we must endure with stamina in the practice of righteousness.

EXCURSUS 3: ORDINATION: BIBLICAL EVIDENCE AND BAPTIST PRACTICE. Ordination is a formal ceremony in which a local church acknowledges the evidence of a special call to ministry in the life of a candidate. The ceremony of ordination symbolizes God's act of setting aside and empowering a person to carry out that ministry in a specific place of service. In understanding the practice of ordination, it will be of importance to investigate the practice in the New Testament, the purpose and form of the ceremony, and tensions and difficulties connected with the practice. New Testament evidence will be related to Baptist practice.

Baptists assume that all believers are to be servants of the Lord, but they also affirm that God calls some leaders to serve in full-time or special capacities. The essence of that ministry can be described as "service," although Baptists acknowledge that these servants must function as spiritual leaders. Even though Baptists readily admit that the practice of ordination involves both Scripture and tradition, they generally find some evidence for the ceremony in Scripture.

The KJV translates no less than thirteen words by the term "ordain," but most of these usages do not refer to the ceremony of ordination. In

Titus 1:5 and Acts 6:3 the Greek word *kathistēmi* is used to describe an appointment to a task, but there is no clear mention of a ceremony. In Acts 1:22 Peter spoke of ordaining (KJV uses "ordain"; NIV has "become") a replacement for Judas among the apostles in order to declare the fact of Jesus' resurrection. The word "ordained" (*ginomai*) again signifies an appointment to office, but no mention is made of a formal ceremony. In Acts 14:23 and 2 Cor 8:19 the term *cheirotoneō* is used to indicate a selection for a task or an office. The word originally meant *to raise the hands to express an opinion in a vote*, but it had come to signify selection or choice for a task. None of these passages actually refers to a ceremony of ordination.

Those passages that speak of a ceremony or recognition mention the laying on of hands. This reference appears in Acts 13:3; 1 Tim 4:14; 5:22; and 2 Tim 1:6. In each instance some type of formal ceremony is indicated, but the passages do not describe this ceremony with any detail. Old Testament passages also speak of a laying on of hands (e.g., Deut 34:9). H. Peacock describes the relations of New Testament ordination to the Old Testament by saying, "The background of New Testament ordination is not the transfer of personality or even of authority from one person to another; it is the prayer-blessing concept of laying on hands seen in healing, blessings, and the gift of the Spirit."[112]

In summary, we say that the New Testament does present evidence for the practice of an ordination ceremony in setting aside men for special ministry in the service of God. The purpose of the ceremony is unclear, and its form is not evident from the New Testament.

The Baptist expression of the purpose of ordination has more to do with church tradition than with biblical teaching. This statement does not suggest that the practice of ordination is totally unwarranted, but it serves as a reminder that all elements of Baptist ordination practice are not clearly outlined in Scripture. Baptists usually emphasize two purposes in the practice of ordination. First, ordination becomes the ceremony in which a congregation affirms that a candidate possesses the gifts necessary for ministry. It is an expression of congregational approval on the spiritual endowment and personal character of the candidate. Second, ordination acknowledges a divine call to ministry. It is a recognition by God's people that the candidate has a special calling from God for service. The ceremony of ordination commissions the candidate to the task.

The New Testament does not provide a specific form for the ceremony of ordination. Christ used a verbal commission to send out his apostles (Matt 28:19-20). The early church incorporated prayer and the laying on of hands (Acts 13:3). Baptist ordination ceremonies today involve an

---

[112]H. F. Peacock, "Ordination in the New Testament, *RevExp* 55 (1958): 270.

ordaining council composed either of all ministers or jointly of ministers and laypersons. This group questions the candidates on their doctrine and Christian experience. If the candidates give the proper evidence of conversion and calling to the ministry, a local church will schedule an ordination service consisting of verbal commissions to the candidate, a testimony from the candidate, and a ceremony of prayer or laying on of hands.

The unstructured nature of the practice and the absence of definitive biblical data have led to numerous tensions in the Baptist practice of ordination. Baptists have generally affirmed the nonsacramental nature of ordination. F. Stagg expresses this view: "The laying on of hands, or ordination in any sense, did not confer new rights or authority upon the one ordained; rather, it was a recognition of the presence already of some charismatic gift of ministry, an intercessory prayer for the continuation of the gift of the Holy Spirit, and the acceptance on the part of the church and the person ordained of new responsibility."[113] However, the mere fact that ordination is especially sought after today signifies that some view it as conferring a desirable position or influence.

In line with this emphasis on the nonsacramental nature of ordination, Baptists have stressed that ordination does not provide the candidate an opportunity to rule over a congregation (1 Pet 5:1-4). Baptists emphasize that "the possession of ministerial gifts places the minister in service to the church, and any authority exercised is ministerial in nature."[114]

The practice of ordination has also opened up tensions in the civil and economic realm. When the Selective Service System operated in America, ordained clergymen were generally exempted from the draft. Tax laws also provide a tax-sheltered housing allowance for ordained senior pastors and certain other ordained people. This feature has opened up the possibility that some will seek ordination for other than spiritual reasons.

The practice of ordination has also uncovered tensions between local church autonomy and wider cooperation between churches. In Baptist life the local church is the guiding authority in the practice of ordination, but the local church performs the function of ordination on behalf of other congregations also. The role of an association in the practices of ordination varies in different geographical areas of Southern Baptist life. In some instances a Committee on Ordination from an association functions as an ordaining council.

---

[113]F. Stagg, *New Testament Theology* (Nashville: Broadman, 1962), 256.

[114]W. T. Stancil, "Tensions in Southern Baptist Ordination Theology," *Search* 15 (1984): 12.

In summary, we can say that the practice of ordination clearly affirms the presence of gifts for ministry and the evidence of a divine call. The practice should be used only for those who will perform a special or specific ministry. It should not be seen as granting special spiritual power or an oppressive authority to the candidate. The person who is ordained will indeed have authority, but the authority is derived from the moral example of unselfish, faithful service for Christ rather than merely from a position.[115]

7. Responsibilities toward Church Groups (5:1-16)

In 1 Tim 5:1-16 Paul gave Timothy directions for meeting the needs of three groups within the church at Ephesus. First, he spoke in 5:1-2 about Timothy's attitude in dealing with church groups that differed by age and sex. Paul urged Timothy to treat men and women, young and old, as family members. In 5:3-8 Paul instructed Timothy in meeting the needs of genuine widows in the church. He said that the godly widows are deserving of financial help from their families and honor from the church. In 5:9-16 Paul focused on the special needs of younger widows. He urged that younger widows not receive regular financial help from the church but that they plan to remarry and assume domestic responsibility. Paul's statements, particularly in 5:11-15, suggest that younger widows were a source of problems in the church.

Paul wanted the action of Timothy and the church toward these various groups to win the esteem of the largely heathen population in Ephesus. Proper behavior toward all of these groups demanded respect, compassion, and the giving of financial help where needed. Christians who did this would demonstrate a life-style the pagan population could understand and admire.

(1) Proper Treatment for All Ages (5:1-2)

[1]Do not rebuke an older man harshly, but exhort him as if he were your father. Treat younger men as brothers, [2]older women as mothers, and younger women as sisters, with absolute purity.

---

[115]Among helpful discussions of the subject of ordination in addition to the sources above are W. L. Hendricks, "Ordination: A Composite View and Practical Suggestions," *SWJTh* 11 (1969): 87-96; E. G. Hinson, "Ordination: Is a New Concept Needed?" *Search* 2 (1972): 40-46; W. B. Hunt, "Ordination in the New Testament," *SWJTh* 11 (1969): 9-27; P. Patterson, "The Meaning of Authority in the Local Church," *Recovering Biblical Manhood and Womanhood*, ed. J. Piper and W. Grudem (Wheaton, Ill.: Crossway, 1991), 248-59. See also the July 1988 issue of *Baptist History and Heritage* for articles on the subject of "Ordination in Baptist Heritage."

Paul and his readers were aware of the spiritual sense in which Christians were related to one another as brothers and sisters (Mark 3:31-35). Paul requested treatment that recognized these family relationships. In giving these directions, Paul was aware of Timothy's youthfulness; and he wanted Timothy to avoid disrespect, insecurity, or temptation to immorality.

5:1 In dealing with the older men[116] Paul urged Timothy to avoid a harsh, insensitive treatment which would not appreciate their age. The term "rebuke," mentioned here only in the New Testament, describes a severe verbal pounding. Such treatment would show no appreciation for age. The youthful Timothy faced a ticklish situation in appealing to older men, but differences of age did not make admonition to these men any less necessary.

Timothy was not to talk down to younger men, but he was to treat them as equals. The term "exhort" demands a kindlier, more considerate approach than the previously denounced "rebuking." Those who err would need to receive some rebuke for their behavior, but Timothy was to avoid a pompous approach in relating to them.

Much of what Paul advised here involved action based on sensible maturity. Kelly suggests that Paul modeled his appeals on "some Hellenistic paradigm traditional in popular ethics."[117] If Paul were aware of this Hellenistic pattern, he also was certainly aware of the special family relationship among believers.

5:2 Paul directed Timothy to treat the older women respectfully as mothers (cf. Rom 16:13). A church leader would find it virtually impossible to heap verbal abuse on an older woman if he showed personal respect for her.

Younger women posed a special problem for Timothy. He was to treat them as sisters and maintain a purity which would banish all evil in thought and deed. The lack of purity among the younger women may have caused special problems for the entire Ephesian church (see 2 Tim 3:6-7; 1 Tim 5:11). The word "purity" calls for modesty and chastity in all relationships.

Paul intended to mold Timothy into a wise leader who could deal individually with his flock. He did not want Timothy only to give admonitions. He wanted him to provide an example which other Ephesian Christians could imitate.

---

[116]The Greek word for "older man" (πρεσβύτερος) is also used to describe the church leader known as an "elder," but the context here clearly indicates that Paul made reference to an older man.

[117]Kelly, *Pastoral Epistles*, 110.

(2) The Care of True Widows (5:3-8)

³Give proper recognition to those widows who are really in need. ⁴But if a widow has children or grandchildren, these should learn first of all to put their religion into practice by caring for their own family and so repaying their parents and grandparents, for this is pleasing to God. ⁵The widow who is really in need and left all alone puts her hope in God and continues night and day to pray and to ask God for help. ⁶But the widow who lives for pleasure is dead even while she lives. ⁷Give the people these instructions, too, so that no one may be open to blame. ⁸If anyone does not provide for his relatives, and especially for his immediate family, he has denied the faith and is worse than an unbeliever.

Paul identified two qualifications of genuine widows. First, they had no relatives to care for them (5:4,8). Second, they practiced certain spiritual disciplines (5:5). Paul suggested caution in handling a widow whose life goal was merely pleasure (5:6), and he reminded families of their obligation to care for genuine widows (5:8).

5:3 The term "proper recognition" demanded that the church treat the widow with respect. It would have been natural for the church to give financial support as a result of the respect (see Acts 6:1-6). Paul would next explain how the church was to identify the truly needy widows so that they might help and honor them.[118]

5:4 Paul spoke to children and grandchildren who had the means and responsibility to care for aged parents or grandparents.[119] He stated three facts about giving financial help to needy relatives. First, such help is a sign of true piety or godliness. To care for aged parents or other relatives is an evidence of the same godliness which Paul commended in 4:7. Sec-

---

[118]The care of widows has a firm foundation in the OT (Exod 22:22; Deut 24:17; Job 29:13; also cf. Mark 12:40 and Jas 1:27). It also had an honorable tradition in the Greco-Roman world. Winter points out that the Greco-Roman world demanded that a dowry accompany a woman into marriage so that it could provide her care whenever she became a widow. If the woman became a widow but had a son, this dowry came under the control of the son. See B. W. Winter, "*Providentia* for the Widows of 1 Timothy 5:3-16," *TynBul* 39 (1988): 83-99. He feels that the directives in 1 Tim 5:3-16 are intended to encourage individual family members to use the dowry they have in order to carry out the legal responsibility of support.

[119]The verb for "learn" has no expressed subject in the Greek text, and the interpretation above suggests that those who learn are the children or grandchildren who have the means to support aged, indigent parents or relatives. It is possible that Paul intended that the subject of "learn" be widows who have children or grandchildren. These would be expected to give attention to caring for their children or grandchildren before they do other charitable works. However, the term "widow" of v. 4 is singular, and the assumed subject of "learn" must be plural according to the Greek structure. Also it is difficult to understand how the widow could repay her parents or grandparents by caring for her own offspring. It seems best to understand that it is the children or grandchildren who are to learn.

ond, Paul saw the giving of this care as a repayment for the earlier care which children had received. Third, care for older widows is pleasing to God (see 1 Tim 2:3 for a similar statement).

Paul was not merely trying to save the church trouble, but he urged careless offspring to assume responsibility for their parents. The Old Testament had demanded such care (Ex 20:12), and Jesus had taught its importance (Matt 15:4-6).

5:5 Paul described the true widow, who was really in need, with three phrases. His description outlines more precisely the kind of person whom Paul had exhorted Timothy to honor. First, she was "left all alone." There were no relatives to support her, and she had no source of income or encouragement. Second, she "puts her hope" in God ("has fixed her hope on God," Williams). The use of the Greek perfect tense to describe placing this hope shows that the widow had developed a settled and continuous confidence in God. Since she had no one else to care for her, she had learned to depend on God alone. Third, the widow was a woman of prayer who prayed "night and day," a manner of saying that she prayed continually. The translation of Williams ("prayers and entreaties") shows that Paul described prayer with two nouns. Paul had earlier used these nouns in 2:1 ("requests, prayers"). In the NIV the verbs "pray" and "ask God for help" are translations of the nouns. Paul's description of the praying widow resembles Luke's portrait of Anna in Luke 2:36-38.

5:6 A contrast to the godly widow of v. 5 appears in Paul's description of the merry widow. The word translated "lives for pleasure" is a rare New Testament word which indicates luxurious, voluptuous indulgence (used only elsewhere in Jas 5:5 to describe self-indulgent living). The widow who abandons herself to pleasure and comfort is in complete contrast with the godly widow who prays and seeks God. Paul portrayed such a widow as physically alive but spiritually dead, a figure of speech known as an oxymoron. Paul did not indicate what Christians would do to support this kind of widow, but the implication is that she had no claim on the church's support.

5:7 There is disagreement concerning who was to receive the "instructions" here. The translation of the NIV reflects the interpretation that the entire congregation ("the people") was to be warned. The Greek text actually omits the identity of those who receive the instructions. If this is the correct interpretation, then the instructions were those of v. 4. Fee, however, feels that the expressed purpose of giving the instructions ("so that no one may be open to blame") relates more to the widows.[120]

---

[120]Fee, *1 and 2 Timothy, Titus*, 78. Fee also points out that the placing of this charge in the midst of the discussion about widows is such an "urgent interruption" that it is unlikely that a pseudepigrapher would create it. The statement is such an obvious expression of pastoral

His idea is that the widows were to receive the instructions of vv. 5-6 so they would avoid the evil behavior of v. 6. The fact that v. 8 is a strong warning to families makes it likely that v. 7 is a warning to the widows. This imperative appears in the middle of a section (vv. 4-8) which had the primary purpose of defining the category of "widows who are really in need." The sense of urgent importance in Paul's words suggests that widows were causing some of the problems in Ephesus. In 5:11-15 Paul would specifically designate the younger widows as the source of the problem.

5:8 Paul's purpose in this verse was to reprimand those families who neglected their own needy widows. To "provide" involves foreseeing and planning for the needs of dependents. Paul suggested that a Christian has a responsibility to care for all needy relatives, but especially for "those under his own roof" (TCNT). Those living under the roof may also be relatives, but they are more intimately a part of the family and deserving of greater care. The Christian faith requires that children honor their parents as a part of their duty (Eph 6:2). Anyone who does not provide such care has denied the faith. The denial is not like that of a heretical apostate, but such an egregious failure mutes a claim to Christian piety (Titus 1:16). Paul's words may indicate that self-centered greed was motivating some of the families in Ephesus. The "love of money" (see 6:10) was a trait which Paul would later denounce as a "root of all kinds of evil."

The failure of Christians to care for their own loved ones is a more flagrant fault than the same trait would be in an unbeliever. Christians have Christ's example of love to which unbelievers lack access (John 13:34-35). This added incentive to obedience makes the failure of Christians a more obvious flaw. White adds, "One of the most subtle temptations of the Devil is his suggestion that we can best comply with the demands of duty in some place far away from our home."[121]

(3) Warning to Younger Widows (5:9-16)

[9]No widow may be put on the list of widows unless she is over sixty, has been faithful to her husband, [10]and is well known for her good deeds, such as bringing up children, showing hospitality, washing the feet of the saints, helping those in trouble and devoting herself to all kinds of good deeds.

[10]As for younger widows, do not put them on such a list. For when their sensual desires overcome their dedication to Christ, they want to marry. [12]Thus they bring judgment on themselves, because they have broken their first pledge. [13]Besides, they get into the habit of being idle and going about

concern typical of Paul that it adds a difficulty for anyone who denies Pauline authorship. See 85.

[121] White, *Epistles to Timothy*, 129.

from house to house. And not only do they become idlers, but also gossips and busybodies, saying things they ought not to. [14]So I counsel younger widows to marry, to have children, to manage their homes and to give the enemy no opportunity for slander. [15]Some have in fact already turned away to follow Satan.

[16]If any woman who is a believer has widows in her family, she should help them and not let the church be burdened with them, so that the church can help those widows who are really in need.

Paul's chief purpose in this section was to single out the younger widows who were apparently a source of great difficulty for the Ephesian church (5:15). Paul recommended the behavior of true widows as a desirable contrast to the actions of the frivolous younger widows (5:9-10). He counseled the younger widows to marry and assume their domestic responsibilities (5:14). Paul's description of the younger widows in 5:11-13 made concrete his reference to the pleasure-seeking widow in 5:6. Paul's twin concerns in this section were to direct the younger widows into responsible commitment to marriage and family and to direct the church to show genuine concern for true widows.

5:9 In vv. 9-10 Paul restated requirements which the true widow was to possess in order to receive help from the church. Some interpreters (Hendriksen, Bernard)[122] feel that Paul here described a special order of widows with spiritual and charitable duties to perform in order to qualify for financial remuneration. Such an order of widows existed in later centuries, but it would have been an unlikely development at this time.[123] What we see here is a tendency from which the later institution developed.

Guthrie sees it "preferable, . . . to suppose that special duties in the Church were reserved for some of the old widows receiving aid, and some official recognition of this fact was given."[124] It is more likely that Paul was outlining qualifications of those widows who would be able to get personal help from the church and was not giving any official recognition to an order of widows.

To "put on the list" may be a technical term for placing the name of an eligible widow on the list for receiving aid. The existence of this list does not imply that only those on the official list could receive aid. It is likely

---

[122]Bernard, *Pastoral Epistles*, 80-81. See Also W. Hendriksen, *I-II Timothy and Titus*, NTC (Grand Rapids: Baker, 1957), 172-74, who places more emphasis on their duties but less on the financial support they receive.

[123]The third-century *Constitutions of the Holy Apostles* (3.1-3) makes reference to an "order of widows" and suggests that they received income from the church and assumed a definite vow of singleness. The text of the *Constitutions* lacks a clear statement of the duties of these widows.

[124]Guthrie, *Pastoral Epistles*, 102.

that poor widows, like other poor persons, often received help from the church without being placed in this special class (see Acts 6:1-7). Paul named three basic requirements for anyone on the list. First, he required that the widow be not less than sixty years of age. This does not imply that a poor, disabled widow under sixty had to wait some years to qualify for help. It is true, however, that women under this age could normally be expected to work and support themselves. After this age a woman would not normally remarry. Second, Paul asked for the widow to have been "faithful to her husband." The NIV translation conceals that fact that the literal statement of the Greek is: "wife of one husband." The expression Paul employed for the wife is parallel to that used earlier for a husband: literally "a one-man woman" and "a one-woman man" (3:2,12). Some interpreters suggest that Paul was prohibiting a second marriage,[125] but Paul would not prohibit remarriage in v. 9 and command it in v. 14. It is more likely that he was demanding faithfulness during her marriage to the single husband whom she once had. The demand was for lifetime fidelity and not singleness during the remainder of her lifetime.

5:10 Paul's third requirement was to list some of the specific good works that should characterize the life of the widow. The listed good deeds are representative but not exhaustive or completely definitive. These benevolent works do not constitute a list of requirements or duties. They are those actions the widow must already have performed and on which her reputation was based.

The demand that the widow bring up children did not exclude a childless widow but demanded that she show an interest in and aptitude for child rearing. One problem the widow could address was the care of orphans. Paul urged that the widow practice hospitality to traveling Christians (cf. Rom 12:13). The demand that she wash the feet of the saints called for an humble spirit of service, but it may have included the literal demonstration of the practice (John 13:14). Washing the feet was a necessary act of hospitality toward traveling missionaries during this time period. By helping those "in trouble," she would be able to assist persecuted believers. However, the "trouble" with which she helped may have included such needs as poverty and sickness as well as problems with persecution. The request that she devote herself to all "kinds of good deeds" was a general request. Such a general demand makes it likely that the entire list was a collection of representative deeds of mercy and kindness.

---

[125]Kelly (*Pastoral Epistles*) follows this approach, suggesting that early Jewish and Christian inscriptions applied the term "having one husband" as an obvious eulogy of those widows who had been content with a single marriage. The *Constitutions of the Holy Apostles* (3.2) reluctantly permits a second marriage but suggests that "third marriages are indications of incontinency" and states that marriages beyond the third are "manifest fornication, and unquestionable uncleanness."

5:11-13 In these verses Paul made a specific request concerning the younger widows and then explained reasons for his request. The request (5:11a) was to exclude the younger widows from the list of those receiving help from the church. Obviously Paul's request did not exclude genuinely needy younger widows from necessary help. He did not want younger widows to be regular recipients. In vv. 11b-13 he supported the request with two reasons. First, in vv. 11b-12 he wisely indicated that younger widows would normally want to remarry. In eagerness to marry, the widows' concern might race ahead of their commitment to Christ. They could easily desire to marry more eagerly than they desired to serve Christ. The explanation for Paul's strong words apparently lay in his view of widowhood as a spiritual commitment. He did not want younger widows to accept the calling of widowhood and then renounce that call with the appearance of any eligible man. It was better to allow them to plan for remarriage as he directed in 5:14.

The translation that "their sensual desires overcome their dedication to Christ" ("grow restive under the yoke of the Christ," TCNT) suggests that in these widows their sensual desires led them to throw off the restraints of their commitment to Christ. Lenski says that "first pledge" (v. 12) resembles "first love" (Rev 2:4) and suggests that the widows had abandoned their initial commitment to Christ.[126] It is wrong to infer from this statement that the widows were expected to render a formal promise not to marry again. That the widows had pledged to serve only the Lord is apparent. Although Paul did not mention this, the widows' problem may have come when they married an unbeliever in opposition to biblical commands (see the discussion of similar issues in 1 Cor 7:32-40).

Second, Paul pointed out in v. 13 that the behavior of some of the widows reflected disgrace on Christianity. They learned idleness and flitted about from house to house. By occupation they were professional time-wasters who were disrupting the spiritual peace of the community. They were also "gossips," spreaders of rumor and nonsense. (This statement does not imply that older women and men are exempt from the liability of gossip.) They were "busybodies" who meddled in other people's business.[127]

---

[126]Lenski, *St. Paul's Epistles*, 675. Fee (*1 and 2 Timothy, Titus*, 82) discusses three interpretations of the term "pledge" (πίστις). The term may refer to a pledge to widowhood that the widow nullifies by her desire to remarry. It may also refer to her pledge to her first husband, and her desire to remarry reflects her abandonment of the ideal of being married only once. The term may refer to a commitment to Christ, and the remarriage may indicate a turning away from Christ. This third option is Fee's choice and is also the option followed in the discussion in the text.

[127]Kelly (*Pastoral Epistles*, 118) points out that the word for "busybodies" describes occult practices ("sorcery") in Acts 19:19. He suggests that Paul may have expressed the fear that certain young widows would "resort to charms, incantations, and magical formulas

Probably the immaturity of the younger widows made them more prone to spreading canards and rumors than was true of the older widows.

The difference between Paul's advice here and in 1 Cor 7:8-9,39-40 was probably due to the age difference of the widows. The reluctant permission to remarry given in 1 Corinthians indicates the expectation that older widows would not normally remarry. Every normal desire of younger widows aimed toward remarriage, and they would usually have years of productive, joyful family life ahead of them. If they carried out their true task as wives and mothers, many of the satanically inspired problems in Ephesus would end. Paul's teachings in 1 Cor 7 and 1 Tim 5 stress a common ideal: to serve Christ undividedly while dealing with sensual desires. More clearly than in 1 Corinthians, Paul said that some can best serve God by marrying (5:14).

5:14 Paul had stated why the younger widows should not be counted among the real widows. Now he indicated what they were to do. What he stated was not merely a wish or a preference but a command. They were to become wives, mothers, and managers of the homes. The word for "have children" is from the same word family as "childbearing" in 2:15. Perhaps 5:14 indicates the way in which the domestic commands of 2:15 were to be fulfilled. The call for household management suggests giving guidance and direction to the household. Performing such a task would absorb energies which, if unused, could lead to gossiping and other meddlesome activities. Paul desired that the Ephesian Christians stand well before the outside world. The faithful domestic performance of Christian wives would muzzle the ability of Satan to stir up disrespect toward Christianity among outsiders. The "enemy" who would stir up disrespect and slander may well be Satan, but he would use human adversaries to spread his bitter froth.

Paul's words here do not contradict his teaching in the earlier discussion about marriage in vv. 11-12. There he was giving reasons for which these younger widows were not to be placed among the group of true widows. These younger widows failed to meet the requirements of vv. 9-10, and they were not to be eligible for aid. Since they were not to be seen as true widows, what advice did Paul have for these younger widows? He answered this question in v. 14. They were to marry and assume their place in domestic responsibility.

5:15 The urgency of making immediate changes came because the problem with straying young widows was already upon them. It was urgent for Paul to speak and for the younger widows to respond. Some

---

in dealing, e.g., with sick people." Fee suggests that it is best to understand the idea in a manner similar to that of 2 Thess 3:11, in reference to those who dabble in other people's business (Fee, *1 and 2 Timothy, Titus*, 85-86)

who had pledged a commitment to widowhood were not living as the true widow of vv. 5,9-10. They had abandoned their trust in God and had become involved in gossip, false teaching, strife, and discord within the church (5:15). Paul did not specify the exact meaning of turning "away to follow Satan," but White says that "the phrase . . . refers to something worse than a second marriage."[128] It need not mean a formal apostasy from Christianity, but it does suggest a carnal life-style.

5:16 Some Greek manuscripts have the words "male (*pistos*) or female believer" (*pistē*) instead of "woman who is a believer." Most textual critics prefer the reference to the "woman" alone, suggesting that the other reading reflects the work of a copyist anxious to harmonize an obscure statement. Why should Paul have singled out only women believers for advice at this point? We lack information on the historical background of the passage, but two suggestions are possible. First, Paul may have aimed a rebuke at a younger woman, either widowed or married to an unbeliever, who was neglecting the care of a widowed mother or grandmother. Second, Paul may have been thinking of a wealthy Christian woman such as Lydia (Acts 16:14-15), who could care for needy widows in her household (cf. Acts 9:36,39). In both possible instances Paul was urging the women to use their time, wealth, or both to care for the needy widows.

Paul mentioned one benefit of such action. Such generosity would free the church to use its limited funds to care for genuine widows. A second benefit, unmentioned by Paul, would be that such a woman could do something that no man alone could perform—care for aging, needy widows.

Summary. Paul's advice focused on the three terms, *respect, compassion,* and *responsibility.* He called on Timothy (and by extension all Christians) to show respect for age and sexual differences. The call for respect implied the need for courtesy, thoughtfulness, and gratitude. He spoke to the church and to individual families about the urgency for showing compassion for truly needy widows. A demonstration of Christian compassion can draw inquiring and even antagonistic outsiders to the Christ who causes that compassion in his children. Paul also talked about responsibility. He urged younger widows to assume the responsible behavior appropriate to a married woman rather than the idle, meddlesome actions of a peripatetic tattletale. Responsible action by all believers can win credibility for Christianity.

8. Proper Handling of Leaders (5:17-25)

Throughout 1 Timothy, Paul shared information that shows he sensed a severe leadership crisis among the Ephesians. In 4:1-5 he pointed out

---

[128]White, *Epistles to Timothy*, 133.

some of the distinctive emphases of the false teachers. In 5:11-16 he focused on the younger widows who had fallen under the influence of the Ephesian errorists. His discussion of leaders follows naturally after his mention of the younger widows because of the clear relationship between the two groups (see 2 Tim 3:6-7).

In 5:17-20 Paul described how to honor and protect deserving elders, but he also advised discipline for those leaders who stray. Following his directives would provide church leaders protection from unwarranted accusations and also prevent showing partiality toward a powerful church leader.

In 5:21-25 Paul provided warnings and directives Timothy could use in his struggles, both those that were personal and those that would bring him into conflict with church leaders. Some of Paul's words were sensible suggestions for handling Timothy's personal needs. Other suggestions prepared Timothy for wise confrontation with straying elders.

(1) Recognition and Discipline of Leaders (5:17-20)

[17] The elders who direct the affairs of the church well are worthy of double honor, especially those whose work is preaching and teaching. [18] For the Scripture says, "Do not muzzle the ox while it is treading out the grain," and "The worker deserves his wages." [19] Do not entertain an accusation against an elder unless it is brought by two or three witnesses. [20] Those who sin are to be rebuked publicly, so that the others may take warning.

Most churches today resemble the church in Ephesus in that they will have both those leaders who deserve recognition and those who merit correction. Paul addressed advice to both of these groups. In vv. 17-18 he gave advice for recognizing those leaders who do their jobs well. In vv. 19-20 he provided instructions for dealing with those elders who faced accusations.

5:17 The term translated "elders" in 5:17 is the plural of the same word translated "older man" in 5:1. This is the first extended discussion of the term in 1 Timothy in reference to a church leader (see 4:14, where a related term translated "body of elders" appears). Usage in the New Testament suggests that the terms "elder" and "overseer" (3:1) were used interchangeably (see Titus 1:5,7; Acts 20:17,28). W. Hendriksen suggests that the term "overseer" was used when the emphasis was on the character of the work.[129] Elders were a permanent feature of Jewish syna-

---

[129]Hendriksen, *I-II Timothy*, 179. He adds that the term "elder" is used when the emphasis is on the honor they are due to receive.

gogues. It would have been natural for churches to adopt this office into their congregational government.

Paul's practice was to use elders in organizing the churches he founded, not only in Jewish regions but also in Gentile territory (e.g., Acts 14:23). Jews would easily have understood this system of organization. Gentiles, who knew that local governments were controlled by officials who resembled elders, would not find Paul's system strange or totally unacceptable. It is not necessary to assume that Paul used a different system of organization for the Jewish and the Gentile congregations. The evidence suggests that Paul did not do this. For additional discussion of the role of elders, see Excursus 4: Elders in the Pastorals and Today.

The expression "direct the affairs of the church" refers to the act of giving leadership and supervision to church ministries. The usage does not suggest an aggressive, dictatorial style of leadership (cf. "rule," KJV). Paul's previous use of the term in describing the activities of a firm but gracious father in 3:4,12 ("manage") shows that he had more than the mere exercise of authority in mind.

The commendation Paul directed for the dutiful elder was "double honor." The term "honor" does not refer merely to an honorarium, but the failure to give proper pay would imply a lack of honor. The idea of "double" may refer to the double portion the oldest in the family received (Deut 21:17). It probably consisted of the twin benefits of honor or respect and financial remuneration.[130] The fact that pay was at least included shows that those who gave leadership to spiritual affairs could expect financial support from the church (cf. 2 Cor 11:8-9; Gal 6:6).

This passage also gives insight into the duties of elders. All elders were involved in directing church affairs. Some among this former group also had the work (the Greek verb suggests hard work!) of preaching and teaching. The teaching would be especially important to provide a bulwark against heresy. It was these latter upon whom Paul bestowed special honor.

5:18 In this verse Paul supported his directive to reward worthy elders. His statements assume that financial remuneration was at least a part of the "honor" to which he referred in 5:17. First, he quoted Deut 25:4 to justify proper treatment for the pastor. Paul reasoned that if God could show concern for the laboring ox, the congregation needed to

---

[130]Hiebert (*Second Timothy*, 101), Huther (*Epistles to Timothy and Titus*, 172), and Hendriksen (*I-II Timothy*, 180) feel that the double honor comes both from the respect intrinsic to the office itself and the joy of a job well done. Williams's translation suggests an additional option when he says, "Elders who do their duties well should be considered as deserving twice the salary they get." The same emphasis on double payment for the worthy elder also appears in the third-century *Apostolic Constitutions* 2.28.

show proper concern for its pastor.[131] The original intention of refusing to muzzle the ox was to allow the animal an occasional bite as it moved about the threshing floor. Paul saw expressed in this command a principle that is broader than a mere statement about care for animals. The second reference resembles the words of Christ in Luke 10:7.[132] It is not likely that Paul was quoting the Gospel of Luke, a document whose date of writing is uncertain. Paul may have been referring to a collection of Jesus' sayings, some of which appear in Luke's Gospel. It is notable that Paul called both statements Scripture, and it becomes clear that such a collection of Jesus' sayings "was placed on an equality with the Old Testament."[133]

5:19 In vv. 19-20 Paul discussed the process of discipline for erring leaders. First, he warned against accepting an accusation against an elder unless two or three witnesses support it. Paul was not urging special treatment for the elder, but he was urging fair protection from capricious accusations. The church leader should enjoy at least as much protection as the ordinary Jew had under the law (see Deut 17:6; 19:15).

5:20 Paul's directives in v. 20 prompted three questions. First, who were those involved in sinning?[134] Paul's statements did not call them elders, but it is a natural deduction from a context in which he dealt with elders that sinning elders were Paul's concern. The present tense of the word for "sin" suggests that the practice was continuous and not merely an isolated occurrence. Second, who were the persons before whom the public rebuke took place? It could have been either a group of elders or the entire congregation. The word "publicly" (lit., "before all") appears to suggest a group wider than merely the assembled elders. Probably the

---

[131]In 1 Cor 9:8-12,14 Paul made this deduction from Deut 25:4. His inspired interpretation in both passages indicates that God's purpose in the inclusion of the command in Scripture is broader in intent than merely urging care for animals.

[132]Paul's description of the Lord's Supper in 1 Cor 11:24-25 is similar to that in Luke 22:19-20. This similarity gives evidence of a close link between Paul and Luke, a point this present passage further supports.

[133]Guthrie, *Pastoral Epistles*, 105. Spicq supports the view that the reference of the formula "the Scripture says" is to both quotations and that Paul was designating another portion of the New Testament as Scripture (*Saint Paul*, 176-77). Both Kelly and Fee question this interpretation. Kelly (*Pastoral Epistles*, 126) says that the formula may refer only to the first of the two quotations or that the second quote may be to "some apocryphal writing which counted as Scripture in the Apostle's eyes." Fee (*1 and 2 Timothy, Titus*, 93) prefers to emphasize that the quotation formula applies only to the first of the references. He hesitates to say that Paul was calling the second reference "Scripture" because he sees the term used only in reference to the OT by Christians until the end of the second century.

[134]Lenski (*St. Paul's Epistles*) is correct in suggesting that the sins Paul denounced are not serious enough to lead either to expulsion from office or from the church. Paul had already given directives for handling that problem in 1 Cor 5:1-8.

entire congregation was to learn of the rebuke. Third, who were the "others" who would "take warning"? Some link them with the entire church. Other interpreters refer the term to the remainder of the elders. Probably Paul had the entire church in view. The open rebuke Paul proposed was intended to promote the fear of God within the congregation. Paul did not envision a vendetta, but he wanted to avoid partiality toward important leaders and provide fair treatment for all.

(2) Special Directions to Timothy (5:21-25)

21 I charge you, in the sight of God and Christ Jesus and the elect angels, to keep these instructions without partiality, and to do nothing out of favoritism.
22 Do not be hasty in the laying on of hands, and do not share in the sins of others. Keep yourself pure.
23 Stop drinking only water, and use a little wine because of your stomach and your frequent illnesses.
24 The sins of some men are obvious, reaching the place of judgment ahead of them; the sins of others trail behind them. **25** In the same way, good deeds are obvious, and even those that are not cannot be hidden.

Paul charged Timothy to assume initiative in handling the problems of church leadership. Some of Paul's words were a charge (v. 21); others were warnings to Timothy (vv. 22-23); others were general platitudes (vv. 24-25).

5:21 Paul charged Timothy to carry out the instructions of vv. 17-20 in the presence of God's heavenly armies. Timothy was to act as a representative of God and as one whom God would judge. The "elect angels" are the unfallen angels in contrast to the fallen angels (Jude 6). Mention of the angels implies that they watch over human affairs (1 Pet 1:12).

The "instructions" Timothy was to keep were those of vv. 17-20, the directions for dealing with the elders. To do the job "without partiality" prohibits a prejudgment of the case. To practice "favoritism" suggests leaning or inclining in a certain direction so that partisanship can influence the outcome of an investigation. Paul demanded a fair sifting of the evidence without deciding the results beforehand.

Paul's appeal had a certain urgency about it. This insistence suggests that his instructions were not merely general suggestions but an expression of specific concerns. Some of the influential elders had strayed from the truth and probably were having a seriously detrimental influence in the fellowship of believers (see 1 Tim 1:20; 2 Tim 2:17).

5:22 Paul warned Timothy of the danger of making hasty appointments to Christian offices. One need not call the practice here ordination, but it has all appearances of referring to an approval for ministry such as appears in Acts 13:3.[135] Paul hinted that one who participates in such an appointment shares in the sinful results that can easily follow.

Paul also appealed for personal purity in Timothy. If Timothy faithfully followed Paul's emphasis, it would assure that he would find leaders of stable commitment for positions in the church. Paul's awareness of the sins of others may have led him to remind Timothy of the importance of keeping his own life in order. "Purity" involves separation from immorality and also single-mindedness of purpose. Paul's concern for Timothy's purity led him to give other personal advice to Timothy in v. 23.

5:23 One of the problems of the false teachers involved the practice of asceticism concerning foods (4:3). Perhaps Timothy had been influenced by this practice, and Paul now advised him about it. Paul gave fatherly directives to Timothy in urging him to take some wine to help his digestion. Contaminated water may have aggravated Timothy's problems, and both Jews and Greeks had used wine for medicinal purposes. Paul did not intend to lead Timothy into slavery to alcohol. His advice resembles the directive, "Take a tonic for your stomach."

5:24 After his brief, personal note concerning Timothy, Paul discussed the "sins" of the elders and outlined his reason for showing great care in laying on hands. He warned against the demonstration of hasty acceptance in v. 24 and against the practice of hasty rejection in v. 25. A fact warning against hasty acceptance is that the sins of some are quite clear, but the sins of others "trail behind them" ("show up later," *The New Testament: A New Trasnlation* [O. M. Norlie]). The "judgment" Paul mentioned is not God's final judgment but a rejection by Timothy or the church of a sinning leader as unfit to serve. If Timothy did not practice this judgment, then the danger of which he had warned in v. 22 (sharing in other's sins) would occur.[136] Paul did not clearly specify which sins take a long time to appear, but his reference in 6:4-10 to the sins of pride, strife, and materialism suggests that they may have been the hidden sins.

---

[135]M. Warkentin (*Ordination* [Grand Rapids: Eerdmans, 1982], 145-46) denies that this has a reference to ordination and labels such a designation "anachronistic." She feels that Paul wanted to remind Timothy that he would be carrying on as Paul's representative and wanted him to use care in appointing people to carry out that mission. For further information see the discussion at 1 Tim 4:14 and Excursus 3: Ordination: Biblical Evidence and Baptist Practice. An alternative interpretation is to see this as a reference to the official restoration of penitents to fellowship. Penitents in the third century were readmitted by laying on hands, but there is no evidence that this rite was used in the first century. See Kelly (*Pastoral Epistles*, 128), who wisely rejects the interpretation.

[136]Kelly disagrees, preferring to see the judgment as divine judgment. He says that some people, even while alive, "cannot conceal the fact that they are incurring the divine wrath" (*Pastoral Epistles*, 129). The term "judgment" (κρίσις) is used of judgment by a human court in Matt 5:21, and this usage would show the possibility that the reference to human judgment is an option.

5:25 The good actions of some people are clearly obvious. Those with other good qualities, not obvious at first glance, cannot remain permanently hidden. Genuine character, like cream, always rises to the top. These words represent a warning against hasty rejection.

The absence of a bad reputation is no evidence of the presence of truly desirable qualities. On the other hand, the absence of a good reputation should not automatically lead to rejection. Some excellent qualities require time for appearance, and the people who have these excellent qualities can eventually establish themselves.

Summary. Paul's words contain advice for giving recognition, administering rebuke, and practicing caution. At least a part of the "double honor" Paul urged for the competent elder involved a recognition for a job well done. For us today writing a letter of gratitude, making a phone call of appreciation, and expressing a personal word of praise can accomplish the same thing. Paul also discussed the need for rebuking or correcting the leader who persistently sins. With compassion, but yet with boldness, wrongdoers today need a confrontation about their errors. Finally, Paul urged caution. Paul applied the caution primarily in the selection of leaders. As we select leaders today for God's work, we must move slowly, deliberately, reflectively, free of unwise pressures, and with maturity in our evaluations of others.

EXCURSUS 4: ELDERS IN THE PASTORALS AND TODAY. Most biblical scholars agree that "dogmatic claims for the presence in the New Testament of one clearly defined form of church government are not warranted."[137] A variety of organizational patterns appears in the New Testament. Some New Testament writings emphasize the activity of elders without indicating the presence of another official church leader (Jas 5:14; 1 Pet 5:1). In the Jerusalem church the role of the apostles was primary, and many of the leadership decisions were undertaken with their suggestions and insights (Acts 6:1-6). In other congregations a twofold pattern of leadership is mentioned: "overseers and deacons" (Phil 1:1). In the Pastoral Epistles three offices are mentioned: overseer, elder, and deacon. However, it appears that the terms "overseer" and "elder" refer to a similar if not an identical office. In Titus 1:5 Paul referred to officials to be chosen in the church as "elders" (*presbyteroi*), but in 1:7 he designated the same leader as an "overseer" (*episkopos*). A reference to the same offices using the same two words also appears in Acts 20:17,28. The word "elder" can refer to an older man (e.g., 1 Tim 5:1), but the term is used most frequently in the Pastorals in reference to a church leader (1 Tim 5:17,19). Hinson says that the use of the term "overseer" calls attention to the function of this church leader. He had administrative and

---

[137]Stagg, *New Testament Theology*, 265.

leadership responsibilities within the congregation.[138] It then appears that the Pastorals use a twofold system of offices with the term "overseers" and "elders" designating a single office and the term "deacons" making reference to a second office.[139]

Three important questions about the position of the elders must be asked. First, what were the duties of the elders? Second, why do some passages in the Pastorals use the plural for "elders" while others use the singular for "overseer." Third, what is the contemporary application of the function of elders in the Pastorals?

The duties of the elders are never discussed in the Pastorals in great detail, but 1 Tim 5:17 makes references to at least two of them. There Paul discussed elders who directed the affairs of the church and also those who were involved in preaching and teaching. The twin responsibilities of leadership and teaching devolved upon the elders. Although duties of the elders are not discussed specifically in the reference to the "overseer" in 1 Tim 3:1-7, Hinson deduces some duties from the references made to requirements or qualifications.[140] The requirements that the leaders be "able to teach" suggests that they preached and instructed new converts. The insistence that they be "hospitable" suggests that they directed some of the charitable ministries of the church. The demand that they not be "lovers of money" suggests that they had some responsibility for the financial affairs of the church. The requirement that they have a good reputation with outsiders suggests that they led out in the missionary work of the church. Such duties as these are reasonable expectations for the elder or overseer to assume.

In the Pastorals elders as church leaders are frequently mentioned in the plural (e.g., 1 Tim 5:17; Titus 1:5). Both appearances in the Pastorals of the word for "overseer" are in the singular (e.g., 1 Tim 3:2; Titus 1:7). The singular for "overseer" is understandable because each reference to this term is a description of the office or position itself. On the other hand, the above references to the elders refer to the occupants who hold the offices, a reference that would more naturally appear in the plural. Hinson makes the logical suggestion that while a board of elders may have taken

---

[138]E. G. Hinson, "An Elder's Life in the Apostolic Age," *BI* 6 (1980): 75-77.

[139]For a further discussion of the relationship between the terms "elder" and "overseer," see Meier, "*Presbyteros* in the Pastoral Epistles," 328, who agrees that they are similar but hesitates to use the word "identical." Note also the interpretation in J. Jeremias, *Die Briefe an Timotheus und Titus; Der Brief an die Hebräer* (Göttingen: Vandenhoeck & Ruprecht, 1981), 41, who insists that the term "elder" in the Pastorals is always a reference to "older men." Against his interpretation is the statement by G. Bornkamm (*TDNT* 6:651-83) that outside of 1 Tim 5:1 the term is obviously a title "for the bearers of an office of leadership in the churches."

[140]E. G. Hinson, "Ordination: Is a New Concept Needed? *Search* 2 (1972): 77.

responsibility for all the congregations in a city, "individual elders possibly assumed a special responsibility for a particular congregation, although evidence for this is not overpowering."[141] Multiple elders then served collectively in planning and supervising churches in a given area. The individual elder may have presided over a house-church that functioned like a family unit.

Is it necessary from the standpoint of Scripture for churches to designate their leaders today as elders? Some Christian leaders demand the term, citing its biblical use. Sometimes they will centralize the authority of the church in a group of ruling elders, who make administrative decisions, and in a teaching elder, who functions as the pastor but who possesses no greater authority than any other member of the elder board. This development is occurring among some denominations that in the past have used a congregational system of government. Several features may explain the interest in using the term "elder" and the office of a ruling elder. First, it is attractive to use New Testament terminology for the office, and the term "elder" is certainly a New Testament term. Second, some undertake a move toward elder leadership in reaction against the lack of spirituality in their present church leaders. They suggest that using a smaller, compact board of elders can guarantee more spiritual and committed leadership locally. Third, it may be more efficient and less time consuming to work through a board of elders than through a congregation. Those churches which have moved toward this system are often described as abandoning a congregational practice and moving toward a presbyterian system of government.

It is not biblically mandatory for churches to use the term "elder" in reference to their leaders, nor is it necessary to leave a congregational system of government. Each church should have the freedom to assign duties to its leaders in accordance with local needs, and they should have the freedom to use whatever term they desire including "elders," "pastors," or "deacons" to describe the office. The use of the term "elder" does not guarantee a more spiritual form of leadership. Indeed, some churches that have experimented with elder rule have found it autocratic, divisive, and prone to some unforeseen failures.

Baptist churches today generally follow a twofold system of leadership in their churches with a pastor and a board of deacons. Some of the functions once carried out by the elders (such as dealing with financial affairs) are now handled by deacons. Other functions of the elders (such as teaching and preaching) are now seen primarily as the work of the pastor. It is mandatory that Baptist churches not make the deacons a mere board of

---

[141]Ibid., 76.

directors and that the church not give all responsibility for spiritual development of the church to the pastor. Changes in the functions of leaders of churches can be made without changing the system of twofold leadership. Merely substituting the name of "elder" for a smaller, more cohesive board of church leaders may not result in a shared, dynamic, and more spiritually based role by leaders. Introducing biblical requirements for all leaders (e.g., 1 Tim 3:1-13) would provide a step toward a more vigorous body of spiritual leaders.

9. A Warning to Slaves and Sinners (6:1-10)

Paul was concerned that the internal life of the Ephesian church might harm its external witness. Some features of the false teaching Paul denounced might have led slaves to look on their servant-master relationship as an antiquated bondage from which Christ had freed them. Christian slaves may have emphasized their new freedom in Christ so that they chafed at the restrictions of slavery. Paul felt it necessary to call the many believing slaves to a behavior that would honor Christianity (6:1-2a). He provided instructions for life under both non-Christian and Christian owners.

He also renewed a warning to Timothy about the false teachers. The "things" Timothy was to teach the church to avoid (6:2b) appear in vv. 3-10. In 6:3-5 Paul described the contentious habits of the false teachers, their corrupted mental condition, and their capitulation to materialism. Some of Paul's warnings were similar to those in chap. 1, but the denunciation of greed added another element to the weaknesses of the errorists. Paul's discussion in vv. 6-10 pointed out the evils of materialism. With clarity he outlined the importance of practicing contentment in this life. He also sketched the tragic end for a confirmed materialist.

Already in 1 Timothy Paul had made reference to the content of the false teaching of the errorists. He discussed their spurious use of the Old Testament (1 Tim 1:6-10), and this probably contributed to their emphasis on asceticism (1 Tim 4:1-3). In this passage he placed more emphasis on the erroneous behavioral emphases of the heresy. He spotlighted their pride, arrogance, contentious attitude, but above all their greed. The more traditional Judaism that probably lay behind his reference in 1 Tim 4:3 ("abstain from certain foods") had probably also encountered Hellenistic influence in Ephesus and had freely imbibed some of its content (note the "opposing ideas of what is falsely called knowledge" in 6:20). Paul was preparing Timothy to remain in Ephesus as his representative to meet and oppose this false teaching.

(1) The Responsibility of Christian Slaves (6:1-2a)

¹All who are under the yoke of slavery should consider their masters worthy of full respect, so that God's name and our teaching may not be slandered. ²Those who have believing masters are not to show less respect for
them because they are brothers. Instead, they are to serve them even better,
because those who benefit from their service are believers, and dear to them.

Slavery in America was based on ethnic distinctions. New Testament
slavery developed more often from economic or political conditions. Victors often enslaved their victims in military struggles. The spread of
Christianity modified the nature of the servant-master relationship by providing masters a sense of accountability to the heavenly Master. For
slaves Christianity gave an incentive to avoid surliness and to expect a
heavenly reward for obedient behavior (Eph 6:5-9; Col 3:22–4:1; Phlm 8-
21). In this section Paul explained the effect of this modification.

6:1 The phrase "under the yoke" describes the galling, humiliating
result of slavery. However, Paul was not suggesting that only those who
were more oppressed than usual needed to respond to his words. The contrast in v. 2 suggests that Paul was thinking in this verse particularly of
those slaves who had unbelieving masters.[142] Paul insisted that Christian
slaves have a genuine respect for their owners. This produced an outward
expression in word, manner, and performance. The "so that" clause
shows that the purpose of Paul's concern was to prevent misbehavior by
the slaves from covering Christianity with disgrace. The great object of
concern for Paul was the glory of God. Malevolent behavior by professing Christian slaves could only lead an owner to mock Christianity.

How could a Christian leader such as Paul tolerate the existence of
oppressive, dehumanizing slavery without denouncing it? To answer this
question, we must note that the time was not propitious for a Christian to
secure freedom for slaves by denouncing slavery. Paul's modification of
the servant-master relationship in Eph 6:5-9 destroyed the very essence
of slavery. Also the New Testament consistently calls Christians to a role
as servants (Mark 10:43-45). Paul "aimed to destroy slavery without
waging a war to do so!"[143] To Paul "it was more important . . . to avoid
reproach against the name of God and his doctrine . . . than to make an

---

[142]Both Fee (*1 and 2 Timothy, Titus,* 96) and Kelly (*Pastoral Epistles,* 131) suggest that
v. 1 speaks of a general situation whereas v. 2 speaks specifically of those slaves who have
believing masters. The effect of seeing v. 1 as a reference to slaves with unsaved masters
will not greatly change the emphasis of the text, but it seems warranted to see the verse as
speaking more precisely of those slaves with unbelieving masters because of the specific reference to believers in v. 2.

[143]Hendriksen, *I–II Timothy,* 192.

abortive revolutionary attempt to undermine the social structure."[144] The "teaching" the unbelievers would slander was the gospel. Paul felt that disrespect for the gospel would lead to disrespect for the author of the gospel. He wanted believers to make no response that would cause that to happen.

6:2a Paul spotlighted those slaves whose masters were believers. The Greek text contains the adversative *de*, normally translated "but." This word is not translated in the NIV, but its presence further supports the suggestion that Paul contrasted slaves who had believing masters with those in v. 1 who had unbelieving masters. A definite contrast with the types of masters or owners of v. 1 seems to have been intended.[145]

Believing slaves could have shown less respect for a Christian master than an unbelieving master because they would have higher expectations from a Christian master. The first clause introduced by "because" supplied the motive for the extra service due to a Christian master. The fact that slaves had a Christian master ought to have inspired them to render even better service.[146] The expression "even better" does not imply that Christian slaves ought to have served Christian owners better than they would have served pagans. The emphasis was that they should give all the more enthusiastic service to their Christian owners. The NIV translation suggests that "those who benefit from their service" were the Christian owners who reaped the added benefit of service with a smile. Hanson, however, points out that the term "service" in common Greek "never means a service done by an inferior to a superior."[147] He sug-

---

[144]Guthrie, *Pastoral Epistles*, 109.

[145]Fee disagrees with this interpretation, preferring to see the δε as intensive in meaning with the translation of "indeed." He sees v. 1 as a general reference and v. 2 as a specific example of those who have believing masters. See Fee, *1 and 2 Timothy*, 97.

[146]The phrase "because they are brothers" can be understood in two ways. It may have provided Christian slaves a reason to respect their Christian masters by urging them to regard the owner as a Christian brother and perform enthusiastic service (see Fee, *1 and 2 Timothy*, 97, and Hiebert, *Second Timothy*, 108). This is the understanding advocated above. However, it may also have provided a ground on which the servants might regard their masters of little worth. Under this view a slave would respond to his Christian owner with the attitude, "How dare he, a Christian brother, treat me in such a shabby way!" Presumably a Christian slave might hope for manumission and expect some favorable treatment from a Christian brother. Lock (*Pastoral Epistles*, 65) and Earle (*1 & 2 Timothy*, 383) adopt the latter interpretations and are supported by the NIV translation "not to show less respect for them [just] because they are brothers." Under this interpretation Paul was suggesting that although the treatment of believing slaves by Christian owners was shabby, the Christian slaves were nevertheless to serve them.

Fee says that the "because" clause more likely explains why the slaves must not despise their owners. They were not to despise them because they were Christian brothers who deserved respect. This seems to fit best with the context.

[147]Hanson, *Pastoral Epistles*, 105-6.

gests that the best translation of the text should emphasize that "the masters, who share with slaves in Christian service, are believers and beloved."[148] His view, which has much to commend it, emphasizes that both Christian masters and Christian slaves were servants to God.[149] Under this view the incentive for the service rendered by the slave was not that the Christian owners would benefit from the service but that both believers and masters were joining together in following Christ as servants (Mark 10:45). This emphasis fits well with this context and other teaching of Scripture.

Paul did not emphasize individual rights but individual responsibilities. The chief concern for Paul was the glory of God, not manumission of the slaves or an increase in privilege for the owners. Equality before God (Gal 3:28-29) does not guarantee that all human beings enjoy equal roles and life status. While Paul accepted a different status for master and slave, he demanded a changed attitude from both.

(2) An Indictment of the False Teachers (6:2b-5)

These are the things you are to teach and urge on them.
[3] If anyone teaches false doctrines and does not agree to the sound instruction of our Lord Jesus Christ and to godly teaching, [4] he is conceited and understands nothing. He has an unhealthy interest in controversies and quarrels about words that result in envy, strife, malicious talk, evil suspicions [5] and constant friction between men of corrupt mind, who have been robbed of the truth and who think that godliness is a means to financial gain.

After a brief diversion to deal with the servant-master relationship, Paul exposed further the shortcomings of the false teachers. He vigorously denounced their penchant for controversy and pointed out their greed. He continued the discussion of greed and its results in 6:6-10.

6:2b Paul's words in v. 2b can refer either to the preceding verses or to the following (6:3-10). Paul referred to "these things" or "these instructions" in 3:14; 4:6,11; 5:7,21. In each instance Paul was making some reference to the preceding statements. The primary "things" Paul wanted Timothy to emphasize here were respect and service by the

---

[148] Ibid.

[149] It is also possible by a change in punctuation of the Greek text to refer the phrase "those who benefit from their service" to the slaves so that the emphasis is "let the slaves, who take part in the benefit, serve all the better because the masters are believers and beloved." This translation finds support in the marginal reading of the Westcott-Hort text. Most commentators follow the view of Lock, who notes the uncertainty of the statement (in the Greek) but feels that a reference to the masters is the more sensible interpretation (see Lock, *Pastoral Epistles*, 65-66).

slaves for their masters (6:1-2). With these issues clearly in mind, Paul now pointed out some additional flawed emphases of the heretics.[150]

6:3 The "if" clause describes the shortcomings of the false teachers. They were not giving "sound instruction." They were broadcasting "false doctrines." The term "sound" is a medical term pressed into service to describe healthy doctrine (cf. 1:10, where "sound" is the same word). Paul taught that anyone who feasts on sound doctrine is spiritually healthy and vigorous. Paul's reference to the instruction of "our Lord Jesus Christ" does not imply that he was reading a text of the Gospels or even a collection of Jesus' sayings. The term refers to Jesus as the ultimate source of sound doctrine, and the entire phrase ("sound instruction of our Lord Jesus Christ") serves as a substitute for the gospel message. The term "godly teaching" is an explanatory addition to the "sound instruction." This godly teaching stands opposed to the ungodly myths of 4:7-10.

6:4 The unhealthy teaching of the false teachers stood in contrast to the healthy instruction from Jesus' teaching. Paul mentioned three unhealthy traits of the heretics, and he then designated the products of their impaired instruction. First, the false teachers were pompous or "conceited," a term that describes a temptation facing the neophyte in 3:6. Second, despite their arrogance they lacked genuine spiritual knowledge. Williams combines both of these terms in calling the false teacher a "conceited ignoramus." Paul had earlier talked about the spiritual ignorance of these heretics in 1:7. His conviction was that those who depart from gospel truth actually lack all spiritual understanding. Third, they were ailing with the disease of controversy and word battles: "Controversies and arguments . . . have impaired their mental health to such a degree that they have become diseased."[151]

The products of such crippled teaching include an envy that shows annoyance at the success of others and a spirit of dissension that brings envy into the open. Also included are "malicious talk," wicked denunciations of others, "evil suspicions," faultfinding, and misgivings about the integrity of others. The vividness of Paul's description suggests that he was facing a concrete situation which aroused his indignant protest. Paul saw that a sense of real community had been destroyed.

---

[150]Fee suggests that the "things" Timothy was to emphasize extend back at least to 5:3; but in 5:7,21 Paul had emphasized some "instructions" Timothy was to instill in the people, and his statements there seem to refer to the directives that immediately preceded those respective verses. Here also it seems best to refer the "things" Timothy was to emphasize to the recently mentioned emphasis on respect and service by slaves for masters. See Fee, *1 and 2 Timothy, Titus*, 100.

[151]Guthrie, *Pastoral Epistles*, 111.

6:5 Paul mentioned a final product of the unhealthy teaching of heresy and then discussed the character of a person who could produce such diseased behavior. The "constant friction" refers to incessant quarreling that came from the contentious nature of the sectaries. As to their personal make-up, they were mentally corrupted and completely lacking in the truth. Paul's statement in v. 4 that the heretics understood nothing was a similar emphasis. Guthrie notes: "When reason is morally blinded, all correctives to unworthy behavior are banished, and the mind becomes destitute . . . of the truth."[152]

The heretics viewed religion as a means of making a quick dollar. In character they were greedy and materialistic. Paul's strong words described false teachers who exploited the church for their own ends without caring about the havoc they created. Paul had no objection to giving money to a religious leader, but he was opposing the goal of materialism that was primary for the heretics. It is interesting to note how many of the qualifications for church leaders in 3:2-12 these false teachers lacked. Paul would now elaborate on the developing dangers of materialism.

(3) The Greed of the False Teachers (6:6-10)

⁶But godliness with contentment is great gain. ⁷For we brought nothing into the world, and we can take nothing out of it. ⁸But if we have food and clothing, we will be content with that. ⁹People who want to get rich fall into temptation and a trap and into many foolish and harmful desires that plunge men into ruin and destruction. ¹⁰For the love of money is a root of all kinds of evil. Some people, eager for money, have wandered from the faith and pierced themselves with many griefs.

Paul expanded his brief reference to materialism among the false teachers (v. 5) into a pointed review of the dangers of greed. Addressing his words specifically to those who willed to become rich, he affirmed that godliness and not wealth brings great gain (v. 6). He explained two reasons for which contentment should be a companion of godliness (vv. 7-8). In vv. 9-10 he presented the desire for wealth as a trap that plunges the unwary into spiritual ruin.

6:6 Paul commended the benefits of godliness with contentment in v. 6 (see Ps 37:3-5). The word "contentment" (*autarkeia*) "was a great word in Stoicism, expressing the essence of the Stoic ideal, which was to be independent of external circumstances."[153] Paul Christianized the

---

[152]Ibid., 112.

[153]Hanson, *Pastoral Epistles*, 107. Dibelius and Conzelmann explain the Stoic understanding of "self-sufficiency" with a quotation from Stobaeus, "Self-sufficiency is nature's

term, using it to refer to an attitude of mind independent of externals and dependent only on God. He was not advocating godless self-sufficiency as a source of contentment. Paul believed that true sufficiency is Christ-sufficiency (Phil 4:13).[154]

The word "but" (de) should be translated more with the intensive idea of *indeed*. Paul was affirming that those who felt that godliness leads to gain were indeed correct, for there is great profit (spiritual profit) in a brand of godliness that possesses a contentment in the realm of its material possessions. True godliness is a means of much gain, for it promises benefits for this life and the next (4:8). Adding contentment to this godliness would promote gratitude for God's gracious gifts in this life (see 1 Tim 4:4-5).

6:7-8 Why do godliness and contentment represent great gain? Paul's "for" clause introduced an eschatological reason for this contentment.[155] Since after a brief stay we shall depart this life as we came in, it is sheer folly to concern ourselves with earthly matters. Material gain is irrelevant, and greed is irrational (see Job 1:21).[156]

The second reason (v. 8) is that we must be content when we possess life's necessities. The use of the adversative "but" (de) suggests that Paul wanted to contrast the believer's attitude to that of the greedy heretics. The term "clothing" is general enough to include both clothing and shelter, but the immediate context favors limiting it to personal possessions such as dress. Paul's words reflect the teaching of Jesus (Matt 6:25-34; Luke 12:22-31). Paul referred to food and clothing as symbols of life's necessities. His expression is a figure of speech known as synecdoche in which a part ("food and clothing") refers to the whole. What is actually a

---

wealth," and a statement from Epictetus, "The art of living well . . . is contingent upon self-control, self-sufficiency, orderliness, propriety, and thrift." See Dibelius, Conzelmann, *Pastoral Epistles*, 84.

[154] The adjective "content" in Phil 4:11 comes from the same word family as "contentment" in 6:6.

[155] Ellis feels that the "for" (γαρ) clause beginning in v. 7 may represent the "quotation of an ethical maxim" which represented Christian tradition accepted by Paul. The saying may plausibly represent a general conviction that early Christians held. See Ellis, "Traditions in the Pastoral Epistles," 246.

[156] A variety of textual readings exists for the "and" in v. 7 (ὅτι—normally translated "because" or "that"), including support for such translations as "and" (καὶ), "but," "it is clear that" (δῆλον ὅτι) and "it is true that" (ἀληθὲς ὅτι). Most commentators agree that the Greek ὅτι is the likely reading but differ on the meaning of the term. Lenski (*St. Paul's Epistles*, 705-6) says that the ὅτι clause explains why we did not bring anything into the world. Lenski's observation is certainly true, but it is unnecessarily trite. Bernard suggests that the ὅτι is to be taken as a resumptive idea, "a somewhat irregular construction, but not impossible." He prefers the translation, "*We brought nothing into the world*; I say, *that neither can we carry anything out*" (*Pastoral Epistles*, 95). The best view is to follow BAGD, who understand ὅτι as introducing a result clause with the meaning *so that*.

necessity will vary somewhat in different societies. However, all of us face the temptation of greedily coveting more than we need. Paul's use of the future tense "we will be content" contains an imperative idea directing Christians to practice contentment once they have life's necessities.

It is interesting to observe that Paul made an allusion to an Old Testament text (v. 7) followed by a reference to Jesus' teaching (v. 8). Although his statements would resemble the teachings of the Stoics, he was clearly influenced more by the Old Testament and the teaching of Jesus than by Stoic philosophy.

In these verses Paul warned that godliness is not a trait from which to make material profit (v. 5). True godliness has contentment for its companion (v. 6). Since we cannot take life's luxuries into God's presence, we should be content with life's necessities (vv. 7-8). Greed can find no place in an attitude like this.

6:9-10 Paul spoke the words of vv. 9-10 to those who "want to get rich" ("men who keep planning to get rich," Williams). There is no condemnation of wealth as such, and the words do not apply to someone who wistfully longs, "It would be nice to have more money."

In v. 9 Paul painted three progressive pitfalls in which the willful wealth-seeker becomes entangled. First, wealth tempts like a lure and causes people to covet the wrong objects. Second, individuals become entangled like animals dangling in a trap. The "desires" that trap them are probably more materialistic than sexual or personally grandiose. Third, the trapped ones drown in an almost personified wealth that becomes "a personal monster, which plunges its victim into an ocean of complete destruction."[157] The "desires" are "foolish" because instead of bringing gain, they only produce harm. Kelly suggests that "ruin" and "destruction" may signify material and spiritual disaster, respectively,[158] but it is probably best not to distinguish between the types of disasters these words suggest.

Paul supported this warning about wealth with a contemporary proverb the wayward Ephesian elders validated by their behavior.[159] We can make three comments about the proverb. First, it does not condemn money but the love of money. Second, it does not state that all evil comes from the love of money, but such misplaced love can cause a great variety of ("all kinds of") evil. It is incorrect to say that the love of money causes all sins. Ambition and sexual lust are also fertile breeding grounds

---

[157]Guthrie, *Pastoral Epistles*, 113. For a more literal use of the verb, note the translation "sink" in Luke 5:7.

[158]Kelly, *Pastoral Epistles*, 137.

[159]A proverb similar to this is well attested in ancient writings. For the proverb see *T. Judah*, 19.

of sin. Third, the wandering elders from Ephesus who had sold out to greed were living proof of this maxim. The concern about materialism Paul had expressed in v. 5 had become a reality in the false teachers. Judas and Ananias and Sapphira were New Testament figures who "drowned" because of this inordinate love.

There is a link between the "faith" of the gospel and the blessedness God promises to his people (6:10b; Ps 1). The denial of one negates the other. Some translations (e.g., "spiked themselves on many thorny griefs," NEB) capture the intensely painful idea behind the word "pierced." Kelly notes that the entire metaphor describes the "thorns of remorse and disillusionment that now lacerate them."[160] With these graphic words Paul concluded his description of the heretics, their false teaching, and their false practice. He now turned his attention to specific words of guidance for his beloved Timothy.

Summary. Paul focused on three important issues in these verses. He called for service among Christian slaves. He warned all his readers against a love for controversy and the all-consuming aims of materialism as seen in the Ephesian heretics.

It is human nature to return cruelty with more cruelty or a mean-spirited petulance. The Christian slaves to whom Paul wrote were not exempt from this temptation. It was needful to warn them, as it is to warn us, that unkindness or injustice by an owner, employer, or enemy does not excuse our reciprocating with the same trait. We are to honor God's name by responding respectfully even to those who berate us.

Conceit leads to a love for controversy. Those who think well of their opinions like to argue them with others. Where a spirit of controversy seizes a family, office, or institution, all sense of community and unity disappears. When we learn of the unhealthy results of indulging a spirit of controversy, we should want to avoid the experience.

Materialism is a desire to possess things instead of a love for the God who made those things. Paul showed that materialism is foolish because it fails to make preparation for eternity and leads to great sorrow in this life. Paul's posting of such warning signs should cause believers to steer clear of the sickness of materialism, but many drive straight through the warning signs to ruin and grief.

10. Instructions to Timothy and the Wealthy (6:11-21)

Paul had earlier referred to the false teachers in 1:3-7; 1:18-20; and 4:1-5. He normally linked indictments of the teachers with a personal admonition to Timothy (1:3; 1:18-19; 4:6-16). The admonitions fre-

---

[160]Kelly, *Pastoral Epistles*, 138.

quently included an appeal to an earlier point in Timothy's spiritual life (1:18; 4:14). After warning the false teachers in 6:3-10 against word battles and godless greed, Paul added another persuasive reminder to Timothy (6:11-16). He followed this reminder with a warning to the wealthy, this time to those who already had wealth (6:17-19). In a concluding word to Timothy, Paul directed him to guard the gospel and avoid foolish discussions about silly speculations (6:20-21).

(1) A Program for Godliness (6:11-16)

[11] **But you, man of God, flee from all this, and pursue righteousness, godliness, faith, love, endurance and gentleness.** [12] **Fight the good fight of the faith. Take hold of the eternal life to which you were called when you made your good confession in the presence of many witnesses.** [13] **In the sight of God, who gives life to everything, and of Christ Jesus, who while testifying before Pontius Pilate made the good confession, I charge you** [14] **to keep this command without spot or blame until the appearing of our Lord Jesus Christ,** [15] **which God will bring about in his own time—God, the blessed and only Ruler, the King of kings and Lord of lords,** [16] **who alone is immortal and who lives in unapproachable light, whom no one has seen or can see. To him be honor and might forever. Amen.**

Paul's statements in these verses consist of a series of commands (vv. 11-12), a solemn charge (vv. 13-14), and an outpouring of praise to God (vv. 15-16). He called Timothy to complete the ministry for which God had placed him in Ephesus. This was more than an appeal to deepen his personal commitment to Christ. Timothy was to finish a job.[161]

6:11 The beginning words, "But you," show that Timothy's behavior was to provide an utter contrast to that of the false teachers mentioned in vv. 3-10. Bernard states that Paul's appeal to Timothy as a "man of God" reminded Timothy that he had received a divine message just as had the Old Testament prophets (see Josh 14:6; 1 Kgs 12:22).[162] It pictured Timothy as one with a special calling for God's service. The twin commands of v. 11 contain a warning and a challenge. Timothy was warned to flee the heresy, divisiveness, and greed that Paul had denounced in vv. 3-10. He was challenged to "pursue" ("constantly strive for," Williams) six virtues mentioned in three pairs. Each trait represents a must to insure Timothy's effectiveness in his ministry. The term "righteousness" refers primarily to upright conduct before human beings, and "godliness"

---

[161]Ellis is puzzled about the source and content of 6:11-20. Although it resembles an entire section of preformed tradition, he notes that it contains a commission (6:11-14), a doxology (6:15-16), and a closing section to Timothy, probably written in Paul's own hand (6:17-20). He suggests that at least 6:11-16 is traditional material that has been reworked by Paul. See Ellis, "Traditions in the Pastoral Epistles," 246-47.

[162]Bernard, *Pastoral Epistles*, 97.

describes an open and obedient relationship before God.[163] The words "faith" and "love" reflect trust in God and benevolence and goodwill toward others (see 2 Thess 1:3; Titus 2:2). Timothy would need "endurance" (*hypomonē*) in order to guarantee staying power for his difficult task. He needed "gentleness" in order to deal effectively with cantankerous heretics and wavering believers.

6:12 Having urged Timothy to avoid the false vagaries of the heretics and to develop needed Christian graces, Paul gave directives for perseverance. First, he borrowed an image from the athletic sphere to urge Timothy to "keep up the good fight for the faith" (Williams). The metaphor can imply either running or boxing or wrestling. To fight for "the faith" includes at least a struggle for the truth of the gospel, but it may also refer "in a broader way to the whole of his Christian life as a great contest requiring discipline and purpose."[164] The use of the present tense for "fight" suggests a continuous struggle.

Second, Paul used a command focusing on eschatology urging "Timothy . . . to continue in the contest until it consummates in triumphant conclusion."[165] Depending on the context, Paul could present eternal life as a blessing to be realized at the end (here and in Rom 6:22) or as a present experience (2 Cor 4:10-12, though the expression differs in this passage). The fact that God had "called" Timothy to eternal life suggests that it was already in his grasp but not completely held.

Timothy made his "good confession" at his public profession of faith through baptism.[166] Paul frequently used the term "called" to show God's initiative in salvation and service. Sometimes the reference has more to do with the experience of salvation (e.g., Rom 8:30; 2 Thess 2:14; 1 Tim 6:12). Sometimes it refers to a vocation of service or to the Christian life seen as a vocation (e.g., 1 Cor 7:17-24). In 1 Tim 6:12 the reference has more to do with the experience of salvation. Paul's command was intended to stir up Timothy to renewed vigor, but it does not imply that Timothy earned eternal life by self-effort. It suggests that "eternal life" is

---

[163]This is Paul's eighth and final usage of this term (εὐσέβεια) in 1 Timothy. The significance of the word in this letter is seen in that Paul used the term only ten times. The other two usages are in 2 Tim 3:5 and Titus 1:1. Sometimes the term is used as a synonym for the gospel (e.g., "godly teaching" in 6:3); and sometimes, as here, it refers to a respect for God which profoundly alters behavior.

[164]Fee, *1 and 2 Timothy, Titus*, 109.

[165]Ibid.

[166]Other alternatives for interpretation are that Timothy made such a good profession during a time of persecution that is unnamed. It could also refer to the time (mentioned in 4:14) when the elders laid their hands on Timothy. It seems wiser to view the "confession" and "calling" both as references to Timothy's baptism rather than to another event in his life. See Huther, *Epistles to Timothy and Titus*, 192, and Kelly, *Pastoral Epistles*, 141-42, for additional discussion of alternatives.

more of a goal toward which Timothy was to orient his efforts rather than a prize that God would give him as a reward for that effort. The fact that God had called him was an incentive for his response.

6:13-14 To drape his commands with seriousness, Paul summoned Timothy to stand in the presence of the all-seeing Father and Son. He described the Father as one "who gives life to everything" ("maintains all life," Goodspeed). This can suggest either that God is the source of all life or that he can protect his own in the face of all danger. Perhaps an element of both truths lies in the reminder. God had given Timothy life through the gospel and provided him stamina for service. Concerning the Son, Paul spotlighted his "good confession" made in the presence of Pilate,[167] a testimony that was not merely verbal but that also included his suffering and death.

Paul charged Timothy to keep the "command" until Jesus returns. The command may refer to directives given to Timothy at his baptism or during the laying on of hands (see 4:14), or it may be "a commandment to Timothy to persevere in his own faith and ministry."[168] This last option fits better in the context. The term "without spot or blame" describes how Timothy was to maintain the command. The keeping of the command was to be unspotted by the contaminations of the heretics and was to be a type of obedience not exposing God's commands to fault or blame. The "appearing" (*epiphaneia*) of Jesus employs a term frequently used in the LXX to describe manifestations of divine glory. Paul frequently used it in reference to the second coming in the Pastorals (see 2 Tim 4:1,8), but he also used it to refer to the incarnation (see 2 Tim 1:10). Paul commonly used the Greek term *parousia* in reference to Christ's return, but both terms occur together in 2 Thess 2:8. Paul's words about Christ's return contribute a sense of urgency to Christian commitment.[169]

---

[167]The preposition ἐπί used with the Greek genitive may mean *in the time of* (Mark 2:26, "in the days of") or *in the presence of* (Mark 13:9, "before"). Either meaning would be suitable here; but many commentators (see Lenski, *St. Paul's Epistles*, 719-20, and Huther, *Epistles to Timothy and Titus*, 193) see the reference to the specific testimony Jesus gave in his trial before Pilate, and they accordingly prefer "in the presence of." If the translation "in the days of" is used, it would refer to the witness of Jesus' entire life; but the part of Jesus' life with which Pilate was chiefly concerned was only at the trial.

[168]Fee, *1 and 2 Timothy, Titus*, 110.

[169]Although Paul frequently spoke of the return of Christ in the context of emphasizing its suddenness or unexpectedness, he could describe Jesus' return with varied metaphors. He pictured the return as like that of a thief (1 Thess 5:2) and also as incorporating delay (2 Thess 2:3). He included a sense of urgency (1 Cor 7:29-31) in the same Epistle with an appeal for waiting (1 Cor 1:7). The present text does not settle the tension between these passages, but it rightly calls Timothy to a sense of urgent discipleship. It is possible that the use of the term ἐπιφάνεια reflects Hellenistic religious terminology. Following this idea, some infer that its appearance suggests that this letter was written at a time when the fervent hope in the imminent return of Christ was diminishing. That emphasis reads too much into

6:15-16 In vv. 15-16 Paul expressed seven statements of majestic praise to God in a moving doxology. In v. 15 he used three names in a description of God. The phrases are Jewish in style and praise the unique sovereignty of God. As the "blessed and only Ruler" God has the universal authority to decide the precise time of Christ's return. The terms "King of kings and Lord of lords" show God's sovereign authority over all powers, both human and divine (see Deut 10:17; Ps 136:2-3). These two titles refer to Christ in Rev 17:14 and 19:16. All three titles fit well with the emphasis that the return of Christ is certain ("God will bring [it] about") and sovereignly in his hands ("in his own time"). Paul's certainty of Christ's return did not cause him arbitrarily to set a date.

In v. 16 Paul affirmed traits of God that focus on his divine essence. The immortality of God is his deathlessness and self-existence. God alone possesses this immortality. Observe the discussion of "immortal" in 1:17, where a different Greek word is used. The blinding glory of God renders him unapproachable both metaphysically and morally (Exod 24:15-17). God is so infinitely holy that no human being can see him and live (Exod 33:20), but the pure in heart have the vision of God (Matt 5:8). The emphasis here more reflects a Jewish understanding than a Greek emphasis that no mortal can know God. The fact of human sin makes it impossible for us to know a God of impeccable purity. "Honor" refers to God's worthiness in receiving esteem and reverence. "Might" is the power of God expressed in sovereign acts. Paul collected these expressions of praise to emphasize God's majesty and kingship.

Two questions emerge from the study of this doxology. First, what was its source? Kelly has suggested that "it may well be a gem from the devotional treasury of the Hellenistic synagogue which converts had naturalized in the Christian Church."[170] His idea has merit because of Paul's Jewish background and his familiarity with the ways of Hellenistic Jews. Second, why did Paul use this doxology? Paul may have emphasized this moving doxology in order to show that the strength of this omnipotent God could enable Timothy to persevere. He may also have placed the statement here for the benefit of the Ephesian believers, who lived in a center of pagan worship for both Artemis and the emperor. Paul may have given a final reminder to his readers that the God of the church was the supreme Lord of the universe.[171]

---

the usage of this term, and it overlooks the sense of urgency that appears in the Pastorals (e.g., 1 Tim 4:1; 2 Tim 3:1).

[170] Kelly, *Pastoral Epistles*, 146.

[171] For elaboration of this idea see Fee, *1 and 2 Timothy, Titus*, 112-13.

(2) A Promise for the Prosperous (6:17-19)

[17] Command those who are rich in this present world not to be arrogant nor to put their hope in wealth, which is so uncertain, but to put their hope in God, who richly provides us with everything for our enjoyment. [18] Command them to do good, to be rich in good deeds, and to be generous and willing to share. [19] In this way they will lay up treasure for themselves as a firm foundation for the coming age, so that they may take hold of the life that is truly life.

Paul turned from a series of admonitions to Timothy to give advice to those already rich. The preceding words on wealth in vv. 6-10 were spoken to those who aspired to wealth. As a final thought Paul spoke a word to those who already had it. The constructive advice here balances the more extreme prohibitions of the earlier passage. He did not condemn wealth, but he showed the added temptations the wealthy face. He was vitally concerned that Christians have the right attitude toward their wealth and make the proper use of it (cf. Luke 12:13-21; Ps 52:7).

6:17 Paul's beginning reference to the "present world" suggests that the wealthy can have their wealth only in this age. It is good for this present world, but it does not convert automatically into blessedness in the world beyond.

In this verse Paul contrasted right and wrong responses to the possession of wealth. A wrong response involves an arrogant attitude ("haughty," Williams) and the making of wealth as the "hope" of one's life. As a deterrent to trusting in riches, Paul mentioned the transitory, uncertain nature of wealth. The word "uncertain" contains a reminder that it is by no means clear that riches will continue with the one who has them. The right response is to hope in a God who lavishes on his people all their needs. The statement implies that God does not give wealth to promote pride but that we might use and enjoy it in his will (cf. Jas 2:5; 4:13-14; 5:2-3).

Paul's sound advice walks the straight line between a world-denying asceticism and a self-centered indulgence. The advice promotes gratitude toward God for the benefits he bestows. We can express Paul's theology of wealth with the words: "God supplies everything, his purpose is beneficent, and it entails obligation."[172]

6:18 Paul mentioned four ways to use wealth wisely. "To do good" involves using wealth in a positive way instead of letting it feed a life of personal luxury. "To be rich in good deeds" pointed the wealthy in the direction in which they were to be truly rich, in the doing of good deeds. These two verbs probably include more than benevolence. The need for benevolence is emphasized in the next pair of terms. "To be generous"

---

[172]Ward, *1 & 2 Timothy & Titus*, 122.

demands a liberal sharing of wealth with others. One who is "willing to share" shows that the generous act of giving is to spring from internal generosity. Paul was suggesting that genuine wealth is found in what we give, not what we have.

6:19 Paul outlined the outcome of such generosity by stressing two truths. First, he stressed that giving generously to the needy stores for the giver a future treasure. The phrase "for themselves" emphasizes that generous givers may imagine that they are helping others, but they also are storing up significant personal benefits. Paul was not advocating that the giver could earn salvation or favors from God. Good works are solid evidence of salvation and assure us that we have eternal life. Paul may have based these thoughts on such words as contained in Matt 6:19-21. The godless, on the other hand, lay up treasures for themselves of a different kind (Jas 5:1-5).

Second, Paul stressed that generous actions allow the giver to lay hold of eternal life in the here and now. Paul had urged Timothy to lay hold of this in v. 12. Here Paul expressed that taking hold of eternal life is a goal of the unselfish giving he had commanded. Christians who enter the life of love by unselfish behavior will enter gloriously into God's presence in the life to come.

(3) A Concluding Caution (6:20-21)

[20]Timothy, guard what has been entrusted to your care. Turn away from godless chatter and the opposing ideas of what is falsely called knowledge, [21]which some have professed and in so doing have wandered from the faith.
Grace be with you.

In later centuries a false teaching known as Gnosticism infiltrated and led astray some Christian churches. Gnostics felt that a hierarchy of spiritual beings related humanity to God, and they emphasized that salvation came from mastering the "knowledge" of the escape of the soul from the world of matter. Some interpreters have seized upon the word "knowledge" (v. 20) as evidence that Paul was opposing a form of Gnosticism. However, the essential elements of Gnosticism mentioned above are absent from the Pastorals. The discussion by Paul of similar philosophical issues in Colossians 2 indicates that Gnostic-like ideas were widespread in the New Testament world but does not prove the presence of developed Gnosticism.

6:20 Paul gave two final commands to Timothy. First, he directed Timothy to "guard what has been entrusted" to him, literally "guard the deposit." The "deposit" (*parathēkē*) is a banking term denoting a sum deposited to the responsibility of a bank (cf. the same word in 2 Tim 1:12,14). Fee suggests that the deposit Paul had entrusted to Timothy was the task of resisting the false teachers.[173] This also included keeping his life pure and faithfully proclaiming the truth.

Second, Timothy was to "turn away from godless chatter" and avoid the pseudointellectual jargon of the heretics. "Godless chatter" (see 2 Tim 2:16 for the same word) characterizes the prating of the heretics as futile nonsense. Paul did not want Timothy to waste time in refuting these erroneous ideas. He was to ignore them. The "knowledge" of the heretics included empty discussions about fables, genealogies, and asceticism.[174] Paul avowed that what the heretics espoused was knowledge, but he named it "false knowledge." There was such a commodity as genuine knowledge (2 Cor 4:6; Phil 3:8), but these heretics did not possess it.

6:21 Paul warned those who professed the false teaching of the heretics that they would miss the mark of the Christian faith. The false teachers pretended to teach what ought to be believed, and they "shot far wide of the faith" (NEB) with their false knowledge.

Two features of the closing greeting are unusual. First, it is brief (see 2 Cor 13:14 for a lengthy greeting). Second, the pronoun for "you" is plural, suggesting that Paul intended that the letter be read to the assembled congregation.

Some commentators think that the lack of extensive final greetings is evidence against Pauline authorship. If this feature is used as a criterion of authorship, a comparison with the more lengthy final greetings in 2 Timothy and Titus would suggest a different author for these writings. This is an unlikely inference.

Note also the rather brief greeting in Gal 6, a letter that also deals with the business of opposing false teaching. Perhaps the content of both this letter and Galatians contributed to making them center more on the false teaching than on Paul's friends.

The KJV ends with a final "amen," but this word is not in the best manuscripts. It was added at a time when the letter was read in church as Scripture and represented the completion of the reading.

---

[173]Fee, *1 and 2 Timothy, Titus*, 119.

[174]The term for "opposing ideas" (ἀντιθέσεις) is the title of a work by the second-century heretic Marcion, in which he set out the apparent contradictions between the OT and the gospel of Christ. The coincidence of words has led some to suggest that this letter was written to answer the arguments of Marcion. Marcion, however, was violently anti-Jewish; and the error of the heretics is distinctly Jewish (1 Tim 1:3-11; 4:1-5).

The term "opposing ideas" was a technical term from rhetoric that referred to a counter-proposition advanced during a debate or argument. Paul's use of the term here suggests that the heretics had fashioned their propositions in opposition to the truth of Christianity and had truly developed a denial of the gospel. See Kelly, *Pastoral Epistles*, 152, for further discussion.

Paul thus concluded 1 Timothy, absent from the scene of battle but concerned enough about the presence of heresy to write an entire letter of directives to his young colleague Timothy. Timothy was to guard the trust committed to him, avoid the pseudointellectual pretensions of the heretics, and stop the advance of this cancerous heresy in the church at Ephesus.

Summary. In 6:11-16 Paul provided positive action for Timothy to undertake after he warned him to flee the evil desire for wealth. Paul's practice was wise and sensible. Often those who prohibit one action fail to provide a substitute. Paul prohibited Timothy's pursuit of wealth, but he urged him to follow hard after the traits of righteousness and godliness and to continue the struggle for the truth of the gospel in the Christian life.

In 6:17-19 Paul made a final statement on a positive use of wealth. It is vain to denounce wealth to those already wealthy. It would be better to instruct them in its positive use. Paul did that here, urging that the wealthy enrich their lives with all types of good deeds. He particularly urged them to use their wealth to share with the needy.

2 Timothy

SECTION OUTLINE

I. Salutation (1:1-2)
   1. Author (1:1)
   2. Recipient (1:2a)
   3. Greeting (1:2b)

Paul wrote his Second Letter to Timothy from the loneliness of a dungeon while awaiting a likely death (4:6-8). He attempted to fortify Timothy for accomplishment and steadfastness in ministry after his departure. Formal divisions of the letter are difficult to make, for we pass quickly from one exhortation to another. The early parts of the letter contain encouragements for ministerial endurance (1:6–2:13). This is followed by an appeal for doctrinal soundness (2:14–4:8). A conclusion containing many personal requests begins at 4:9.

In 1:6-18 Paul presented the qualities necessary for effectiveness in ministry. He followed these by presenting some images for assessing an effective minister (2:1-7) and outlined some truths that promote an effective ministry (2:8-13).

In 2:14-26 Paul explained proper response to doctrinal errors. He presented practical instruction for facing spiritual defection in 3:1-17. He concluded with a personal warning and charge in 4:1-8.

In the conclusion Paul made personal requests of Timothy and passed on important information. He also sent some final greetings (vv. 19-21) and concluded with a benediction (v. 22).[1]

I. SALUTATION (1:1-2)

Paul's salutation in 2 Timothy is brief and similar to that of 1 Timothy. The apostle gave a lengthy salutation in Titus; but in this, his final letter,

---

[1]D. E. Hiebert's outline elaborates these divisions. The insights mentioned in the excursus reflect a debt to his suggestions (*Second Timothy*, EvBC [Chicago: Moody, 1958], 13-17).

he used a standard form. The threefold wish in the greeting appears also in 1 Timothy but in none of his other writings.

1. Author (1:1)

[1]Paul, an apostle of Christ Jesus by the will of God, according to the promise of life that is in Christ Jesus,

1:1 Paul used the term "apostle" to refer to one selected by God to serve as an ambassador to herald abroad the gospel (cf. 1 Tim 1:1).

His reason for mentioning the term "apostle" differs somewhat from that in 1 Timothy. There he used the term to lend credibility to his directives to Timothy in the face of much opposition. Here the opposition is in the background, although it has not vanished (see 2 Tim 2:17-18). The use of the term here reinforces Paul's urgent appeals to Timothy to heed and follow Paul and his gospel.

Paul emphasized the divine origin of his apostleship by his reference to God's will in his appointment. In 1 Timothy he had used the term "command of God" to express the basis of his apostolic call. Paul used the phrase "by the will of God" in 1 and 2 Corinthians, Ephesians, and Colossians; and it probably served as a spiritual reminder to Timothy that all his experiences, including hardship, should be based on an assurance of the will of God.

The phrase beginning with "according to" emphasizes the goal and purpose of Paul's apostleship. His mission was to make known that eternal life becomes a reality through fellowship with Christ. Paul was teaching that life becomes available only in Christ. Anyone who has responded to Christ in faith has put on Christ (see Gal 3:27). Kelly feels that the expression here has the full force that the "in Christ" phrase normally carries in Pauline writings and that "it stands for the mystical union with Christ which the believer enjoys as the fruit of his faith."[2]

2. Recipient (1:2a)

[2]To Timothy, my dear son:

1:2a In 1 Timothy, Paul had addressed Timothy as "my true son." That expression gave a public legitimacy to Timothy before the Ephesian church. Here Paul was not attempting to authorize Timothy before the Ephesians. He did want to express affection for him, and the expression "my dear son" constitutes an affectionate greeting. Paul's words in Phil 2:19-24 show that a unique bond existed between Paul and Timothy.

---

[2]J. N. D. Kelly, *A Commentary on the Pastoral Epistles* (1963; reprint, Grand Rapids: Baker, 1981), 154.

Many of Paul's appeals to Timothy in the Epistle reflect the uniquely close bond between the older apostle and his younger "son" in the ministry.

3. Greeting (1:2b)

Grace, mercy and peace from God the Father and Christ Jesus our Lord.

1:2b   Paul used the identical wording for expressing the greeting here and in 1 Timothy. For meanings of "grace, mercy and peace," see the commentary on 1 Tim 1:2.

Lenski observes that the presence of "mercy" here and in 1 Tim 1:2 is a feature indicating the genuineness of Pauline authorship of the Epistle. He says: "All the letters that Paul had written up to this time use only 'grace and peace'; a forger would have copied this greeting, would not have even thought of risking the innovation: 'grace, mercy, peace.'" [3]

---

[3]R. C. H. Lenski, *The Interpretation of St. Paul's Epistles to the Colossians, to the Thessalonians, to Timothy, to Titus, and to Philemon*, 93-94.

——————————— *SECTION OUTLINE* ———————————

II. THE GRATITUDE OF PAUL (1:3-5)

——————— **II. THE GRATITUDE OF PAUL (1:3-5)** ———————

³I thank God, whom I serve, as my forefathers did, with a clear conscience, as night and day I constantly remember you in my prayers. ⁴Recalling your tears, I long to see you, so that I may be filled with joy. ⁵I have been reminded of your sincere faith, which first lived in your grandmother Lois and in your mother Eunice and, I am persuaded, now lives in you also.

In most of Paul's letters the apostle moved from a salutation to an expression of thanksgiving.[1] This was the pattern Paul followed in 2 Timothy. The thanksgiving here reflects the more personal nature of 2 Timothy. Paul remembered his own spiritual attachment to Timothy, the emotional attachment Timothy had to Paul, and the genuine faith Timothy had shown.

His thanksgiving consists of a single, involved Greek sentence. Paul expressed his constant gratitude (v. 3), anticipated a joyful reunion with Timothy (v. 4), and recalled Timothy's genuine faith (v. 5).

1:3 After sharing his gratitude, Paul mentioned facts about the manner of his serving God and also about the occasion for his gratitude. Paul never clearly expressed the object of his gratitude. He may have been thankful for Timothy's experience of divine grace, or, as Hiebert[2] suggests, he may have been expressing his feeling of gratitude without stating specifically his object for thankfulness.

Paul's manner of serving God followed the pattern of his ancestors. He moved in the true succession of Old Testament religion. Fee suggests that Paul may have mentioned this fact to contrast his behavior with that of the heretics who followed falsehood (1 Tim 1:7). Paul's reference to his own ancestors also paved the way for him to mention Timothy's family background (v. 5). Paul served his God "with a clear conscience." His

---

[1]Exceptions to this pattern of following the salutation with an expression of gratitude appear in 1 Timothy, Titus, and Galatians. In these three letters Paul was absorbed with the presence of problems in the church and probably was eager to communicate an important demand to his readers. Such letters as 1 Corinthians (1:4-9) and Philippians (1:3-11) show a detailed expression of gratitude to the readers. For samples of the wishes contained in the initial phrases of the letter body, see F. X. J. Exler, *The Form of the Ancient Greek Letter of the Epistolary Papyri* (Chicago: Ares, 1976), 103-12.

[2]D. E. Hiebert, *Second Timothy*, EvBC (Chicago: Moody, 1958), 28.

words do not contradict his statement in 1 Tim 1:13 in which he suggested that he had served in ignorance as an unbeliever. Paul had always served God with a clear conscience. "In his Jewish days he worshiped God according to the Old Testament; on becoming a Christian he worshiped the same God in and through Christ the Mediator, the one who had been sent by the God of Israel."[3] Whatever Paul did in serving God was always done with a full commitment to God as he understood him. Paul, however, had for a time been ignorant of God's provision through Christ. Paul was reflecting a measure of restrained pride in his Jewish religious upbringing. It is easy to spot this same pride in Rom 9:1-5 and in Phil 3:4-6. Kelly says: "It is clear that, while in one sense his acceptance of Christ as his Saviour represented a complete break with his ancestral piety, in another sense it was its proper development and flowering."[4]

The term "constantly" does not mean that Paul was always praying but that day or night Timothy was always mentioned as a prayer-object whenever he did pray.[5] Each time of prayer was an occasion to express gratitude for Timothy. The frequency of prayers for Timothy would have added intensity to Paul's desire to see him.

1:4 None of Paul's disciples had shown greater loyalty to Paul than Timothy (Phil 2:19-24). Paul remembered an emotional expression of that loyalty. We do not know the precise occasion that prompted Timothy's outburst of tears. Some have linked it with the departure mentioned by Paul in 1 Tim 1:3. Others have felt that Timothy was a participant in the scene of Acts 20:37. Paul's loneliness in confinement added to his desire to see Timothy again. He had shown similar strong yearnings to see people in Rom 1:11; Phil 1:8; and 1 Thess 3:6.

Tears from a man like Timothy were more allowable among those of Paul's era than among modern men of the West. Paul's own tender memories reflect the warmth of this large-hearted pastor. The "so that" clause of v. 4 expresses the purpose of Paul's desire to see Timothy. He longed to see Timothy so that he might be filled with joy. The anticipation of that

---

[3]R. W. Ward, *Commentary on 1 & 2 Timothy & Titus* (Waco: Word, 1974), 142.

[4]J. N. D. Kelly, *A Commentary on the Pastoral Epistles* (1963; reprint, Grand Rapids: Baker, 1981), 155-56. In another example of this affection for his background, Paul described the law as superseded (Gal 3:24-25) but as serving its purpose in bringing him to Christ.

[5]The expression "night and day" is also linked with Paul's prayers in 1 Thess 3:10. The RSV and some other versions place the terms "night and day" with the participle "long" to produce the translation "I long night and day to see you." That translation is unwise because it makes the two terms "night and day" modify "long," when they actually modify "constantly." In linking the pair of terms with the adverb "constantly," Paul was describing his prayers in the sense of a frequent repetition and not in the sense of uninterrupted intercession. Every time Paul turned to God in prayer, whether it was day or night, he thought of Timothy.

meeting must have filled Paul with joy. The meeting itself would have been a pure delight.

1:5   Paul pointed to the genuine work of God in Timothy's life as a basis for his gratitude. First, he commended Timothy's faith as "sincere" ("genuine," Williams). The faith to which Paul referred was a faith in the God of the Old Testament who had revealed himself in Jesus. Timothy's trust in Jesus had led him to a faithfulness in action. Second, Paul commended the spiritual heritage Timothy had received. This faith in the God of the Bible had first lived in his grandmother Lois and his mother Eunice.[6] Their faith was the expression of the faith of a "true" Jew (Rom 2:28-29) which found its fulfillment in Jesus Christ. The pair had a genuine expectant faith for the Messiah of the Old Testament. When they heard the gospel, they believed upon Jesus Christ as the Messiah for whom they had hoped. They passed their faith on to Timothy. Paul was tracing the faith of Timothy back to its roots. Third, Paul declared that he was certain of the reality of Timothy's faith. The expression "I am persuaded" ("I am sure," NASB) employs a Greek perfect tense that implies that Paul was thoroughly convinced.[7] Paul did not state what "reminded" him of Timothy's sincere faith, but the expression suggests that some act from outside Paul had prompted his memory.[8] Paul would later express some misgivings about Timothy's moral courage in responding to difficulty (v. 8). He had no doubt about the reality of Timothy's faith.

Summary.   Gratitude is a sacrifice that continually pleases God (Heb 13:15). The imprisoned apostle, lonely and facing death, could have been filled with a morbid foreboding and an attitude of complaint. Instead, he expressed thanksgiving and gratitude at the memory of the faithfulness and love of his younger friend Timothy. Like a ray of moonlight penetrating the darkness of night, Paul's gratitude for Timothy brought light into

---

[6]The Christian faith of Eunice is commended in Acts 16:1. The same passage is silent about the faith of Timothy's father, but no NT passage encourages the belief that he ever became a Christian.

[7]The translation of the NIV (and KJV), "I am persuaded," may not suggest the strong conviction of certainty Paul implied. Paul's use of the Greek perfect tense is much more strongly expressed than with a simple "I am sure." Paul meant, "I am certain; I stand convinced." There was absolutely no doubt in his mind about the reality of Timothy's faith, and he used a strong expression to indicate his conviction.

[8]J. E. Huther suggests that the "tears of v. 4 may have rekindled Paul's memory" (*Critical and Exegetical Handbook to the Epistles to Timothy and Titus* [1884; reprint, Peabody, Mass.: Hendrickson, 1983], 206). Lenski says: "Something had occurred in Rome and under Paul's eyes which vividly reminded him of Timothy and of Timothy's unhypocritical faith, and had done that to such a degree that it left a deep impression on Paul. The apostle must have exclaimed: 'Just like my beloved Timothy's faith!'" R. C. H. Lenski, *The Interpretation of St. Paul's Epistles to the Colossians, to the Thessalonians, to Timothy, to Titus and to Philemon* (Columbus, Oh.: Wartburg, 1946), 750.

Paul's inner man. His spirit of thankfulness prevented a focusing on himself and a preoccupation with discomfort and pain. It permitted him to focus on helping Timothy to fulfill God's plan in his life. It thus allowed the apostle to accomplish more completely the divine will.

─────────────── *SECTION OUTLINE* ───────────────

III. APPEALS FOR MINISTERIAL STAMINA (1:6–2:13)
   1. Qualities Needed in Ministry (1:6-18)
      (1) A Call for Courage (1:6-7)
      (2) A Readiness to Suffer (1:8-12)
      (3) An Imitation of Paul's Example (1:13-14)
      (4) An Incentive for Faithfulness (1:15-18)
   2. Images of Effectiveness in Ministry (2:1-7)
      (1) The Teacher (2:1-2)
      (2) The Soldier (2:3-4)
      (3) The Athlete (2:5)
      (4) The Farmer (2:6)
      (5) The Application (2:7)
   3. Truths That Promote Effectiveness in Ministry (2:8-13)
      (1) A Proper Understanding of Christ (2:8)
      (2) The Goal of Paul's Suffering (2:9-10)
      (3) The Certainty of Reward (2:11-13)

───── **III. APPEALS FOR MINISTERIAL STAMINA (1:6–2:13)** ─────

1. Qualities Needed in Ministry (1:6-18)

Paul urged Timothy to express loyalty to Christ despite hardship. Such loyalty demanded special spiritual qualities. Paul focused on the need for courage (vv. 6-7) and a willingness to suffer (vv. 8-12). He urged Timothy to follow the pattern of ministry Paul had shown (vv. 13-14), and he presented Timothy with a positive example of ministerial stamina for him to imitate (vv. 15-18).

(1) A Call for Courage (1:6-7)

⁶For this reason I remind you to fan into flame the gift of God, which is in you through the laying on of my hands. ⁷For God did not give us a spirit of timidity, but a spirit of power, of love and of self-discipline.

1:6 Paul's conviction that Timothy had genuine faith led him to urge Timothy to fan his gift into an open flame. The phrase "for this reason" is a reference to the possession of that genuine faith. Because Timothy had genuine faith, Paul urged him to set it ablaze. The expression "fan into flame" describes the act of rekindling the embers of a dying fire. The command does not imply that Timothy had let his spiritual flame go out.

It is an appeal for a continual, vigorous use of his spiritual gifts. Timothy was already using his gifts vigorously (2 Tim 3:14). In the face of Paul's impending death, he was to continue an ardent usage of his gifts. Rekindling his gifts would involve fervent prayer, obedience to God's Word, and demonstration of an active faith by Timothy.

The "gift" to which Paul referred was Timothy's gift for ministry. Timothy had to function in an environment of fear, heresy, and challenges to his leadership. His gift related to administration and organization rather than evangelism. The list of duties mentioned in 4:2-5 sounds more administrative and pastoral, although Paul did urge him to "do the work of an evangelist."

The reference to "laying on of . . . hands" is a reference to a time when Timothy's gifts were officially recognized. The exact time and the participants in this event cannot be determined. (See discussion on 1 Tim 4:14 and Excursus 3: Ordination in the New Testament.) Paul focused only on *his* role in the recognition of Timothy's gifts because he wanted to emphasize the close personal relationship between himself and Timothy.[1] Barrett points out that the gift received by Timothy did not function *ex opere operato*. It sprang into action from the faith and commitment of the recipient.[2] The act of laying on hands was itself symbolic. The laying on of hands was not the cause of Timothy's receipt of a spiritual gift but was a visible representation and symbol of it.

In vv. 6-7 and throughout this Epistle, Paul pictured Timothy as a younger and more hesitant colleague. He reminded Timothy of his spiritual gift for ministry in order to encourage a revitalized commitment. Paul's approach to Timothy shows the gentleness of a seasoned pastor. He did not "order" Timothy to stir up his spiritual gift, but he reminded Timothy of the presence of the gift and the need to use it. This is not so much a command as a reminder.

1:7 Paul explained the reason for his directive in the previous verse. His reference to the "spirit" does not refer to the Holy Spirit but to those traits of which the Spirit is the author.[3] These traits represent gifts for performing special ministries.

---

[1]In 1 Tim 4:14 Paul had mentioned the role of the elders in also laying on hands at the time of the recognition of Timothy's gifts. In 1 Timothy, Paul was concerned to give legitimacy to Timothy before the Ephesian church, and he mentioned the role of the elders who shared in the occasion for recognizing Timothy. Here in 2 Timothy, Paul did not need to give added legitimacy to Timothy, and he mentioned only his personal role.

[2]C. K. Barrett, *The Pastoral Epistles*, NCIB, ed. H. F. D. Sparks (Oxford: University Press, 1963), 93.

[3]Used in this way, the term "spirit" becomes a figure of speech known as metonymy. This is a form of substitution in which the name of one thing is used for another of which it is a part or with which it is associated. We use metonymy when we refer to announcements

The Holy Spirit does not produce "timidity" or cowardice. A spirit of cowardice would falter under the load of responsibilities that Paul was placing on Timothy. Instead, the Holy Spirit produces power, a reference to a forcefulness of character that can use authority boldly.[4] The Holy Spirit also produces a love that endures even the most cantankerous opposition and a self-discipline that can use restraint and oppose indulgence. This love is not so much a love that produces ministry as a love that conquers contempt and opposition by forgiveness and refusal to seek revenge. The self-discipline refers to a "wise head,"[5] which provides wise guidance for the use of power and love. N. J. D. White suggests that the "special charismata . . . bestowed on the ministers of the Church . . . are a part of the general stream of the Pentecostal gift which is always being poured out by the ascended Lord."[6] J. H. Bernard points out that Timothy needed "*power* to fulfill his arduous tasks, *love* to suffer gladly all opposition . . . [and] *discipline*, to correct and warn the wayward and careless."[7]

(2) A Readiness to Suffer (1:8-12)

[8]**So do not be ashamed to testify about our Lord, or ashamed of me his prisoner. But join with me in suffering for the gospel, by the power of God,** [9]**who has saved us and called us to a holy life—not because of anything we have done but because of his own purpose and grace. This grace was given us in Christ Jesus before the beginning of time,** [10]**but it has now been revealed through the appearing of our Savior, Christ Jesus, who has destroyed death and has brought life and immortality to light through the gospel.** [11]**And of this gospel I was appointed a herald and an apostle and a teacher.** [12]**That is why I am suffering as I am. Yet I am not ashamed, because I know whom I**

---

from the President of the United States of America as coming from the White House. We use the term "White House," the President's place of residence, as a substitute for the President. Another biblical example of metonymy occurs in Luke 16:31, where the term "Moses and the prophets" is used in place of the message of the Old Testament.

[4]J. N. D. Kelly defines this power as an ability "enabling them to dominate any situation with moral authority" (*A Commentary on the Pastoral Epistles* [1963; reprint, Grand Rapids: Baker, 1981], 160).

[5]This word is used by Fee (*1 and 2 Timothy, Titus*, GNC [San Francisco: Harper & Row, 1984], 177). The term translated "self-discipline" (σωφρονισμός) appears only here in the New Testament. However, related words appear frequently in the Pastorals. In 1 Tim 2:9,15 the noun σωφροσύνη is translated "propriety," and in 1 Tim 3:2 and Titus 1:8 the adjective σώφρον is translated "self-controlled." Other verbal forms of this family of words also appear in the Pastorals. The words suggest the idea of a controlled response that is not seen as a mere natural endowment but as a fruit of the Holy Spirit.

[6]N. J. D. White, *The First and Second Epistles to Timothy and the Epistle to Titus*, ed. W. R. Nicoll (New York: Doran, n.d.), 155.

[7]J. H. Bernard, *The Pastoral Epistles* (1899; reprint, Grand Rapids: Baker, 1980), 109.

have believed, and am convinced that he is able to guard what I have entrusted to him for that day.

Paul began with an appeal for Timothy to join with him in suffering for the gospel (v. 8). He followed with two incentives to support his appeal. First, he mentioned the truths of the gospel which would promote a readiness to endure hardship for Jesus (vv. 9-10). Second, he referred to features of his own life that would provide an example for Timothy to imitate. In v. 11 he mentioned his divine appointment to ministry, recognizing that Timothy would also sense his own appointment to a similar task. Paul mentioned divine appointment in order to emphasize that his imprisonment had come as a result of God's will. In v. 12 Paul presented his own courageous confrontation with suffering to add steel to Timothy's willingness to endure hardship.

1:8 Paul's command that Timothy not "be ashamed" did not imply that Timothy was already ashamed and needed to cease such shame. The use of the Greek aorist tense suggests that at present Timothy was not ashamed. Paul wanted such shame never to begin, but he realized the possibility that it might.

Paul warned Timothy against being ashamed of testifying about the Lord[8] and about him. Timothy may have been embarrassed that some of the mockers saw Jesus as no more than a dead Jew.[9] Timothy may have wanted a more powerful vindication of the Christian message for others to see before he proclaimed the gospel. Timothy could also have been humiliated that his leader was a prisoner. Paul may have viewed himself as the Lord's prisoner, but Timothy may not have been proud to serve in the company of an inmate. Paul clearly did not see himself as a victim of the Roman state but as the prisoner of Jesus. Such an attitude was transforming in its faith and commitment.

Instead of Timothy's feeling shame, Paul wanted him to suffer for the sake of the gospel.[10] The power of the Holy Spirit can produce a strength

---

[8]The phrase translated "to testify about our Lord" is literally "the testimony of our Lord." It may refer to the testimony Jesus rendered, such as his strong witness by a holy life and an open response before Pilate. Most modern versions (including the NIV) more properly view the reference as a testimony given about Jesus ("never be ashamed of your testimony to our Lord," NEB).

[9]The evidence from 1 Cor 1:22-24 is that some Jews viewed the message about a crucified Savior as incomprehensible and that the pagans saw the same message as utter nonsense. It would be tempting for a faint-hearted individual to draw back from the ridicule and scorn that would be inevitable.

[10]Paul always affirmed that suffering for the gospel was the expected lot of believers (see 2 Tim 3:12). He had consistently proclaimed this truth throughout his ministry (see Acts 14:22; 1 Thess 3:4; 2 Cor 4:7-18). Christians today must not be blind to this plain teaching of Scripture and must avoid surprise when opposition to the gospel produces a personal attack.

that bears suffering. Paul knew that divine help was available, and he wanted Timothy to use it richly.

Fee points out that "the two imperatives of this verse entreat Timothy to the three basic loyalties: to Christ (and his gospel), to Paul, and to his own ministry."[11] These loyalties involve our God, our friends (especially believers), and our God-given opportunities for service.

1:9 Paul showed that the gospel provides access to this divine power. He outlined the process, purpose, and basis of salvation. The process of salvation is a call from God to share in his kingdom. The call has been "made outwardly by the preaching of the gospel, inwardly by the influence of the Spirit working through the word."[12] The purpose of salvation is that each believer might produce a life of obedience and holiness to God instead of self. The basis of this salvation is the purpose and grace of God, not human merit.

Paul used the term "called" to describe a stage in the process of salvation occurring after God's choice of the individual (see Rom 8:30). The sense of the statement is that God has called believers to a new quality of life. Here the quality of holiness is emphasized. In 1 Tim 6:12 the goal of the call is eternal life, and in 1 Cor 1:9 the goal of the call is fellowship with Christ. However the call is viewed, believers are called out of the world to begin a new experience of commitment in living fellowship with God and other believers.

The phrase "holy life" (lit. "holy calling") can show either the means or purpose of the calling. The RSV translation, "with a holy calling," shows the interpretation of means; but the NIV shows the interpretation of purpose with its statement of "to a holy life." Although either interpretation could make sense, it seems more likely in this context that Paul was describing the purpose of the call so that the translation "to a holy life" seems more relevant.

The language of this verse and of v. 10 sounds creedal, but Paul did not introduce it with his faithful saying formula. Ideas similar to those stated here appear in other writings of Paul (1 Thess 4:7; Eph 2:8-10).[13]

---

[11]Fee, *2 Timothy*, 178.

[12]J. E. Huther, *Critical and Exegetical Handbook to the Epistles to Timothy and Titus* (1884; reprint, Peabody, Mass.: Hendrickson, 1983), 211.

[13]E. E. Ellis feels that the content of 1:9-10 is preformed tradition probably stemming from a hymnic-type confession ("Traditions in the Pastoral Epistles," *Early Jewish and Christian Exegesis: Studies in Memory of William Hugh Brownlee*, ed. C. A. Evans and W. F. Stinespring [Atlanta: Scholars, 1987], 246). Kelly considers the possibility of a hymnic or liturgical source, but he says: "A more likely explanation would seem to be that, while Paul is drawing on semi-stereotyped catechetical material, he is moulding it freely to his purpose and impressing his own stamp upon it" (*Pastoral Epistles*, 162).

In v. 9 Paul gave a brief expression of the gospel emphasizing particularly divine grace.

Paul also emphasized two facts about Christ in v. 9. First, he affirmed the preexistence of Christ, for the divine grace of Christ became available "before the beginning of time" ("from all eternity," NASB). Second, he pictured Christ as the mediator through whom divine grace comes to human beings. The availability of God's sovereign grace through Christ would brace the wavering resolve of Timothy. It was also important for Timothy to recall that God's saving purpose had been at work before the world was founded. In typical Pauline style, the apostle amplified themes introduced in v. 1. The phrase "the will of God" (1:1) is similar to "his own purpose" (1:9). Likewise, "the promise of life that is in Christ Jesus" (1:1) anticipates the "grace . . . given in Christ Jesus . . . [who] has brought life" (1:9-10). In so doing Paul underscored these themes for Timothy.

1:10 Paul described the powerful effect of the gospel. He moved from a discussion of God's purposes in eternity to Christ's appearance in time. First, Paul stated that God's plan to save had been revealed by Jesus' appearance[14] as our Savior.[15] Second, Paul mentioned that Jesus had destroyed death. Though Christians are not released from physical death, their approach to it means its virtual abolition since it is no longer to be feared (Heb 2:14-15) and has lost its sting (1 Cor 15:55).[16] Third, Paul contended that Jesus had "brought life and immortality to light through the gospel." Christ taught that eternal life began on earth with a knowledge of God (John 5:24; 17:3). The resurrection of Christ brought the nature of life out to public view for the first time.[17] As Lock observes, "There was hope of immortality in the world before, but the Resurrection

---

[14]The "appearing" (ἐπιφάνεια) is a reference to Jesus' incarnation. The term can refer to Jesus' second coming (1 Tim 6:14; 2 Tim 4:1; Titus 2:13), but this context demands the incarnational reference. The revelation Paul described was given in Jesus' teaching, but it appears supremely in his death and resurrection. Christ's appearance on earth made visible God's intent to save sinners.

[15]In 1 Tim 1:1; 2:3; 4:10 the term "savior" is used in reference to God, but here and in Titus 1:4; 2:13; 3:6 it is used in reference to Christ. In Greek religion the term was used in reference to the redeemer gods, and sometimes the emperor of the Roman cult was designated by the term. Jesus did not use the term of himself, but his followers applied it to him (John 4:42). Paul also used the expression in Eph 5:23 and in Phil 3:20.

The use of the term became more common after Christianity spread outside of Palestine. Its use probably indicates a conscious desire to protest the false claims of pagans for their "saving" gods and also to oppose the vain pretensions of the state cult. See Kelly, *Pastoral Epistles*, 163, for additional discussion.

[16]D. Guthrie, *The Pastoral Epistles*, 130.

[17]The term "immortality" means *incapable of decay or corruption*. Paul's most frequent use of the term is in reference to the resurrection body in 1 Cor 15:42,50,53-54. Immortality is an existence only God can give (Rom 2:7).

had converted it into a certainty and shown from beyond the grave the continuity of life there with life here."[18] R. L. Child has described the work of Jesus in abolishing death:

> By his patient endurance of the judgment of God upon sin, and by His steadfast testimony to the character of God as loving and good, Jesus has transformed the significance of death, and in so doing has destroyed its power to hurt us. . . . the resurrection of Jesus exhibited once for all His victory over sin and death, and demonstrated the reality of life beyond death.[19]

Christ is a destroyer in that he put death out of action. He is an illuminator in that his words and actions bring the nature of eternal life into clear view. The preaching of the gospel allows these benefits to become operative within the world. Paul's conclusion of this verse by reference to the "gospel" allowed him to explain in the following verse his role in proclaiming the gospel.

1:11 The mention of the "gospel" provided Paul with an opportunity to describe his role in proclaiming the good news. He elaborated on that role to remind Timothy that he had been imprisoned for the sake of the gospel. If Paul endured imprisonment for a divinely appointed task, Timothy had no reason to be ashamed of him. Paul was not informing Timothy of his call to preach, but he was reminding him that God had put him into his present circumstances. Paul may have been reminding Timothy that he also could expect such an appointment in his preaching of the gospel.[20]

The three nouns ("herald," "apostle," "teacher") of v. 11 also appear in 1 Tim 2:7. Paul's use of the emphatic pronoun "I" indicates that he was placing emphasis on his own appointment to office. The term "herald" stressed the boldness and openness of Paul's evangelistic work. Paul had a message to which he had given wide publicity before audiences of kings, magistrates, and commoners. The term "apostle" reminded Timothy of Paul's special commission and emphasized the authoritative nature of his proclamation. Paul was not emphasizing his own personal authority as much as he was emphasizing the authority of the gospel. The term "teacher" underscored Paul's responsibility to explain the faith with clarity for all believers.

---

[18]W. Lock, *The Pastoral Epistles*, 87-88.

[19]R. L. Child, "The Abolition of Death," *ExpTim* 68 (1957): 218.

[20]If the "Timothy" of Heb 13:23 is identical with the recipient of the Pastorals, we can realize that Timothy did suffer imprisonment for his witness. Paul's words that such hardship was an "appointment" by God must have strengthened and encouraged Timothy as a prisoner.

1:12 Paul connected his present circumstances with his role as a messenger of the gospel. His efforts to fulfill his commission as a herald of the gospel had led to his imprisonment and suffering. The resources that strengthened Paul in this difficulty were also available to encourage and embolden Timothy. Paul stated firmly that he was unashamed of his plight in life and then provided reasons that would banish any shame Timothy might have had (see v. 8 for the mention of shame to Timothy).

Paul's reference to shame means that his imprisonment caused him no personal shame.[21] Even though he faced the prospect of impending execution, Paul shared in no attitude of disgrace. The basis of his confidence was that he knew God and trusted in the power of God.

Paul's word for the translation "have believed" utilizes a Greek perfect tense to emphasize that he had "permanently put his trust and confidence in Him . . . , has been trusting Him all along, and is trusting Him now in the face of impending death."[22] Further, Paul stood convinced (same word as "persuaded" of v. 5) that divine power could preserve him. Paul knew that he had placed his faith in a living person who would never disappoint him.

Paul used a single word to describe what he had entrusted to God.[23] The term can refer either to something God entrusted to Paul or Paul had entrusted to God. If the term refers to something God had given to Paul, it would be a reference to the gospel and would bear the same meaning as the identical word of v. 14 (translated there as "deposit"). In this verse Paul used an idiom that literally means *my deposit*. This suggests more likely that Paul was referring to something he had placed with God for his guarding.[24] The NIV translation clearly emphasizes this. The reference

---

[21]It is entirely possible that Paul meant "I am not ashamed of the gospel" and not the suggestion given above, "I am not ashamed of my imprisonment." If the former alternative were the meaning, Paul would have been asserting that despite all of his persecution and suffering he still had no shame about the Christian message. Paul's boldness and daring for the gospel are such that there is no evidence that he ever considered being ashamed of the Christian message, nor would anyone think that he was ashamed of the gospel. It seems more likely, however, that the imprisoned Paul might have reflected on his condition in prison and have felt embarrassment over his imprisonment. Paul assured his readers that even this type of shame had never been a temptation for him.

[22]D. E. Hiebert, *Second Timothy*, EvBC (Chicago: Moody, 1958), 42.

[23]The Greek word is παραθήκη ("deposit," Berkeley). W. Barclay suggests that this word presents the picture of a man going on a journey and depositing with a friend his most precious and valued possessions. To return such a deposit unharmed was among the highest and most sacred obligations men recognized at the time. "To the ancient world there was nothing more sacred than the duty to return that which had been entrusted, and to return it in safety. It is this very duty that Paul places upon God" ("Paul's Certainties: Our Security in God—2 Tim 1:12," *ExpTim* 69 [1958]: 324-25).

[24]For the opposite interpretation see Kelly, *Pastoral Epistles*, who interprets the term "deposit" here in the same way as in 1 Tim 6:20 and v. 14. He feels that retaining the same

can be either to his life, his converts, or his work. The phrase "for that day" expresses the duration of the time in which God can guard this deposit. God will guard it until the return of Christ. Paul was affirming that God can keep a life or ministry committed to him in a position of perfect safety. God will keep the recipients of his promises safe to the end. Paul's more hesitant but promising friend Timothy could find strength in such truth to propel him to bold witness for Jesus.

(3) An Imitation of Paul's Example (1:13-14)

[13] What you heard from me, keep as the pattern of sound teaching, with faith and love in Christ Jesus. [14] Guard the good deposit that was entrusted to you—guard it with the help of the Holy Spirit who lives in us.

Paul's appeal to Timothy in vv. 8-12 was personal and related to Paul's circumstances of suffering. He could encourage change in Timothy by appeal to their personal relationship, but he also needed to remind Timothy of the imposing threat of false teachers. Paul presented his own pattern of teaching as an outline that Timothy could follow in the encounter with heresy.

1:13 Paul had earlier conveyed to Timothy an outline of doctrinal beliefs that were important. He now wanted Timothy to use them as a model in his own ministry.[25] The term "pattern" ("example," Williams; "standard," NASB) is the same word as "example" of 1 Tim 1:16. Paul desired Timothy to be loyal to the Pauline message, but he left him free to express it with his own personality. Paul had not delivered to Timothy a fixed creedal formula but a general outline of teaching which he was to maintain.

The words "with faith and love" describe how Timothy was to hold the teaching Paul had given. How Timothy maintained orthodoxy was as important as the content of orthodoxy itself. Timothy's faith was to focus on Christ Jesus. The love that flowed from that relationship provided

---

meaning for "deposit" in all three passages is important. He says: "The passage as a whole thus expresses his supreme assurance that, whatever misfortunes overwhelm his ministers, God will himself preserve the faith entrusted to them from corruption, so as to enable them, as it were, to hand back their charge to him intact at the final judgment" (166).

[25] This verse can be translated differently from the NIV. The NEB translates, "Keep before you an outline of the sound teaching which you heard from me." The differences in interpretation, which are not great, revolve around the question of whether Paul was urging Timothy to keep what he had heard from Paul as a pattern of sound teaching (NIV) or to keep an outline of the sound teaching he had heard from Paul (NEB). See J. H. Bernard, *The Pastoral Epistles* (1899; reprint, Grand Rapids: Baker, 1980), 106, 112, for additional discussion. Was Timothy to make an outline of Paul's sound teaching, or was he to keep Paul's sound teaching as a pattern? The NIV seems to render Paul's authoritative statement more accurately.

sensible, compassionate direction in his work of teaching and directing others (see Eph 4:15-16). It would enable Timothy to teach the truth in love. Paul realized that Timothy's faith and love were fruits of his union with Jesus Christ.

1:14 Paul had entrusted Timothy with the sound teaching of the gospel. He could not let heresy erode it. The "deposit" Paul had left with Timothy is a reference to the truth of the gospel Timothy had received (see v. 12, where the Greek term translated "what I have entrusted to him" is identical to "deposit" but is defined differently). Paul's words to Timothy suggest that the apostle was designating Timothy to carry on Paul's work. The task of preserving the truth of the gospel is so demanding and difficult that human strength alone cannot assure it. Maintaining the purity of the gospel demands the might and wisdom of the Holy Spirit. The Holy Spirit dwells within all believers and provides strength for them. Paul focused on that special enabling which the Spirit makes available for use in ministry.[26]

Paul had appealed for an expression of loyalty from Timothy in the service of Christ. He now gave some examples of both disloyalty and loyalty which Timothy could see and apply.

(4) An Incentive for Faithfulness (1:15-18)

15 You know that everyone in the province of Asia has deserted me, including Phygelus and Hermogenes.
16 May the Lord show mercy to the household of Onesiphorus, because he often refreshed me and was not ashamed of my chains. **17** On the contrary, when he was in Rome, he searched hard for me until he found me. **18** May the Lord grant that he will find mercy from the Lord on that day! You know very well in how many ways he helped me in Ephesus.

Paul grieved at the neglect he had suffered from friends in the province of Asia, but the encouragement Onesiphorus had given him greatly cheered him. He wanted Timothy to imitate the latter example but to avoid the shame of the former response.

---

[26] The words here related to the Holy Spirit sound similar to Paul's statement in Rom 8:9, where Paul spoke of the indwelling of the Spirit as a factor in providing spiritual strength and leadership (see Rom 8:14). However, Paul had spoken in 2 Tim 1:6 of the spiritual equipment given to prepare for ministry, and his reference to the Holy Spirit in this context likely provides a reference to this spiritual endowment.

It is only natural that the aging apostle would show concern for the correct transmission of the gospel. Nothing in the words of this verse should be seen as a reference to a post-Pauline period in the church where the leaders of the church formed a succession of teachers charged with passing on apostolic tradition.

1:15 Paul reminded Timothy of the general knowledge of his abandonment by many friends in the province of Asia.[27] This province made up a large part of the western segment of modern Turkey. In New Testament times its largest city was Ephesus. Those who had deserted Paul could have been those believers living in the province of Asia who had neglected Paul or Asian Christians living in Rome who had ignored him. The phrase "in the province of Asia" (lit. "in the Asia") suggests that these deserters lived in Asia at the time of writing. If they had been Asian Christians living in Rome, Paul would likely have described them as "from Asia."

What was the nature of the desertion? Doubtless these former friends of Paul had turned against him personally, but they also seem to have rejected or ignored the gospel he preached. Perhaps a sense of general discouragement had set in after Paul's arrest. Particularly the appeal for faithfulness in 2:11-13 was a call for faithfulness to the gospel. The falling away was more serious than a failure to support Paul in prison. The verb "deserted" (*apostrephō*) is also used in 2 Tim 4:4 and in Titus 1:14 to refer to doctrinal apostasy.[28] Paul's friends were guilty of leaving both Paul and his gospel.

Paul's use of "everyone" is an example of his acceptable hyperbole. Probably the entire Ephesian church had not abandoned the gospel. The friends mentioned in 2 Tim 4:19 had not turned away from Paul or the gospel. The large numbers who had turned against the gospel led Paul to state the outlook as rather bleak, but there were still some who remained obedient to Christ.

We know nothing more in canonical Scripture about either Phygelus or Hermogenes. Hermogenes appears in the apocryphal *Acts of Paul and Thecla* in the company of Demas, where both are described as "full of hypocrisy." The apocryphal reference is likely not to a historical incident but is probably inspired by the mention of both men in 2 Timothy. The mention of the pair Phygelus and Hermogenes suggests that they may have served as ringleaders of the trouble in Ephesus along with Hymenaeus and Philetus (see 2 Tim 2:17-18).

1:16 Quite in contrast to the behavior of this profane pair was the commendable behavior of Onesiphorus. Paul spoke affectionately of his diligent, unselfish service. What is unclear is the situation Onesiphorus faced. Was he alive or deceased? Further, if Onesiphorus were dead, was

---

[27]Bernard (*Pastoral Epistles*, 112) points out that "you know" (οἶδας) denotes hearsay knowledge that was all Timothy could have known about Paul's situation at Rome. The "You know" (γινώσκεις) of v. 18 indicates that Timothy had personal knowledge of the ministry of Onesiphorus in Ephesus.

[28]A different verb (ἐγκαταλείπω) is used in 4:10 to describe Demas's departure, which is evidently of a more personal nature.

Paul's expression in v. 16 (and in v. 18) a prayer for the dead? Disagreements among interpreters are widespread.

Fee finds evidence for the death of Onesiphorus in the request of mercy for Onesiphorus's family and also in the request for future mercy to Onesiphorus at the final judgment (v. 18).[29] In opposition to this, Lenski suggests that Paul mentioned the "household of Onesiphorus" because the entire family allowed Onesiphorus to go to Rome. Further, he feels that if Onesiphorus had died, Paul would have sought for comfort and not mercy.[30] The evidence for and against his death is not totally decisive, but Paul's statements present no clear evidence of his death. The belief that he was dead is more an assumption than a direct teaching.

Even if he were dead, Paul's expression need not be seen as a prayer for the dead. Fee calls the request a "wish-prayer" and suggests that it represents Paul's desires for the family but can hardly be called intercession.[31]

Paul commended Onesiphorus for two responses. First, he "refreshed" ("cheered," Williams) Paul. This involved personal visits and gifts to relieve the rigors of imprisonment.[32] Paul would explain in v. 17 how devoted Onesiphorus was in his ministry to Paul.

Onesiphorus's family appears again in 2 Tim 4:19, but we hear nothing more about the man himself. The kindness of Onesiphorus doubtless led to his inclusion in the apocryphal *Acts of Paul and Thecla*, where he is introduced as a citizen of Iconium who along with his wife Lectra hosted Paul and was converted by him. The story in the apocryphal writing has little or no historical authenticity.

1:17   Paul presented the action of Onesiphorus as a model for the hesitant Timothy to imitate. In the first imprisonment in Rome[33] (Acts 28:30-

---

[29]Fee, *1 and 2 Timothy, Titus*, 186.

[30]Lenski, *St. Paul's Epistles*, 773-74. It should also be noted that the mere mention of Onesiphorus's household in v. 16 does not imply his death. Stephanas, whose household is mentioned in 1 Cor 16:15, was very much alive at the time of writing of 1 Corinthians (see 1 Cor 16:17).

[31]Fee, *1 and 2 Timothy, Titus*, 186. Proponents of the view that Paul was here praying for the dead cite 2 Macc 12:44-45 as a Jewish example of prayer for the deceased. Christian theology, filled with hope for this life and the life beyond, holds out no hope for spiritual reform among the already dead (see Heb 9:27).

[32]Paul's expressions in Rom 15:32; 1 Cor 16:18; and 2 Cor 7:13 show that friendly contacts cheered and encouraged him. The fact that he received gifts during the imprisonment suggested in Phil 4:10-22 points to the likelihood that Onesiphorus had brought gifts at this later time as well as personal solace.

[33]The imprisonment mentioned in Acts 28:30-31 clearly took place in Rome. A more difficult question asks if Paul wrote the Prison Epistles of Ephesians, Philippians, Colossians, and Philemon from the same imprisonment. Paul had spent two years in a Caesarean imprisonment (see Acts 24:27). Some church tradition and biblical statements (see 1 Cor 15:32; 2 Cor 1:8-11) point to the possibility of an Ephesian imprisonment. For a discussion of possibilities of the location of the writing of the Prison Epistles, see J. A. T. Robinson (*Redating*

31) Paul had stayed in "his own rented house." Some church tradition has suggested that Paul suffered a subsequent imprisonment in Rome that was the occasion of his martyrdom.[34] At the time of the writing of 2 Timothy, Paul was in a hard-to-find location. Friends had apparently lost contact with him. Their efforts to make contact with him could have made Paul's imprisonment more difficult. Onesiphorus went to much trouble to track Paul down, and he found him after diligent effort. He shamelessly identified with the imprisoned Paul. Paul wanted Timothy to follow this example and put aside any shame (v. 8) in experiencing suffering for the gospel.

1:18 Paul used the same word found in v. 16 (*dōē*; "may the Lord show," v. 16) to express a wish that Onesiphorus might find mercy on the day of judgment. Fee notes that this "is not, in fact, intercessory prayer . . . ; rather, it is an acknowledgment that even one like Onesiphorus has only God's mercy as his appeal."[35] The term "day" is a reference to the time of Christ's second advent when he will begin judgment. It is probably best to take the first noun "Lord" as a reference to Christ and the second "Lord" as a reference to God the Father. Paul was expressing the wish that God the Son might commend Onesiphorus to God the Father on the day of judgment.

Paul concluded his comments to Timothy by remarking that Timothy well knew the many services Onesiphorus had rendered to Paul in Ephesus. He had a reputation for unselfish service that had apparently spread throughout the Ephesian Christian community. It is impossible to determine exactly when the service Onesiphorus rendered to Paul in Ephesus took place. It could have occurred when both Paul and Timothy were in Ephesus (1 Cor 4:17; 16:8). It could also have occurred while Paul was in Ephesus with Timothy before he went into Macedonia (1 Tim 1:3). Whenever it occurred, Timothy saw it, and Paul used their common memory of this incident to spur Timothy onward in service.

The courtesy and compassion of Christians often leads them to express a desire for God's blessings on their friends. "God bless you, brother," is a frequent Christian wish. The important feature of Paul's wish here is that he asked God's eschatological blessings on his friend. The fact that Paul made a similar request in 1 Thess 5:23-24 for another Christian group who were then alive provides additional basis for belief that Onesiphorus was yet alive.

---

the New Testament [Philadelphia: Westminster, 1976], 57-67), who leans toward a Caesarean origin, and D. Guthrie, *New Testament Introduction*, 2nd ed. [London: Tyndale, 1963], 92-178, who favors a Roman origin but thoroughly discusses all options.

[34]Eusebius, *Ecclesiastical History* 2.22.

[35]Fee, *1 and 2 Timothy, Titus*, 187.

Summary. Paul called on Timothy to demonstrate both courage (vv. 6-7) and a readiness to suffer (vv. 8-12). He provided Timothy with some examples of traits to imitate and to avoid (vv. 13-18).

Moral behavior is best learned by observing such commitment in others. Children learn this behavior from parents. Young Christians learn it from older Christians. Ultimately moral behavior cannot be taught merely by character-building courses in the public schools. Christians must see moral commitment as a sterling example in others.

Paul was not ashamed to present himself as the initial example he gave to Timothy. He had no doubt that his behavior was worth imitating. Christian leaders today need to have such a commitment to Christ that they are unashamed to say in humility, "If you want an example to follow, look at me!"

2. Images of Effectiveness in Ministry (2:1-7)

After appealing for qualities such as courage, willingness to suffer, and faithfulness in the life of a minister, Paul borrowed images from daily life to illustrate the traits necessary for effective service. He pictures the effective minister in terms of a teacher (2:1-2), a soldier (2:3-4), an athlete (2:5), and a farmer (2:6). He concluded with an appeal for Timothy to consider carefully the application of these images (2:7).

(1) The Teacher (2:1-2)

¹You then, my son, be strong in the grace that is in Christ Jesus. ²And the things you have heard me say in the presence of many witnesses entrust to reliable men who will also be qualified to teach others.

Paul charged Timothy to send on faithfully the message he had received. Timothy was not to be an innovator of religious novelties but was to show loyalty and commitment to the gospel message. Paul demanded Timothy's active involvement in the training of a future generation of Christian servants.

2:1 Paul began with an emphatic repetition of the personal pronoun the GNB translates "as for you." Timothy's behavior was to stand in contrast to that of the disobedient Asians (1:15) and was to imitate the pattern of Onesiphorus (1:18). The "then" of the NIV text translates the Greek term for "therefore" (*oun*) and reinforces the emphasis of the pronoun by suggesting that Timothy was to resume the obedient behavior of Onesiphorus.[36]

---

[36]The conjunction οὖν is most commonly translated with an inferential meaning (*therefore*), but it is also frequently used with a resumptive meaning (*then*). In this passage it is more likely resumptive. Paul was urging Timothy to follow in the path Onesiphorus followed.

Paul used a vigorous word to express his command. To "be strong," a present passive imperative, implies that Timothy was to keep on being empowered by God (cf. 4:17; Eph 6:10; Phil 4:13; 1 Tim 1:12, where the same Greek word is used). The command demanded Timothy's continuous active cooperation with God.

The quarry from which Timothy was to mine such strength was God's grace made available in Christ Jesus. The term "grace" refers to the unmerited gift of help God gives to the needy. As Fee observes: "Though it is true that grace is the means by which we are saved and by which we are enabled to walk in God's will, it is also true that same grace is the sphere in which all of Christian life is lived."[37]

The phrase "in the grace" may show either the means by which Timothy was to receive Christ's strength ("by means of grace") or the sphere in which Christ's strength was to be experienced ("in the sphere of grace"). Paul used a similar idea in Eph 6:10 ("in the Lord"), and the same idea appears in 2 Tim 1:1 ("life that is in Christ Jesus"). Probably both there and here Paul intended to show the need for living constantly in the sphere of strength afforded by God's grace.

2:2 Having been strengthened by God's dynamic grace, Timothy was to serve as a teacher. Paul's chief concern in giving this command was not merely to transmit beliefs through the proper ecclesiastical channels. Paul had a deep concern for the truth of the gospel in Ephesus. He would later ask Timothy to leave Ephesus and join him in Rome (4:9,21). Paul wanted Timothy to pass gospel truths to reliable men. These trustworthy men could keep the home front secure against heresy. Note the close relationship between the task of this verse and the imperatives of 1:13-14.

The "things" Timothy was to send were the foundational truths of the gospel.[38] The men who were to receive these truths had to be "reliable" ("faithful," KJV) in that they were trustworthy believers. They also had to be "qualified to teach others" ("capable of teaching others," Moffatt). They had to "be able and competent in turn to pass on to others this treasure by their ability and willingness to teach."[39] The specific people Paul had in mind probably were the elders of 1 Tim 3:1-7 and 5:17-22.

He had used Onesiphorus as an example in 1:15-18. Now he resumed an address to Timothy, urging him to claim grace so that he might show loyalty in performing his task. Examples of the inferential use of the conjunction appear in John 4:6,33,40. Other examples of the resumptive use of the conjunction appear in John 4:5,28. For a fuller discussion of the use of the word, see H. E. Dana and J. R. Mantey, *A Manual Grammar of the Greek New Testament* (New York: Macmillan, 1942), 252-58.

[37]Fee, *1 and 2 Timothy, Titus*, 190.

[38]The command "entrust" (παρατίθημι) comes from the same word family as the noun "deposit" (παραθήκη) of 1:14. The clear reference to the gospel in that verse makes it likely that Paul here conveys the same idea.

[39]Hiebert, *Second Timothy*, 53.

An uncertainty in interpretation comes from the ambiguous phrase "in the presence [*dia*, ordinarily *through*] of many witnesses." The NIV's rendering suggests either the time of laying on hands for Timothy or his baptism, where many witnesses would have heard the charges given by Paul to his "son." The translation "through" suggests that many witnesses joined in communicating the truth to Timothy. These witnesses would include Barnabas, his mother and grandmother, and other significant Christian leaders. If this is the sense, it shows that the Christian teaching given to Timothy had a publicly acknowledged content verified by the testimonies of many others. This emphasis on a widespread knowledge of the truth fits well in Ephesus, which had been riddled with enervating heresy.

This passage shows that Paul was concerned that the correct traditions about the gospel were transmitted from one generation of Christians to another. This concern about correct transmission of truth has already appeared in 2 Tim 1:13-14. An emphasis on tradition was also a part of earlier letters by Paul (e.g., 1 Cor 11:23; 15:1-8). Paul was not showing an interest in tradition in order to emphasize apostolic succession. We do not find Paul's discussion of apostles in their relationship to overseers and deacons. What we find are Paul's instructions to Timothy concerning the importance of holding to the truth of the gospel message. Paul's "interest is in the reliability rather than the status of the men Timothy will select."[40]

(2) The Soldier (2:3-4)

[3]**Endure hardship with us like a good soldier of Christ Jesus. [4]No one serving as a soldier gets involved in civilian affairs—he wants to please his commanding officer.**

Because of the soldierlike hardship of his life, Timothy desperately needed an abundant supply of the grace Paul had described. He also needed a singleness of purpose that could provide a detachment from the ordinary cares of life.

2:3 Paul wanted Timothy to take his share in the rough treatment and suffering that is the lot of committed Christians (Acts 14:22). The command to "endure hardship" is similar to the comand in 1:8. Paul's statement suggests either that Timothy had been reluctant to face hardship or that he had not maintained courage in the face of a new challenge.[41] The

---

[40]Kelly, *Pastoral Epistles*, 174. Kelly provides a lengthy discussion refuting the idea that this verse contains a device by a pseudonymous author who reflects second-century ecclesiastical practices.

[41]Fee points out that the translation of the NIV ("endure hardship") more resembles a general appeal to toughen up in order to face the general adversities of ministry. The verb in

appeal to "endure hardship" means literally *to suffer together with some-one*. The Greek text mentions no specific person with whom Timothy was to share this suffering, but Goodspeed's translation ("join the ranks of those who bear suffering") catches the sense of the command.

Paul illustrated his appeal for enduring suffering by a simile drawn from the military. He wanted Timothy to suffer as a good soldier of Jesus Christ. Paul had previously used military metaphors in 2 Cor 10:3-5; Eph 6:10-17; and 1 Tim 1:18. In each of the foregoing instances, Paul used a military analogy to illustrate the struggle against those who oppose the gospel. Fee adds: "While the imagery here may indeed reflect that con-cern [with heresy], . . . it more likely is a general metaphor for Timothy as a minister of the gospel, whose ministry has some analogies to the life of the soldier."[42]

2:4 Paul also used military imagery to commend growth or accom-plishment in some aspect of Christian behavior (1 Cor 9:7; Phil 2:25). The soldier was concerned to obey his commander twenty-four hours a day, and Paul wanted Timothy to display the same zeal in commitment to the Lord.

The ambition of the Christian soldier must be that of pleasing the Commander. The phrase "one serving as a soldier" is not merely a refer-ence to someone's serving as a minister or a full-time Christian worker. Paul desired that all believers live as soldiers. To get "involved in civil-ian affairs" called for Timothy not to be absorbed in merely living or existing. It was not a prohibition of marriage,[43] nor was it merely an appeal to escape from worldliness. It called for Timothy to give himself fully to the service of his commanding officer: "Singleness of purpose and detachment from extraneous cares are essential conditions of suc-cessful service."[44]

Paul's appeal shows the importance of developing an ability to distin-guish between doing good things and doing the best things. Servants of Christ are not merely to be well-rounded dabblers in all types of trivial pursuits. They are tough-minded devotees of Christ who constantly choose the right priorities from a list of potential selections. Paul prohib-ited the loss of single-mindedness and the longing for an easy life.

---

this verse is an identical form to that in 1:8 ("join with me in suffering") and probably more refers to sharing suffering than to persisting through difficulties. See Fee, *1 and 2 Timothy, Titus*, 191

[42]Ibid.

[43]Paul had indicated that marriage would be the norm among Christian leaders (1 Tim 3:2,12; Titus 1:6). He was not concerned with the mere existence of an additional occupa-tion, for he himself was a tentmaker. What he prohibited was excessive entanglement in the occupation or in any avocation that hinders full service for Christ.

[44]Bernard, *Pastoral Epistles*, 117.

(3) The Athlete (2:5)

[5]Similarly, if anyone competes as an athlete, he does not receive the victor's crown unless he competes according to the rules.

2:5 Paul used the picture of the athlete to illustrate the importance of complete devotion and stamina in Christian living. Performing as an athlete demands a commitment to a regimen of training and to the rules for the game. Paul may have been emphasizing either or both, but the context appears to spotlight the self-discipline and stamina needed for training and preparation.[45] He implied that the Christian athlete could expect suffering, but he also held out the promise of a prize for the committed devotee. The ultimate prize would come at the time of final judgment for the believer (2 Cor 5:10). The type of training that would prepare for this reward is godliness (1 Tim 4:7-8).

In the Pastorals, Paul had used athletic images in 1 Tim 4:7-8; 6:12 in order to emphasize that the Christian life demands the practice of self-discipline which affects both personal behavior and inner attitude. Christians must practice self-control. Each Christian must also have an inner preparedness to endure cheerfully the demands and hardships that spiritual commitment will bring. Paul made a similar point in 1 Cor 9:24-27.

(4) The Farmer (2:6)

[6]The hardworking farmer should be the first to receive a share of the crops.

2:6 Paul used the analogy of the farmer to show that the one who works hard has the first claim on the fruits of the work. The phrase "to receive a share of the crops" is not an appeal for a diligent worker to receive an adequate salary. It promises a spiritual reward from God for a job devotedly done. The time of this reward may be either in this life or at the last judgment. The reward may consist of honor and recognition from the church or a divine approval and blessing by God.

Paul frequently used the verb for "hardworking" to describe the work of ministry (Rom 16:6,12; 1 Cor 15:10; Gal 4:11). He was underscoring the fact that the farmer who works hard will be the first to enjoy the

---

[45]Kelly and Fee take opposite positions on this issue. Fee feels that the rules refer to the regulations of the game, for "the concern is not with Timothy's need for discipline as such but with his taking his share 'in suffering'" (*1 and 2 Timothy, Titus*, 192). Kelly asserts that Paul was emphasizing the importance of "arduous self-discipline" and suggests that the ultimate referent of the term "rules" is the official regulations imposed on athletes who take part in public games. Athletes in the Olympian Games had to swear that they had observed ten months of strict training (see Pausanias, *Descriptions of Greece*, 5.24.9). The appeal for self-discipline does seem to have been in the forefront of Paul's concerns, and Kelly's arguments are more compelling. See Kelly, *Pastoral Epistles*, 175-76.

fruits, and the diligent Christian servant can expect the same. He was deliberately contrasting the energetic farmer with the farmer who is afraid of work. As Bernard aptly observes, "The main thought is that labor, discipline, striving are the portion of him who would succeed in any enterprise, be he soldier or athlete or farmer."[46]

The term "first" suggests that the energetic Christian "has the priority over those who have either done nothing or been thoroughly idle."[47] The time of enjoyment of these fruits is eschatological, at the time of Christ's return (2 Cor 5:10).

Hanson believes the emphasis in the verse stresses that the pastor should also expect proper financial support from a diligent ministry. He does not rule out that the remuneration may include joy in ministry and also eternal reward, but he stresses the anticipation of salary.[48] The context, however, is not discussing earning a livelihood from the gospel, although Paul did broach that subject in other passages (e.g., Gal 6:6). This passage emphasizes the anticipation of a final reward from the Lord for earnest, steady work in Christ's service.

(5) The Application (2:7)

[7] Reflect on what I am saying, for the Lord will give you insight into all this.

2:7 Just in case Timothy had missed the point of Paul's illustrations, Paul urged him to ponder them ("Consider these three illustrations of mine," Phillips). He encouraged his meditation by promising that God would grant him help in understanding their intent.

The term "insight" refers to the faculty of right judgment or comprehension. Timothy was to put his mind to use in reflecting on Paul's metaphors, but genuine understanding would come from the Lord (1 Cor 2:10).

Paul had used three of these metaphors in 1 Cor 9:6-7,24-27. He indicated there that the Christian worker could normally expect financial support from his converts. He also stressed the importance of stamina in ministry. Barrett summarizes Paul's purpose in 2 Tim 2:3-7 as "to exhort Timothy to take his share of hardship; and the metaphors, when duly pondered, suggest that beyond warfare is victory, beyond athletic effort a prize, and beyond agricultural labour a crop."[49]

Application. Paul emphasized traits that believers need to demonstrate in their service for the Lord. These include (1) the faithful skills of a competent teacher, (2) the willingness to suffer and the choice of priorities of

---

[46]Bernard, *Pastoral Epistles*, 118.

[47]Kelly, *Pastoral Epistles*, 176.

[48]Hanson, *Pastoral Epistles*, 130, says, "The salary (or at least remuneration) motif grows clearer and clearer as one reads through vv. 4-7."

[49]Barrett, *Pastoral Epistles*, 102.

a soldier, (3) the self-discipline of an athlete, and (4) the hard work of a farmer. Paul demanded the pursuit of excellence in the Christian life. He tolerated no images of mediocrity for the believer. Can you imagine Paul illustrating the Christian life with the images of a dropout or a turncoat?

The positive images Paul presented demand consideration and reflection for proper application. As we reflect on the images, God will provide the understanding for applying the truths (v. 7).

3. Truths That Promote Effectiveness in Ministry (2:8-13)

Paul used this paragraph to conclude his appeal for Timothy to show stamina in Christian work. In 1:6-18 he had appealed for Timothy to demonstrate courage, willingness to suffer, and faithfulness in his conduct of ministry. In our previous paragraph he had used the figures of a teacher, soldier, athlete, and farmer to build readiness for suffering hardship into Timothy's life. In this paragraph Paul discussed the proper understanding of Christ (2:8), the goal of Paul's suffering (2:9-10), and the certainty of reward (2:11-13) as incentives to produce effectiveness and stamina in Timothy's work.

(1) A Proper Understanding of Christ (2:8)

8 Remember Jesus Christ, raised from the dead, descended from David. This is my gospel,

2:8 Paul made frequent appeal to the memory in addressing Timothy in this Epistle (1:6; 3:14-15). Here he urged Timothy to rivet his attention on Christ. Two features of Christ's person and work attracted Paul's attention. First, he stressed Christ's resurrection. The perfect tense of the participle for "raised" suggests that Paul was stressing the result of Christ's resurrection, the demonstration of his lordship (Rom 1:4), rather than the fact of the resurrection. Jesus' resurrection from the dead is the prime example of eschatological victory after death. It provides an encouragement for anyone facing suffering.[50] The affirmation of the resurrection here also prepares us for the exposure in 2:14-18 of some who denied the future resurrection of believers by affirming that it had already occurred.

Second, the mention that Christ "descended from David" shows that Christ has messianic qualifications and is the heir to the glorious promises of God for David. As the Messiah he is now seated in glory on his heavenly throne and will come again to reign over this world (Heb 1:3; 10:12-13). Paul presented Christ as the fulfillment of God's promise. Timothy would be the transmitter of a gospel which was rooted in the past and which looked with optimism toward the future because of Jesus' resurrection.

---

[50]Fee, *1 and 2 Timothy, Titus*, 196.

The phrase "my gospel" helps us to recognize that the twin emphases of this verse were a part of the gospel Paul proclaimed. The phrase does not suggest that Paul alone was the source of the emphasis but, in line with Paul's statements in 1 Tim 1:11, asserts that these are truths God had revealed to Paul.[51]

The memory of Christ cloaked with resurrection power and messianic dignity is an inspiration for Christian service. Such a powerful Savior can stimulate a diffident disciple such as Timothy to new vigor and hope.

(2) The Goal of Paul's Suffering (2:9-10)

⁹for which I am suffering even to the point of being chained like a criminal. But God's word is not chained. ¹⁰Therefore I endure everything for the sake of the elect, that they too may obtain the salvation that is in Christ Jesus, with eternal glory.

2:9 Paul elaborated on the fact of his suffering and expressed his optimism despite hardship. Paul's imprisonment involved "being chained like a criminal." The chains impeded Paul's movement and added to his misery. The term "criminal" (*kakourgos*) is used in Luke 23:32 to refer to the brigands who died with Jesus. Its use shows that Paul had serious charges lodged against him. The harshness of this second imprisonment made his earlier imprisonments seem mild (cf. Acts 24:23-27; 28:23-31).

Paul's indomitable spirit broke out in the declaration "God's word is not chained." Men could silence Paul, but they could not silence the power of God's Word (see Phil 1:12-18). As Lock observes, "God buries His workers but continues His work."[52] Paul was affirming that the bonds did not hinder his bold proclamation of the gospel.

The boldness of Paul's statement should not blind us to the fact that the spread of the gospel is, above all, a work of divine power (2 Tim 1:7). Success in preaching the gospel does not depend on mere human stubbornness, cleverness, or aggressiveness. God himself is the author of all success in preaching his message, and we who proclaim it must remember that God must drive the message home to the human heart with a spirit of conviction.

2:10 Paul articulated the aim of his suffering. He had suffered so as to enable God's chosen people to obtain their salvation. The "therefore" points back to v. 9. The knowledge that the gospel was not chained or bound provided Paul with an incentive to endure. Paul's endurance

---

[51]Lock suggests that this phrase implies, "not invented by me but entrusted to me" (*Pastoral Epistles*, 95). Bringing Paul to understand these truths could involve either special revelation to Paul (e.g., Gal 1:12) or receiving tradition held by other early believers (e.g., 1 Tim 3:16).

[52]Lock, *Pastoral Epistles*, 95.

involved an unrelenting commitment that moved straight ahead through difficulty. It was much more than a mere absence of complaint.

The "elect" for whom Paul suffered were "His chosen people" (Williams). He applied Old Testament language for God's people (Deut 7:6) to New Testament believers. Paul was not concerned to settle the theological status of God's people but to picture them as objects of his saving action.

Paul did not clarify the nature of the relationship between his suffering and the salvation of God's people.[53] He could not have meant that his sufferings were redemptively effective for them. Such an emphasis would contradict the statements of Rom 3:21-26, which emphasize the fullness of the satisfaction of Christ's death. Kelly explains that Paul was not merely saying that his endurance would be an inspiring example for others but "that the deeper motive of his patient acceptance of hardships was the conviction that he was thereby actually making it easier for them to attain salvation."[54] Paul felt that the church would face a predetermined amount of suffering before Christ returned.[55] The more Paul took upon himself, the less his Christian friends would have to bear themselves. In line with other New Testament passages (2 Cor 1:6; 4:8-15), he emphasized that his suffering would bring some relief to other believers.

The salvation to which Paul referred is that final consummation of salvation to be made clear at Christ's return (Heb 9:28). This is the result of that experience initiated by faith in Jesus Christ.

---

[53]In Phil 1:12-28 Paul indicated that his sufferings had emboldened his friends (v. 14) and aided them in pushing the gospel forward with unity (v. 27).

[54]Kelly, *Pastoral Epistles*, 178.

[55]The classical passage for dealing with this theme is Col 1:24. There Paul said that he was completing those afflictions of Christ that are yet to be endured on behalf of the church. Four thoughts give insight into this verse.

First, Paul's statements show "the oscillation in Hebrew thought between individual and corporate personality" (see F. F. Bruce, *The Epistles of Paul to the Ephesians and to the Colossians*, NIC [Grand Rapids: Eerdmans, 1957], 215). Bruce says Paul was asserting that the sufferings of the Servant of Jehovah (the Messiah) are to be carried on by the disciples of Christ, namely Paul.

Second, his suffering in no way supplements the saving work of Christ. Vaughan follows Lightfoot's suggestion that the sufferings relate to Christ's ministerial afflictions, not his redemptive sufferings (see C. Vaughan, "Colossians," *EBC* [Grand Rapids: Zondervan, 1978], 11:190).

Third, Christ does continue to suffer in the sufferings of his people. This is implied in the words of Christ to Ananias in Acts 9:16: "I will show him how much he must suffer for my name."

Fourth, there is the possible thought that Paul's own suffering may relieve "his converts and other members of the body of Christ of part of the suffering that would otherwise fall to their lot" (see Bruce, *The Epistle to the Colossians*, 216-17). The quote from Kelly in the text affirms this viewpoint.

(3) The Certainty of Reward (2:11-13)

[11] Here is a trustworthy saying:
If we died with him,
  we will also live with him;
[12] if we endure,
  we will also reign with him.
If we disown him,
  he will also disown us;
[13] if we are faithless,
  he will remain faithful,
  for he cannot disown himself.

2:11 Paul introduced these verses with his "trustworthy saying" formula (cf. 1 Tim 1:15; 3:1; 4:9). For additional information on the trustworthy sayings, see the discussion of 1 Tim 1:15. Scholars divide over the identity of the trustworthy saying. The statement of v. 8 has the appearance of an aphorism or maxim, but it is too far from v. 11 to be considered seriously.[56] The best decision is to regard the content of 2:11b-13 as the trustworthy saying, for the parallel structure of the passage and its rhythmic character identify it as a possible extract from a hymn or saying of the early church.

The saying of 2:11b-13 has four conditional clauses. Each protasis (the "if" clause) describes an action of a believer. Each apodosis (the conclusion) presents the results in terms of either Christ's individual action or joint action with the believer. The initial two sayings describe positive actions. The final two sayings refer to negative actions.

The initial line of the first saying ("If we died with him") reads like Rom 6:8. If this is a hymn, Paul could have been its author.[57] The Greek construction in this context suggests a definite past event such as the conversion and baptism of a Christian (Col 2:12). Paul presented Christian

---

[56] One feature in favor of referring the faithful saying back to an earlier verse is the presence of "for" (γάρ) in v. 11 (untranslated in the NIV). To many interpreters it seems unlikely that a "faithful saying" would begin with "for."

Both Fee and Lenski identify the "faithful saying" with 11b-13, and they explain the presence of "for" in keeping with their views. Fee views the conjunction as explanatory, giving the reason for which Timothy ought to take his share of suffering and referring to the idea in 2:1-10. The idea would be that those who have died with Christ and endured for him would receive a heavenly reward (Fee, *1 and 2 Timothy, Titus*, 198). Lenski views the γάρ as confirmatory and suggests that a proper translation for 11b would be, "If, '*indeed*' [γάρ; italics mine] we died" (Lenski, *St. Paul's Epistles*, 792). Williams's translation makes the same emphasis, "If we indeed have died with Him."

[57] Kelly identifies the saying as a hymn "of Jewish-Christian provenance" (see Kelly, *Pastoral Epistles*, 179). He despairs of identifying its original setting precisely.

Fee feels that all the content is Pauline and says, "If he did not compose it, then it was certainly composed in his churches" (*1 and 2 Timothy, Titus*, 199).

conversion as a dying and rising with Christ. The type of commitment demonstrated in baptism would prepare a believer for the expression of his obedience as a martyr, but the primary reference is to death to self and not merely to martyrdom.[58] The future tense of "we will . . . live" suggests that this is a reference to life in heaven.[59] Although the reference is to heavenly life, there is a sense in which believers experience a beginning of eternal life now (John 5:24). White says: "There is a beginning of eternal life even while we are in the flesh, . . . in that newness of life to which we are called, and for which we are enabled, in our baptism."[60]

2:12 The first conditional clause of v. 12 urged Timothy to remain loyal even in the face of suffering. To "endure" demands a "continuing experience of bravely bearing up under the hardships and afflictions heaped upon the believer because of his relation to Christ."[61] The apodosis of this clause promises a victory in the end times for faithful believers. The reigning does not occur until after the return of Christ. Believers will participate in the reign of the glorified Messiah, perhaps during the millennium described in Rev 20:1-6.[62]

The second conditional clause of v. 12 was a warning to Timothy and to all believers. With this clause the emphasis shifts from positive actions of believers to negative actions of believers. The language resembles that of Matt 10:33, and the disowning of Christ is a verbal or behavioral denial to avoid suffering. Those who deny Christ in persecution will have denial by him in the final judgment (Mark 8:38). Those whom Christ denies in the judgment will enter eternity in lostness. Paul's awful warning did not apply to a temporary denial such as Peter demonstrated (Luke 22:54-62) but to a permanent denial such as Judas illustrated (Acts 1:15-19). The threat of "disown[ing]" would have been a warning to Timothy

---

[58]Hiebert feels that the reference is "to a martyr's death now viewed from the standpoint of the crowning day. It is the purpose of the passage to give encouragement to suffer for Christ even unto death" (Hiebert, *Second Timothy*, 63). Kelly feels that the reference is to "the death to sin and self that every Christian undergoes in baptism" (*Pastoral Epistles*, 179-80); and Lenski says, "This is the death which occurs in baptism by contrition and repentance" (*St. Paul's Epistles*, 793).

[59]Fee disagrees with this understanding, suggesting that "the future . . . has primarily to do with life in Christ in the present" (*1 and 2 Timothy*, 199). He suggests that such language as Paul used contains latent in it the idea of an eschatological consummation still to be realized. Bernard interprets it as a reference to "the life of the blessed in heaven" (*The Pastoral Epistles*, 121).

[60]White, *Epistles to Timothy*, 163. This writer would agree with White's statement on the present possession of eternal life but would link it with the act of "believing," not the experience of baptism.

[61]Hiebert, *Second Timothy*, 63.

[62]This statement is not intended to advocate a specific millennial viewpoint. The truth of the statement does not depend on the definition of *millennium* accepted by the reader.

and other believers and a threat of judgment to the Asians of 1:15 who had deserted.[63]

2:13 Paul's statement here has raised varied interpretations. To be "faithless" is a present tense,[64] implying that the readers were developing a pattern of failure to live up to their profession or were proving unstable and disobedient in trials. We would expect Paul to have concluded his statements with a promise that God would also be faithless to us, but Paul could not bring himself to state that about God. The statement that "he will remain faithful" may mean that God will be faithful to mete out punishment to the guilty.[65] However, in keeping with Paul's statements in Rom 3:3-4 and 8:35-39, he seems to have suggested that "however wayward and faithless men may be, God's love continues unalterable and he remains true to his promises."[66]

The human faithlessness only serves to decorate the faithfulness of God. Paul was asserting that despite human unfaithfulness God's saving purpose has not retreated. Timothy and all those with him were to continue their endurance that they might experience God's blessing. Paul did not state these words to open the door to apostasy and disobedience but to soothe a troubled conscience and to provide encouragement to return to God.

Paul supported his affirmation by stating that God cannot deny or change himself. Kelly maintains, "To be faithful through everything, in spite of the worst that men can do, is the essence of his nature."[67] Paul's warnings in these verses promised that God will reward loyalty to Christ and steadfastness in persecution. Disloyalty will receive punishment. May these warnings not fall on deaf ears!

Summary. Several ringing certainties dominated Paul's thinking in this section. Paul's gospel proclamation in 2:8 emphasized the certainties

---

[63]In such verses as Heb 10:35-39 and Mark 13:13, the New Testament emphasizes that endurance in Christian commitment is the evidence of genuine conversion. The mere claim that one is a believer is shown to be true only when the one making the claim endures in obedience. Paul's words assume that one who endures in commitment proves a genuine faith (v. 12a). They also assume that one who denies shows the lack of such faith (v. 12b). Jesus offered mercy to a repentant, remorseful Peter (John 21:15-17). Peter could only speak of judgment for the stubborn refusal of Judas to return to God (Acts 1:15-20).

[64]The translation "to be faithless" is more accurate than the KJV's "if we believe not." The present tense of the Greek verb suggests a failure to render obedience or commitment, not an existence in the state of an unbeliever.

[65]This is the interpretation of Hendriksen, who says: "Divine faithfulness is a wonderful comfort for those who are loyal . . . It is a very earnest warning for those who might be inclined to become disloyal" (*I-II Timothy*, 260). G. W. Knight offers a detailed discussion and refutation of the position held by Hendriksen (*The Faithful Sayings in the Pastoral Letters* [Grand Rapids: Baker, 1979], 126-31).

[66]Kelly, *Pastoral Epistles*, 180.

[67]Ibid., 181.

of Christ's resurrection and his messianic majesty. The certainty of the power of God's word provided stamina and motivation for Paul's endurance of hardship even as a "criminal" (2:9). This verse has similarities to Paul's affirmation in 1 Cor 1:18b. In 2:11-13 Paul's certainty of reward derived largely from the certainty that God was faithful to care for and love his people. God's faithfulness means future life and glory for believers.

The warning of 2:12b presents relevant truth. Those who persist in a denial of God by a refusal to suffer for him can expect to enter eternity separated from fellowship with God.

— SECTION OUTLINE —

IV. APPEALS FOR DOCTRINAL SOUNDNESS (2:14–4:8)
   1. The Confrontation of False Teaching and Living (2:14-26)
      (1) Resistance of the False Teachers (2:14-19)
      (2) An Appeal for Separation (2:20-21)
      (3) Timothy's Response to Error (2:22-26)
   2. The Stubborn Character of Human Beings (3:1-9)
      (1) What They Are (3:1-5)
      (2) What They Do (3:6-9)
   3. Sources of Strength for Endurance (3:10-17)
      (1) The Example of Paul (3:10-13)
      (2) The Enrichment of Scripture (3:14-17)
   4. A Charge for Consistent Behavior (4:1-5)
      (1) Basis of the Charge (4:1)
      (2) Timothy's Charge to Ministry (4:2)
      (3) Reason for the Charge (4:3-4)
      (4) Timothy's Personal Charge (4:5)
   5. Reward for Self-sacrifice (4:6-8)
      (1) The Sacrifice of Life (4:6)
      (2) The Service of Ministry (4:7)
      (3) The Reward for Obedience (4:8)

—— IV. APPEALS FOR DOCTRINAL SOUNDNESS (2:14–4:8) ——

1. The Confrontation of False Teaching and Living (2:14-26)

In 2 Timothy, Paul still faced the problem of false teaching that was common in 1 Timothy, but the problem was much more in the background than it had been in 1 Timothy. A concern for dealing with false teachers is prominent in Paul's directives from 2:14 through 4:8. In this present section Paul urged Timothy to take the lead in resisting falsehood by warning of the danger from heresy and exposing its error (2:14-19). Paul used an illustration to appeal for separation from the false teachers and their teaching (2:20-21). He also outlined Timothy's response to the error he faced (2:22-26).

(1) Resistance of the False Teachers (2:14-19)

¹⁴Keep reminding them of these things. Warn them before God against quarreling about words; it is of no value, and only ruins those who listen. ¹⁵Do your best to present yourself to God as one approved, a workman who

does not need to be ashamed and who correctly handles the word of truth. [16] Avoid godless chatter, because those who indulge in it will become more and more ungodly. [17] Their teaching will spread like gangrene. Among them are Hymenaeus and Philetus, [18] who have wandered away from the truth. They say that the resurrection has already taken place, and they destroy the faith of some. [19] Nevertheless, God's solid foundation stands firm, sealed with this inscription: "The Lord knows those who are his," and, "Everyone who confesses the name of the Lord must turn away from wickedness."

Paul had poured out many words urging Timothy to endure suffering with courage and commitment. Now he cast a watchful eye on the still-present threat of heresy. Paul warned Timothy about the false teachers and their errors (2:14). He also wanted Timothy to take the lead in resisting them and their teaching (2:15-18). He spoke a word of encouragement to the church, reminding them of God's protective love and appealing for separation from evil (2:19).

2:14 The beginning imperative in v. 14 contains a strong appeal, directing Timothy to do his duty for the people. He was to continue reminding his audience of the emphases Paul had made in 2:11-13, namely, that they were to endure in their commitment and proclaim the Christian message (2:2). Paul charged Timothy to add solemnity to his exhortation by warning the Ephesians "before God." The content of the warning includes an appeal to avoid "quarreling about words." This wrong emphasis can lead to aimless word splitting.[1] "In the end disputing about words seeks not the victory of truth but the victory of the speaker."[2] This word splitting involved useless verbal quibbling, but it did not focus on the aims of Christianity.

Paul outlined two results of such verbal quibbles. First, it accomplishes no good purpose ("is useless," NASB; "is of no value," NIV). Second, it works to the ruin of those who participate in it ("brings destruction on those who hear it," Williams). The word for "ruins" (*katastrophē*) describes the tearing down of believers. It is the opposite of edification. Word splitting whets an appetite for argument rather than building commitment to the living God. In the heat of debate we must always ask ourselves if the subject is actually worth a fight and a searing disagreement.

2:15 What could Timothy personally do to prevent a growing interest in such misdirected actions? M. Dibelius and H. Conzelmann say, "The best medicine against the disease of 'disputes about words' is Timothy's

---

[1] "Quarreling about words" (2:14), a verb, comes from the same family of Greek words as "quarrels about words" (1 Tim 6:4), a noun. The same error of which Paul had earlier warned still persisted.

[2] R. W. Ward, *Commentary on 1 & 2 Timothy & Titus* (Waco: Word, 1974), 171.

good conduct itself."[3] This good conduct included three features. First, Timothy was to make it his supreme ambition to obtain God's approval ("Try hard to show yourself worthy of God's approval," NEB).[4] Second, he was to be a workman with no reason to be ashamed. The term "workman" is frequently used in reference to an agricultural laborer (e.g., Jas 5:4), but here Paul used the term to describe a laborer for God. Paul was urging his Christian friend to work with such diligence that he would have no fear of shame for poor quality work. Third, this same workman (specifically, Timothy but by application today all believers) was to be accurate in delivering the message of truth. The truth is the gospel. Paul showed concern that Timothy would present the gospel without perverting or distorting it.[5] He was not to be turned aside by disputes about words or mere empty prattle.

2:16 Paul urged Timothy to make a positive contribution to the fight against false teaching. He was continually to keep away from "godless chatter." The use of the present imperative for "avoid" suggests that Timothy had to remain continually alert to the threat of heresy. The term "godless" shows that the debates of the heretics had nothing to do with real godliness. The term "chatter" pictures the discussions of the heretics as aimless and empty. Paul had used the same words in 1 Tim 6:20.

The reason for avoiding these foolish discussions was that they led to progress in the wrong direction. Though Paul left unstated in the original language the subject of the verb "will become," it is clear that the verb (*prokopsousi*) is third person plural. What is unclear in the original language is who the "they" refers to, but the context and the pronoun "their" of v.17 suggest that the false teachers themselves will develop in ungodliness. With a twist of irony Paul stated that the heretics would indeed

---

[3]M. Dibelius and H. Conzelmann, *The Pastoral Epistles* (Philadelphia: Fortress, 1972), 111.

[4]The KJV's translation of "study" has led many English-speaking Christians to think wrongly that Paul was urging a diligent preparation of academic assignments. Paul's focus was on showing diligence to win divine approval. The verb (σπουδάζω) expresses an ardent striving in Eph 4:3; 1 Thess 2:17. Paul had earlier described the heretics as only concerned about personal gain (1 Tim 6:6-10), and he wanted Timothy to seek only God's favor.

[5]Interpreters find a variety of possible sources for the derivation of the term ορθοτομέω ("handling aright the word of truth," ASV; "driving a straight furrow, in your proclamation of the truth," NEB). Lock presents the possibilities as a plow cutting a straight furrow, a road engineer's building a straight road, or a mason's squaring and cutting a stone to fit its proper place. He questions whether any one of these were consciously present in Paul's mind (*The Pastoral Epistles*, ICC [Edinburgh: T & T Clark, 1924], 99).

J. E. Huther properly suggests that the notion of cutting falls quickly into the background so that the meaning is "deal rightly with something so as not to falsify it" (*Critical and Exegetical Handbook to the Epistles to Timothy and Titus* (1884; reprint, Peabody, Mass.: Hendrickson, 1983], 234). Paul wanted Timothy to perform the task opposite that of a peddler of God's word (2 Cor 2:17).

advance but only in the direction of ungodliness.[6] Paul limited the effect of their ungodly behavior by describing the exposure of their folly to the Christian public (see 2 Tim 3:9).

2:17 Not only would these people advance in ungodliness, but their teaching would spread to cause ruin. The spread of their heresy furthered the spread of ungodliness. Their influence on other believers would be disastrous. The term "spread" is an idiom with the literal meaning of *have pasture*. Alford suggests that "pasture" is "the medical term for the consuming progress of mortifying disease."[7] Paul compared the spread of the heresy to the spread of gangrene through the body. The term for gangrene, used only here in the New Testament, describes the death of bodily tissues due to the loss of blood supply. Just as gangrene progressively brought death to the human body, the sickening progress of the heretical teaching worked havoc with the body of Christ in Ephesus.[8]

Paul presented the names of two heretics. Hymenaeus was not a common name, and he was probably the same as the "Hymenaeus" of 1 Tim 1:20. Apparently he was brazen enough in his impiety to have ignored Paul's earlier ban. The fact that he could ignore Paul's earlier ban demonstrates the circumstances in Ephesus. Nothing more is mentioned in the Bible about Philetus.

2:18 Paul asserted that these two ringleaders had "wandered away from the truth." The term "wander away" suggests that they had missed the mark. Paul had also used the term in 1 Tim 1:6; 6:21.

Paul identified the nature of the heresy. The two heretics had asserted that the general resurrection had "already taken place."[9] Greeks often

---

[6]The term "ungodly" or "ungodliness" (ἀσέβεια) is the opposite of "godliness" (see 1 Tim 2:2; 3:16; 4:7). G. Fee suggests that the heretics had used this term, borrowed from Hellenism, to describe their own practices. Paul adopted it from them, but he defined it differently. Fee uses the term "godliness" to refer to genuine religion, and its opposite "ungodliness" shows the absence of true fear of God (*1 and 2 Timothy, Titus*, GNC, ed. W. W. Gasque [San Francisco: Harper & Row, 1984], 27).

[7]H. Alford, "The Second Epistle to Timotheus," *GT*, 5th ed. (Boston: Lee and Shepherd, 1888), 3:385.

[8]Interpreters debate whether the term translated "gangrene" refers to the disease of gangrene or to cancer. Both A. T. Hanson (*The Pastoral Epistles*, NCB [Grand Rapids: Eerdmans, 1982], 135) and C. Spicq (*Saint Paul: Les Epitres Pastorals* [Paris: Gabalda, 1947], 353-54) favor the translation as "gangrene." Alford (*Second Epistle to Timotheus*, 385) quotes Hippocrates' opinion that the term referred "to the state of a tumour between inflammation and entire mortification." Williams translates, "Their message will spread like a cancer." The GNB compares the sickness to "an open sore that eats away the flesh." Most interpreters favor the translation "gangrene," but too much argument about the precise identity of this medical term may be an unnecessary word battle.

[9]For all of his warning about false teaching, Paul gave little precise definition to the content of the false teaching he denounced. This passage and the statement in 1 Tim 4:3 present the clearest expressions of the content of the false teaching in the Pastorals.

showed a contempt for the concept of physical resurrection. Because they viewed the body as evil, they eschewed the concept of a future bodily resurrection. For such people a spiritualized or sacramental view of resurrection was more congenial. Paul had taught the concept of spiritual resurrection (see Eph 2:6; Rom 6:3-4), but he had also asserted the reality of a future resurrection (1 Cor 15; Phil 3:21). The Ephesian teaching concerning the resurrection may have denied a future bodily resurrection. It probably asserted that the resurrection had already occurred in the spiritual renewal of the believer by regeneration.[10]

For Paul the result of such heresy was to "destroy the faith of some." In asserting that the resurrection had already occurred, the false teachers could deny both the past resurrection of Christ and the future resurrection of believers. They could depreciate the body and promote asceticism. Both emphases can lead to moral indifference. D. Guthrie says, "Christianity without a resurrection ceases to be a living faith."[11] For Paul the resurrection hope was foundational in Christianity. In 1 Cor 15 Paul had shown that a denial of the possibility of resurrection jettisoned the gospel (15:3-11), brought the credibility of the apostles into question (15:14-15), and robbed believers of an incentive for sacrifice and service (15:29-34). Paul did not specify in this passage all the negative results he expected from an affirmation that the resurrection had already occurred, but he clearly viewed it as an unacceptable perversion and as a threat to all spiritual progress.

2:19 Although Paul was saddened at the denial of Christian truth by Hymenaeus and Philetus, he recognized the durability of the main structures of Christianity. God's solid foundation is unshakable.

The "foundation" may refer to the church as a whole, the genuine work of God in Ephesus, the deposit of faith, or it may be a general statement of truth without a definite reference. Paul's description of the church as "the pillar and foundation of the truth" (1 Tim 3:15) makes the term in v. 19 appear to be a reference to the church as a whole, but certainly with a special reference to the Ephesian congregation.

A seal is a sign or a stamp of approval that shows genuineness or attests ownership. Paul pictured God's people as stamped with two seals. First, God owns and cares for his people. The statement is a reference to Num 16:5, which was spoken on the occasion of the rebellion of Korah, Dathan, and Abiram. "Paul's object in citing it was to give encouragement

---

[10]Evidence of a spiritualized view of the resurrection appears in Irenaeus's words about the heretic Menander: "For his disciples obtain the *resurrection* by being baptized into him, and can die no more, but remain in the possession of immortal youth" (*Against Heresies*, 1.23.5).

[11]Guthrie, *The Pastoral Epistles*, TNTC (London: Tyndale, 1957), 149.

to Timothy, and others who were worried by backsliding in the community, by reminding them that God can be relied upon to discriminate between his loyal and disloyal servants."[12]

Second, God's true servants must practice holiness. The statement reflects the sentiment of Ps 34:14 and Prov 3:7. God's action in salvation demands a response of holy commitment (2 Cor 5:15). Paul was effectively saying that Hymenaeus and Philetus did not belong to the people of God. God knew who his true people were. Those who were truly God's people would turn away from the false teaching in Ephesus.

(2) An Appeal for Separation (2:20-21)

[20] In a large house there are articles not only of gold and silver, but also of wood and clay; some are for noble purposes and some for ignoble. [21] If a man cleanses himself from the latter, he will be an instrument for noble purposes, made holy, useful to the Master and prepared to do any good work.

Paul's description of the false teachers in 2:14-19 contained an implicit appeal to avoid and separate from them (vv. 16,19). Paul introduced the metaphor of a house containing two kinds of vessels in order to elaborate his appeal for turning away from wrongdoing. In v. 20 he outlined the features of the metaphor, and in v. 21 he made its application.

2:20 The large house to which Paul referred is a metaphor for the church. Some of the articles are expensive ("gold and silver"), and some are inexpensive ("wood and clay"). Some of these expensive vessels are used for important ("noble") occasions, and some for the less expensive, ordinary ("ignoble") purposes. In using the expression "articles . . . of gold and silver," Paul referred to worthy, commendable Christians. In using the expression "articles . . . of wood and clay," he spoke of unworthy Christians, who were to be avoided. Paul was suggesting that the church contained both faithful and unfaithful believers; some served for desirable ends, and others accomplished shameful ends. In v. 21 Paul would urge his committed readers to avoid those who would hinder their good work, namely, the false teachers.

2:21 Paul presented his description without comment in v. 20 but made his intent more obvious in v. 21. His purpose was not to advocate that all types of vessels are useful to the Lord (1 Cor 12:21-24), nor was it to suggest that good and evil inevitably will appear in the kingdom (Matt 13:24-30). His purpose was to urge Timothy and others in the church to seek cleansing from ("keeps himself clear of," Montgomery)

---

[12] J. N. D. Kelly, *A Commentary on the Pastoral Epistles* (1963; reprint, Grand Rapids: Baker, 1981), 186.

the false teachings represented by Hymenaeus and Philetus. The separation from sin implied in v. 19 is specifically urged in v. 21.

Paul was more concerned that Timothy separate from the false teaching than that he break all contact with the false teachers. His emphasis on what Timothy should avoid in 2:14,16 related more to the content of the false teaching than to the person of the false teacher. Later in this chapter Paul would appeal for Timothy to instruct false teachers so that they could repent of heretical views (2:24-26).

Paul had three encouraging words about an instrument "for noble purposes." First, such a person is "made holy," set apart for a special purpose before God. Second, he is "useful to the Master."[13] Third, he is "prepared to do any good work." He will be ready to undertake whatever the Lord calls him to do. Those who are most useful to God will find that there are ignoble practices, attitudes, and ideas they must avoid (v. 20). Paul had urged his readers to effect that separation.

(3) Timothy's Response to Error (2:22-26)

[22] Flee the evil desires of youth, and pursue righteousness, faith, love and peace, along with those who call on the Lord out of a pure heart. [23] Don't have anything to do with foolish and stupid arguments, because you know they produce quarrels. [24] And the Lord's servant must not quarrel; instead, he must be kind to everyone, able to teach, not resentful. [25] Those who oppose him he must gently instruct, in the hope that God will grant them repentance leading them to a knowledge of the truth, [26] and that they will come to their senses and escape from the trap of the devil, who has taken them captive to do his will.

With the dangerous false teaching Paul had described, there were some specific actions Timothy needed to take. Negatively, he was to avoid certain traits and action (vv. 22-23). Positively, he was to try to rescue false teachers from their involvement with error (vv. 24-26).

2:22 The two imperatives ("flee" and "pursue") are identical with the commands of 1 Tim 6:11. In this context the "evil desires of youth" are not so much a reference to sensual allurements as to expressions of youthful immaturity. Hotheaded answers and extended discussions of trivia can hinder effectiveness, not only for youthful disciples but for those of all ages. Young men can be characterized by partiality, intolerance, halfheartedness, and unwarranted self-assertion. These were the qualities Timothy was to avoid.

---

[13]"Useful" (εὔχρηστον) appears in Paul's description of Mark (2 Tim 4:11) and Onesimus (Phlm 11).

Paul encouraged Timothy to follow hard after righteousness, an open rectitude in attitude and action. He was to show faith—a sincere confidence in God—and love—a growing affection for others. He was to seek peace—a genuine fellowship and harmony with other Christians. In urging Timothy to frequent the company of "those who call on the Lord out of a pure heart," Paul was not suggesting that Timothy was to practice faith, love, and peace only with believers. His statement implies that traits of righteousness, faith, love, and peace are best developed whenever a Christian stays in the company of other believers.[14] Williams brings out this idea in his translation "in association with those who call upon the Lord with pure hearts."

2:23 Timothy needed to cultivate a sense of what to avoid. Some questions were "foolish and stupid" ("silly and ill informed," Phillips). The result of discussing them would be further quarrels and strife, and because of this result Paul directed Timothy to avoid even the discussion of the questions. Paul had discussed a similar subject in vv. 14,16. The cure for overcoming all of these irrelevances was to refuse to listen. As Ward observes, "The irrelevancy of much of the controversy then prevalent among Christians seems to have deeply impressed St. Paul; again and again he returned to this charge against the heretical teachers, that their doctrines are unprofitable and vain, and that they breed strife about questions either unimportant or insoluble."[15] Paul was not prohibiting intelligent, probing theological discussion but useless wrangling over recondite questions that divide and confuse. We must cultivate a judgment that can distinguish between these options.[16]

The solution to dealing with such ignorance and strife lies in a positive effort to teach truth to those in the grip of error. In 24-25a Paul reminded Timothy of the attitude needed to deal with false teachers. In 25b-26 he outlined the aim in talking with them.

2:24-25a Any believer can be called "the Lord's servant," but the designation was especially proper for a Christian leader such as Timo-

---

[14]Kelly, agreeing with the statements above, feels that what Paul is really referring to "is the brotherly accord which should flourish among Christian people" (*Pastoral Epistles*, 189). He points to the presence of a similar idea in Rom 12:18. Fee, differing slightly, feels that the prepositional phrase preceded by "with" modifies the verb "pursue" and is describing a distinctive trait of believers. Believers are those who "call upon the Lord with a pure heart." The differences between Fee and Kelly do not greatly affect the meaning (see Fee, *1 and 2 Timothy, Titus*, 216).

[15]J. H. Bernard, *The Pastoral Epistles* (1899; reprint, Grand Rapids: Baker, 1980), 126.

[16]"Uninformed men rejoice in a verbal victory and angels weep at the damage done to the witness of the church. *Controversies* are prolific, spawning *quarrels* and fights to the third and fourth generation" (see R. W. Ward, *Commentary on 1 & 2 Timothy & Titus* [Waco: Word, 1974], 181).

thy.[17] Paul prescribed both negative and positive instructions for the
Lord's servant. Negatively the Christian leader was not to be quarrelsome.
Paul had earlier prescribed this requirement for the overseer or elder of a
congregation (1 Tim 3:3).[18] Paul outlined four positive traits needed by a
servant who seeks to prevent quarrels. First, he must be "kind to everyone" ("gentle to everybody," Williams). He need not be a jellyfish, but he
must have a kindliness in his outward manner. Second, he must be "able
to teach" ("a skillful teacher," Williams). The term in this context calls
for both the ability and the willingness to teach. Third, he must avoid
resentfulness ("patient when wronged," NASB). The word describes
someone who can control irritability because he has learned to bear
patiently the wrong in others. Fourth, he is to "instruct" his opponents so
as to correct their error of heresy. The call for gentleness demands a tol-
erance in spirit without a weakening of evangelical orthodoxy. Timothy's
opponents included both hardened antagonists (see 1 Tim 1:20) and those
duped by their deceitful ways, and Timothy had to be prepared to deal
wisely with either group.

2:25b-26 Paul stated the purpose of the gentle instruction by using
two verbs that follow the phrase "in the hope that." First, Paul wanted the
false teachers to experience repentance so that they would acknowledge
the truth. To acknowledge the truth involved understanding the gospel so
that they might experience a genuine commitment to Christ. The phrase
"in the hope that" does not imply that God hesitates to give repentance
but that human beings often refuse to accept it. Paul presented repentance
as a gift given by God.[19]

Second, Paul wanted the false teachers to return to sober thinking and
win release from Satan's stranglehold. To think soberly in the spiritual
realm demands clear, sound insight about spiritual realities.[20] Some had
muddled thinking because they had been taken captive in the snare of the
devil. The verb for taking them captive (*zōgreō*) means literally *to capture*

---

[17]The idea is applied to all believers in 1 Cor 7:22.

[18]The word for quarrel (μάχομαι) can refer to a physical fight (e.g., Acts 7:26), but it can
also refer figuratively to a verbal quarrel or dispute. The latter was Paul's idea in this context. He basically was warning a person not to develop a contentious attitude by verbal
fighting.

[19]Kelly says that this repentance "will be wholly God's work; but while love will open a
door to his grace, violence can only obstruct it by exasperating those who desperately need
it" (*Pastoral Epistles*, 190).

[20]The verb for "come to their senses" (ἀνανήφω) appears only here in the NT. In its
background it referred to regaining sobriety after a bout of drinking, but it was used largely
in the spiritual or ethical realm. Huther says, "The error into which they had fallen is to be
compared with the intoxication which beclouds men's wits" (see *Epistles to Timothy and
Titus*, 240).

alive and is used in Luke 5:10 to describe capturing men for God's purposes. Here it was Satan who took individuals captive to do his will.[21] Judas, into whom Satan entered (Luke 22:3), was an example of someone taken captive by Satan to do his will. Paul advocated a style of teaching God could use both to correct error and to rescue from error those who were entrapped. The emphasis on error and false teachers provided Paul a launching pad with which to enter into another accusation against the false teachers in 3:1-9.

Summary. Paul had given Timothy a warning to resist the false teachers (vv. 14-19), an appeal for separation (vv. 20-21), and an outline for a proper response to error (vv. 22-26).

In resisting error Timothy was to avoid the discussion of empty, aimless questions that would only stir up strife. He was to provide a reasoned explanation of the Christian message as an antidote to error. He could serve with the confidence that God knew and protected him.

Paul appealed to Timothy to separate from the false teaching of the heretics, but he urged him to seek to reach and inform the teachable among the heretics. Timothy himself was to live a righteous life-style.

The best prescription for avoiding enticing errors is a proper presentation of the truth. Paul urged this on Timothy. Further, some questions, if pursued and investigated, will only produce more strife and confusion. God can provide us the wisdom to know when to provide an answer to inquiries and when to pass beyond the question to deeper goals.

2. The Stubborn Character of the False Teachers (3:1-9)

In this section Paul concluded his brief emphasis in 2 Timothy on the heresy Timothy was to oppose. Paul provided a vivid description of the false teachers (3:1-5a) along with a personal appeal to Timothy in v. 5b. Paul assumed that Timothy would not be surprised by the appearance of

---

[21]Interpreters differ concerning the antecedents of the pronouns represented by the "who" and "his" of the NIV text. Some argue that the Greek personal pronoun (represented in English by "who," αὐτοῦ) cannot refer to the same antecedent as the Greek demonstrative pronoun (represented in English by "his," ἐκείνου). The possibilities are: (1) both "who" and "his" refer to the devil (the position advocated by this author); (2) both "who" and "his" refer to God; (3) "who" is a reference to the Lord's servant, who takes the false teachers captive to do "his" (i.e., God's) will; (4) "who" is a reference to the devil, and "his" refers to God. Here Paul would have been suggesting that some taken captive by the devil are rescued by God so as to do his (God's) will.

To refer the antecedent of the pronouns to either God or to the Lord's servant makes them depend on words too distant from the pronouns. Huther points out that it is possible for both the "who" and the "his" to refer to the same subject (*Epistles to Timothy and Titus*, 241). One could view the repetition of the demonstrative pronoun translated "his" as emphatic. It is indeed the devil's will Satan captures people to do. For further study consult Hanson, *Pastoral Epistles*, 142-43, who has a lengthy discussion of the issues.

the false teachers, but he wanted Timothy to know the perniciousness of their character. In 3:1-5 he outlined the nature of the heretics, and in 3:6-9 he described the actions that came from this perverse nature. Paul's description made it clear that Timothy was facing religious pretenders representative of the quacks and mythomaniacs that populated the ancient world. After making this statement about the heretics, Paul would not mention the false teachers again except in passing references in 3:13 and in 4:3.

(1) What They Are (3:1-5)

¹But mark this: There will be terrible times in the last days. ²People will be lovers of themselves, lovers of money, boastful, proud, abusive, disobedient to their parents, ungrateful, unholy, ³without love, unforgiving, slanderous, without self-control, brutal, not lovers of the good, ⁴treacherous, rash, conceited, lovers of pleasure rather than lovers of God— ⁵having a form of godliness but denying its power. Have nothing to do with them.

In 2:24-26 Paul had expressed hope for the spiritual recovery of some deceived individuals whom Satan had trapped. Paul wanted Timothy to realize that despite the positive hope expressed in 3:9, opposition to the truth would grow even more intense. Wicked men would arise among professing Christians.

3:1 Paul called on Timothy to "mark" ("realize," NASB) this fact. The fact is that "terrible"[22] times will come in the last days. The term "last days" sounds as if it applies "especially to the last days of this age, before the Second Coming."[23] However, in the New Testament the phrase refers to that entire time from the completion of Christ's redemptive work until his return. Christ's life, death, resurrection, and ascension have inaugurated the last days. Peter's speech at Pentecost in Acts 2:16-39 proclaimed this fact, and the writer of Heb 1:2 reaffirmed its truth. Paul's description of moral declension has been used to denounce outbreaks of corruption that have appeared throughout church history. Today we are living in the last days, that period between Christ's exaltation and his return.[24]

---

[22]This adjective (χαλεπός) is translated "times of stress" (RSV) and "dangerous" (Norlie). It is used in Matt 8:28 to describe the bizarre actions of a pair of demoniacs.

[23]R. Earle, *1 & 2 Timothy*, EBC, ed. F. E. Gaebelein (Grand Rapids: Zondervan, 1978), 406.

[24]Not all exegetes define "the last days" in this way. Some believe that the term "denotes the period just before the Parousia and the end of the present age" (see Kelly, *Pastoral Epistles*, 193). It is true that the apostolic church expected that the return of Christ would be preceded by a time of great evil that includes the rising of religious charlatans and a widespread turning away from God (Matt 24:3-28; Mark 13:5-23; 2 Thess 2:3-4,8-11). Jewish apocalyptic writings emphasized that a decline of morality would occur before the

In vv. 2-5 Paul presented a list of vices that resemble a similar collection in Rom 1:29-31 and 1 Tim 1:9-10. The presence of people who had these vices demonstrated that the times were truly terrible. Paul's list referred to professing Christians, while the list in Rom 1:29-31 described pagan society. C. Spicq points out that all the vices come from a love of self.[25] Unlike the list in 1 Tim 1:9-10, this list lacks evidences of discernible order. Some of the terms are grouped in pairs, and sometimes they are joined by assonance, the repetition of an identical initial sound in the Greek text.

3:2 The first two terms of v. 2 and the final pair in v. 4 have the prefix *phil* (meaning *fond of*) in Greek. Several terms have the Greek *a* (alpha privative) meaning *not* (note its presence in our word "atheist," meaning *not a believer in God*). The list contains eighteen or nineteen terms depending upon whether the final term of v. 4 is reckoned as a single item or as a pair.

The key to understanding the list is the initial term, "lovers of themselves" ("utterly self-centered," Phillips). When the center of gravity in an individual shifts from God to self, a plethora of sins can spring up. Self-love leads to materialism ("greedy for money," Phillips). The accumulation of things becomes a means of gratifying self. Self-centeredness also produces people who are "boastful" ("full of big words," Phillips) and "proud" ("conceited," GNB). The two terms "emphasize boastfulness in words and thought, respectively."[26] Those who are "abusive" use scornful language in heaping injuries on others. A related word refers to those who blaspheme God (see Mark 7:22; Rev 13:5), but here people receive the brunt of the insults.

---

return of the Messiah. Paul clearly felt that such events were occurring in the breakdown of godliness in Ephesus, but he may only have been asserting that this breakdown, typical of that period between Christ's exaltation and his return, was occurring. He need not be seen as asserting that the return of Christ was just around the corner.

Ward attempts to explain why the moral breakdown and violence linked with wars can be considered as signs of the final days. He says: "The answer is that in any period of history they may not be 'the' signs but just signs. In other words the spirit of the age may have an eschatological flavor without necessarily being the herald of the actual End" (*1 & 2 Timothy & Titus*, 187).

[25] Spicq, *Saint Paul: Les Epitres Pastorales* (Paris: Gabalda, 1947), 368.

[26] Fee, *1 and 2 Timothy, Titus*, 220. The two words appear in a list together in Rom 1:30. The first term, "boastful," appears in the NT twice, both times appearing in lists of vices. The second term, "proud," appears five times, but the type of usage does not make it easy to distinguish between the two terms in meaning. The term "proud" is used in Jas 4:6 and in 1 Pet 5:5 to describe people whom God resists. Kelly says that both "express different but related aspects of the pride which springs from self-centeredness. The former has to do with words, gestures, and outward behavior, and the latter with inward feelings" (*Pastoral Epistles*, 194).

The final three terms of v. 2 and the first two of v. 3 all begin with the Greek *a*. To be "disobedient to . . . parents" suggests someone who lacks parental respect and will obviously violate the reprimands of 1 Tim 5:8. Such rebellious offspring will also be "ungrateful" ("no gratitude," NEB) and "unholy" ("irreverent," Williams). They lack all gratitude for benefits given by their parents, and they sullenly hold nothing as sacred.

3:3 The two terms with which v. 3 begins describe people who are inhuman because of their lack of family love and who are "unforgiving" ("irreconcilable," Williams) in their resistance to all overtures of reconciliation. The first term suggests that the evildoers have become almost beastlike in the breakdown of love for their kin, especially parents. There is a certain natural affection between parents and children. This term pictures those who lack even the normal compassion linking family members together. The second term pictures someone who adamantly refuses to come to terms with the conciliatory approaches of an opponent.

Continuing his picture of moral heresy in v. 3, Paul described the false teachers as slanderers who took delight in spreading rumors by malicious talk (see 1 Tim 3:11, where "malicious talkers" is the same Greek word). They lacked any semblance of "self-control" ("dissolute," Moffatt), indulged their passions, and resorted to violence. They were "brutal" ("savage," Williams); and they resembled fierce, untamed animals in their attitudes and actions. They hated the good and lacked a love for anything virtuous. This was the complete opposite of the behavior anticipated in the elders of Titus 1:8, who were to "love what is good." The final three terms ("without self-control, brutal, not lovers of the good") all have the alpha privative, denoting a negative meaning.

3:4 The heretics were "treacherous" in that they were ready to betray their friends. We need not see this as proof that they were betraying fellow Christians to antagonistic authorities during periods of persecution. They may have undertaken their treachery for personal, selfish gain. They were also "rash" ("reckless," Williams). They would stop at nothing to gain their ends and were foolhardy in their behavior. They were "conceited" ("swollen with self-importance," NEB) in that they were blinded by their pride and arrogance. They displayed the same traits against which Paul had warned in 1 Tim 3:6; 6:4.[27] Because they loved

---

[27]This list of vices represents the third of four lists that appear in the Pastorals. The other lists appear in 1 Tim 1:9-10; 6:4-5; and Titus 3:3.

Hanson feels that an anonymous pseudepigrapher has styled this list after the example in Rom 1:29-31 (*Pastoral Epistles*, 144). N. J. McEleney has given an excellent analysis of this list and other vice lists in the Pastorals, but he takes no firm position on the Pauline authorship of these lists, referring to the writer as "the biblical author" (see "Vice Lists of the Pastoral Epistles," *CBQ* 36 [1974]: 219.

The similarity of the lists in the Pastorals to those in other Pauline writings (e.g., Rom 1:29-31;

themselves, they also loved sensual pleasures. They were controlled by the quest for the thrill of pleasure. Given a choice, they would always please themselves rather than God. The substitution of pleasure and materialism for piety had led to irreligion. Barrett says that these descriptions "constitute a shocking picture of Church life, for it is part of the indictment that the sinners maintain a religious profession and in fact pass themselves off as Christian propagandists."[28]

3:5 Paul concluded with a summary of the despicable behavior of the errorists and gave a warning to Timothy. In this verse Paul made clear that he was referring his descriptions in 3:2-4 to the false teachers in Ephesus.

The summary contains two elements. First, the heretics maintained a "form of godliness." They affected its outward appearance but lacked its essence. They enjoyed arguing about religious trivia (1 Tim 1:6-7) and practiced asceticism (1 Tim 4:3), assuming that being religious proved that they were also righteous. Paul's vigorous denunciation of such hypocrisy provides a shocking warning for modern purveyors of religion who deny God's moral claims but use religious jargon.

Second, Paul indicated that they were denying the essence of Christianity. The perfect tense of "denying" (lit. "having denied") suggests that they had denied the truth of Christianity and continued to do so. Such denial was a way of life for them. For Paul there was only one solution. Timothy had to turn his back constantly on such people. The present tense of the Greek verb indicates a continuous action Timothy was to apply rigorously. He had to continue to keep away from people like this. The command did not demand a termination of all personal relations (Paul had called for kindness to all in 2:24), but it does suggest that he had to practice a separation in spirit from the actions and attitudes of the errorists.[29]

Gal 5:19-21) is a feature favoring Pauline authorship. Fee says: "The evidence speaks favorably for Pauline authorship. Such lists are a common feature, yet none closely resembles the others and each is adapted to its context—as here" (*1 and 2 Timothy, Titus*, 223).

[28]C. K. Barrett, "The Pastoral Epistles," NClB, ed. F. F. D. Sparks (London: Oxford University Press, 1963), 111.

[29]At several places in the Pastorals, Paul appealed for separation from the false teachers whom he addressed (1 Tim 4:7; 6:20; Titus 3:9-11). At the same time he also urged an effort to teach the truth even to those who are self-contradictory and deceived (see 2 Tim 2:24-26). Several features stand out in his statements. First, his general calls for separation often relate to a separation from accepting the teaching of a heretic rather than from personal contact (e.g., 1 Tim 4:7; 6:20). Second, it is likely that his appeals for rejection of individuals relate to people who are stubbornly refusing instruction and are intent on following a path of destruction (Titus 3:9-11). Those to whom Paul urged the practice of "gentleness" seem to be more open and teachable (2 Tim 2:24-26).

Ward describes the attitude Paul sought in his readers when he says: "It was not the separation of quarantine but a separateness of spirit, a freedom from contagion or infection. . . .

(2) What They Do (3:6-9)

⁶They are the kind who worm their way into homes and gain control over weak-willed women, who are loaded down with sins and are swayed by all kinds of evil desires, ⁷always learning but never able to acknowledge the truth. ⁸Just as Jannes and Jambres opposed Moses, so also these men oppose the truth—men of depraved minds, who, as far as the faith is concerned, are rejected. ⁹But they will not get very far because, as in the case of those men, their folly will be clear to everyone.

In vv. 6-7 Paul described the victims affected by the sinister activities of the false teachers. Their insidious methods were most effective among gullible women whose instability tilted them to seek new and exciting experiences. By comparing these hucksters with the Egyptian magicians of v. 8, Paul intimated that they were religious humbugs with an assured limitation to their successes (vv. 8-9).

3:6 Before Paul described the victims of the false teachers, he used two verbs in v. 6 to portray their victimizers as deceitful and ruthless in their desire for control. The verb translated "worm their way" ("some of that ilk sneak into," Berkeley) is a pejorative term that pictures the actions of the deceivers as sinister and treacherous. They had entered homes under false pretenses. Once admitted, they proceeded to "gain control" ("get . . . into their clutches," NEB). In this context the terms suggest that the false teachers had gained a complete psychological dominance over their victims.[30]

The victims of these false teachers were weak-willed women who certainly lacked spiritual insight and perhaps also moral substance. Paul's words were not a general statement about the female sex but referred specifically to the credulous women in Ephesus.

Paul's words represented a condemnation for the women in Ephesus who had permitted themselves to be deceived by clever religious propagandists. Not all the women in Ephesus were as unstable and spiritually immature as these women were (see 2 Tim 4:19), but those women who had responded to the heresy were a source of much confusion and instability in the church. Fee uses these verses as sources of information for the women about whom Paul wrote in 1 Tim 2:9-15; 3:11; and 5:3-16. He feels that Paul's reasons for forbidding the women to teach, encouraging submission to their husbands, and directing the younger widows to marry were related to the moral and spiritual conditions among these

---

Their aims, ideals and activities are not to be shared, but as persons they are to be won" (*1 & 2 Timothy & Titus*, 188-89).

[30] The latter verb can be used to describe a control or possession of something for a positive spiritual purpose as is suggested in the verb "take captive" in 2 Cor 10:5.

women.[31] For additional sources and discussion of the contemporary relevance of Paul's prohibition of female teaching, see the exegesis of 1 Tim 2:9-15 and Excursus 2: Women in Ministry.

Five features characterize Paul's statement about these female victims. First, Paul described them as "weak-willed women" ("weak and silly women," Williams). The term is a Greek diminutive, literally suggesting "little women" but more precisely showing them as easily deceived and prone to temptation. Their weakness was primarily moral, not intellectual.

Second, they were "loaded down with sins" ("overwhelmed with the weight of their sins," Williams). The verb *sōreuō* means *to heap up* and is metaphorically used to express a cumulation of sins which has become so unbearable that any solution offered is clutched at.[32]

Third, they were "swayed by all kinds of evil desires." This may refer to some sexual involvement between the false teachers and the women. It *certainly does* describe them as dominated by curiosity, novelty, and self-centeredness.

3:7 Fourth, they were "always learning" ("forever getting information," Berkeley). Hiebert notes: "In their restless quest for the new and novel they turn to every new doctrine that comes to their attention."[33] They had an insatiable curiosity about religion but little discernment to distinguish truth from error.

Fifth, they were "never able to acknowledge the truth." They traveled more and more along the path of religious bondage without coming to experience the truth that could set them free (John 8:31-36).

All five of these phrases in vv. 6-7 referred to the women in Ephesus who were being led astray by the false teachers. These women were morally weak, emotionally unstable, and forever dabbling with religious novelties.

3:8 The names Jannes and Jambres do not appear in the Old Testament, but there are references to them in Jewish, pagan, and Christian literature as two of Pharaoh's magicians who tried to demonstrate that they could work miracles as effectively as Moses (Exod 7:11; 9:11).[34] Their

---

[31]Fee, *1 and 2 Timothy, Titus*, 221-22. For a contrary opinion see P. W. Barnett, "Wives and Women's Ministry," *EQ* 61 (1989): 225-38, who doubts that the directives concerning the immature women here apply to the women addressed in 1 Tim 2:9-15. He feels that Paul's directions about the role of women in teaching (1 Tim 2:9-15) are valid today, not because a woman is unable to hold the office of a teacher but because of the "effect this incumbency would have on marriages within the church and indeed on the value of the mothering role."

[32]Guthrie, *Pastoral Epistles*, 158-59.

[33]D. E. Hiebert, *Second Timothy*, EvBC (Chicago: Moody, 1958), 88.

[34]The names appear in the *Damascus Document* 5.18, where "Jannes and his brother" are mentioned as opponents of Moses and Aaron. In Targum Pseudo-Jonathan on Exod 7:11

names may have come into the New Testament from Christian acquaintance with Jewish traditions about Moses in which these were the names given to Pharaoh's magicians. The word for "oppose" (*anthistēmi*) shows strong resistance to a person or an idea and is used in Acts 13:8 to show the resistance of Elymas the Sorcerer to the gospel. The similarity between Jannes and Jambres and the false teachers may refer to their common use of magical or occult methods. It is more likely, however, that their commonality is that both groups resisted the truth.

Paul asserted two additional statements in v. 8 about the false teachers. First, he saw them as possessing "depraved minds" ("Their minds are distorted," Phillips). That avenue through which the truth could reach the will had ceased to function. This led to Paul's second statement, the evaluation of their faith content as worthless or rejected. The term for "rejected" is used in the New Testament to describe someone whose actions or abilities prove the person unfit for spiritual usefulness (see "disqualified" in 1 Cor 9:27). It is an apt term to use in reference to false teachers whose empty professions were only a caricature of the true faith.

3:9 Paul gave a hopeful prediction of the ultimate demise of the spread of the false teachers. In 2 Tim 2:16 Paul had suggested that the heretics would increase more and more in the direction of ungodliness. Eventually the folly of the heretics would become obvious and would contribute to their defeat. The "folly" of the heretics was probably more a reference to the conduct of the heretics than to their doctrines. A sample of this conduct appears in 3:6.

The participants would indeed grow worse in their depravity (see 3:13). They could not continue to spread their views because their empty practices would be patently absurd to listeners and observers. Added exposure would contribute to their downfall. Paul may have deduced this observation from the experience of Jannes and Jambres in Exod 9:11.

Summary. Two principles emerge from Paul's description of the false teachers in this passage. First, it is obvious that character determines behavior. What we are is seen in what we do. Even though we can adjust our behavior temporarily to correspond to what is socially acceptable or in our self-interest, we will eventually show our character by what we do.

---

both names appear, and Pliny mentioned Jannes in *Natural History* 30.2.11. Origen, *Against Celsus* 4.51, discussed the pair so as to suggest that a work now lost contained stories about the exploits of Jannes and Jambres. Variant spellings also appear, such as "Johanna" for "Jannes" and "Mambres" for "Jambres."

An interesting discussion of the tendency in early Christians to name the nameless in the NT appears in B. Metzger, "Names for the Nameless in the New Testament: A Study in the Growth of Christian Tradition," *New Testament Studies: Philological, Versional, and Patristic* (Leiden: Brill, 1980), 23–45.

This fact leaves us with the challenge of allowing God to mold and alter our character.

A second principle is that the love of self (just as the love of money) produces all kinds of evil. Self-love is the basic shortcoming mentioned in the list of vices in 3:2-5. This vice leads to action in vv. 6-9 that is deceitful, determined to dominate, stubborn, and rejected by God. The best term to describe self-centered action is Paul's term "folly" (v. 9). Only God, who enables us to love him, can keep our lives from being filled with folly.

3. Sources of Strength for Endurance (3:10-17)

Paul had used a frightening picture to portray the opposition Timothy would face. Where could anyone find the strength and wisdom for resisting and overcoming such opposition? Two sources of help were the sterling example Paul had demonstrated (vv. 10-13) and the instruction of Scripture (vv. 14-17). Paul directed Timothy to consider and use the strength each resource could provide.

(1) The Example of Paul (3:10-13)

[10] **You, however, know all about my teaching, my way of life, my purpose, faith, patience, love, endurance, [11] persecutions, sufferings—what kinds of things happened to me in Antioch, Iconium and Lystra, the persecutions I endured. Yet the Lord rescued me from all of them. [12] In fact, everyone who wants to live a godly life in Christ Jesus will be persecuted, [13] while evil men and impostors will go from bad to worse, deceiving and being deceived.**

Paul introduced his word to Timothy by a personal address that literally says, "But as for you" (sy de), the same Greek phrase employed in v. 14. Timothy was familiar with Paul's life-style and his trials. Paul gave Timothy an abridged description of his life and its sufferings (vv. 10-11) followed by an explanation of the sufferings (vv. 12-13).

3:10 Paul expressed active examples of his commitment in order to urge Timothy to resolute action. In v. 11 he used examples of his passive commitment in the face of persecution and affliction. The verb "know" described Timothy as someone who had carefully traced out the events of Paul's life. It "does not imply that Timothy has always been at the side of Paul but that he has observed that life with close interest."[35] The verb is used in Luke 1:3 ("carefully investigated") to describe Luke's careful checking of the truthfulness of Christian traditions about Jesus.

---

[35]Hiebert, Second Timothy, 91.

The knowledge Timothy had gained was not theoretical but practical (cf. 1 Tim 4:6, where "followed" is the same verb translated as "know").

Paul condensed his biographical summary to seven Greek nouns in v. 10 with two additional nouns added in v. 11. In presenting these descriptions Paul was not guilty of either egotism or boasting but was drawing out lessons from his life for the benefit of his younger disciple. The "teaching" was the gospel message he had proclaimed. His "way of life" referred to those guiding principles of his life which he had demonstrated in conduct. His "purpose" was his resolve to show "single-minded commitment to Christ."[36] His "faith" described his stalwart confidence in God. The term "patience" (*makrothymia*) reflected a forbearance toward people and circumstances (4:2), and the term "love" embraced both friend and foe alike. His "endurance" (*hypomonē*) was an attitude of perseverance that controlled discouragement under trying circumstances.[37]

3:11 The difficulties Paul mentioned in v. 11 had demanded his obedience to Christ whenever he had confronted their challenge. The "persecutions" and "sufferings" involved whatever hardships Paul had endured in faithfully spreading the gospel. Timothy had not been with Paul to see his suffering in Antioch (Acts 13:48-52) and Iconium (Acts 14:1-7), but he could have personally observed Paul's trials in Lystra, his probable hometown (Acts 14:8-20; 16:1-2). Even when Timothy had been absent from Paul's side, he would have heard people discuss the events and use them as patterns of what other devoted followers of Christ could expect.

Paul concluded his observation of hardship with a reference to Ps 34:19, exclaiming that God had indeed rescued him from death and disobedience to his calling. Hendricksen notes: "The Lord ever rescues his people, frequently from death, sometimes by means of death. Either way, nothing ever separates them from his love (Rom 8:38-39)."[38] Paul's words reminded Timothy of the certainty of suffering, but they also contained a promise of divine protection.[39]

3:12 What did Paul's experiences teach about the expectations of the godly servant of Christ? Godly followers of Christ should expect to

---

[36]Fee, *1 and 2 Timothy, Titus*, 226.

[37]Huther says that the difference between the terms "patience" and "endurance" is "that the former is applied to one who is not irritated, the latter to one who is not discouraged" (*Epistles to Timothy and Titus*, 252).

[38]Hendricksen, *I-II Timothy and Titus*, NTC (Grand Rapids: Baker, 1957), 293.

[39]Paul's words to Timothy were not a promise that God would snatch him out of all difficulties. It was true that Paul had been exempted from some trials (e.g., Acts 18:9-11; 2 Cor 1:8-11). However, the lengthy list of sufferings in 2 Cor 11:23-33 suggests that Paul was not always removed from his trials and difficulties. Even though Paul had not been removed from the difficulties, his life had been spared; and God had preserved him from spiritual compromise and fickle commitment in all of his actions.

suffer. Paul's experiences were not isolated or exceptional. These words were an emphatic appeal for Timothy to join Paul in suffering.[40]

Persecution "may vary in degree and take different forms in different countries and in different ages, but the basic hostility of the world to the godly man remains unchanged."[41] Christians will suffer because the world is hostile to the kingdom of God. Both Christ (Matt 5:11-12; Mark 8:34) and Paul (2 Cor 12:9-10; 1 Thess 3:4) had prepared their followers to anticipate such hardship. Paul's words about the expectation of suffering were frightening to a timorous disciple. They are also a reminder to every Christian to expect opposition for devotion to Jesus. Such forewarning allows the thoughtful Christian to be armed with commitment for spiritual battle.

The phrase "in Christ Jesus" carries the usual Pauline meaning of union with Christ. The believer experiences fellowship with Christ in suffering as a part of the mystical union with him.

3:13 Paul's explanation for the certainty of suffering was that evil would grow in its intensity. Paul described the false teachers as "evil men" and branded them as religious swindlers or "impostors." Although the word "imposter" is used outside the New Testament to refer to a dabbler in the occult or a wizard, Paul may have been designating them as impostors, not magicians. The term does link them with Jannes and Jambres, whom he had mentioned in 3:8. The only progress of these ungodly heretics was in the direction of evil. They succeeded in deceiving others and also in losing their own ability to distinguish between truth and falsehood. They were to be pitied!

Paul's description of the progress of evil in v. 13 outlined its growth in intensity and in its effect on the false teachers themselves. They would progress more deeply into bondage. Observers could see through their folly (see 3:9). The heretics themselves would be caught up in their own practices as unwilling slaves (John 8:34). They would deceive others, but sadly they themselves were deceived.

Paul introduced an implied contrast between the destinies of the persecuted believers and the persecuting false teachers. The persecutions and difficulties of the godly made it appear as if the future were frightening, but they were in reality bound for glory (Rom 8:28-30). The evil persecutors, who appeared to be in charge of events that were going on, were progressing from bad to worse and were heading blindly for destruction.

---

[40]The translation "in fact" represents an emphatic usage of the Greek conjunction καί. Other passages that use the conjunction in this way include Phil 4:10 ("indeed") and 2 Cor 11:1 ("already").

[41]Hiebert, *Second Timothy*, 94.

(2) The Enrichment of Scripture (3:14-17)

[14] But as for you, continue in what you have learned and have become convinced of, because you know those from whom you learned it, [15] and how from infancy you have known the holy Scriptures, which are able to make you wise for salvation through faith in Christ Jesus. [16] All Scripture is God-breathed and is useful for teaching, rebuking, correcting and training in righteousness, [17] so that the man of God may be thoroughly equipped for every good work.

Paul penned a second personal appeal to Timothy beginning with the phrase "But as for you." The repetition of the phrase (see v. 10) marks out the beginning of a new emphasis. In v. 14 he focused on the people who had been influential in instructing Timothy. In vv. 15-17 he discussed the usefulness of Scripture in providing spiritual enrichment. The combined impact of his godly teachers and his inspired source of knowledge in Scripture was to promote endurance in Timothy.

3:14 Timothy had learned the gospel and its demands from a compassionate cadre of teachers. They had not only taught him its outline but had assured him of its reality and truthfulness. Timothy's need was not to search out new novelties on which he might squander his energies but to remain in the truths he had learned.

The term "continue" (menō) is the same term translated "hold to" or "remain" in John 8:31; 15:5-6. It demands more than merely continuing in orthodoxy. It called for a commitment to live and abide in what Timothy had learned.

An incentive for remaining in these truths was the personal impact of his teachers upon him. The reference to the "whom" who had instructed Timothy is a plural pronoun in the Greek. Paul was thinking of the moral impact made on Timothy's life by his mother Eunice and grandmother Lois (1:5) as well as by Paul himself. Perhaps the term also included a reference to other godly Christian instructors such as some of the "many witnesses" of 2 Tim 2:2. As White observes, "The truths for which St. Paul is contending were commended to Timothy by the sanction of the best and noblest personalities whom he had ever known or heard of."[42] That fact alone should have led Timothy to continue to stand fast in the truths of the gospel.

3:15 Paul reminded Timothy of his inspired source of instruction in the Scriptures. Paul knew that Timothy had received instruction in the Scriptures from the time of childhood. Jewish parents normally began instructing children in the Scriptures from their fifth year. Timothy's

---

[42] N. J. D. White, *The First and Second Epistles to Timothy and the Epistle to Titus*, ed. W. R. Nicoll (New York: Doran, n.d.), 174.

godly background would have assured that he began the study at a proper age.[43]

Paul used a rare term in his reference to the "holy Scriptures." Used only here in the New Testament, the phrase literally means *sacred writings* (*hiera grammata*).[44] Josephus used the identical term in referring to the Old Testament.[45] The phrase may have been used to stress the sacred character of Timothy's learning as an utter contrast to the mindless heresies of the false teachers (see 3:8).[46] Paul's use of the term was a reference to the Old Testament writings. He was not suggesting that a part of Timothy's childhood instruction involved the New Testament.

The aim of the content of the sacred writings is to relate God's saving purpose in Christ. Timothy's study of the Scriptures had grounded him in that wisdom and enlightenment that leads to faith in Jesus Christ. The Scriptures lead to salvation but only as they point to Christ. The Scriptures themselves do not provide salvation, but they do point to the Savior who can provide it. The phrase "through faith in Jesus Christ" shows how the Scriptures make individuals wise. They enlighten them to the necessity for faith in Jesus Christ.

The instruction of the Scriptures about salvation relates to two different areas. First, the Scriptures describe the process of conversion. They outline the method by which individuals can be saved (cf. Rom 5:9). The Scriptures also show believers how they are to live, grow, and serve. The Scriptures will provide directions for believers who want to work out their own salvation (cf. Phil 2:12). The themes are present in both the Old Testament and New Testament Scriptures. Paul and his early readers, following a Christological interpretation, thought of the Old Testament as the Scriptures that make us "wise for salvation" (cf. Luke 24:25-27,44-49; John 5:39).

3:16 Paul's observation about the effect of Scripture in Timothy's life led him to make an assertion about the inspiration and usefulness of

---

[43]Josephus, *Against Apion* 1.60, comments about the Jewish emphasis on training children: "Above all we pride ourselves on the education of our children, and regard as the most essential task in life the observance of our laws and of the pious practices, based thereupon, which we have inherited."

This instruction extended also to women as indicated in the compliment paid to the parents of the Jewish heroine Susanna: "Her parents also were righteous, and taught their daughter according to the law of Moses" (*Susanna* 3). Additional information on Jewish education of children appears in A. Edersheim, *The Life and Times of Jesus the Messiah* (Grand Rapids: Eerdmans, 1956), 1:226-34.

[44]The term "writings" (translated as either "what he wrote" or "learning") appears without the adjective in John 5:47; 7:15, where it refers to Scripture. The usual term for Scripture is the Greek αἱ γραφαί (lit. "the Scriptures"). The singular word "Scripture" appears in 3:16.

[45]Josephus, *Antiquities* 10.210.

[46]Guthrie, *Pastoral Epistles*, 162.

Scripture. We must not view Paul as attempting to inform Timothy of the inspiration of Scripture. Timothy had heard this truth since childhood. Paul was reminding Timothy that Scripture was profitable and "that the basis of its profitableness lies in its inspired character."[47] For additional discussion on the subject of the inspiration of Scripture, see Excursus 5: Inspiration, Infallibility, Inerrancy, and Authority.

Four questions confront us as we begin an exegesis of this important verse. The four questions stem from the statement "All Scripture is God-breathed."

First, to what did Paul refer by his use of "Scripture"? The term "Scripture" (*graphē*) is usually a reference to the Old Testament (just as is "holy Scriptures" in the preceding verse).[48] Paul's reference to the "holy Scriptures" in 3:15 is clearly a statement about the Old Testament. He continued to refer to the Old Testament in 3:16.

Second, what is the meaning of the phrase "all Scripture"? Did he refer to (1) an individual passage of Scripture, (2) the entire Old Testament, or (3) all parts of Scripture? It is clear from the context that Paul was not merely referring to a single passage of Scripture. He was making either a collective reference to all of Scripture or a partitive reference to each passage of Scripture. The Greek phrase (*pasa graphē*) lacks the definite article, and this would normally suggest that the reading "every Scripture" is preferable (e.g., Jas 1:17, *pasa dosis agathē*, "every good gift"). However, the collective sense of "all" sometimes occurs even in texts without the article (e.g., Acts 2:36, "all" [*pas*] Israel). Kelly opts for the translation "every,"[49] but Kaiser feels that the emphatic position of the adjective *pas* in the sentence requires the translation of "all."[50] To this writer the translation "all" seems preferable, but the meaning comes out similarly with either translation. If we affirm that each part of Scripture is inspired, we come eventually to assert that its entire content is inspired.

Third, should we read the opening phrase as "all inspired Scripture is also useful" or as "all Scripture is inspired and useful"? The NIV, Williams, KJV, and GNB take the latter option; and ASV takes the former. Since reputable translations take opposing sides in the interpretations, it is obvious that the decision is difficult. It seems preferable to take the

---

[47]Ibid., 164.

[48]Peter used the term γραφάς in reference to the writings of Paul in 2 Pet 3:16. The evidence seems to suggest that he was putting Paul's writing on the level of OT Scripture although not all evangelicals follow this interpretation. For a discussion of the issue, see M. Green, *The Second Epistle of Peter and the Epistle of Jude*, TNTC (Grand Rapids: Eerdmans, 1968), 147-49.

[49]For additional insight into the issue, see Kelly, 202.

[50]W. C. Kaiser, *Toward Rediscovering the Old Testament* (Grand Rapids: Zondervan, 1987), 27.

latter translation, "Each Scripture is inspired and useful." Kelly lists four reasons for this translation. (1) It seems natural, since the phrase does not contain a verb in the Greek, to take the two adjectives in the same way. (2) If "inspired" were to be translated before "Scripture," it would be natural to place it here in the Greek text, but this is not the case. (3) The phrase "each inspired Scripture" contains a hint that certain passages of Scripture are not inspired, which Paul certainly did not desire to assert. (4) The construction of this phrase exactly parallels that of 1 Tim 4:4 ("everything God created is good and nothing is to be rejected"), and the translation of that passage seems suitable here.[51] Paul was not raising the question of the inspiration of certain passages of Scripture. He affirmed the usefulness of Scripture based on its inspiration.

Fourth, what is the meaning of the adjective "God-breathed"? Is it active in meaning, suggesting that all Scripture has an inspiring effect? Is it passive in meaning, suggesting that all Scripture has its origin in God, is the product of the breath of God? The Greek word (*theopneustos*) contains a suffix (*tos*), which frequently suggests a passive meaning (e.g., *agapētos*, "loved [by God]," Rom 1:7). The term in our text is passive in its meaning.[52] The idea the term presents is that God has breathed his character into Scripture so that it is inherently inspired. Paul was not asserting that the Scriptures are inspiring in that they breathe information about God into us, even though the statement is true. The Scriptures owe their origin and distinctiveness to God himself. This is the abiding character of Scripture.[53] In affirming the inspiration of Scripture, Paul declared the fact of inspiration without discussing the process by which inspiration took place.

The affirmation of the inspiration of Scripture leads to a discussion of its usefulness. Paul described four uses to which Scripture can be put.

First, it is useful for teaching. This suggests that Scripture is a positive source of Christian doctrine. Paul used the term "teaching" (*didaskalia*) fifteen times in the Pastorals, and in the remainder of the New Testament it occurs only six times. (In the Pastorals, cf. 1 Tim 1:10; 4:1,6,13,16; 5:17; 6:1,3; 2 Tim 3:10,16; 4:3; Titus 1:9; 2:1,7; 2:10. In the remainder of the New Testament, cf. Matt 15:9; Mark 7:7; Rom 12:7; 15:4; Eph 4:14; Col 2:22.) Because of the prominence of heresy among his readers, Paul emphasized the importance of sound teaching. In commending the Scriptures as a source for teaching, Paul was actually commending the Old

---

[51]Kelly, *Pastoral Epistles*, 203.

[52]Corroborating evidence for this viewpoint comes from the use of the passive in 2 Pet 1:21 to describe men "carried along by the Holy Spirit" as they spoke God's word in Scripture.

[53]For additional discussion on the meaning of θεόπνευστος ("God-breathed"), see B. B. Warfield, *The Inspiration and Authority of the Bible* (Philadelphia: Presbyterian and Reformed, 1948), 245-96.

Testament as a source of doctrine. Such doctrines as creation (Gen 1–2), the fall of man (Gen 3), and the nature of the atonement (Isa 53) have a foundational statement in the Old Testament.[54]

A second use for Scripture is for "rebuking." The term (*elegmos*) may refer to a rebuke that exposes the errors of false teachers. It may also refer to the reproof in our personal lives. Whether the reproof is personal or doctrinal, Scripture can show sinners their failures, clarify the point of the mistake, and lead them to a new sense of peace and wholeness.

The third use of Scripture is to provide correction. The terms "correcting" and "training" show a positive use for Scripture. Negatively, the Scripture is helpful for convicting the misguided and disobedient of their errors and restoring them to the right paths. The term "correcting," used only here in the New Testament, suggests that Scripture helps individuals to restore their doctrine or personal practice to a right state before God. Correction is one means God uses in order to restore people to spiritual positions they have forfeited. This emphasis frequently appears in the wilderness experience of Israel (see Deut 8:2-3,5).

A final use of Scripture is to provide moral training that leads to righteous living. This positive purpose is expressed by a term (*paideia*) that also appears in Eph 6:4 ("training"). There it denotes a system of discipline used by a parent to develop Christian character in a child. Here it describes a system of discipline in Scripture that leads to a holy life-style.

Paul's words here have affirmed both the inspiration and the usefulness of Scripture. The relationship between inspiration, authority, and inerrancy are much discussed in contemporary Evangelicalism. For an elaboration of the subject of inspiration and inerrancy, see the following excursus, "Inspiration, Infallibility, Inerrancy, and Authority."

3:17 Paul outlined the result of the use of Scripture.[55] He used "man of God" as an oblique reference to Timothy. The statement in the verse holds true of any Christian leader. The phrase "thoroughly equipped" conceals the fact that Paul used an adjective he elaborated with a participial clause. The adjective (*artios*) describes someone who is "in fit shape or condition."[56] The participial phrase described him as furnished completely to do whatever God called him to perform. The use of the Greek perfect tense for "equipped" suggests that this is an abiding condition. If Timothy would nurture his spiritual life in the Scriptures that he would

---

[54] Kaiser, *Rediscovering the Old Testament*, 29.

[55] Kaiser defends the designation of this verse as a result clause by suggesting that the four phrases of v. 16 introduced by "for" (πρός) represent the purpose of the use of Scripture. He feels that another purpose clause is unnecessary and that this clause fits better when it is seen as a result clause (*Rediscovering the Old Testament*, 31-32).

[56] Lenski, *The Interpretation of St. Paul's Epistles to the Colossians, to the Thessalonians, to Timothy, to Titus, and to Philemon* (Columbus, Oh.: Wartburg, 1946), 847.

use in his ministry, he would be fully qualified and prepared to undertake whatever tasks God put before him. What a tragedy for any Christian to be labeled as spiritually unprepared for a task when the means of instruction and preparation are readily at hand! With these words Paul prepared the way to give a final personal charge to Timothy in 4:1-5.

Summary. Christians can receive strength for the Christian pilgrimage from two sources. First, they can observe the lives of other believers. Paul urged Timothy to look at his life in order to learn and apply Christian truth (vv. 10-13). Timothy could observe two features from Paul's life. He could learn that persecution was certain (v. 12). He could also be reminded of divine strength and protection (v. 11). Even though hardship was certain, divine strength was even more pervasive.

The second source of strength for the Christian pilgrimage is Scripture. Paul focused on three contributions Scripture can provide for the believer. The Scriptures contain the explanation of God's plan of salvation (v. 15). They contain an outline of doctrine and truth that support the plan of salvation (v. 16). The Scriptures also provide warning to keep Christians from wandering afield from God's will.

Those who obey the commands and respond to the promises of Scripture can find the strength to live a life of such arresting quality that it can encourage and enlighten others.

EXCURSUS 6: INSPIRATION, INFALLIBILITY, INERRANCY, AND AUTHORITY. Theologians have frequently distinguished between the concepts of revelation, inspiration, and illumination.[57] Revelation is the process by which God communicates to human beings a knowledge of himself. Paul described himself as a recipient of such revelation in Eph 3:3. The term "inspiration" relates to that influence of the Holy Spirit by which human beings become organs to communicate the truth of God in words to others. The process of writing Scripture is an example of inspiration. The term "illumination" refers to the work of the Holy Spirit which enables a believer to understand and apply divine truth (John 14:26). The three concepts are related to one another because the concept of revelation, the disclosure of truth, demands inspiration to guarantee its accurate disclosure. The concept of inspiration demands the concept of illumination in order for the written record to be understood properly. The terms "inspiration" and "revelation" appear in Scripture. The term "illumination" does not appear in Scripture with the theological meaning given above, but the concept of illumination is thoroughly biblical.

Sometimes the term "inspiration" is used without the more precise theological meaning given earlier. When we say today that a person is

---

[57] R. A. Finlayson, "Contemporary Ideas of Inspiration," *Revelation and the Bible*, ed. C. F. H. Henry (Grand Rapids: Baker, 1958), 222.

"inspired," we do not suggest that the person has become the organ for infallible communication of a message from God. Individuals may be inspiring in that they speak with moving emotion, but the process whereby the Holy Spirit operates within human beings to produce Scripture is not occurring today. That process became complete when the New Testament was written.

Three views of inspiration are frequently discussed in relationship to Evangelicals. These are (1) a dictation theory, which asserts that God spoke through the writers as though they were dictating machines; (2) verbal plenary inspiration in which the result of inspiration is that God produced in all Scripture the very words he wanted; (3) a dynamic view in which the thoughts of Scripture are viewed as inspired but the choice of words is left to the individual writers. Many evangelical Christians hold to the second view, a position advocated by B. B. Warfield in his classic writing *The Inspiration and Authority of the Bible*.[58] No respected Evangelicals maintain that God dictated the words of Scripture. The dynamic view of inspiration is discussed by D. M. Beegle in *Scripture, Tradition, and Infallibility*.[59]

The fact that the Bible is inspired by God leads us to assert that the Bible is infallible, inerrant, and authoritative.[60] The term "infallible" suggests that the Bible does not mislead, is a sure, reliable guide, and is fully trustworthy in all matters about which it speaks. Some scholars limit the term "infallible" to spiritual, religious, or redemptive themes; but it is difficult to separate trustworthiness in historical matters from trustworthiness in issues of theology. Also, any errors in the field of history would undermine the confidence of the reader in the theological trustworthiness of Scripture. It is better to find the Bible to be a sure, safe guide even in issues that touch on history and related issues of truth.[61]

The term "inerrant" suggests that the Bible is free from all falsehood or mistakes, and it provides a safeguard for the confidence that Scripture is reliable in all of its assertions. Some evangelical Christians use the terms "infallible" and "inerrant" in almost a synonymous sense. Others distinguish between them by linking the term "infallible" more closely with theological truth and the term "inerrant" more closely with historical truth. Two features about the affirmation of inerrancy are important.

---

[58]Warfield taught at Princeton Theological Seminary, 1887-1921, and this volume is a reprint edition of his original work. He discusses at length the concepts of revelation and inspiration.

[59]*Scripture, Tradition, and Infallibility* (Grand Rapids: Eerdmans, 1973), 225-41. Beegle uses the term "content inspiration" instead of "dynamic inspiration."

[60]A more complete discussion of this subject appears in "The Chicago Statement on Biblical Inerrancy," *JETS* 21 (1978): 289-96.

[61]For a fuller discussion of the ideas of infallibility, inerrancy, and authority, see I. H. Marshall, *Biblical Inspiration* (Grand Rapids: Eerdmans, 1982), 49-73.

First, we who affirm inerrancy must realize that the Bible sometimes uses approximations (e.g., Mark 9:2, "six days" and Luke 9:28, "eight days"), irregularities of spelling (e.g., some manuscripts of Matt 27:46, "Eli" and Mark 15:34, "Eloi"), and observational descriptions of nature (Matt 5:45, "he causes his sun to rise"). These and other related features do not negate an affirmation of inerrancy.

Second, an affirmation of inerrancy by an individual is no complete guarantee of full orthodoxy or godliness. Some cultic religious groups, who question or deny correct views of Christ's person, have very high views of Scripture. Also, we who hold to inerrancy must always hold the truth in love (Eph 4:15). It is possible to negate orthodox doctrine by unorthodox lovelessness.

An assertion of the authority of Scripture is an outgrowth of an affirmation of inspiration. Evangelicals who hold to the authority of Scripture do so because they feel that the Scripture is truth. They also realize that the authority of Scripture is derived by virtue of its inspiration by God. Some Evangelicals who hold to the authority of Scripture are reluctant to affirm inerrancy. Evangelicals hold to the authority of Scripture because they recognize that they cannot find out the truth by themselves. They believe that God must reveal the truth to them, and they feel that the locus of that revelation is Scripture. We who hold to the authority of Scripture turn to the Scripture for statements of our beliefs and practices.

Paul's affirmation of the inspiration of Scripture in 2 Tim 3:16 provides us a statement of the divine origin of Scripture. His statement encourages us to turn to Scripture with the confidence that it provides an infallible, inerrant guide for our beliefs and practices. Our affirmation of this high view of Scripture provides us the challenge of obeying Scripture in all of its parts.

A Bibliography on Inspiration, Infallibility, Inerrancy, and Authority. Baptists have long affirmed the inspiration of Scripture, and this affirmation has led them to turn to it for their doctrines and practices. In 1888 Basil Manly, then a professor at the Southern Baptist Theological Seminary, wrote *The Bible Doctrine of Inspiration.* It recently has been republished (1985) by Gano Books of Harrisonburg, Virginia. A generation ago J. I. Packer authored an excellent defense of the inerrancy and infallibility of Scripture in his *"Fundamentalism" and the Word of God* (Grand Rapids: Eerdmans, 1958). In the same year C. Henry edited *Revelation and the Bible* (Grand Rapids: Baker, 1958), a collection of Evangelical thought on the subject of revelation, inspiration, and authority.

During the last fifteen years a spate of books and articles by Evangelicals on the subject of inspiration, inerrancy, and authority has appeared. H. Ridderbos, a European scholar from a Dutch Reformed background, has authored *Studies in Scripture and Its Authority* (Grand Rapids: Eerdmans, 1978). In the same year a group of Evangelical scholars meeting in session in Chicago, Illinois, authored the "Chicago Statement on Biblical Inerrancy," a contemporary affirmation on the subject of inerrancy (see "The Chicago Statement on Biblical Inerrancy," *JETS* 20 [1978]: 289-96). British Evangelical I. H. Marshall has offered an excellent analysis of contemporary discussions on the relationship of inspiration to authority in his *Biblical Inspiration* (Grand Rapids: Eerdmans, 1983). Canadian biblical scholar C. Pinnock, who formerly taught at New Orleans Baptist Theological Seminary, has authored *The Scripture Principle* (San Francisco: Harper & Row, 1984). Three collections of articles on the subject of Scripture and inerrancy are *Inerrancy and Common Sense*, ed. R. Nicole and J. R. Michaels (Grand Rapids: Baker, 1980), authored by the faculty of Gordon-Conwell Theological Seminary; *Scripture and Truth*, ed. D. A. Carson and J. D. Woodbridge (Grand Rapids: Zondervan, 1983); and *Authority and Interpretation: A Baptist Perspective*, ed. D. Garrett and R. Melick (Grand Rapids: Baker, 1986). Southern Baptist Theological Seminary President R. Honeycutt has authored "Biblical Authority: A Treasured Heritage!" *Review and Expositor* 83 (1986): 605-22.

4. A Charge for Consistent Behavior (4:1-5)

In this section Paul continued an appeal for doctrinal soundness that began in 2:14. He underscored Timothy's special role in thwarting the advance of heresy in Ephesus. Paul outlined the basis of the charge in v. 1 and delivered a ministry-related charge to Timothy in v. 2. He explained a reason for the charge in vv. 3-4 and repeated directives of a mostly personal nature in v. 5. The intensity of Paul's feeling is evident from the use of nine imperatives in this section. Five of these appear with machine-gun precision in v. 2, and four others are in v. 5.

(1) Basis of the Charge (4:1)

[1] In the presence of God and of Christ Jesus, who will judge the living and the dead, and in view of his appearing and his kingdom, I give you this charge:

4:1 Paul grounded his charge to Timothy in four realities. The first two of these are God the Father and Christ Jesus the Son. Summoning Timothy into the majestic presence of the Father and reminding him of Christ's role as judge, Paul prepared Timothy to shoulder the duties of his ministerial office. The "living" are those who will be alive at the time of Christ's return, and the "dead" are those who will experience a resurrection to a personal meeting with the Lord (1 Thess 4:16-18).

Two other realities that pressed Timothy into consistently active commitment were the return of Christ and the eternal kingdom he will establish at that time.[62] The term "appearing" (*epiphaneia*) is used in 1:10 in reference to the incarnation, but in 4:8; 1 Tim 6:14; and in Titus 2:13 it describes Christ's second coming. There is a sense in which the kingdom of Christ is a present reality (see Col 1:13), but the emphasis on the judgment of Christ locates the beginning of this "kingdom" at the time of his return.

The solemn language resembles Paul's statements in 1 Tim 5:21; 6:13. The fact that all believers including Timothy will give an account at Christ's coming (see 2 Cor 5:10) prepared Timothy to shoulder the demanding duties of ministry in Ephesus. Because Paul viewed his departure from the scene as near, he passed the baton of the office into the hands of his younger colleague.

The phrase "the living and the dead" was frequently used among Christians to describe the future judgment (e.g., Acts 10:42; 1 Pet 4:5). The terms referred to those who were physically alive or dead. The statement emphasized that no one would escape divine judgment. The dead would be raised for judgment, and the living would also face the divine tribunal.

Both believers and unbelievers will be included among the living and the dead. The judgment of unbelievers will involve a determination of eternal destiny (see Rev 20:11-15). The judgment of believers will not determine eternal destiny but will concern itself with an evaluation of works for the purpose of recognition or reward (see 1 Cor 3:1-15; 2 Cor 5:9-10).

(2) Timothy's Charge to Ministry (4:2)

²Preach the Word; be prepared in season and out of season; correct, rebuke and encourage—with great patience and careful instruction.

4:2 Five aorist imperatives in this verse set forth commands with the crisp forcefulness of a military order. The first command, "Preach the Word," is the basis for all others. The command urged Timothy to declare the gospel.[63] That was the word on which he had to focus. Every com-

---

[62]The reading of the KJV ("at his appearing and his kingdom") is based on a variant text that presents the Greek preposition "at" (κατά) instead of the conjunction "and" (καί). Many modern translations (NIV, Williams) omit the preposition, accept the conjunction, and regard the pair of nouns as the accusative with a verb of oath-taking. Verbs implying an oath sometimes take a noun in the accusative to indicate the basis on which the oath is made. Paul fortified his charge to Timothy by reference to the glorious realities of the return of Jesus and the kingdom which he will establish.

[63]Many American Evangelicals use the term "the word of God" as a reference to the words of Scripture. In the Pastorals the term "word," "word of God," or "word of truth" is

mand that follows in this verse told Timothy how he should proceed about the task of preaching the word. To "preach" does not imply that an ordained minister is to stand behind a stately pulpit and expound Scripture. It called Timothy to a public heralding of the gospel message, whether done in a mass meeting or person-to-person. An example of the "Word" Timothy was to declare is found in 1 Tim 1:15. The following four commands indicate how Timothy's heralding the truth was to be carried out.

First, Timothy was to stand "prepared in season and out of season" ("press it home on all occasions, convenient or inconvenient," NEB). The command implies that each Christian leader must always be on duty and take advantage of every opportunity for service. Paul urged Timothy to stand by his message. The reference is probably to all of the varied tasks of ministry and not merely to the work of preaching. The phrase "in season and out of season" may point either to Timothy or to his listeners. If the former is true, then Paul was saying that Timothy should stay with the task whether or not he felt like it (see 2 Tim 1:6-7). If the latter is true, Paul urged Timothy to declare the truth whether or not his hearers found it a convenient time to listen. In light of Paul's words in vv. 3-4, the latter reference is probably what Paul intended. We should not apply the command so as to violate Jesus' warning in Matt 7:6, but we should realize that the occasion is always "seasonable" for proclaiming the gospel.

It is not certain that Paul intended this, but his next three imperatives may refer respectively to intellect, conscience, and will. Timothy was to correct error by the use of reasoned argument. He was to rebuke a straying conscience whenever the need appeared. He was to give hope to the fainthearted by providing tender encouragement in the face of discouraging opposition.

Paul qualified the manner of Timothy's obedience by use of the phrase "with great patience and careful instruction." He had to use patience to prevent the display of a grating anger or a tendency to quit under pressure. (Cf. 2:24.) To make the correction and rebuke profitable, it must be accompanied by sound, reasonable teaching. Guthrie observes: "Christian reproof without the grace of long-suffering has often led to a harsh, censorious attitude intensely harmful to the cause of Christ. . . . To rebuke without instruction is to leave the root cause of error untouched."[64]

---

frequently a reference to the gospel. In the following passages from the Pastorals, this is the usual meaning of the term: 1 Tim 5:17; 2 Tim 1:13; 2:9; 2:15; Titus 1:3; 2:5. The term "gospel" has a wider reference than a mere explanation of the plan of salvation. It refers to the message of salvation along with the truths and moral demands that accompany it and support it.

[64] Guthrie, *Pastoral Epistles*, 167.

(3) Reason for the Charge (4:3-4)

[3]For the time will come when men will not put up with sound doctrine. Instead, to suit their own desires, they will gather around them a great number of teachers to say what their itching ears want to hear. [4]They will turn their ears away from the truth and turn aside to myths.

Paul gave a stern charge to Timothy in declaring the truth because even professing Christendom would increase its appetite for error rather than for truth. Only sturdy pastors can put up with such unstable congregations. Paul foresaw future times that would be even less favorable spiritually than his own, but the germ of stubborn resistance to the truth was present in his day (2 Tim 3:6-8). The future difficulties would build upon the foundation of present opposition to the gospel.

4:3 Paul described three features that would develop as evidence of a restless craving for novelty. First, listeners would no longer "put up with sound doctrine" ("listen to wholesome teaching," Williams). They would find the content and demands of the gospel unpalatable to them. Second, they would amass teachers "to suit their own desires." They would pack the pulpits of their churches with preachers who would tell them only what they desired to hear. Third, they would do this because they wanted only to satisfy the "itching" in their ears. This description refers to people who crave spicy bits of information due to mere curiosity. This statement explains the reason for which people have gathered around them teachers who suit their desires. They have a desire to dabble with novelty. They covet new, fashionable ideas and long for the excitement of having their ears teased by the satisfying but harmless mumbling of pseudoscholarship. Such speakers toy with the minds of the hearers but leave the intellect uninformed, the conscience unchallenged, and the will set in a direction away from God.

It is important to recognize that Paul was speaking these words to believers. In 2 Tim 3:6-9,13 Paul had described the actions of false teachers. Now he warned that even professing believers would feel the influence of this wanderlust for unfamiliar ideas and the unbeaten moral path.

4:4 Paul outlined in this verse two results of spiritual wandering. First, the listeners would turn away from hearing the truth of the gospel (see 2 Tim 2:18). Second, they would "turn aside to myths." The verb translated "turn aside" is a strong term used medically to describe wrenching a limb out of joint.[65] The term "myths" is a reference to all

---

[65]Hiebert, *Second Timothy*, 107. See also the discussion in *The Vocabulary of the Greek Testament*, ed. J. H. Moulton and G. Milligan (1930 ed.). The verb also appears in 1 Tim 1:6; 5:15; 6:20; Heb 12:13.

those religious errors that can flood the mind of the listeners because they desire to turn away from the truth (see the discussion on 1 Tim 1:4). Because they looked for someone to soothe the itch rather than to satisfy the thirst, they would leave the truth without an awareness of their desertion. Many who have turned from a commitment to the gospel in our time fall within the description of these words. This verse represents Paul's last reference in 2 Timothy to the false teachers.

(4) Timothy's Personal Charge (4:5)

⁵But you, keep your head in all situations, endure hardship, do the work of an evangelist, discharge all the duties of your ministry.

4:5 Paul opened his personal appeal to Timothy with a pointed statement, "But you" ("As for you," RSV).[66] In contrast to those listeners who have itching ears, Timothy was to respond with spiritual intelligence. Paul indicated the nature of Timothy's response by issuing four quick imperatives, the first in the present tense and the other three in the aorist.

"Keep your head in all situations" called Timothy to live continually in a state of alertness as he met heretical teaching. The Greek present tense underscores the need for continuous alertness. While other people were racing off in an empty quest for trendy religious innovations, Timothy was to be composed and self-possessed. The alertness Timothy was to practice was not merely a calmness of spirit but an ability to be watchful and cautious with reference to the false teaching around him.

In remaining composed, Timothy would face hardship; but he was to endure it without flinching. Paul had warned Timothy about suffering in 1:8; 2:3; and 3:12, and he would describe his own suffering for the gospel in 4:6-8.

"The work of an evangelist" involved spreading the gospel. This was a function of Timothy's work as a pastor and not a special office. The noun "evangelist" appears also in Acts 21:8 and Eph 4:11. The term does not establish itself in reference to a special class of church officers because "it was so evidently the duty of every Christian to 'spread the Gospel' that the existence of a special class of 'evangelists' would have seemed otiose."[67]

Although it is true that some Christians have the gift of evangelism more obviously than others, that fact must not discourage active sharing of the gospel by all believers. The Great Commission (Matt 28:19-20) and the example of the Book of Acts make clear that witnessing is not simply a responsibility for ordained leaders but for all believers. No

---

[66]This is the same expression we have earlier seen in 3:10,14.
[67]Barrett, *The Pastoral Epistles*, 117.

single spiritual obligation is more natural for committed believers or more important than the practice of this conviction. Although he recognizes the significance of the work of the apostles in spreading the gospel, M. Green says, "It was axiomatic that every Christian was called on to be a witness to Christ, not only by life but by lip."[68] Such is Christ's desire for the church of the twentieth and the twenty-first centuries.

Timothy was to "discharge all the duties" of his ministry by filling his work to the brim with those tasks on which Paul had urged him to focus. The Greek word for "ministry" refers to "service for the Lord," a general reference to all kinds of work in the name of Christ and for the help of believers. It does not have the specialized connotation of our modern term "the ministry."

With these words Paul concluded this charge to Timothy. He would outline his own final testimony in 4:6-8. Paul had completed the great race of service for Christ, but Timothy was in the midst of a torrid battle.

Summary. In these verses, Paul presented a foundation, a command, an explanation, and a reminder. The foundation for Paul's words to Timothy was the awareness that he had to answer God for his discharge of his responsibilities (v. 1). This recognition of accountability to God would provide Timothy a jarring incentive to obey. The command Paul gave was to continue to preach the gospel no matter how stubborn and indifferent the opposition (v. 2). Christians have no alternative plan for carrying out God's work other than declaring the gospel. The explanation Paul gave for his insistence on continued preaching was that some listeners would refuse to hear God's message. Indifference by the listeners must not be permitted to shut off the proclamation of the gospel by believers. The reminder Paul gave was that Timothy was to remain alert and watchful of opposition but endure all necessary afflictions in spreading the gospel.

Christians committed to declaring God's message to indifferent audiences can expect God's strength, power, and ultimate blessing.

5. Reward for Self-sacrifice (4:6-8)

When Paul penned 1 Timothy, he hoped to see Timothy soon; but he was prepared for the possibility of delay (1 Tim 3:14-15). In 2 Timothy Paul again confronted the heresy that had troubled him in 1 Timothy, and he also hoped to see Timothy soon. However, in vv. 6-8 he injected a new feature for Timothy's consideration: the expectation of his approaching death. This anticipation gave Paul an added sense of urgency in the charge he had just completed (4:1-5). Paul's testimony in this passage provided an additional motivation that could spur Timothy to continued

---

[68]M. Green, *Evangelism in the Early Church* (London: Hodder and Stoughton, 1970), 175.

obedience. Paul outlined the sacrifice he had made (v. 6), the service he had rendered (v. 7), and the reward he anticipated (v. 8).

(1) The Sacrifice of Life (4:6)

⁶For I am already being poured out like a drink offering, and the time has come for my departure.

4:6 Paul linked this verse with the preceding verse by use of an emphatic "I" (*egō*), which the NEB renders "as for me." He also used an explanatory "for" to introduce the verse. Paul was saying to Timothy in vv. 5-6, "As for you, keep your head . . . because as for me I am going to depart" (author's translation). The apostle used two metaphors to describe his anticipated death.

First, he compared the pouring out of his energy in ministry to the pouring out of the wine of an Old Testament drink offering.[69] Such offerings (see Num 15:1-10) were probably a substitute for the blood used in heathen sacrifices (Ps 16:4). They were totally expended or poured out as an accompaniment to the burnt offering in the sanctuary (Num 28:7). Paul had used this metaphor in Phil 2:17. The present tense of the verb for "being poured out" suggests Paul's awareness that this was an act then underway. Paul was aware that he was slowly dying in God's service, and he felt that the shedding of his blood in martyrdom would complete the drink offering to God. He viewed the entire ordeal as a libation to God.

Second, he described his "departure" or death with a verb that pictures the departure of a ship by lifting its anchor or the breaking up of camp by a group of soldiers. Both the ship and the soldiers were going home, and the idea of going home was an accepted euphemism for death. Paul used the verbal form of the noun "departure" in Phil 1:23 ("depart") to picture the possibility of his death. By faith Paul gave a marvelous appraisal of the grim prospects of his death. Timothy may have read the story of this buoyant faith through a covering of tears.[70]

---

[69] A libation normally was a part of a burnt or a peace offering. The entire libation was poured out in the sanctuary. The priests received none of the drink offering. These facts make Paul's use of the image all the more significant. For further information on the drink offering, see A. F. Rainey, "Sacrifice and Offerings," ZPEB 5.208-11; S. Langston, "Sacrifice and Offering," HBD, 1218.

[70] Paul's statement in these verses contains two significant features. The personal nature of the testimony has long been used as an indication of the authenticity of the section. Even those who question the Pauline authorship of the Pastorals often affirm that this is a true Pauline fragment.

A second feature about this section is its link with Philippians. Twice in this verse links with Philippians have appeared. Some have used this link to suggest that the pseudepigraphic author used Philippians as his source. For a discussion of this idea and an explanation opposing it, see Fee, *1 and 2 Timothy, Titus*, 240.

(2) The Service of Ministry (4:7)

⁷I have fought the good fight, I have finished the race, I have kept the faith.

4:7 Paul found three metaphors to reflect the struggles of his ministry, not merely the difficulties of his life. His use of three Greek perfect tenses suggests that something was completed with consequences that still abide. The fight and the race were over, but the victory still abides. Paul had kept the faith, and it remains unshaken. Interpreters differ over whether the "fight" is a race ("I have done my best in the race," GNB) or a boxing or wrestling match as the NIV suggests. Fee supports the former, and Kelly opts for the latter. Fee is probably correct in suggesting that Paul was not commenting about having done his best in the contest but was saying that he "has been running in the noblest, grandest run of them all—the ministry of the gospel."[71]

To "have finished the race" involves a foot race as a metaphor. Paul was not commending himself for having "run the full distance" (GNB) but was stating that he had followed the course laid out by his Lord. For a similar metaphor see Paul's expression in Acts 20:24.

To keep the "faith" may have involved either maintaining the sound doctrine of Christianity intact or keeping a loyalty to the trust the Father had given him. In light of the fact that the phrase "kept the faith" seems to be a fixed formula for maintaining a personal trust, the latter option seems more likely.[72] Certainly Paul did hold to the Christian faith, but he emphasized here his fidelity to his commission.

Paul was not boasting of his accomplishments but was reflecting on his life course with a statement of confidence. He was describing what the grace of God had produced in him.

(3) The Reward for Obedience (4:8)

⁸Now there is in store for me the crown of righteousness, which the Lord, the righteous Judge, will award to me on that day—and not only to me, but also to all who have longed for his appearing.

4:8 The victory Paul received as a consequence of his accomplishments in the good fight is described as a "crown of righteousness." The crown was a reward given to a victorious athlete for prowess in a contest (see 1 Cor 9:25). It was usually a perishable wreath woven from ivy, leaves, or flowers.

---

[71] Ibid., 238. The use of the Greek article with the noun "fight" suggests that Paul had a specific fight, for the gospel, in mind.

[72] Josephus (*Wars* 6.345) used the phrase to describe the Roman general Titus's keeping his word by giving sanctuary even to his military opponents who came to him in surrender.

The phrase "of righteousness" may refer to the crown either as a reward for righteous behavior or as a gift consisting of righteousness awarded by the Judge when he returns. Fee defends the latter view, suggesting that the statements in Jas 1:12 and 1 Pet 5:4 support this interpretation.[73] Kelly, joined by Hiebert and Guthrie, feels that Paul was describing a recompense given by God in recognition of an upright life.[74] This need not be seen as a reward for personal achievement but as an explanation of expected recognition due to the righteous. Kelly's arguments seem the more convincing.

Jesus Christ is the Judge who will bestow the award in connection with his return, both to Paul and to all those whose righteous actions demonstrate their longing for Christ's return. The perfect tense for the Greek participle "have longed" suggests that those in mind had loved Jesus' appearing in the past and continued to do so up until the moment of reward. To long for Christ's "appearing" is not a demand for constant discussions of eschatology but a requirement that believers would perform the life-style of Titus 2:12-13. The behavior Paul sought in Timothy formed a distinct contrast with the behavior exhibited by Demas in 4:10. Paul also wanted to avoid any appearance of special claim for himself while offering encouragement to Timothy.

Summary. The knowledge that God rewards and recognizes faithful Christian service is an incentive to godly living. A confidence in God's bestowal of rewards is encouraged by a knowledge of his faithfulness. God is faithful to believers; he will not ignore their works; he will justly evaluate all of them. This knowledge is a prod to devoted obedience to God. An expectation of reward is also a recognition of God's grace. Those who anticipate reward will not be able to boast, "Look at my accomplishments." They should be able to offer praise to God by saying, "Thank you, Lord, for what you have produced in me." The very expectation of reward is an acknowledgment of God's grace.

---

[73]Fee, *1 and 2 Timothy, Titus*, 239.

[74]Kelly, *Pastoral Epistles*, 209-10. Kelly admits that the reading of Jas 1:12 ("the crown of life") provides an analogy in translation that opposes his view. He argues that the interpretation "the crown which consists of righteousness" seems to oppose the idea that the believer is already justified, and he objects to this implication.

─────────────── SECTION OUTLINE ───────────────

V. PERSONAL APPEALS FROM PAUL TO TIMOTHY (4:9-18)
1. A Few Requests and Warnings (4:9-15)
2. A Reminder of God's Delivering Power (4:16-18)

── **V. PERSONAL APPEALS FROM PAUL TO TIMOTHY (4:9-18)** ──

This section reads like a personal letter from Paul to Timothy. Paul gave Timothy some requests and warnings (vv. 9-15), and he reminded him of God's delivering power (vv. 16-18). Paul still wanted to see Timothy very much (1:4), but he also wanted Timothy to assume some of the Pauline responsibilities in light of his approaching death. Paul's reminders here were not the demoralized rantings of a self-pitying wretch but the response of God's premier apostle gripped by the purposes of his apostolic call. Paul was still making plans for additional service despite the nearness of the end. Christianity produces stalwart disciples who can live courageously and single-mindedly in the face of intimidating circumstances.

1. A Few Requests and Warnings (4:9-15)

⁹Do your best to come to me quickly, ¹⁰for Demas, because he loved this world, has deserted me and has gone to Thessalonica. Crescens has gone to Galatia, and Titus to Dalmatia. ¹¹Only Luke is with me. Get Mark and bring him with you, because he is helpful to me in my ministry. ¹²I sent Tychicus to Ephesus. ¹³When you come, bring the cloak that I left with Carpus at Troas, and my scrolls, especially the parchments.

¹⁴Alexander the metalworker did me a great deal of harm. The Lord will repay him for what he has done. ¹⁵You too should be on your guard against him, because he strongly opposed our message.

Paul made requests of Timothy in vv. 9,11, and 13. He explained his request for Timothy's quick travel in v. 10, indicating that he was alone and eager for the solace of faithful friends. The warning in vv. 14-15 was intended to steer Timothy away from the trouble Alexander might have caused him.

4:9 The reference to "quickly" in v. 9 indicates the urgency of the Pauline request. Paul had a foreboding of his fate, but he was not expecting immediate execution. Paul's previous experience with the Roman judicial system had led to a lengthy confinement (Acts 24:27; 28:30-31), and he anticipated normal delays. Timothy, if he left soon, could arrive at

Rome in three or four months. Paul expected to be alive still at this time. He also wanted Timothy to come soon to avoid the dangerous conditions of winter on the Mediterranean (v. 21). Apparently the difficulties at Ephesus did not demand that Timothy remain there permanently. The request to Timothy was considerably more urgent than the appeal to Titus in Titus 3:12.

4:10 Paul's reason for the urgent request to Timothy was that all his coworkers except Luke had left him. Demas had left for dishonorable reasons, but Crescens and Titus may have been sent by Paul to new positions of ministry. The name "Demas" is a shortened form of Demetrius. It is impossible to know whether this Demas was identical with others in the New Testament named Demetrius (Acts 19:24; 3 John 12). Paul had commended Demas as a "fellow worker" in Phlm 24. It is clear from a reading of Col 4:11,14 that Demas was not Jewish. His love for this world probably involved a preference for ease and comfort along with a reluctance to share Paul's sufferings. Paul's words did not picture him as an utter apostate but reflected disappointment at his self-interest.[1] Thessalonica could have been his hometown. Demas's profession of love for this age contrasted sharply with Paul's call to love Jesus' appearing (4:8).

This passage provides our only sure information about Crescens in the New Testament. Some manuscripts read "Gaul," modern France, instead of "Galatia"; but students of the New Testament text have not regarded it as original.[2] Later Christian writers who comment about Crescens presumed that he went to Gaul. They thus provided apocryphal information about him. Titus's travel to Dalmatia probably terminated his work on Crete (Titus 1:5). Dalmatia was a city in the southern part of the province of Illyricum (Rom 15:19), modern Yugoslavia. It was north of Nicopolis (Titus 3:12). We have no additional biblical information about Titus's ministry in Dalmatia.

---

[1] In the apocryphal writing *Acts of Paul and Thecla* 1, 4, 12-14, 16 he appears as a jealous and hypocritical companion of Paul who gave evil counsel intended to destroy Paul.

[2] The reading of "Galatia" has strong support from a diversity of manuscripts stemming from both the Eastern and the Western church. It is easy to understand how the Greek for "Galatia" (Γαλατίαν) could be altered to the Greek for "Gaul" (Γαλλία). The *a* in Galatia (A) could be mistaken for the *l* in Gaul (Λ), and the *t* (T) could have dropped out. For further discussion on the textual reading, see B. Metzger, *A Textual Commentary on the Greek New Testament* (n.p.: United Bible Societies, 1971), 649.

Kelly adopts an unusual approach. He assumes that the correct reading of the text is Galatia, but he interprets the term "Galatia" as a possible reference to Gaul. He finds support for this view from some of the early fathers (Eusebius, Epiphanius) and the proximity of Paul to Gaul if we accept the Roman origin of 2 Timothy. Kelly says, "The verse thus becomes an important witness to the expansion of the Church westwards" (*Pastoral Epistles*, 213).

Kelly's view is creative but highly speculative. It is best to retain the understanding of Galatia as the destination of Crescens.

4:11 Of Paul's trusted companions only Luke remained with him. He had been with Paul during the first Roman imprisonment (Col 4:14; Phlm 24).[3] His presence here has led some to suggest that he played a role in writing 2 Timothy for Paul, perhaps as an amanuensis.[4] The fact that Paul later (v. 21) mentioned some Roman Christian friends who were with him is not a contradiction to his stating that Luke alone was with him. They were not among Paul's trusted coworkers and could provide friendship, but not much assistance in ministry. Luke's presence with Paul showed his personal devotion and may also indicate that Luke had given a physician's care to Paul for his physical needs.

Paul had earlier refused to carry Mark on his second missionary journey (Acts 15:36-41) because Mark had deserted Paul in the field (Acts 13:13). Paul's magnanimity showed itself in his regarding Mark as a fellow worker (Col 4:10-11; Phlm 24) during his first imprisonment. Now he indicated his desire to have Mark with him again because of his great helpfulness in service. The "ministry" Mark performed could have been gospel preaching and teaching, a personal ministry to Paul, or a combination of both. Since Paul was discussing personal needs in this context, it is likely that meeting such needs was at least a part of Mark's proposed duties. Mark was presumably somewhere along Timothy's route to Paul in Rome.

4:12 Tychicus was a native of the province of Asia (Acts 20:4-5) who had accompanied Paul on the third missionary journey and preceded him to Troas. He had likely carried the Letters of Colossians (Col 4:7-9) and Ephesians (Eph 6:21). Paul had intended to send him to Crete to replace Titus (Titus 3:12). The Greek aorist verb "sent" is likely an epistolary aorist. The verb would thus indicate "I am sending" from the standpoint of the writer or "I have sent" from the viewpoint of the readers. Tychicus likely would carry 2 Timothy to its destination and replace Timothy in ministry in Ephesus while Timothy journeyed to be with Paul in Rome.

4:13 Paul's instruction to Timothy here suggested the route Timothy was to follow in his journey westward. He was to leave Ephesus, journey

---

[3] Some NT scholars lean toward the possibility of a Caesarean origin for the Prison Epistles (Acts 24:27) or toward an Ephesian origin (1 Cor 15:32). A full discussion of the possibilities for the origin of the Prison Epistles is beyond the scope of this commentary, but this writer assumes a Roman origin. See R. Melick, *Philippians, Colossians, Philemon*, NAC (Nashville: Broadman, 1991), 168-70.

[4] There is nothing improbable in suggesting that Luke served as amanuensis with Paul in writing 2 Timothy. Some of the vocabulary similarities between Luke-Acts and the Pastorals (e.g., "the living and the dead" appearing in Acts 10:42; 2 Tim 4:1) suggest possible authorship by Luke. The suggestion is possible, but its validity can never be more than a matter of conjecture.

to Troas, cross the Aegean Sea, follow the Egnatian Way through Macedonia, cross the Adriatic Sea to Brundisium, and proceed on to Rome.

Carpus was a believer from Troas, but how Paul came to leave anything at his home is unknown. Fee offers the possible explanation that Paul was arrested in Troas and had left a coat behind.[5] Some years had elapsed since Paul's visit to Troas in Acts 20:6, and that visit would not be the occasion when the cloak was left.

The "cloak" Paul requested was a large sleeveless, woolen outer garment made of a single piece of heavy material with a hole in the middle for allowing the head to pass through. It would have resembled the poncho and would have provided excellent protection against the damp cold of a dungeon during winter (v. 21).[6]

Most commentators regard the "scrolls" as papyrus rolls and the "parchments" as an expensive, durable writing material made of animal skin.[7] It is impossible to know the contents of the parchments, but suggested contents include personal documents of Paul, the Old Testament Scriptures, or blank sheets of writing paper. Sentiment often favors viewing them as Old Testament Scriptures.

T. C. Skeat has suggested a view of the latter phrase of v. 13 which links the scrolls and the parchments together. Considering it unlikely that Paul would carry a library with him, Skeat views the adverb "especially" (*malista*) as equating the "scrolls" and the "parchments" instead of differentiating between them. In his view Paul would have been saying, "Bring the books—I mean the parchment notebooks."[8] This view still leaves us uncertain about the contents of the books, but Skeat's explanation seems the best solution.

4:14-15 The reference to Alexander in vv. 14-15 leaves us uncertain both of his identity and his action but thoroughly convinced of his deliberate malice. The name Alexander was linked with Hymenaeus in 1 Tim 1:20. Alexander was also the name of a little-known Ephesian Jew in Acts 19:33-34. Fee presents an imaginative reconstruction that the excommunicated Alexander left Ephesus (1 Tim 1:20), perhaps went to

---

[5]G. Fee, *1 and 2 Timothy, Titus*, GNC, ed. W. W. Gasque (San Francisco: Harper & Row, 1984), 244.

[6]Some interpreters discuss the possibility that the "cloak" was a cover for books, a view suggested by Paul's discussion of the "scrolls" in the same verse. Modern interpreters have not followed this view. For details see Bernard, 146-47.

[7]J. N. D. Kelly (*A Commentary on the Pastoral Epistles* [1963; reprint, Grand Rapids: Baker, 1981], 215-16) advocates these views.

[8]Skeat discusses these views in "'Especially the Parchments': A Note on 2 Timothy 4:13," *JTS* n.s. 30 (1979): 174. He also presents information on the preparation of papyrus and parchment in "Early Christian Book-Production: Papyri and Manuscripts," *The Cambridge History of the Bible*, ed G. W. H. Lampe (London: Cambridge University Press, 1969), 2:54-79.

Troas, and there informed on Paul so as to cause his arrest.[9] Paul
reminded Timothy of his identity by designating him as "the metalworker" and urged him to be "on . . . guard against him." Spicq presents
evidence that the verb for "did . . . harm" (*endeiknymi*) could suggest
supplying information to the authorities as an informer.[10] If we identify
Alexander with the excommunicated leader of 1 Tim 1:20, it is plausible
to follow Fee's suggestions.

Alexander had vigorously resisted Paul in deed (v. 14) and in word
(v. 15). Paul expressed confidence in God's justice in dealing with Alexander. The use of the future tense ("The Lord will repay him") is more a
prediction of what God would do than a curse invoked by an angry, vin-
dictive Paul. There should be no objection to a Christian's approval of
God's right to punish the guilty, for "if God is a moral governor, if sin is
a reality, those who know themselves to be on God's side cannot help a
feeling of joy in knowing that evil will not always triumph over good."[11]
Paul did not appear to be uttering the words due to his own personal
pique but in response to Alexander's resistance to the gospel.

2. A Reminder of God's Delivering Power (4:16-18)

**[16] At my first defense, no one came to my support, but everyone deserted
me. May it not be held against them. [17] But the Lord stood at my side and
gave me strength, so that through me the message might be fully proclaimed
and all the Gentiles might hear it. And I was delivered from the lion's mouth.
[18] The Lord will rescue me from every evil attack and will bring me safely to
his heavenly kingdom. To him be glory for ever and ever. Amen.**

Paul gave Timothy fresh information about his lack of support from
Christian friends (v. 16) and the magnificent strength the Lord had supplied (v. 17). The memory of the divine protection led Paul to an outburst
of praise (v. 18).

4:16 Many earlier commentators identified Paul's "first defense" with
his trial during his imprisonment of Acts 28:16-31. However, nothing in
Acts suggests that Paul was abandoned by callous Christian friends as
indicated in v. 16. Further, Timothy would not need to receive information from Paul about events that occurred so long ago.

More recent interpreters view the occasion as a preliminary investigation during a later imprisonment, called in Latin legal language the *prima
actio*. This would have a purpose similar to a grand jury hearing. After

---

[9]Fee, *1 and 2 Timothy, Titus*, 245.

[10]C. Spicq, *Saint Paul: Les Epitres Pastorales* (Paris: Gabalda, 1947), 394.

[11]N. J. D. White, *The First and Second Epistles to Timothy and the Epistle to Titus*, ed.
W. R. Nicoll (New York: Doran, n.d.), 181.

this first investigation the judge had been unable to resolve his doubts for or against Paul and called for a further investigation, known as a *secunda actio*. This would involve considerable delay, and Timothy might not have known about these developments. For discussion of information about Paul's second Roman imprisonment, see the discussion of "Conflicting Circumstances" under the "Authorship of the Pastorals."

The only blot on events at the trial was that Paul's friends, both Christian and others, had deserted him. In Acts 19:31 Paul had some leading officials of Ephesus who gave him sound advice in a troublesome moment. Likely these were interested non-Christians. However, no one similar to these Ephesian friends stepped forward to speak for or to Paul during this trial. Perhaps weakness of character or fear led to the absence of patrons willing to risk loss of standing for Paul. Such Christian friends as were there may have proved unacceptable as witnesses. Perhaps we should put Luke and Tychicus in this category. Paul's wish that God would not hold this action against his friends resembles the response of Jesus in Luke 23:34.

4:17 In contrast to the desertion of friends, the Lord stood beside Paul to provide strength. Two results developed from the help and strength God provided in the trial. First, the gospel was fully proclaimed so that the heathen world heard it. God gave Paul the courage and opportunity to preach, and Paul had fulfilled his plans of reaching Rome with the gospel. In defending himself before the judge, Paul had used the occasion to proclaim the gospel (cf. Acts 26:2-29). In proclaiming the gospel before such a cosmopolitan audience, it would have been possible for Paul to say realistically that he had reached all the Gentiles with the message. Jesus' own words in Matt 10:17-33 would encourage Paul to feel that preaching the gospel before a tribunal represented a significant opportunity for advancing the truth.

A second result was Paul's deliverance from the lion's mouth. Interpreters have identified the lion as the literal lions of the amphitheater, the emperor Nero, or Satan. The phrase appears in Ps 22:21 in reference to an experience of great danger. This was Paul's meaning here, and it is best not to be too specific beyond this. God intervened by giving Paul the strength to proclaim the gospel, confounding the judge in reaching a conclusion, and saving Paul from a cruel death. The lion had been robbed for the moment.[12]

---

[12]Lock makes an interesting comparison between the entire section of 2 Tim 4:9-19 and Ps 22. The similarity is especially obvious in the use of the phrase "the lion's mouth," which Lock feels that Paul "probably consciously borrowed" from the psalm. Echoing the same view of the phrase as advocated in the text, Lock feels that there is no need to link the term with any historical personality but only to view it as "a proverb of extreme danger" (see W. Lock, *The Pastoral Epistles*, ICC [Edinburgh: T & T Clark, 1924], 116, 119).

4:18 Paul's enthusiastic assertion of the Lord's rescue from every evil attack could refer either to physical or spiritual protection. However, if Paul were expecting a physical deliverance from his imprisonment, this expectation would contradict the outlook he expressed in 4:6-8. Further, Paul never led any of his converts to expect protection from all physical harm (see Acts 14:22). It is best to see Paul expressing an optimism of rescue from the many spiritual attacks against him. Kelly says that Paul "is affirming his confidence that no assault of his enemies will undermine his faith or his courage, or cause him to lapse into disastrous sin."[13] It was not that Paul expected a deliverance from a threatened martyrdom. Paul expected divine protection so that he would triumphantly overcome the spiritual forces arrayed against him and enter into a glorious heavenly kingdom. Paul expressed a hope that would be a fulfillment of the Lord's promise in Luke 9:24.

The kingdom for which Paul expressed hope of entrance was already a present reality initiated by the person of Christ (Matt 12:28). It is also a goal Christians can anticipate in full consummation at the end of the age (1 Thess 2:12; Gal 5:21; 1 Cor 15:50).

Frequently when Paul dwelt on divine power and goodness, he concluded with a doxology (e.g., Rom 9:5; 11:33-36). His anticipation of a powerful deliverance led him to express a doxology. His words resemble the doxology in Gal 1:5 addressed to God the Father. Here it was addressed to Christ.[14]

Application. Paul's rapid listing of events involving Christian friends presents a glimpse of God's grace in action in many lives. Three features of Paul's attitude can provide us help and encouragement for today. First, Paul avoided indulging his disappointments. Doubtless he was saddened that one as promising as Demas (Phlm 24) should have walked away from commitment. However, he did not allow that setback to dominate his outlook, and he moved on to a more positive expression of what God was doing. Second, Paul could rejoice in the victory won in the life of Mark. This young man had performed so poorly that Paul had rejected him (Acts 15:36-41), but now he had proven himself. Surely this was cause for joy and happiness. Third, Paul found no room for vindictiveness toward those who hurt or opposed him. Perhaps the memory of Alexander (v. 14) was a painful experience for Paul, but the apostle simply

---

[13]Kelly, *Pastoral Epistles*, 220.

[14]There is some uncertainty concerning whether the reference to the "Lord" in these verses refers to Christ or to God the Father. Kelly (*Pastoral Epistles*, 220) feels it is a reference to the Father, and Fee (*1 and 2 Timothy, Titus*, 246) takes it as a reference to Christ. The fact that Paul in v. 17 could speak of the "Lord" at his side suggests an experience similar to that of Acts 23:11, where the reference is clearly to Christ. Likely that is Paul's meaning here.

left the responsibility for dealing with him to God. He did not grit his teeth in anger and wish him disaster. As Christians we must learn to rejoice in divine victory and avoid succumbing to disappointments and a spirit of vindictiveness.

————————— *SECTION OUTLINE* —————————

VI. CONCLUSION (4:19-22)
1. Greetings to Friends (4:19)
2. Information about Mutual Friends (4:20)
3. Final Request and Greetings to Timothy (4:21)
4. Benediction (4:22)

————————— **VI. CONCLUSION (4:19-22)** —————————

Paul had concluded 1 Timothy without a personal greeting[1] to his faithful disciple. In v. 19 Paul sent greetings to his friends Priscilla and Aquila, and in v. 20 he passed on information about mutual friends. In v. 21 he penned a final request to Timothy and also included greetings from Roman believers to him. A concluding benediction appears in v. 22.

1. Greetings to Friends (4:19)

[19] **Greet Priscilla and Aquila and the household of Onesiphorus.**

4:19 Priscilla and Aquila were a devoted Christian couple who planted churches and nurtured believers wherever their many travels took them. We meet them first in Acts 18:2, where Aquila, a Jew from Pontus, had arrived in Corinth with his wife, Priscilla, after expulsion from Rome. Fee assumes that Priscilla was also a Jew,[2] but W. Ramsay infers that Luke's intention in Acts 18:2 was to imply that Priscilla was not Jewish.[3] Subsequently the pair accompanied Paul to Ephesus (Acts 18:18-26) and established a house-church there (1 Cor 16:19). Later they had established another house-church in Rome (Rom 16:3-5). Here in 2 Timothy they had returned to Ephesus.

In four of six instances the name of Priscilla appears before that of Aquila. Most interpreters assume that this indicated her greater social prominence or more forceful personality. Ramsay indicates that her name was that of a prominent Roman family and that *Aquila* was frequently

---

[1] For a discussion of typical closings to Hellenistic letters, see F. X. J. Exler, *The Form of the Ancient Greek Letter of the Epistolary Papyri* (Chicago: Ares, 1976), 69-77. He also includes samples of final phrases including greetings on 111-15.

[2] G. Fee, *1 and 2 Timothy, Titus*, GNC, ed. W. W. Gasque (San Francisco: Harper & Row, 1984), 249.

[3] W. M. Ramsay, *St. Paul the Traveller and the Roman Citizen* (1897; reprint, Grand Rapids: Baker, 1966), 268-69.

used of freedmen.[4] They were a remarkable couple who had risked their lives to save Paul's life and had sacrificed time, money, and reputation for the cause of the gospel.

The name of Onesiphorus appears in 1:16-18. Paul's mention of only the family of Onesiphorus may suggest that Onesiphorus was not with them, but it need not indicate that Onesiphorus was dead.

2. Information about Mutual Friends (4:20)

[20] **Erastus stayed in Corinth, and I left Trophimus sick in Miletus.**

4:20 The mention of this pair of friends to both Timothy and Paul picked up a thread last suggested in v. 12. Paul wanted to explain that the absence of these friends from his side was not due to unfaithfulness.

Erastus was the name used for a companion of Timothy in Acts 19:22 and also for a Corinthian city official in Rom 16:23. Two problems emerge in comparing these references with the reference in our text. First, are the two references to Erastus outside of 2 Timothy speaking of the same person? Second, if they are not identical persons, to which of these was Paul referring? Answers to these questions are not easy, and all we can suggest are possibilities.

The Erastus in Acts 19:22 was a traveling companion on a missionary journey. The journey took place sometime during the mid-to-late fifties while Paul was in Ephesus. The Erastus of Rom 16:23 was a city official serving in Corinth in the late fifties. It is unlikely that the two individuals were identical.

The proposed date for writing 2 Timothy is a decade later than the date of the reference in Rom 16:23. The reference in 2 Timothy sounds more like a description of an individual sent on a specific ministry and remaining in Corinth to do that ministry. The Erastus of Acts 19:22 seems the more likely person to be linked with the name mentioned in our text because a city official of Corinth would have less freedom to travel about. It is uncertain how Erastus arrived at Corinth, but it is at least possible that after Paul's arrest he dropped out of the group that was escorting Paul to Rome.

Trophimus had been a part of Paul's traveling group returning from Corinth to Jerusalem (Acts 20:4; 21:29) and was the unintentional cause of Paul's seizure by a Jerusalem mob. We do not know the occasion for Paul's leaving Trophimus in Miletus, although the visit would likely have occurred after Paul's release from a first Roman imprisonment. Paul wanted Timothy to know of the illness of a friend in the nearby city of

---

[4]Ibid.

Miletus. The passing reference to Trophimus's sickness indicates that miracles of healing were not produced at the demand of an apostle but were evidences of divine power carried out by the will of God.

3. Final Request and Greetings to Timothy (4:21)

²¹Do your best to get here before winter. Eubulus greets you, and so do Pudens, Linus, Claudia and all the brothers.

4:21 Paul wanted Timothy to come before winter not only because he needed his coat but because transportation on the Mediterranean stopped from November through March. Mention of this season indicated that the letter was probably written in late spring or early summer. If Timothy wanted to make it to Rome during that year, he needed to leave at once.

The four friends who sent greetings to Timothy appear to have been Roman believers, friends of Timothy, and perhaps leaders in the church. The only person whose name is mentioned further in Christian history was Linus. Irenaeus presented him as the leader of the Roman church following Peter and Paul.[5] The reference in Irenaeus is probably not historically accurate because it assumed that Peter and Paul organized the Roman church and selected their successor. Christians already lived in Rome before Paul arrived (see Acts 28:11-16).[6]

4. Benediction (4:22)

²²The Lord be with your spirit. Grace be with you.

4:22 In the benediction Paul expressed a personal word for Timothy. He wished that the Lord might strengthen Timothy personally so that the younger leader might faithfully discharge his task (see Gal 6:18). Only the strong presence of the Lord could sustain the hesitant disciple in the face of the suffering and opposition that lay ahead.

If 2 Timothy is indeed the last of Paul's writings, these words represent the last of Paul's surviving words. Note that this letter has a double benediction (cf. 1 Cor 16:23-24). Most of Paul's epistles lack a double benediction. The first benediction was directed toward Timothy; the second expressed a word for the entire church.

This letter represented a special message to Timothy, but Paul had an obvious concern for the full fellowship. Nothing could sustain the Ephesian Christians with more stamina and holiness than an abundant supply of God's grace. All of God's people always need all of his grace.

---

[5]Irenaeus, *Against Heresies* 3.3.3.

[6]For a further discussion of the historical background to the references about Linus, see Hanson, *The Pastoral Epistles*, NCB (Grand Rapids: Eerdmans, 1982), 164.

Titus

I. SALUTATION (1:1-4)
   1. Author (1:1-3)
   2. Recipient (1:4a)
   3. Greeting (1:4b)

I. SALUTATION (1:1-4)

1. Author (1:1-3)

¹Paul, a servant of God and an apostle of Jesus Christ for the faith of God's elect and the knowledge of the truth that leads to godliness— ²a faith and knowledge resting on the hope of eternal life, which God, who does not lie, promised before the beginning of time, ³and at his appointed season he brought his word to light through the preaching entrusted to me by the command of God our Savior,

In his letters to churches or to individuals, Paul used the form of introductory greeting customary in first-century letter writing. In the Epistle to Titus, Paul identified himself as the source of the letter and Titus as the recipient, followed by his stated desire for God's blessing upon Titus. With the exception of the Thessalonian correspondence, Paul typically added some words or phrases that described himself (e.g., "an apostle of Christ Jesus," "a prisoner of Christ Jesus," "a bond-servant of Christ Jesus"). These self-descriptions at the beginning of his letters served to establish his authority and right to speak. In Titus, Paul also used these self-descriptive phrases to introduce theological statements that indicate the scope and nature of God's plan for redemption of persons. Romans and Galatians are the only other epistles in which Paul expanded his greeting.

1:1 Paul began by identifying himself as "a servant of God and an apostle of Jesus Christ." In Romans and Philippians, Paul introduced himself as "a servant of Christ Jesus." The interchangeability of "Christ

Jesus" and "God" as referents within the Pauline Letters indicates Paul's affirmation of the deity of Jesus Christ. Paul continued to express this certainty throughout the Epistle to Titus. (See comments on 1:4; 2:13.)

Having established his authority as God's servant and Christ's apostle, Paul amplified his role as an apostle with two prepositional phrases contained in a compound construction that is governed by the same preposition, *kata*. Although *kata* with the accusative is usually rendered "according to, in accordance with," in this context the NIV correctly renders *kata* as "for." This suggests purpose or goal with regard to Paul's apostleship (cf. BAGD, *kata*, II.4). The purpose and goal of Paul's apostleship was to encourage both "the faith of God's elect" and "the knowledge of the truth that leads to godliness." Whereas Paul used these prepositional phrases to describe his apostleship, they are rich in theological content and mark the beginning of an outstanding summary of God's redemptive plan contained in vv. 2-3.

By referring to Christian believers as God's elect (cf. Rom 8:33; Col 3:12), Paul employed a descriptive term that calls attention to God's activity in human salvation, known theologically as "election." This doctrine is not exclusively Pauline. It reflects Jesus' own teaching (e.g., Matt 22:14; 24:22,24,31 and parallels; Luke 18:7; John 6:37-44; 10:27-29) and that of other New Testament writers (e.g., Acts 13:48; 1 Pet 1:1-5; 2:9; 2 Pet 1:3,10-11; Rev 17:14). Divine election constitutes a basic element in the doctrine of salvation (also known as Soteriology). Although this element contains mysteries for human understanding, election is biblically emphasized as a central part of God's dealing with his people. It is clearly evident in his choice of Israel (Deut 7:6-9; 14:2; Ps 33:12; Isa 41:8-10; Ezek 20:5; Acts 13:16-17) and his choice of the church (Col 3:11-12; 2 Thess 2:13-14; 1 Pet 1:1; 2:9-10; Rev 17:14). Paul specifically taught throughout his epistles that God is the Source, Initiator, Implementer, and Guarantor of salvation (cf. Rom 8:28-39; 9:10-16; Eph 1:4-14; 2:4-10; 1 Thess 1:4-5).

Because of the mysteries concerning God's election of believers, many Christians have ignored this doctrine or have rejected it outright. Perhaps this discomfort with election is due to the logical, yet unbiblical, extensions sometimes made by systematic theology concerning God's activity. It is unfortunate when systematic theology goes beyond the express teaching of Scripture. In the case of election, this biblical teaching has sometimes been extended to necessitate a doctrine of divine reprobation. Simply put, this doctrine states that if God chooses individuals for salvation, then he must likewise choose individuals for eternal damnation. This may appear to be a logical extension of divine election, but the Scriptures do *not* teach this doctrine. The biblical theologian must stop where the biblical text stops, even though some issues appear to remain unresolved.

Another common objection to the doctrine of election is that it severely diminishes the challenge to evangelism. Once again, the believer must be obedient to the biblical mandate, which is unmistakably presented and easily understood. Evangelism is commanded in Scripture, demonstrated by examples in Scripture, and is therefore an obligation and privilege of every believer (Ps 51:10,13; Prov 11:30; Matt 5:13-16; 28:19-20; Acts 1:8; 5:42; Rom 1:14-15; 10:13-15). Rather than being viewed as unnecessary because of election, evangelism is to be seen as another essential element in God's overall plan and purpose in salvation.

The doctrine of election inevitably produces a certain intellectual tension, particularly with regard to "free will" or personal activity in one's own salvation (cf. Rom 5:18; 1 Tim 2:5; Titus 2:11; 2 Pet 3:9). Such tensions are also to be found in other New Testament doctrines, most notably in the fully divine and fully human natures in the person of Jesus Christ. Balanced biblical theology requires that such tensions remain. Rejecting clear biblical teaching because of limited human understanding is dangerously shortsighted. After setting forth the doctrine of election in Rom 9–10, Paul said: "Oh, the depths of the riches of the wisdom and knowledge of God! How unsearchable his judgments, and paths beyond tracing out!" (Rom 11:33).

The doctrine of divine election firmly establishes the believer's eternal security. God has not left the believer's assurance of salvation captive to changing feelings or faltering faith. Rather, the faithfulness of God demonstrated in his divine election secures the believer's salvation in the will and purposes of God himself.

In addition to giving assurance of salvation, the doctrine of election leaves no room for human pride or an "elitist" Christian mentality. Rather, it is a source of genuine humility as believers recognize that their salvation is in reality God's work alone.

Finally, the doctrine of election is best, and possibly only, understood within the context of the believer's personal experience of salvation. Most believers, when reflecting upon their own salvation, will attribute it totally to God's working in their lives. They understand that they are redeemed only because of God's love and grace.[1] The doctrine of election, although partially eclipsed by our finite minds, ultimately rests here,

---

[1] J. S. Stewart, *A Man in Christ* (London: Hodder & Stoughton, 1935), 222, states: "No other position was indeed possible for a man like Paul in whose thinking grace—that is to say, the divine initiative—was fundamental. Everything in religion that matters starts from God's side." Stewart adds: "In the words of Baron von Hugel, 'The passion and hunger *for* God comes *from* God, and God answers it with Christ.' Man's intelligence and will and heart and conscience never initiate anything in religion; and over the best moral and spiritual triumphs of this life the saints can only cry, 'Not unto us, O Lord, not unto us, but unto Thy name give glory.'"

in God's love, grace, and mercy. Once grasped by the believer, it offers a foundation for comfort, security, and true worship, not uncertainty and confusion.

Just as Paul's apostleship was "for the faith of God's elect," it is also "for [same governing preposition, *kata*] the knowledge of the truth that leads to godliness." A brief glance through a concordance at the Greek terms for "knowledge" (*gnōsis*, and its derivative forms) indicates Paul's preoccupation with "knowledge," both its content and function within the Christian experience. In Titus 1:1 Paul used the derivative term *epignōsin* for "knowledge." This term, frequent in Paul, is used here in a technical sense to denote a defined body of Christian knowledge. Paul clearly used the phrase "the knowledge of truth" to indicate the "gospel" in its fullest sense. He did so by modifying "knowledge" with the term "truth." This knowledge of the truth in all of its theological and practical dimensions is further amplified as being "that [which] leads to godliness." The term for godliness (*eusebeia*) denotes an everyday way of living (or conduct) that displays devotion to God.[2] This initial reference to the transforming power of the gospel that results in godly living is a recurrent theme throughout this letter as Paul contrasted the expected behavior of Christians with the behavior of their opponents and unbelievers.

The sequence of these three significant terms Paul used in this first verse—faith, knowledge, godliness—suggests a pattern of true Christian growth. Saving faith that opens one's eyes to the knowledge of the truth should result in a transformed life characterized by godliness. All too often, in our evangelistic efforts to produce faith, we have neglected the hard work of encouraging the knowledge of the truth. Because the results of our evangelism are easily measured by recording decisions and baptisms, we may become content with our "success" as reflected by statistical data. We may be "substituting statistical records for spiritual reality, which is something like reading the recipe instead of eating the meal."[3] The cultivating of the knowledge of the truth is not so easily defined or measured. It is a much more disciplined, difficult, and undramatic process. A. W. Tozer so aptly comments: "The Christian is strong or weak depending upon how closely he has cultivated the knowledge of God. Paul was anything but an advocate of the once-done, automatic school of Christianity. He devoted his whole life to the art of knowing Christ (Phil 3:8,10,14). Progression in the Christian life is exactly equal to the growing knowledge we gain of the triune God in personal experience. And

---

[2]W. Foerster, TDNT 7:182-83. Of the fifteen occurrences of this term in the NT, 1 Timothy contains eight occurrences, 2 Peter contains four occurrences, and one occurrence each is found in Acts, 2 Timothy, and Titus.

[3]W. W. Wiersbe, *The Integrity Crisis* (Nashville: Thomas Nelson, 1988), 44.

such experience requires a whole life devoted to it and plenty of time spent at the holy task of cultivating God. God can be known satisfactorily only as we devote time to Him."[4] The disciplined study of the knowledge of the truth is necessary to convince our minds and hearts of our fallen human condition, of God's higher purposes and plans for us, and, therefore, our desperate need to change. This understanding, empowered by the Spirit of God, will transform us from self-centered and self-controlled to God-centered and God-controlled. In his characteristically pithy manner, V. Havner describes the church as it has ignored the necessity of a progression from faith to knowledge to godliness: "We are challenged these days, but not changed; convicted, but not converted. We hear, but do not; and thereby we deceive ourselves."[5]

Paul's concern was that as a servant and an apostle he would be used to produce faith (salvation), knowledge (of God and all his work in Jesus Christ), and godliness (being "conformed to the image of Christ Jesus," Rom 8:29). This progression of faith to knowledge to godliness should be a pattern for every Christian, both in living their lives and in giving their lives in the communication of the gospel. Indeed, the cultivation of godliness becomes the ultimate evidence of God's divine election (2 Pet 1:5-11).

1:2 In v. 2 the prepositional phrase "on the hope of eternal life" is not without grammatical difficulties and has yielded two interpretations. Some understand the phrase to be a third amplification of Paul's apostleship, following faith and knowledge.[6] This interpretation requires that the phrase modify "apostle of Jesus Christ" and assumes a parallelism of this prepositional phrase beginning with *epi* (meaning *on*) to the preceding compound prepositional phrase beginning with *kata* (which clearly modifies "apostle"). In support of this interpretation, note that in

---

[4]A. W. Tozer, *The Root of the Righteous* (Harrisburg: Christian Publications, 1955), 11-12. Tozer's continuing comments are pertinent: "Without meaning to do it we have written our serious fault into our book titles and gospel songs. 'A little talk with Jesus,' we sing, and we call our books 'God's Minute,' or something else as revealing. The Christian who is satisfied to give God His 'minute' and to have 'a little talk with Jesus' is the same one who shows up at the evangelistic service weeping over his retarded spiritual growth and begging the evangelist to show him the way out of his difficulty. We may as well accept it: there is no shortcut to sanctity."

[5]D. J. Hester, *The Vance Havner Quote Book* (Grand Rapids: Baker, 1986), 63.

[6]See C. K. Barrett, *The Pastoral Epistles* (Oxford: Clarendon, 1963); M. Dibelius and H. Conzelmann, *The Pastoral Epistles, Her* (Philadelphia: Fortress, 1972); D. Guthrie, *The Pastoral Epistles* (Grand Rapids: Eerdmans, 1957); A. T. Hanson, *The Pastoral Letters* (Cambridge: University Press, 1966); A. E. Humphreys, *The Epistles to Timothy and Titus* (Cambridge: University Press, 1895); J. E. Huther, *Critical and Exegetical Hand-Book to the Epistles to Timothy and Titus* (New York: Funk & Wagnalls, 1885); J. N. D. Kelly, *The Pastoral Epistles* (Peabody, Mass.: Hendrickson, 1960); and R. C. H. Lenski, *St. Paul's Epistle to Titus* (Minneapolis: Augsburg, 1961).

2 Tim 1:1 Paul characterized his apostleship as being "according to the promise of life that is in Christ Jesus."

The alternative interpretation of "on the hope of eternal life" understands this phrase as modifying "the faith of God's elect" and "the knowledge of the truth." The NIV embraces this interpretation and actually inserts the terms "faith and knowledge" into the translation, thus rendering "a faith and knowledge resting on the hope of eternal life." Supporters of this interpretation note the remote position of "apostle" in relation to the preposition *epi* and suggest that the compound prepositional phrase "for the faith . . . and the knowledge" constitutes the more natural antecedent for the preposition *epi* ("on," "on the basis of").[7] No significant doctrinal question rests upon either interpretation. Yet the context of the phrase, particularly regarding Paul's statements following it, appears to indicate that he intended that "the faith . . . and the knowledge" are modified by "on the hope of eternal life." Restricting the application of this phrase to Paul's apostleship unnecessarily limits Paul's thought, particularly since it appears to be the starting point for his statements that follow. Having already mentioned faith and knowledge with regard to his apostleship, Paul also noted that these elements are based on the hope of eternal life. Hiebert succinctly states, "'The hope of eternal life' is the basis on which the superstructure of Christian faith and service is built."[8] (Cf. Col 1:4-6.)

Paul continued by establishing the absolute certainty of this hope. He simply stated that this hope of eternal life is based on God's own promise. It is noteworthy that elsewhere in the New Testament Paul combined the concepts of *hope* and God's *promise* (cf. Rom 4:13-20; Acts 26:6). Indeed, to be without the promise is to be "without hope" (Eph 2:12). His use of the term "hope" indicates the human attitude toward God's promises. Because the promised person, thing, or event is from God himself, the certainty of fulfillment is assured. Therefore biblical hope does not reflect a doubtful, tremulous wishing for that which may or may not occur. Neither is it based on what is humanly evident or at times logically expected. Instead, biblical hope is based on the immutable nature and promise of God and therefore results in encouragement, confidence, strength, and security for the believer.[9]

---

[7]See P. Fairbairn, *Commentary on the Pastoral Epistles* (1874; reprint, Grand Rapids: Zondervan, 1956); G. D. Fee, *1 and 2 Timothy, Titus* (Peabody, Mass.: Hendrickson, 1988); W. Hendrickson, *I-II Timothy and Titus* (Grand Rapids: Baker, 1957); D. E. Hiebert, *Titus*, EBC, vol. 11, ed. F. E. Gaebelein (Grand Rapids: Zondervan, 1978); and N. J. D. White, *The Epistle to Titus*, EGT, vol. 4, ed. W. R. Nicoll (Grand Rapids: Eerdmans, 1970).

[8]Hiebert, *Titus*, 427.

[9]Hebrews 6:17-20 provides an excellent commentary on God's trustworthiness and hope. See also C. F. D. Moule, *The Meaning of Hope* (Philadelphia: Fortress, 1963).

A basic presupposition of Scripture is that God cannot lie or deceive; therefore God's truthfulness is unquestioned. God's absolute trustworthiness is often demonstrated in contrast to the inherent lying nature of humans (Num 23:19; cf. also 2 Sam 15:29; Rom 3:4; Heb 6:18). Paul's use of the expression "who does not lie" ("unlying," *apseudēs*) with reference to God's character has a twofold effect in this passage. Primarily, it establishes that the certainty of "the hope of eternal life" is rooted in the character of God and that such hope actually will be realized. In the Scriptures, God is often presented as the object of his people's hope (Jer 17:7; Pss 38:15; 42:5; 43:5; 71:5). Secondarily, Paul's use of the term "who does not lie" with reference to God effectively serves as a stark contrast to the lying character of the Cretans, which Paul noted in 1:12-13.

Many people would agree that the fall of humanity in the garden of Eden is the single most disastrous event in human history. The willful disobedience of the man and woman to God's command resulted in death (Gen 2:17; Rom 6:23; 1 Cor 15:22) and produced a sinful nature shared by all humankind (Rom 3:23; 5:12-21; 1 Cor 15:21-22). It also made necessary a "rescue operation" whereby God in his mercy redeemed humankind through a plan that ultimately resulted in the sacrificial death of his only Son, Jesus. At its foundation, Christian theology is concerned with regaining eternal life lost through disobedience to God's word.

Paul affirmed that the God "who does not lie promised before the beginning of time" this eternal life for which the Christian believer now hopes. A promise is a personal declaration made to another person (or perhaps to oneself) that certain conditions will be met. The promise of God is a central element in the history of redemption. Israel itself was created by God's personal promise to Abraham, and the nation was continually sustained by that promise and other promises related to it, particularly the messianic promise.[10] In the Old Testament, God's promises of redemption were sometimes direct, sometimes veiled, and sometimes amplified by ceremony and symbolism. As the writer to the Hebrews stated, "In the past God spoke to our forefathers through the prophets at many times and in various ways" (Heb 1:1). Yet the New Testament is best understood in light of the fulfillment of all that the Old Testament awaits. Jesus himself traced the thread of promise for his companions on the road to Emmaus: "Beginning with Moses and all the Prophets, he explained to them what was said in all the Scriptures concerning himself"

---

[10]God's promise to Abraham was still in effect, though Abraham, doubting God's promise, took matters into his own hands with Hagar. Yet this blatant action of unbelief did not thwart God's original promise, which he honored in the birth of Isaac (Gen 16–21). In the same way, the sin of Adam did not thwart the original intention of God that people would have eternal life.

(Luke 24:27). The continuity and correspondence of the Old and New Testaments depend on God's promises.[11] God's trustworthiness is vividly demonstrated as the promises are fulfilled in the unfolding plan of redemption.

At times God's promises have been understood as prophecy, i.e., the foretelling of future events. The divine authenticity of the prophetic message depended upon the fulfillment of the foretold event. Thus the fulfilled prophecy contained an inherent apologetic for the prophet's claim to divine authority. The history of Israel is replete with the fulfillment of God's promises: the national promise to Abraham that God would bless him and make from him a nation, the promise of Davidic kingship, and the promise of a national homeland. Indeed, to many biblical students the reestablishment of the state of Israel in Palestine in 1948 represents yet another example of God's absolute faithfulness to his promises. The apologetic value of God's promises, made and fulfilled, should never be ignored by the believer.

Paul's phrase "before the beginning of time" (lit. "before times eternal," *pro chronōn aiōniōn*) has been understood in two ways. This phrase may be interpreted as an idiomatic expression meaning *a long time ago* or *in the distant past*, thus keeping God's promise within the framework of human history. So understood, the "promise" referred to in this passage is usually cited as God's promise contained in Gen 3:15, declaring the final ruin of Satan by a human conqueror.[12] Although feasible, this interpretation is too limited in view of the clarity of the phrase "before the beginning of time." Paul's words are best understood to mean that God's original intention before creation was for people to enjoy eternal life. In a sense, it was "promised" (as a birthright, so to speak), although there is no specific biblical record of God having made this promise before crea-

---

[11]For further study of the implications of God's promises and fulfillment for OT and NT continuity, see W. J. Beecher, *The Prophets and the Promise* (1905; reprint, Grand Rapids: Baker, 1963); W. C. Kaiser, Jr., "The Old Testament as the Promise-Plan of God," *Toward Rediscovering the Old Testament* (Grand Rapids: Zondervan, 1987), 83-100; and T. E. McComiskey, *The Covenants of Promise* (Grand Rapids: Baker, 1985).

[12]Traditionally, Christians have interpreted Gen 3:15 as the first biblical reference to the gospel. Hence, Gen 3:15 has been labeled the *"protevangelium"*: the "offspring of the woman" being understood as a direct reference to the Messiah and his redemptive work in ultimately destroying the serpent. It is also clear that in some Jewish circles, Gen 3:15 was considered to be a messianic prophecy as early as the third century B.C. See R. Martin, "The Earliest Messianic Interpretation of Genesis 3:15," *JBL* 84 (1965): 425-27. Commentators on Titus suggesting the "promise" of 1:2 as referring to Gen 3:15 include J. J. Van Oosterzee, *The Epistle of Paul to Titus, Lange's Commentary on the Holy Scriptures* (Grand Rapids: Zondervan, 1960), 6; and W. Lock, *The Pastoral Epistles*, ICC (Edinburgh: T & T Clark, 1924), 125. Cf. also A. T. Robertson, *WP* 4:597. Commenting on this same phrase in 2 Tim 1:9, Guthrie (*Pastoral Epistles*, 129) notes that this may be a reference to Gen 3:15.

tion. The fact that death itself was the punishment for human disobedience suggests that eternal life was the original plan for men and women.

1:3 In this context Paul's use of the aorist of the verb *phanerō*, meaning *to show, make known, make manifest, make visible, reveal* (NIV renders "brought to light"), indicates that at a definite period in time, once for all, and in a public and visible manner, God's promise was fulfilled. By modifying this thought with the words "at his appointed season" (lit. "in his own times," cf. 1 Tim 2:6; 6:15), Paul contrasted the *promise fulfilled* with the *promise made* "before the beginning of time," thus indicating God's complete faithfulness to his word. The expression "at his appointed season" is characteristic of Paul's firm belief in God's sovereignty with regard to historical events within his own plan and purposes (Gal 4:4; Rom 5:6; Eph 1:9-12; 3:4-11; 1 Tim 2:5-7).

God has revealed "his word." In this context "his word" is simply "his message" (i.e., "the gospel of Jesus Christ"). Paul's epistles, unlike the Johannine writings, do not employ *logos* ("word") as a technical "title" for Jesus. Paul did affirm, however, that the historical person Jesus Christ, encompassing both his teaching and complete redemptive work, is "the gospel" (cf. 1 Cor 1:23; 15:12; 2 Cor 1:19; 11:4; Phil 1:15-18). The coming of Jesus Christ into human history constitutes the visible fulfillment of God's promise of eternal life for humanity.

"His word," the "gospel," is now made visible "through the preaching entrusted to me [Paul] by the command of God our Savior." Paul used the more common New Testament Greek term for "preaching" (*kērygma*). This noun form, literally rendered "in preaching" (*en kērygmati*), has the basic meaning of *proclamation*. In the New Testament, and especially in Paul's epistles, *kerygma* appears to be used frequently as a technical term expressing both the *content* and the *method of conveying* the message of redemption through faith in Jesus Christ. By referring to "preaching," Paul focused on his own primary role in God's plan of redemption. He expressed here, as in other writings, that God had "entrusted" preaching the gospel to him (cf. Gal 2:7; 1 Tim 1:11). Paul considered the gospel message to be of tremendous importance, and he realized his serious obligation to protect, as well as proclaim, the gospel.

The term "entrusted" also serves to reiterate that Paul's authority was derived solely from God. Paul received this responsibility and authority "by the command of God our Savior," which is an apparent reference to God's specific commission to him at the time of his conversion (cf. Acts 9:15-16; 22:10,14-15; 26:16-21; Gal 2:7). Even though Paul used terms that imply obligation and duty, there is also an element of divine compulsion that accompanies God's specific call to preach. Paul's own admission in 1 Cor 9:16 ("Yet when I preach the gospel, I cannot boast, for I am compelled to preach. Woe to me if I do not preach the gospel") is echoed throughout the Scriptures by other servants of God and apostles of Jesus Christ (Jer 20:9; Acts 4:20).

The application of the title "Savior" to God, common in the Old Testament, appears only six times in the New Testament. It is found twice in 1 Timothy (2:3; 4:10), three times in Titus (1:3; 2:10; 3:4), and once in Luke's Gospel (1:47). Whether Paul purposely applied this title to God in direct contrast to this same title being applied to Nero is uncertain.[13] It would appear more likely (especially in light of the Lukan usage in Mary's prayer and Paul's own traditional Jewish background) that its usage in the Pastoral Epistles simply reflects Paul's choice of a typical Jewish expression. This being the case, Paul's use of the pronoun "our" is significant, thus attributing the salvation of both Paul the Jew and Titus the Gentile to the same gracious and merciful God.

2. Recipient (1:4a)

⁴To Titus, my true son in our common faith:

1:4a Having completed a rather long yet theologically rich introduction, Paul finally identified his recipient: "To Titus, my true son in our common faith." The possessive pronoun "my" does not appear in the Greek text. The term "true son" (literally "true child") is one Paul also used with reference to Timothy (1 Tim 1:2). The term "son" can be used as an expression of affection, or it may suggest that Titus was one of Paul's own converts. This relationship is further defined by Paul's addition of the phrase "in our common faith" (lit. "in accordance with a common faith," *kata koinēn pistin*). In this way Paul also alluded to the legitimacy of Titus's authority to receive and implement his instructions in Crete.

Titus is mentioned by name in the New Testament only in 2 Corinthians, Galatians, 2 Timothy, and Titus.[14] Personal facts known about Titus are not extensive. He was a "Greek" (Gal 2:3), probably one of Paul's own converts (Titus 1:4) and subsequently one of Paul's "coworkers" (2 Cor 8:23).[15] Although the personal data are limited, Titus's role as Paul's coworker in the missionary endeavors of the early church is impressive. Even though Titus is not mentioned by name in Acts, all the evidence strongly indicates that Paul presented Titus to the Jerusalem

---

[13]Guthrie, *Pastoral Epistles*, 55-56.

[14]Second Corinthians 2:13; 7:6,13,14; 8:6,16,23; 12:18; Gal 2:1,3; 2 Tim 4:10; Titus 1:4. Titius Justus, mentioned in Acts 18:7, is not to be confused with Titus, the recipient of this letter.

[15]E. E. Ellis, "Paul and His Co-workers," *NTS* 17 (1971): 437-52. For a detailed investigation of Titus's work in Corinth, see C. K. Barrett, "Titus," *Essays on Paul* (Philadelphia: Westminster, 1982), 118-31.

Council in Acts 15 as living proof that the Jewish rite of circumcision was not necessary for salvation (see Paul's account in Gal 2:1-10, especially noting v. 3). This indicates that Titus had received the Holy Spirit and that this fact was clearly and undeniably evident to others. Second Corinthians, containing the most direct references to Titus, offers a portrait of a devoted and trusted associate of Paul. Titus is seen working in difficult and sensitive situations within the troubled Corinthian church. His duties with regard to that church included delivering Paul's "severe letter" (2 Cor 7:6-7) and taking the leadership role in encouraging and administering the church's contribution to the collection for the Jerusalem church (2 Cor 8:6-24). We can reasonably infer from 2 Corinthians that Titus possessed considerable people skills (naturally acquired or Holy Spirit given) and that he was a man of unquestioned integrity, especially with regard to financial resources.

Finally, Paul's instructions to Titus in this letter indicate his high regard for his coworker's missionary zeal, as well as his considerable abilities to organize local churches for effective and solid Christian ministry. In a day when many Christian institutions have been marred by financial irresponsibility, lack of integrity, division over nonessential issues, and the ever-present threat of false doctrine, Titus serves as a challenging example of a man of character who was consistently available to do God's work.

3. Greeting (1:4b)

Grace and peace from God the Father and Christ Jesus our Savior.

1:4b The terms "grace and peace" are a standard feature in Paul's salutations. It is likely that Paul developed the term "grace" (*charis*) in this context as a wordplay on the Greek term "Greeting" (*chairein*), customarily used in Greek letters in Paul's day. To the Christian, however, the term "grace" suggests the "unmerited favor" given to us by God. "Peace" (Hebrew *shalom*), on the other hand, is a customary form of greeting in Jewish letters.[16]

Paul "Christianized" both *grace* and *peace* by stating that their sources are "God the Father and Christ Jesus our Savior." The concept of the fatherhood of God is rarely expressed in the Old Testament. The term "Father" is applied to God only fifteen times, and then strictly with relation to his people, Israel, or to Israel's king. With the exception of Israel's king, God is never referred to as the Father of an individual. Nor does the Old Testament refer to God as the Father of humankind in general. In the

---

[16]W. G. Doty, *Letters in Primitive Christianity* (Philadelphia: Fortress, 1973), 29. See also J. L. White, "Saint Paul and the Apostolic Letter Tradition," *CBQ* 45 (1983): 433-44.

New Testament, although references to God as "Father" are quite numerous, only Christians are within the sphere of God's fatherhood.[17] Both Old Testament and New Testament references indicate that the biblical concept of God's fatherhood is restricted to those belonging to him through faith. Whereas the Scriptures may suggest a *universal* brotherhood of man, the idea of a *universal* fatherhood of God is absent from biblical teaching.

The title *Savior*, used in this letter six times, is applied to God three times (1:3; 2:10; 3:4) and to Jesus three times (1:4; 2:13; 3:6). Each occurrence of *Savior* applied to God is closely followed by *Savior* applied to Jesus. This interchange of such an important New Testament title (Savior, *sōtēr*) suggests the mutual role of God and Jesus Christ in redemption, as well as the high Christology found in this letter. The use of the possessive pronoun "our" with "Savior" further demonstrates the "common faith" of Paul and Titus. The cultural and religious barriers between Jew and Greek are dissolved in a common faith characterized by a personal relationship with God as Father that is based upon the redeeming work of the Savior, Jesus Christ.

Summary. This theologically rich introduction to the Epistle to Titus moves in scope from Paul's reflections on the sovereignty of God in human salvation to Paul's role in achieving God's purposes. Although he touched on some of the deep mysteries of God, he recognized his own God-given role to protect and proclaim the message of the gospel God had entrusted to him. He was a servant of God and an apostle of Jesus Christ who embraced the trustworthy promises of God, knowing that they would be fulfilled at God's appointed time. Likewise, believers of all ages reflecting upon God's will and purposes for the world should be challenged to see their own role as God's instruments for promoting faith and knowledge that leads to godliness.

---

[17]H. F. D. Sparks, "The Doctrine of the Divine Fatherhood in the Gospels," *Studies in the Gospels: Essays in Memory of R. H. Lightfoot*, ed. D. E. Nineham (Oxford: Blackwell, 1955), 241-62; G. Schrenk, TDNT 5:990-91; and O. Hofius, NIDNTT 1:615-21. For an opposing view, see H. W. Montefiore, "God as Father in the Synoptic Gospels," *NTS* 3 (1956-57): 31-46.

SECTION OUTLINE

II. INSTRUCTIONS FOR ESTABLISHING CHURCH LEADERSHIP
   (1:5-16)
   1. The Charge to Appoint Elders on Crete (1:5)
   2. The Qualifications for Elders on Crete (1:6-9)
      (1) Marriage and Family Qualifications (1:6)
      (2) Personality and Character Qualifications (1:7-8)
      (3) Devotion to Sound Doctrine (1:9)
   3. The Need for Qualified Church Leadership (1:10-16)

II. INSTRUCTIONS FOR ESTABLISHING CHURCH LEADERSHIP (1:5-16)

1. The Charge to Appoint Elders on Crete (1:5)

[5] The reason I left you in Crete was that you might straighten out what was left unfinished and appoint elders in every town, as I directed you.

Paul now turned his attention to Titus's immediate task within the churches on Crete. Crete, although relatively small, is one of the larger islands in the Mediterranean Sea. By the second century B.C., Crete had a substantial Jewish population, powerful enough to obtain the protection of Rome. Acts 2:11 reports that Cretan Jews were among those visiting Jerusalem who witnessed the unique moving of the Holy Spirit on the Day of Pentecost. The large and influential Jewish population on Crete, as well as the initial exposure of Cretan Jews to the gospel at Pentecost, suggests that Crete was a fertile location for missionary work.

1:5 Paul's statement, "the reason I left you in Crete," suggests that Paul and Titus had actually been involved in a joint missionary effort on the island. For unknown reasons, Paul left Crete before the churches were fully organized. However, Paul temporarily left Titus behind (3:12) in order to complete the organization.

Attempts to place the missionary work of Paul and Titus on Crete within the framework of Acts is problematic. Acts contains no record of missionary activity on Crete or the establishment of Christian churches. The only recorded visit of Paul to Crete is found in Acts 27:7-9. It is unlikely that Paul had the opportunity for establishing churches on Crete at this time. There is also no indication in the Acts 27 passage that Titus accompanied Paul on this voyage to Rome. For this reason, most scholars who maintain the Pauline authorship of Titus accept the theory that Paul experienced two Roman imprisonments and that his work with Titus on Crete was done after his first Roman imprisonment, the account of which concludes Acts.[1]

Paul instructed Titus to complete their work in Crete. Grammatically, it is possible that Paul gave Titus two tasks, namely, to "straighten out what was left unfinished" *and* "appoint elders in every town." If two specific tasks are intended here, then the content of the first task is unexplained. It is possible that Paul's command to appoint elders in every city actually defines what was unfinished.[2] However, this interpretation unduly limits the phrase "that you might straighten out what was left unfinished." A more likely interpretation is that Paul intended for Titus to take care of several unfinished tasks referred to in the body of the letter as involving organizing the churches, refuting false teachers, and instructing in doctrine and conduct for the church family.[3] However, Paul's primary task for Titus was the appointment of elders in every Cretan town where a Christian congregation was located. With the words "as I directed you," Paul reminded Titus that these instructions were previously given to him, as well as confirming to the Cretan churches that Titus's work there was supported by Paul's apostolic authority.

This directive to Titus to "appoint elders" is one reason 1 and 2 Timothy and Titus have been labeled the "Pastoral Epistles." For centuries these letters have been generally understood as manuals on church order. However, upon closer inspection, these letters clearly are *not* church manuals containing rigid instructions for church organization. Instead, they are letters to different churches, addressing very different situations.[4] In fact, the entire New Testament contains little specific instruction concerning how the church should be organized.[5] Assuming that some form of

---

[1]For an explanation of the second Roman imprisonment theory and its bearing on this epistle, see D. Guthrie, *The Pastoral Epistles* (Grand Rapids: Eerdmans, 1957), 20-21. Also see F. F. Bruce, *Paul, Apostle of the Heart Set Free* (Grand Rapids: Eerdmans, 1977), 444ff. Even some scholars denying Pauline authorship do not deny the plausibility of two Roman imprisonments; cf. C. K. Barrett, *The Pastoral Epistles* (Oxford: Clarendon, 1963), 9.

[2]G. D. Fee, *1 and 2 Timothy, Titus* (Peabody, Mass.: Hendrickson, 1988), 172. Fee's position appears to reflect a reaction to Hanson's emphasis on the phrase "straighten out what was left unfinished," 176, "Additional Note."

[3]D. E. Hiebert, *Titus*, EBC, vol. 11, ed. F. E. Gaebelein (Grand Rapids: Zondervan, 1978), 429.

[4]G. D. Fee, "Reflections on Church Order in the Pastoral Epistles, with Further Reflection on the Hermeneutics of *ad hoc* Documents," *JETS* 28 (1985): 141-51. On the difference in church situations between Crete and Ephesus, see J. P. Meier, "*Presbyteros* in the Pastoral Epistles," *CBQ* 35 (1973): 323-25.

[5]F. Filson (*A New Testament History* [London: SCM, 1965], 345-48) demonstrates that there was no fixed form or order in the church. Filson concludes his survey of church organization by

organization is necessary, the basic biblical pattern for New Testament church organization appears to be that the leadership was (1) to come from within the church (i.e., local in nature), (2) to meet certain standards of behavior (i.e., qualified), and (3) to be plural in composition (i.e., not a leadership dominated by one personality). These elements, excluding the behavioral qualifications for leadership, are demonstrated by Paul's action in Acts 14:23.

Having identified these constant elements in the New Testament representation of early church organization (i.e., that elders are to be local, plural in number, and qualified), it is also noted that the New Testament reflects a variety of differences within the leadership of the early churches.[6] Factors contributing to these differences may have included cultural distinctions, the proportion of Jewish to Gentile Christians within the congregation, the size of the congregation, or the growth rate of the congregation. Even the manner in which the elders are chosen and appointed in each local church is not specifically delineated in the New Testament.[7] Because so much of our knowledge of early church organization is based upon incidental references within Acts and the New Testament epistles and because so little direct instruction on church organization is given, extreme caution should be used in making dogmatic statements or taking dogmatic positions on church organization. The flexibility afforded the church by this absence of rigid rules and regulations allows the local congregation to be organized in ways appropriate to its own situations and circumstances.

The term "elder" (*presbyterous*) simply means *an aged man*. However, in the context of New Testament church organization, *elder* is a technical term signifying a *church leader*.[8] It is likely that this term was carried over from the synagogue, which probably served as a limited model for

---

stating: "The foregoing sketch shows that the New Testament depicts no fixed church order. Church leadership takes a variety of forms. There are apostles, the Twelve and others. They play a basic role and exercise real influence and authority; but they have no formal successors. There are the Seven, and they have no successors. There are elders and deacons; to indicate their function, the elders are sometimes called "overseers." There are prophets, teachers, and other gifted leaders, but they fit into no formal pattern." Cf. also E. Schweizer, *Church Order in the New Testament*, trans. F. Clark, SBT 32 (London: SCM, 1961).

[6] B. Reicke, "The Constitution of the Primitive Church in the Light of Jewish Documents," *The Scrolls and the New Testament*, ed. K. Stendahl (New York: Harper & Row, 1957), 143-56. Reicke states: "In fact, it seems that objective arguments for each of the constitutional ideas to be considered, for the monarchic as well as for the oligarchic and democratic forms, can be found in the New Testament" (144-45).

[7] Barrett, *Pastoral Epistles*, 128-29; Hiebert, *Titus*, 430.

[8] This distinction is widely accepted by scholars, with the notable exception of J. Jeremias, *Die Briefe an Timotheus und Titus* (Göttingen: Vandenhoeck & Ruprecht, 1968), and his article, "PRESBYTERION ausserchristlich bezeugt," *ZNW* 48 (1957): 127-32.

early church organization.[9] Titus was to "appoint elders [plural] in every town [local]." It is unlikely that Titus made such appointments without the advice and consent of the local Cretan congregation.[10] In vv. 6-9, the qualifications for becoming a Cretan elder are presented. These qualifications are similar to those Paul enumerated in 1 Tim 3:1-7; they are not exact parallels, however, and their differences suggest the flexibility in church organization required for different church situations.[11]

2. The Qualifications for Elders on Crete (1:6-9)

Before considering these specific qualifications, some preliminary observations may be helpful for better understanding the selection of church leaders. First, the creation of a specific group of "elders" within the church membership should facilitate harmony and effective ministry by means of an organizational structure, not discord and discontent based on a holier-than-thou mentality (either assumed by the elders or projected upon the elders by members of the church). It should be noted that *all* church members, by virtue of their conversion experience, have come to realize they were rebels against a holy God. By God's grace they are *reconciled* rebels and thus no longer at enmity with God.

Second, church leaders are to serve as "shepherds of God's church" (Acts 20:28). They accept increased responsibilities for the spiritual welfare of the members. Their firm devotion to the authentic gospel message

---

[9]G. Bornkamm, TDNT 6:651-83. Also J. P. Meier, *CBQ* 35 (1973): 323-45; D. D. Bannerman, *The Scripture Doctrine of the Church* (Grand Rapids: Eerdmans, 1955), 410. Bannerman observes that the NT office of elder "continued in substance what it had been hitherto under the Jewish synagogue system in its best days, with suitable modification and development in accordance with the free spirit of the gospel, and the Providential circumstances in which the Christian congregations found themselves placed. This presumption is confirmed by all the evidence, direct and indirect, bearing upon the point in the NT documents which belong to this period of history."

[10]See W. Lock, *The Pastoral Epistles*, ICC (Edinburgh: T & T Clark, 1924), 129 on καταστήσομεν in Acts 6:3. This clearly indicates that the term does not exclude the congregation's participation in the selection process.

[11]The most noticeable difference in the qualifications for an elder in Titus and 1 Timothy is the omission of "not a recent convert" in Titus. This omission may suggest that the Cretan churches were recently established and much less developed than the church at Ephesus. It is also noteworthy that Titus contains no references to "deacons." This suggests two important points. (1) Paul obviously was willing to be flexible in certain matters of church organization as the local situation dictated. (2) The tendency to emphasize the similarities between 1 and 2 Timothy and Titus because of their being grouped together (somewhat superficially) as "Pastoral Epistles," without exploring their significant differences in content and historical context, can present a distorted picture of the material in each letter. Meier's analysis, based upon the use of the term *presbyteros*, is instructive. He states, "Moreover, the interesting differences between 1 Tim and Titus tend to be ignored in the rush to schematize and fit the data into the prefabricated synthesis" (323).

requires that they encourage others toward faith that leads to godliness. They should also demonstrate to those opposing the true gospel message their erroneous position in an effort to convince them of the truth (1:9).[12]

Third, increased responsibilities mean increased accountability and visibility. Whereas all believers are ultimately accountable to God, the elder (church leader) has an additional accountability to the church in which he serves. His conduct, both within and outside the church, must be exemplary. Of course, this does not mean that he must be perfect, for such a standard would be impossible. But the fact remains that the increased visibility of the church leader, both to the church and the non-believing community, requires that his personal conduct clearly reflect the saving gospel of God's redemptive grace *and* the ongoing process of sanctification in his life.

And finally, it is noted that the elder (church leader) be selected as a result of his already exemplifying these qualifications. The qualifications are to be met *before* he becomes an elder. Simply put, these are qualifications that a man must meet in order to become an elder; they are not characteristics that a man should assume after he becomes an elder.

Paul set the overall tone for the qualifications of being an elder in a Cretan church by stating, "An elder must be blameless" (lit., "If anyone is blameless," v. 6). This primary condition of blamelessness is repeated and strongly emphasized by the verb form "he must" (*dei*) in v. 7. It should be understood as the basic condition for evaluating the prospective elder with regard to the specific qualifications that follow. Paul was especially sensitive that the witness of the church as a whole could be compromised by valid objections to its chosen leaders. The importance of this basic qualification for any church leadership position is especially noted since Paul used the same term ("nothing against them," *anegklētoi*) in his *deacon* qualifications in 1 Tim 3:10, while choosing a synonym, "above reproach" (*anepilēmpton*), to begin his elder qualifications in 1 Tim 3:2.[13]

The qualifications presented require acceptable conditions in three basic areas of the prospective elder's life, namely, (1) his marriage and family (v. 6), (2) his personality and character traits (vv. 7-8), and (3) his devotion to God's Word and his commitment to teaching and protecting the true gospel message.

---

[12]F. Büshsel, TDNT 2:473-76. The verb ἐλέγχειν in 1:9 suggests an active pursuit of convincing the erroneous party, not just an attitude of "defending the faith."

[13]Guthrie, *Pastoral Epistles*, 184, observes: "The same Pauline word *anenkletos* used to describe the blamelessness of the Cretan *elders* is applied in 1 Tim. iii. 10 to the Ephesian *deacons* reflecting the need for an irreproachable moral standard in all types of Christian office."

(1) Marriage and Family Qualifications (1:6)

6 An elder must be blameless, the husband of but one wife, a man whose children believe and are not open to the charge of being wild and disobedient.

1:6 The home life of the elder must reflect this blamelessness. Two aspects of the prospective elder's family life are noted: his marriage and the faith and conduct of his children. First, Paul stated that the elder must be "the husband of but one wife" (lit. "one woman's man," *mias gynaikos anēr*).[14] These simple words have proved difficult to understand, and the interpretations derived from them are many and varied.[15]

A basic question concerning this qualification is whether the elder is restricted to *one* marriage to *one woman* in his lifetime. Obviously, this phrase would eliminate a bigamist or polygamist from consideration. However, there is a question about whether this qualification would also prohibit a man who is remarried after the death or divorce of his wife from serving as an elder. Since the Scriptures do not prohibit remarriage after the death of one's spouse, and actually encourage it in some cases (cf. 1 Tim 5:14), it is unlikely that such a remarried man should be disqualified. Under the normal circumstances of the death of a spouse and a subsequent remarriage, it would not appear likely that the man would be considered blameworthy. However, if a man is divorced and subsequently remarries, there appears to be a legitimate question about whether this man is disqualified. The interpretation of Paul's phrase "husband of one wife" is determined in large measure by the interpretation of biblical teaching with regard to divorce.[16] There is also a question of how to apply this qualifi-

---

[14]This exact phrase appears in 1 Tim 3:2 regarding elder qualifications, and a similar phrase is used in 1 Tim 3:12 regarding deacon qualifications.

[15]Commentators offer considerable discussion on the exact meaning of this phrase. For a survey of patristic discussion, see C. H. Dodd, "ΜΙΑΣ ΓΥΝΑΙΚΟΣ ΑΝΗΡ 1 Tim 3:2, 12: Titus 1:6," *BT* 28 (1977): 112-16. Also see R. L. Saucy, "The Husband of One Wife," *BibSac* 131 (1974): 229-40. Saucy argues that the dissolution of a marriage by divorce effectively ends that marriage relationship and that subsequent remarriage does not constitute continually living in a sinful state, i.e., having more than one wife. He maintains that the issue is how the man presently lives in relation to his present marriage. In a similar argument P. Trummer, "Einehe nach den Pastoralbriefen. Zum verstandnis der Termini *mias gynaikos aner* und *henos andros gyne*," *Bib* 51 (1970): 471-84, maintains that this text as well as 1 Tim 3:2,12; 5:9 does not address the question of second marriages but rather emphasizes that the elder's (or widow's) married life be exemplary, whether married one or more times.

[16]The discussion of biblical teaching with regard to divorce is full and varied, and many interpretations have been offered. For fuller exploration of this subject, see commentaries on these texts: Matt 5:31-32; 19:3-12; Mark 10:2-12; Luke 16:18; 1 Cor 7. See also C. E. B. Cranfield's essay entitled "The Church and Divorce and the Remarriage of Divorced Persons in the Light of Mark 10:1-12," *The Bible and Christian Life* (Edinburgh: T & T Clark, 1985), 229-34.

cation to marriages contracted or dissolved before Christian conversion. It would appear reasonable that Paul's all-encompassing condition, "blameless," should be used to influence the decision about a man's qualification for being an elder if the man is divorced (whether or not he remarries).

Perhaps most significantly, a man under consideration to become an elder (or any other church leader) and who has been divorced and remarried should evaluate his own personal situation and the public perception of his circumstances before taking such a position. The spiritual maturity and personal characteristics required of a man to become an elder (cf. 1:9) should be evident in his choice to allow or refuse to allow himself for consideration to serve in formal church leadership. If he can reasonably assume that those in the Christian community, as well as those in the unbelieving community, regard him as blameless, and therefore not compromising the witness of the church, then he may allow himself to be considered. If, on the other hand, there is reason to believe that the church's witness would be compromised by his serving as a church leader, then he should not allow himself to be considered. However, whether a Christian is considered qualified or disqualified to serve as an elder because of his previous marriage experience, the fact remains that there are places of significant Christian leadership available outside the formal structure of the church.

Attempts to prohibit unmarried men from becoming elders on the basis of this phrase misinterpret Paul's intention as well as ignore his teaching on marriage in 1 Cor 7. Surely, remaining unmarried would not be considered blameworthy. However, it may be assumed that the majority of candidates would be married and that Paul may have preferred married men to hold these positions because of their experience in leading the family unit (cf. 1 Tim 3:5).

The second aspect of the prospective elder's family life concerns his children, specifically their faith and personal conduct. Paul stated that the elder should be "a man whose children believe and are not open to the charge of being wild and disobedient." The qualifications regarding the elder's children in Titus 1:6 and 1 Tim 3:4 are similar in that they both require that the children be well behaved and obedient.[17] However, the addition of "whose children believe"[18] in Titus makes this condition

---

[17]Paul's use of ἀσωτίας recalls Luke 15:13, where this same term is used to describe the prodigal son. Cf. also Eph 5:18 and 1 Pet 4:4. According to Foerster, TDNT, 1:507, "In all these passages the word signifies wild and disorderly rather than extravagant or voluptuous living."

[18]KJV renders τέκνα ἔχων πιστά "having faithful children." This interpretation is supported by Lock, 130, who states: "Perhaps 'believing,' 'Christian.' More probably, as suiting the following qualifications better, 'trustworthy,' 'loyal'; cf. 1 Cor. 4:17 and 1 Tim. 3:5."

But Hiebert (*Titus*, 430) states: "The original (tekna pista) may mean 'faithful children' but 'believing children' is intended here, referring to those who are old enough to have made

even more stringent. This additional requirement that the elder be capable of influencing his own children to become Christians demonstrates
Paul's conviction that effective spiritual leadership in the home suggests
the probability of effective spiritual leadership in the church.[19] Not only
is the elder to be a good father as reflected in his children's behavior,
but he is also to be a spiritual father as reflected in the spiritual commitment of his children.

(2) Personality and Character Qualifications (1:7-8)

**[7] Since an overseer is entrusted with God's work, he must be blameless—
not overbearing, not quick-tempered, not given to drunkenness, not violent,
not pursuing dishonest gain. [8] Rather he must be hospitable, one who loves
what is good, who is self-controlled, upright, holy and disciplined.**

1:7 The logical connection between what Paul required concerning
the elder's home life and his responsibilities within the church should not
be overlooked. The conjunction "since" (*gar*) which begins v. 7 indicates
that Paul was continuing his thought from v. 6 and actually making a logical connection between his statements on the elder's home life and the
church. This is apparent not only because of the use of "since" (*gar*), but
also from Paul's repetition of the necessity (note the verb form, *dei*) that
the elder be blameless and his description of the elder as one "entrusted
with God's work" (*theou oikonomon*, lit. *God's steward*). It is unfortunate
that the NIV rendering "since an overseer is entrusted with God's work"
fails to bring out this significant logical connection, as well as the implications of Paul's use of the term "steward" (*oikonomon*). In Greek the
root of the term *oikonomon* is *oikos*, meaning *house*. The "steward" is
responsible for his master's "house." The fact that the elder is referred to
as "*God's* steward" is noteworthy. The elder is clearly considered to be

---

a personal decision. If they remained pagans, it would throw into question the father's ability
to lead others to faith." Contrary to the KJV rendering, the RSV, NEB, NASB, as well as the
NIV render the phrase to mean that the children are to be Christian believers. This view is
accepted by most recent commentators.

It should be noted that there may be an indirect connection between this additional qualification of "believing children" in Titus 1:6 and the qualification in 1 Tim 3:4 ("not a recent
convert"), which is omitted from Titus. White, *EGT* 4:187, observes: "It must be supposed
that a Christian father who has unbelieving children is himself a recent convert, or a very
careless Christian. The fact that St. Paul did not think it necessary to warn Timothy that such
men were not eligible for the presbyterate is a proof that Christianity was at this time more
firmly established in Ephesus than in Crete."

[19]Guthrie, *Pastoral Epistles*, 185, comments: "As in 1 Timothy, the home is regarded as
the training ground for Christian leaders." He also states, "Bernard is nearer the truth when
he understands the point to be that elders who have children are expected to have a Christian
household."

God's servant. He is to do God's work, and he is ultimately accountable to God for his performance.[20] Paul's concern for the elder's home life is clear. Just as a father functions as the "overseer" (*episkopon*) in his own house, so also the elder functions as "overseer" in God's house. A man whose home life is blameless will, in all probability, be blameless in a leadership role in God's house. There is no indication from the text that Paul made a distinction between "elder" and "overseer" in this letter. The terms appear to be used either synonymously or with "overseer" being employed generically, thus describing a function of the elder's role in the church.[21]

Paul followed these domestic qualifications with a succinct list of five negative and six positive personality and character traits.[22] Concerning the negative traits, F. D. Gealy observes, "Since the office of bishop is one of authority and power, the vices named are those to which persons in such positions are tempted."[23] Each negative trait is presented as one word preceded by "not" (*mē*). Each negative trait should be considered in light of Paul's fundamental qualification of "blameless," which is repeated at the beginning of these five traits. The elder should be characterized as "not overbearing" (*mē authadē*) or "self-willed" (KJV). He should be flexible in his own opinions, considerate of other viewpoints, and especially open and eager to do God's will. The Christian leader should be sensitive to use authority in ways that truly promote God's work and not any personal agenda.

"Not quick-tempered" is a necessary prerequisite for leading people. One who cannot control his own emotions cannot exercise proper judgment over church matters, especially those issues that inevitably evoke strong feelings. This qualification may not preclude an elder's strong personal feelings concerning any given issue. It does prohibit an impulsive or divisive reaction that would do more to complicate the problem than to solve it.

Paul disqualified a drunkard from serving as an elder. The elder must "not be given to much wine" (author's translation). Even in light of

---

[20]J. E. Huther (*Critical and Exegetical Hand-Book to the Epistles to Timothy and Titus* [New York: Funk & Wagnalls, 1885], 284) comments: "Even if they are elected by the church, they bear their office as divine, not exercising it according to the changing pleasures of those by whom they are elected, but according to the will of God."

[21]See the excellent study by R. E. Brown, "*Episkope* and *Episkopos*: The New Testament Evidence," *TS* 41 (1980): 322-38. Also J. Meier, *CBQ* 35 (1973): 323-45.

[22]Although the content of the qualifications for elders appears to be *generally* the same in Titus 1:6-9 and 1 Tim 3:2-7, the *form* in which they are presented varies significantly, both verbally and in arrangement of material. This raises serious questions regarding the existence of a supposedly specific, detailed list of qualifications from which Paul drew.

[23]F. D. Gealy, *The First and Second Epistles to Timothy and the Epistle to Titus*, IB, vol. 11 (Nashville: Abingdon, 1955), 528.

Paul's other comments regarding the abuse of wine, one cannot be dogmatic that he requires total abstinence in the elder.[24] However, considering the addictive qualities of alcohol, any Christian (whether an elder or not) should seriously consider Paul's statements concerning the responsibilities of the "strong" to the "weak."[25] Remaining blameless in any situation that gives offense should be the governing rule with regard to any questionable practices allowed by Scripture yet not encouraged by Scripture.

The elder should not be "violent" (*mē plēktēn*, lit. *a striker*). Physical violence is certainly unnecessary and unbecoming to a position of leadership. It should be noted that words often strike harder than fists.

The final negative trait is that the elder not pursue dishonest gain. This final trait offers several interpretations, suggesting that the elder either (1) be reputably employed, (2) be absolutely honest in money matters including those involving the church, or (3) not use his Christian service as an opportunity for financial profit.

1:8 Paul began v. 8 with the adversative particle "but" (*alla*), thus indicating a contrast between the preceding five negative traits and the six positive traits that follow. The elder must be "hospitable." Generally understood, the elder should be "devoted to the welfare of others."[26] Specifically understood, the elder's duties may require him to entertain Christian or non-Christian visitors on behalf of the church.[27] The elder must be "one who loves what is good." The neuter form indicates *good things*, as well as "good men" (KJV). "Self control" includes mastery of his mind, his emotions, his words, and his deeds. This positive trait is stressed in Titus as applicable to all Christians generally.[28] The elder is to be "upright" ("just," "righteous"). He must be committed to doing what is right. He must be "holy," committed to a life especially separated to devotion and service of God. He must be "disciplined" (*egkratē*). This final trait also concludes Paul's list of the fruits of the Spirit in Gal 5:23. The term "denotes power of lordship . . . over oneself or over something."[29] Although some may have acquired many of these personality/character traits naturally, others may have developed them only through

---

[24]Cf. 1 Tim 5:23, where Paul recommended wine for Timothy's health; but also note his warnings in Rom 14:21; 1 Tim 3:3,8; Titus 2:3.

[25]See 1 Cor 8:4-13; Rom 14:1-23, noting especially vv. 13-23.

[26]Guthrie, *Pastoral Epistles*, 186.

[27]J. N. D. Kelly, *The Pastoral Epistles* (Peabody, Mass.: Hendrickson, 1960), 232. Fee, *1, 2 Timothy, and Titus*, 81, states that hospitality "was a thoroughgoing expectation of all Christians in the early church (cf. 1 Tim 5:10; Rom 12:13; 1 Pet 4:9)." Also see D. W. Riddle, "Early Christian Hospitality," *JBL* 57 (1935): 141-54.

[28]The Greek term σώφρονα, with its cognate forms, appears in Titus 1:8; 2:2,4-6,12.

[29]W. Grundmann, TDNT 2:339.

growth in the grace of God and the knowledge of his Word. It is the elder's devotion to the Word of God and his facility in it that constitutes Paul's third and final area of elder qualifications found in v. 9.

(3) Devotion to Sound Doctrine (1:9)

⁹He must hold firmly to the trustworthy message as it has been taught, so that he can encourage others by sound doctrine and refute those who oppose it.

1:9 That "he must hold firmly to the trustworthy message as it has been taught" constitutes the basis of the elder's doctrinal function as a teacher and apologist of the gospel. The gospel is referred to as "the trustworthy message" (*tou . . . pistou logou*, "the faithful word").[30] The NIV rendering, "as it has been taught," inadequately expresses the phrase *kata tēn didachēn* (lit. "according to the teaching"). The message is "trustworthy" precisely because it is according to, in harmony with, and in conformity to "*the* teaching" (author's translation). This use of the noun "teaching" with the definite article suggests that Christian doctrine was beginning to be formed into some type of recognized, orthodox propositions, perhaps even written.[31] The elder "must hold firmly" to orthodox biblical teaching. However, maintaining correct beliefs or doctrines is not enough. Two basic functions of the elder's role in the church emanate from his own personal devotion to the truth of God's Word. Paul expressed this clearly with "so that" (*hina*) followed by two infinitives: "*so that* he can *encourage* others by sound doctrine and *refute* those who oppose it" (author's emphasis). The first function, to encourage, is expressed by the Greek infinitive *parakalein*. This Greek term is widely used throughout the New Testament and displays a wealth of meanings

---

[30]Although this phrase is similar to the formula expression "πιστὸς ὁ λόγος," which is unique to the Pastoral Epistles, it should not be interpreted as such in this passage. Here "πιστοῦ λόγου" refers to the whole gospel message, whereas the phrase "πιστὸς ὁ λόγος" refers to a *specific* statement or statements. Cf. 1 Tim 1:15; 3:1; 4:9; 2 Tim 2:11; Titus 3:8. For an extended study on πιστὸς ὁ λόγος, see G. W. Knight III, *The Faithful Sayings in the Pastoral Letters* (Grand Rapids: Baker, 1979).

[31]Kelly, *Pastoral Epistles*, 233, states: "It is also noticeable that the primitive kerygma is already beginning to take shape as a fixed body of orthodox doctrine. (See notes on 1 Tim vi. 20; 2 Tim i. 13f.; ii.2)." Guthrie (186), referring to "teaching," states, "It may possibly refer to some written records." C. H. Dodd (*According to the Scriptures* [London: Fontana, 1965], 126) demonstrates that use of certain OT passages throughout the NT documents may indicate the formation of a body of teaching. Dodd concludes: "The evidence suggests that at a very early date a certain *method* of biblical study was established and became part of the equipment of Christian evangelists and teachers. This method was largely employed orally, and found literary expression only sporadically and incompletely, but it is presupposed in our earliest sources."

within a variety of contexts.[32] Used here, within the context of the elder's function toward believers, "to encourage others by sound doctrine" indicates comfort and edification in "the trustworthy message." This is especially true in light of the false teachers and the false teaching Paul would address in vv. 10-16.

The most prominent false teaching Paul encountered and vigorously opposed throughout his ministry was false teaching that promoted a works righteousness *in addition to* "the righteousness which comes by faith." This false teaching, promoted by Jewish converts to Christianity (known as "Judaizers," or the "circumcision," cf. Eph 2:11) is referred to in Acts and the New Testament epistles. The severity of this false teaching resulted in the repudiation of the Jewish rite of circumcision as a necessary condition for Christian conversion at the Jerusalem Council in Acts 15. The resulting instructions contained in Acts 15:28-29, however, appear to have left some opportunity for interpreting dietary regulations (clean and unclean) as either conditional for salvation or representative of acceptable Christian behavior. Paul absolutely and vehemently opposed any attempt to connect Christian conversion with human effort. From his knowledge of the apostolic "teaching" (i.e., the "trustworthy message"), the elder is to "encourage" the believers with "sound doctrine," i.e., in teaching that is not tainted with error.[33] This function of the elder necessarily requires that he be a "student of the Word," willing to learn and willing to communicate his learning.

The second doctrinal function of the elder is that he "refute those who oppose it" (i.e., "the trustworthy message"). The Greek verb employed here, *elegchein*, suggests an educative dimension in confronting false teachers who contradict the gospel message. The goal of the refutation of

---

[32]O. Schmitz, TDNT 5:793-99. In Acts and the Pauline Epistles, παρακαλέω is especially linked with the message of the gospel. It can have an evangelistic nuance of "invitation" when used in reference to an invitation to salvation for unbelievers (e.g., Acts 2:40; 13:15), or it can be used in the context of believers (e.g., Heb 13:22) with the nuance of encouraging, comforting, and edifying believers by biblical teaching.

[33]The Pastorals express preference for the term διδασκαλία ("teaching"). Of twenty-one NT occurrences, it is employed fifteen times in the Pastorals and four times in Titus (1:9; 2:1,7,10). The term may refer to a written body of doctrine or oral teaching, but its usage appears to imply definite, known propositions or tenets of Christian faith. K. H. Rengstorf, TDNT 2:162, points out that the term can denote the essential difference between Christian proclamation and the various movements that threaten the community.

On "sound doctrine," U. Luck, TDNT 8:312, observes: "To be avoided is the mistake of thinking that the reference is to the teaching which makes whole, whose goal is the health of the soul. Sound doctrine is true and correct teaching in contrast to perverted doctrine." See further A. J. Malherbe, "Medical Imagery in the Pastoral Epistles," *Texts and Testaments, Critical Essays on the Bible and Early Church Fathers*, ed. W. E. March (San Antonio: Trinity University Press, 1980), 19-35.

false teaching is not to destroy the opponent but rather to restore him to
"sound doctrine." This necessarily implies that the false teaching to
which Paul referred was coming from *within* the church, i.e., from those
who professed Christian faith. Such a situation would also require that the
elder be courageous in his willingness to confront a so-called Christian
brother.

In summary, Paul presented qualifications for church leaders. They
must meet certain standards with regard to their home life, their personality and character traits, and their doctrinal integrity. While most of these
qualifications are simple and straightforward, others are verbally ambiguous and are therefore susceptible to a variety of interpretations. This is
especially true of Paul's requirements concerning the elder's marriage and
the faith of his children. Must a divorced man or the father of children
who have rejected the gospel message be disqualified regardless of the
circumstances involved in either case? The answer to such questions will
inevitably involve the issues of the authority and the interpretation of
Scripture, especially with regard to what the Scriptures authoritatively
prescribe as normative for the Christian believer and the church regardless of the time in history or the cultural circumstances involved. The
difficulty of applying these scriptural standards consistently in any given
situation is all too apparent. For example, in what sense is a church or
denomination "unbiblical" if it does not employ *both* elders and deacons
in its organizational structure (cf. 1 Tim 3:1-13)? Fortunately, most issues
subject to inconsistent applications are not theological in nature but
involve practical matters, thus allowing local congregations to exercise
judgment within the context of their own particular situation. Such room
for judgment is contained in the all-encompassing term of "blameless"
which Paul specifically applied to the home life situation of the prospective elder. In any given situation, good Christian judgment requires exam-
ining such practical matters on their merits or demerits with the
understanding that the resulting conclusion not compromise the witness
of the church.

The need for doctrinally trained elders is evident as Paul continued to
explain the situation on Crete in vv. 10-16.

3. The Need for Qualified Church Leadership (1:10-16)

[10] **For there are many rebellious people, mere talkers and deceivers, especially those of the circumcision group. [11] They must be silenced, because they
are ruining whole households by teaching things they ought not to teach—
and that for the sake of dishonest gain. [12] Even one of their own prophets has
said, "Cretans are always liars, evil brutes, lazy gluttons." [13] This testimony is
true. Therefore, rebuke them sharply, so that they will be sound in the faith
[14] and will pay no attention to Jewish myths or to the commands of those who**

reject the truth. [15]To the pure, all things are pure, but to those who are corrupted and do not believe, nothing is pure. In fact, both their minds and consciences are corrupted. [16]They claim to know God, but by their actions they deny him. They are detestable, disobedient and unfit for doing anything good.

1:10 In the history of the early church, it appears that as the good seed of the gospel was sown and began to grow, false teachers also followed, sowing their seeds of error. This consistently resulted in discomfort, confusion, and divisions within the church. The churches on Crete were no exception. Having instructed Titus that the elders must be committed to sound doctrine, Paul indicated that their ability to "refute those who oppose it" (1:9) must be demonstrated on Crete: "For there are many rebellious people, mere talkers and deceivers, especially those of the circumcision group."

Just how great this opposition was cannot be determined by the indefinite term "many." The direct attention given to false teachers and false teaching in this letter is limited to 1:10-16 and 3:10-11. However, the instructions given to Titus in chap. 2 may well reflect Paul's knowledge of specific areas of behavior that were open to criticism from the opposition (cf. 2:7-8).[34] Whereas the sense of urgency concerning the false teaching is not as great as that expressed in 1 Timothy, the "many rebellious people" had created a situation of significant concern for the young churches on Crete. Paul's use of the term *anypotaktoi* (*rebellious, insubordinate*) suggests that the false teaching was coming from within the ranks of those professing Christian faith on Crete. Their rebelliousness was against the truth of the gospel (cf. v. 14). Paul described them as "mere talkers," a term that may be associated in the Jewish mind with the activity of heathen idolaters.[35] Since what they taught was error, they were therefore "deceivers."

Paul identified the troublemakers as "especially those of the circumcision group." The English rendering of "especially" might suggest that Jewish believers formed a significant part of the problem. However, Fee argues that the Greek term *malista* (rendered "especially") can also mean *in other words*. In this context the false teachers would be solely limited to Jewish converts, i.e., "the circumcision" group (cf. Eph 2:11).[36] Paul

---

[34]Fee, *1, 2 Timothy and Titus*, 177, states: "Along with 3:10-11, this is the only indication in the letter of the presence of false teachers. Yet their lack of genuine good works (v. 16) plus the emphasis throughout on observable good works by those who know the truth (2:5, 7, 8, 10, 14; 3:1, 8, 14) suggest that their presence is a major reason for the letter—even if it lacks the urgency of 1 Timothy."

[35]Cf. Lock, 133.

[36]F. D. Gealy, *First and Second Epistles to Timothy, Titus*, 530, argues: "The most reasonable conjecture is that, given a later date for the Pastorals, 'those of the circumcision' were neither Jews nor Jewish Christians, but Gentile Christians who were attached to Jewish

had encountered opposition from this group before. (See comments on v. 9.)

1:11 Using strong language, Paul asserted, "They must be silenced." The picture contained in Paul's words is that of an animal with a muzzle over its mouth. His words were strong "because they are ruining whole households by teaching things they ought not to teach." In the Greek the verb *dei* ("it is necessary") is used twice in v. 11. The first usage expresses that *it is necessary to silence* the opponents. The second usage, appearing as a negative (*mē dei*), expresses the thought that the opponents were teaching *things which are not necessary.* This indicates that the false teaching here, as found elsewhere in the New Testament, is the attempt to add "works" in some form as a requirement for Christian salvation.[37] The Cretan churches were clearly troubled by such false teaching, as evidenced by Paul's comments in vv. 10-16. In any age churches must not tolerate obvious and blatant error to be taught within the sphere of their authority, particularly when such error involves the issue of salvation. The church must not allow the gospel to be held captive to a free-speech mentality that compromises God's clear revelation.

The term "households" may refer specifically to actual family units; however, the term probably refers to house-churches where most Christian instruction was conducted. These false teachers were motivated by "dishonest gain," a motive Paul also condemned in 1 Tim 6:5. No details are given concerning the source of this dishonest gain. Perhaps these false teachers were receiving gifts from their followers. At any rate, Paul condemned the practice of religion for profit and clearly associated it with those in opposition to Christian truth.

1:12 In an almost parenthetical manner, Paul quoted Epimenides, a well-known and highly esteemed sixth-century Cretan philosopher. The line, which offers an unflattering assessment of the Cretan character, is introduced by Paul in a direct manner to emphasize its source to be none other than a revered Cretan: "Even one of their own prophets has said, 'Cretans are always liars, evil brutes, lazy gluttons.' "[38] Paul evidently applied this quotation to the Cretan false teachers, not to Cretans in general.

---

practices and were concerned to retain as obligatory for Christians a more considerable body of Jewish customs than Paul or 'Paul' could admit." This is indicative of the far-fetched interpretations produced by a determined hold on a late-date theory.

[37] Paul's argument in Galatians provides the classic response to attempts to add human works to the free grace of God's salvation to humanity. Paul's question in Gal 3:3 is pertinent to the Cretan situation: "Are you so foolish? After beginning with the Spirit, are you now trying to attain your goal by human effort?"

[38] This statement, attributed by most scholars to Epimenides, probably reflects the Cretan boast that Crete contained the tomb of Zeus. Of course, being a god, Zeus could not possibly have died! For details on the history of this quotation, see Lock, 134-35 and Kelly, 235.

As applied to these false teachers, Paul agreed with this assessment, declaring, "This testimony is true."

The Greek world of that day also concurred since the verb "to cretize" (*kretizein*) was used to express *lying* or *cheating*.[39] The details of the quotation are applicable to these false teachers because "teaching things they ought not to teach" proved them to be liars; their rebellious, out-of-control nature proved them to be "evil brutes"; and their desire for "dishonest gain" proved them to be "lazy gluttons." These Cretan false teachers, who evidently claimed to be Christians (1:16), were in fact living up to the reputation given them as unregenerate people centuries before Christ.

1:13 Paul's response to their rebelliousness and false teaching was to command Titus to "rebuke them" (imperative mood): "Therefore, rebuke them sharply, so that they will be sound in the faith." The term for rebuke (*elegche*) is the same term Paul used in 1:9 to describe the elder's duty regarding false teaching in the church. Titus's rebuke was to be sharp or severe. Paul's only other use of this adverb (*apotomōs*, "sharply") is in 2 Cor 13:10. In that context the adverb is associated with correction based upon Paul's authority: "That I may not have to be harsh [lit. deal sharply] in my use of authority." It is interesting that although Paul instructed that the elders should refute or rebuke false teachers in 1:9, he specifically instructed Titus to rebuke them sharply in 1:13. This may indicate that Paul thought Titus's rebuke of the Cretan false teachers would carry more apostolic authority since Titus was his personal delegate. Furthermore, Titus's dealings with the false teachers would serve as an excellent example for the Cretan elders to follow.

Paul continued to define this sharp rebuke by insisting that it must contain the educative and restorative quality inherent in the verb *elegche*. Paul stated, "Therefore, rebuke them sharply, *so that they will be sound in the faith*" (author's emphasis). In dealing with error in the church, the primary goal should always be the correction *and* restoration of those teaching error.

Failure to confront problems within the church, whether theologically or practically based, may be indicative of a basic indifference with regard to God's truth or the nurturing of truly Christian relationships. The fear of giving offense and a highly individualized view of personal faith may discourage church leaders from following the biblical mandate to rebuke. The restoration that is possible both in fellowship and in sound doctrine is compromised by this reluctance to confront. Loving, sensitive, yet firm confrontation can result in stronger relationships and restored unity or perhaps a needed purging of those who deny the truth. (See comments on 3:9-11.)

---

[39]Kelly, *Pastoral Epistles*, 235.

In v. 9 Paul employed the phrase "sound doctrine" (*en tē didaskalia tē hygiainousē*) as a figure of speech for correct doctrine.[40] Again in v. 13 this same figure of soundness or health is used with the phrase "in the faith" (*en tē pistei*), still emphasizing the importance of sound doctrine. In this context Paul's use of "faith" (*pistei*) with the definite article and the use of "sound" (*hygiainōsin*) clearly refers to "the faith" as a body of doctrine (oral or written) and not "faith" as personal experience.[41]

1:14 Paul's description of the false teaching as "Jewish myths" and "the commands of those who reject the truth" indicates its nature and suggests its content. The fact that the nature of the false teaching was Jewish is confirmed not only by Paul's use of the term "Jewish myths" but also from his reference to the "circumcision" in v. 10. The myths referred to possibly were concerned with Jewish and Gnostic ideas combined in Hellenistic Judaism and transferred to Christianity by Jewish-Christian converts.[42] The actual influence of Gnostic beliefs on first-century Judaism remains questionable, however, and there is no compelling reason to interpret Paul's description of the false teaching as anything less than completely Jewish in character.[43] The actual content of these Jewish myths remains unknown.

Paul's second description of the false teaching as "the commands of those who reject the truth" is more suggestive of its content, especially in light of his concluding comments that follow in vv. 15-16. The literal phrase "commandments of men" (*entolais anthrōpōn*) recalls Isa 29:13 (LXX): "These people come near to me with their mouth and honor me with their lips, but their hearts are far from me. Their worship of me is made up only of *rules taught by men*." Jesus quoted this same passage from Isaiah to the Pharisees (Mark 7:7 // Matt 15:8) when they disputed with him concerning religious ceremony and the matter of being clean or unclean. It appears obvious that the "commandments of men" in the New Testament refers to Jewish ceremonial rituals involving the religious concept of "clean" and "unclean." Those persons who tenaciously hold to these human commandments or traditions (i.e., religious rituals that have no real meaning) are "those who reject the truth," according to Paul

---

[40]Cf. 286, n. 33.

[41]Guthrie, 189.

[42]G. Stahlin, TDNT 4:783, states: "In fact it is highly probable that the Past. are concerned with the early form of a Gnosticism which flourished on the soil of Hellenistic Jewish Christianity, like the rather different Gnosticism to which Colossians refers." For a similar view, cf. Kelly, 236.

[43]It is difficult to believe that false teaching coming from "the circumcision" would contain any religious or philosophical ideas foreign to basic Jewish beliefs and practice. On "myths and genealogies" in 1 Timothy and Titus, with arguments against a possible Gnostic influence, see Fee, 41-42.

(1:14), or who "have let go of the commands of God," according to Jesus (Mark 7:8).

1:15 In a concluding remark, Paul summed up his comments on dealing with the Cretan false teachers with a proverbial sounding statement concerning "the pure" (lit. "clean," *kathara*). This confirms that a significant element of the false teaching concerned Jewish ceremonial practices (e.g., dietary regulations), which were being taught as necessary for true Christian living. Paul stated: "To the pure [clean], all things are pure [clean], but to those who are corrupted and do not believe, nothing is pure [clean]." "The pure" are those persons who are pure by virtue of their faith alone. This is clear because "those who are corrupted" (i.e., "unclean") are specifically referred to as "those who do not believe." Therefore, to those who are pure, all things are pure in the sense that ceremonial cleanliness is totally unnecessary and of no value.

This basic truth reflects Jesus' teaching in Mark 7:1-23, and it was impressed upon Peter in Acts 10:9-15; 11:1-18. Such dietary rules are only the commands of men and therefore do not please God. Obviously Paul was *not* suggesting that the pure cannot sin or be tainted with moral failure and sinful behavior. On the other hand, those who are corrupted and do not believe cannot make themselves pure by strictly adhering to human commands (i.e., ceremonial or ritualistic practices of purity or cleanliness). Even the Old Testament gives expression to the fact that external religious ceremonies, originally designed as an outward expression of inward repentance, are absolutely ineffective alone (1 Sam 15:22; Isa 1:11-18; Hos 6:6; Mic 6:6-8). David also clearly expressed the inability of any religious ceremony to cleanse from sin. Rather, he declared that God values the internal cleansing of moral evil by a "broken and contrite heart" of repentance (Ps 51:16-17).

Paul added, "In fact, both their minds and consciences are corrupted." By maintaining their steadfast position with regard to the necessity of ceremonial purity (which is in fact unacceptable to God), they effectively demonstrated that their minds were corrupted (i.e., their intelligence was corrupted), and their consciences were corrupted (i.e., they could no longer discern right and wrong).

1:16 These false teachers were very religious, just as the Pharisees who confronted Jesus were very religious. "They claim to know God," and in 1:16 the "claim" is literally the term "confession" (*homologeō*). They confessed that they knew God. This usage of the term "confess" indicates that these false teachers actually claimed to be Christian believers.[44] Yet

---

[44]O. Michel, TDNT 5:199-220. See especially 209, where Michel points out the connection between confession and faith in Rom 10:9-10. It appears likely that at baptism, new converts were required to make some "confession of faith." Cf. O. Cullmann, *Baptism in the New Testament*, SBT (First Series), I (London: SCM, 1950), 71-80.

"by their actions they deny him." This judgment, spoken against these false teachers, is the same that God spoke through his prophet Isaiah, "Their hearts are far from me" (Isa 29:13). Instead of being pure before God due to their observance of religious ceremonies, Paul asserted that they were "detestable." This strong adjective "denotes what causes horror and disgust to God."[45] In actuality, to God they were exactly opposite of what they strove to be by their works. They were "disobedient" both to the truth of the gospel and to the apostolic authority (i.e., "rebellious," v. 10). And they were "unfit for any good work" (author's translation). C. S. Lewis's observation is noteworthy: "Of all bad men religious bad men are the worse."[46] There is an obvious irony here. Those who trusted in "works" are unfit for those "good works" which God desires (cf. Eph 2:8-10).

Titus 1:14-16 should be studied in light of Jesus' teaching in Mark 7:1-23 and its parallel passage in Matt 15:1-20. The connections and correspondences both conceptually and verbally indicate that Paul was thoroughly knowledgeable about the content and the full meaning of Jesus' teaching. When Paul proclaimed God's grace in the person and work of Jesus Christ, he was consistently confronted by those who perverted the true gospel by requiring a works righteousness. The damaging influence and results of such false teachers were all too apparent to him. To add requirements to the free gospel of God's grace offered through faith in Jesus Christ was to distort it beyond any rightful measure. Jesus said it best to the Pharisees: "Thus you nullify the word of God by your tradition that you have handed down" (Mark 7:13).

Summary. Paul in vv. 10-16 attempted to expose and rebuke those false teachers who were endangering the Cretan churches. He used strong language as he exposed their error of adding external religious requirements to the gospel of God's grace. This issue of works righteousness had to be confronted in the Jerusalem church (cf. Acts 15) and apparently became an issue within many churches established throughout the Mediterranean world. Paul's most complete theological refutation of this problem is contained in his Epistle to the Galatians.

Unfortunately, we must recognize that both historically and currently many of the church's problems are from within. What Satan cannot destroy through external forces, he will insidiously attack through internal confusion. Although many of the issues that cause division may be insignificant, there must be no compromise on the most significant issue about what constitutes salvation. Just as Paul faced this problem with regard to Jewish heresy, so have church leaders through the ages (e.g., Martin Luther) struggled with clarifying to the church that salvation is by faith alone.

---

[45]Kelly, *Pastoral Epistles*, 238.
[46]C. S. Lewis, *Reflections on the Psalms* (London: Collins, 1961), 32.

The source of this recurrent problem of works righteousness is found in the very nature of humans. Proud, self-centered human nature desires to have some control and to make some contribution toward salvation. To become utterly dependent on God's grace for forgiveness and salvation requires a genuine confession aptly summed up in the words of a familiar hymn: "Nothing in my hand I bring, simply to Thy cross I cling" (A. M. Toplady). The free gift of salvation involves repentance and acceptance of God's grace alone, but self-sufficient humans would rather add something that can be externally observed and for which they can claim credit (see comments on 3:5-7).

Because of this serious perversion of the doctrine of salvation, it is evident how much the churches of Crete needed strong, qualified leaders. Godly leaders should be capable of protecting the gospel, particularly in light of Titus's impending departure. The leaders should also be qualified by their own personal integrity and conduct so as to validate what they profess to be true. So it is in any age.

────────────── *SECTION OUTLINE* ──────────────

III. INSTRUCTIONS FOR EXHORTING VARIOUS GROUPS (2:1-15)
  1. Exhortations for Right Behavior (2:1-10)
    (1) Behavior in Accord with Sound Doctrine (2:1)
    (2) Exhortations for Older Men (2:2)
    (3) Exhortations for Older Women (2:3)
    (4) Exhortations for Younger Women (2:4-5)
    (5) Exhortations for Younger Men (2:6-8)
    (6) Exhortations for Slaves (2:9-10)
  2. The Theological Basis for Christian Behavior (2:11-15)

────────── **III. INSTRUCTIONS FOR EXHORTING** ──────────
VARIOUS GROUPS (2:1-15)

1. Exhortations for Right Behavior (2:1-10)

Having addressed Titus's duties with regard to church organizational leadership and the confrontation of false teaching, Paul encouraged Titus to exhort various groups within the church to meet certain standards of behavior. Five specific groups were to receive specific exhortations: the older men (v. 2), the older women (v. 3), the young women (vv. 4-5), the young men (vv. 6-8), and slaves (vv. 9-10). These groups, designated by age, sex, and social position, would certainly include each believer and church member on Crete. Van Oosterzee correctly observes, "No condition and no period of life is to remain unaffected by the sanctifying influence of the gospel."[1]

The basic structure of 2:1-10 is easily determined because each group is specifically designated (e.g., "older men," "older women"). Certain grammatical forms, such as the use of verbal infinitives (i.e., "to be" [*einai*] in vv. 2,4,9; or "to be self-controlled" [*sōphronein*] in v. 6) and the use of the adverb "similarly, likewise" (*hōsautōs*) in vv. 3,6 provide a simple literary framework for 2:2-10. This is especially evident since only one verb, "to encourage, to exhort" (*parakalei*) in the imperative mood (v. 6) governs these grammatical forms.[2] The repeated use of the

---

[1] J. J. Van Oosterzee, *The Epistle of Paul to Titus, Lange's Commentary on the Holy Scriptures* (Grand Rapids: Zondervan, 1960), 15.

[2] E. W. Bullinger, *Figures of Speech Used in the Bible* (1898; reprint, Grand Rapids: Baker, 1968), 110, states, "Supply the verb "exhort" from verse 6 here, and also in verses 4 and 9:—'[Exhort] that the aged men be sober, etc.'" Both grammatically and logically it seems

Greek conjunction "in order that" (*hina*) four times (vv. 4,5,8,10) is especially noteworthy. Each *hina* clause expresses the goal or purpose of the
behavior that is encouraged. Furthermore, these *hina* clauses indicate that
proper Christian behavior has a significant impact on pagan attitudes
toward Christianity (v. 5), silencing opponents by correct Christian teaching (v. 8), and attracting a lost world to Christianity (v. 10), thus affecting
the entire missionary enterprise of the church.[3]

Any similarities between the list of behavioral expectations in Titus
2:1-10 and the so-called Pauline household rules in Col 3:18–4:1 and Eph
5:21–6:9 are superficial.[4] Paul's primary concern was to indicate that the
Christian's faith, both *subjectively* as experience and *objectively* as a body
of doctrine, must result in a life that consistently demonstrates appropriate behavior. Such behavior must be free of censure and be complimen-
tary to the gospel of Jesus Christ, which Christians publicly profess as the
source of their salvation.

In contrast to the opponents in 1:10-16, who taught error that resulted
in their being "unfit for doing anything good" (v. 16), Paul emphasized in
2:1-10 that good works are a necessary and natural result of believing
"sound doctrine." To be rescued from sin and death through faith in Jesus
Christ must result in a changed life that displays self-control and reflects
God's love and grace.

(1) Behavior in Accord with Sound Doctrine (2:1)

[1]You must teach what is in accord with sound doctrine.

2:1 Paul began chap. 2 with a command for Titus: "You must teach
what is in accord with sound doctrine." Paul's emphatic use of the phrase,
literally "but you" (*sy de*), clearly suggests a contrast with the opponents
of 1:10-16. He asserted Titus's personal responsibility for instructing the
Cretan believers regarding their own appropriate Christian behavior and

---

best to take 2:1 as a completely independent sentence. So understood, each group is thus
"exhorted."

[3] C. K. Barrett, *The Pastoral Epistles* (Oxford: Clarendon, 1963), 133-34, states: "Three
times, in 2:5, 8, 10, he lays emphasis on the impression Christian life should make upon
onlookers; 2:14 and 3:2 are similar. He evidently valued this impression, and there can be
little doubt that it proved eventually to be one of the strongest missionary forces."

[4] See the excellent study by W. Lillie, "The Pauline House-tables," *ExpTim* 86 (1975):
179-83. Lillie excludes Titus 2:1-10 and 3:1-8 from the "housetables" genre, noting the
absence of (1) familial relationships (including children), (2) reciprocal duties, and (3) a
three-part structure. On Titus 2:1-10 specifically, see G. D. Fee, *1 and 2 Timothy, Titus* (Peabody, Mass.: Hendrickson, 1988), 184 and M. Dibelius and H. Conzelmann, *The Pastoral
Epistles* (Philadelphia: Fortress, 1972), 139, who comment, "The section looks more like a
catalogue of duties than a list of rules for the household."

responsibilities. The message that Titus was to "teach" (lit. "speak," imperative mood) concerns "what is in accord with sound doctrine" (*ha prepei tē hygiainousē didaskalia*).[5]

(2) Exhortations for Older Men (2:2)

[2]Teach the older men to be temperate, worthy of respect, self-controlled, and sound in faith, in love and in endurance.

2:2 Perhaps out of respect for age, Titus's exhortations began with the older segments of the church. First, Titus was called to address the "older men." The Greek term used here, *presbytas*, meaning *old men*, must not be confused with the similar term *presbyteros*, which designates a church official (see comments on 1:5). The older men in general are designated. There is no indication about what specific age a man must attain before he is considered an "older man." Generally speaking, this group may have referred to men of an age sufficient to have raised a family and seen their children begin families of their own. Titus was to exhort or encourage "the older men to be temperate, worthy of respect, self-controlled, and sound in faith, in love, and in endurance." The term rendered "temperate" (*nēphalious*) is from a Greek word group that literally means *soberness* in contrast to drunkenness. If Paul was using this term figuratively, it indicates "complete clarity of mind and its resulting good judgment."[6] The term rendered "worthy of respect" (*semnous*) suggests dignity and therefore reflects upon the older man's manner of behaving.[7] He is not to be frivolous or silly.

---

[5]The Greek verb τρέπει was used by Paul precisely to indicate that Titus was to speak that which is *"in accord with* sound doctrine." Although these "appropriate things" are obviously to be practical and ethical in nature, Paul indicated that they were to be in harmony with "sound doctrine." Sound doctrine is clearly linked to practical and ethical behavior. Cf. C. Brown, NIDNTT 2:668-69. Both A. T. Hanson (*The Pastoral Letters* [Cambridge: University Press, 1966]) and F. D. Gealy (IB 11) completely miss the point of ἅ πρέπει. This is obvious from their observations that the writer in vv. 1-10 did not teach "theological doctrine" but rather dealt with practical and ethical matters. Hanson remarks: "It is remarkable that the advice which follows has very little to do with Christian doctrine as such. . . . The author was certainly not much interested in theology as such" (112). Gealy comments, "The discussion is carried on, less on a doctrinal than on an ethical and practical basis" (533). This teaching constitutes practical standards of behavior and certain responsibilities. Whereas in v. 1 Titus was to instruct verbally ("speak"), in v. 7 he was to instruct by personal example. In 2:1, as in 1:9, the phrase "sound doctrine" is used in the objective sense of a body of Christian teaching (perhaps written), in contrast to the errors of false teachers.

[6]P. J. Budd, NIDNTT 1:514.

[7]It is worth noting that this term (σεμνούς) and the term εὐσέβεια (1:1) are used predominately in the Pastoral Epistles within the NT (σεμνούς, three of four NT occurrences, and εὐσέβεια, ten of fifteen NT occurrences). The close relationship between these two concepts is apparent since both terms are often studied together; cf. W. Foerster, TDNT 7:168-96, and W. Gunther, NIDNTT 2:91-95.

The third characteristic desired for this group is "self-controlled" or "sensible" (NASB, *sōphronas*). The importance of this characteristic being demonstrated by all Christians becomes apparent when we realize this term and its cognate forms are applied directly not only to the "older men" in v. 2 but also to the "older women" (v. 4), the "young women" (v. 5), and the "younger men" (v. 6). The instructions to the believing "slaves" in vv. 9-10 also assume the adoption of this characteristic. As W. Lock observes, "It is one of the essential characteristics of the Christian life, one of the purposes of the Incarnation (Titus 2:12)."[8] Because Paul directed that self-controlled, sensible behavior be evident in every believer, he definitely indicated that it is *needed* and *attainable* by all Christians. It should be a distinguishing feature of Christian character consistently practiced within the home, the church, and among nonbelievers.

Finally, the older men were to be sound "in faith, in love and in endurance." Once again the metaphor of good health or soundness (*hygianontas*) is employed. The definite article is used before each noun—faith, love, and endurance—suggesting their personal faith unlike other articular uses of "faith" in the Pastoral Letters where it refers to a body of doctrine (cf. 1:4,13; 2:1). Here it refers to their personal love and their personal endurance. It is possible, as has been suggested, that Paul varied the early Christian triad of faith, hope, and love by substituting "endurance" for "hope," thus emphasizing the need of perseverance for the older men.[9] The latter years of life, especially for men, can be filled with regrets, a sense of uselessness or worthlessness, feelings of despair, self-absorption, or even a tendency to relax moral standards because of old age. However, Paul desired for the older men what he desired for himself as he approached the end of life: To have fought the good fight, to have finished the race, to have kept the faith (2 Tim 4:7). Biblical history, as well as secular history, sadly reports the lives of those who did not finish well.

(3) Exhortations for Older Women (2:3)

[3] **Likewise, teach the older women to be reverent in the way they live, not to be slanderers or addicted to much wine, but to teach what is good.**

Paul continued by instructing Titus to encourage the older women (*presbytidas*). As suggested for the "older men," the age at which one is

---

[8]W. Lock, *The Pastoral Epistles*, ICC (Edinburgh: T & T Clark, 1924), 139. Also see his "Additional Note," 148-50.

[9]See comments by Fee, *1, 2 Timothy, Titus*, 185-86, and J. N. D. Kelly, *The Pastoral Epistles* (Peabody, Mass.: Hendrickson, 1960), 234. Also see A. M. Hunter's treatment of this early Christian triad in *Paul and His Predecessors*, 2nd ed. (London: SCM, 1961), 33-35 or his article "Faith, Hope, Love—A Primitive Christian Triad," *ExpTim* 49 (1937-38): 428-29.

considered an older woman would probably be the age attained at the time children are raised and establishing their own homes. As children grow up and leave home, the older woman's focus may become less defined as her familial responsibilities become less demanding. This may contribute to feelings of uselessness, loneliness, low self-esteem, and self-pity. Paul suggested in this passage that older women should possess personal godliness, be worthy of respect, and play an essential role in the lives of the young women in the church. The concept of spiritual mentoring is evident in this passage.

2:3 The term "likewise" (*hōsautōs*) indicates that the verb forms, which are lacking in the exhortations to the older women, are to be supplied from the exhortations to the "older men" given previously. "Encourage" (from v. 6) the older women "to be" (from v. 2) "reverent in the way they live." The term translated "in the way they live" (*katastēmati*) indicates the outward expression of an inner character. The adjective rendered "reverent" comes from a Greek compound term, *hieroprepeis*, combining *hieron* (*temple*) and *prepeis* (*is appropriate to, fitting,* cf. same term in 2:1). Paul possibly used this unusual compound (only here in the NT) to suggest that the "way of life" for the older women should be appropriate to a "priestess" serving in God's temple. So considered, these women (a number of whom would probably be widows) would see themselves as given to God and his service. Such women were not to be "slanderers." The term for *devil* comes from the Greek root *diabolos*, meaning *slanderer*. Those persons who cannot control their tongues in speaking lies, false accusations, and spreading malicious gossip (whether true or untrue) do the work of Satan himself. They cannot be slanderers and serve God. This exhortation to self-mastery of the tongue is especially directed toward women (cf. 1 Tim 3:11); however, self-control in this area applies to all Christian believers (cf. Jas 3:1-12).

The older women must not be "addicted to much wine." Paul's inclusion of this item suggests that alcohol may have been an especially troubling problem among Cretan women. By contrast, the older women would have self-mastery over their emotional lives and physical appetites. In addition, the older women are to teach what is good (*kalodidaskalous*). Kelly states: "This does not envisage formal instruction (this is forbidden in 1 Tim 2:12, and there is no reason why Paul should take a different line in Crete), but rather the advice and encouragement they can give privately, by word and example."[10] Paul's purpose in encouraging the older women to be teachers of good relates directly to the exhortations he proposed for the young women. This purpose is explicitly expressed in the Greek by the following *hina* clause in v. 4: in order that ("then," NIV)

---

[10]Kelly, *Pastoral Epistles*, 240.

they might advise/bring to their senses (*sōphronizōsin*) the young women. Here this important concept of self-control, self-mastery, sensibleness (*sōphronas*) for all believers is again evident. As applied to both the older women and the younger women, the former must possess it in order to effectively advise the latter.

(4) Exhortations for Younger Women (2:4-5)

⁴Then they can train the younger women to love their husbands and children, ⁵to be self-controlled and pure, to be busy at home, to be kind, and to be subject to their husbands, so that no one will malign the word of God.

2:4 Communicating Paul's exhortations for the younger women was not Titus's direct responsibility. Rather, this was to be the duty of the older women. Because of the domestic focus of Paul's encouragements to this particular group, it is certainly reasonable to assume that the older women would be better qualified to communicate effectively with the younger women. The very specific characteristics proposed by Paul suggest that he primarily had younger wives in mind. Of the seven adjectives used to describe the desirable qualities for Christian young women, four implicitly presuppose a life involving marriage and family. The absence of punctuation in the Greek text allows for interpreting each adjective independently (as NASB, KJV), or some adjectives may be grouped as pairs (as NIV, RSV, NEB).

The young women are "to love their husbands and children." This compound phrase in English expresses two Greek terms that were often used in Paul's day to describe characteristics highly desirable in a woman.[11] This specific exhortation, given first, may suggest the extremely high value Paul gave to the congenial and cohesive Christian family unit. The next two adjectives, also paired by the NIV, are "self-controlled and pure."

2:5 Self-controlled (*sōphronas*) is the recurring Greek term that is an essential element in the exhortations for each group represented in this section of the letter. Self-control, coupled with "pure" (*hagnas*, i.e., *morally pure, chaste*) may express Paul's concern for marital fidelity. The two Greek terms rendered "to be busy at home" (*oikourgous*) and "to be kind" (*agathas*) may be taken together to simply mean *good workers at home*.[12] Taken independently, "to be busy at home" (*oikourgous*) would indicate

---

[11]Kelly (ibid., 240-41) states: "In antiquity, among pagans and Jews alike, these twin virtues were regarded as the glory of young womanhood, and are frequently mentioned on funerary inscription."

[12]Dibelius and Conzelmann, *Pastoral Epistles*, 141, state, "The two words οἰκουργούς and ἀγαθάς should be taken together and translated 'fulfill their household duties well.'"

an efficient management of household responsibilities, and "kind" (*agatha*) would indicate a lack of irritability in light of the nagging demands of mundane and routine household duties.

Finally, the younger women are "to be subject to their husbands." In the Greek this phrase literally states, "Being subject to their *own* husbands." Both the NIV and the RSV have omitted translating *idiois* ("own"), obviously taking this term to be superfluous and therefore not contributing to the meaning of the phrase. It should be noted, however, that this identical phrase appears in 1 Pet 3:1. E. G. Selwyn's comment is pertinent: "This word delivers the passage from any charge of inculcating the 'inferiority' of women to men, and shews that the subordination is one of function, within the intimate circle of the home."[13] The use of the term "to be subject to" (*hypotassomenas*) is common to specific New Testament instruction regarding the relationship between husband and wife (cf. Eph 5:24; Col 3:18; 1 Pet 3:1,5). The term is also used in a variety of other contexts including, for example, the subjection of all things to Christ, the subjection of persons to civil authorities, the subjection of slaves to masters, and the subjection of one Christian to another. Cranfield has demonstrated that this term (*hypotassō*) does not mean *obey*. Rather, he argues: "The *hupotassisthai* which Paul here [Rom 13:1] and elsewhere enjoins is to be understood in terms of God's *taxis* or 'order.' It is the responsible acceptance of a relationship in which God has placed one and the resulting honest attempt to fulfill the duties which it imposes on one."[14]

It must also be noted that to "be subject to" does not imply a position of innate inferiority of being. As a general rule, all Christian theological discussion concerning the relationships between men and women should begin with Paul's statement (possibly an early Christian confession) in Gal 3:28 that "there is . . . neither male nor female . . . in Christ." This statement concerning the equality of the sexes succinctly expresses the attitude of Jesus, as seen in his encounters with women in the Gospels; of the early church, as seen in the role played by women in worship and outreach in Acts; as well as the attitude of Paul demonstrated in his Epistles.[15]

---

[13]E. G. Selwyn, *The First Epistle of St. Peter* (London: Macmillan, 1958), 182.

[14]C. E. B. Cranfield, *The Epistle to the Romans*, vol. 2 (Edinburgh: T & T Clark, 1979), 662. Cf. Delling, TDNT 8:43, who states, "So also in the commonly required subjection of wife to husband according to the biblical understanding (Col 3:18; Eph 5:22-24; 1 Pet 3:1; Titus 2:5) the issue is keeping a divinely willed order; cf. 1 Cor 11:3; 14:34 (Gen 3:16); also 1 Pet 3:6, with a reference in v. 5 to the ὑποτάσσεσθαι of the women of the OT."

[15]See the excellent, yet succinct, treatment of the whole NT issue of "male and female" in R. N. Longenecker's *New Testament Social Ethics for Today* (Grand Rapids: Eerdmans, 1984), 70-93.

However, the equality of the sexes does not negate the distinctives of the sexes. The fact is that God created male and female. Each sex has distinctive features, not only physically but emotionally and psychologically. Such features are for the mutual benefit of the other. Yet *in the context of the home*, wives are "to be subject to their [own] husbands," thus recognizing and accepting a God-given order and responsibility. In the context of male-female relationships, the terms "subjection," "subordination," and "submission" can stir emotional feelings and responses. Each term contains some acquired nuance that seems to suggest forced compliance or inferiority. That such a meaning is not intended by Paul in this particular text is further demonstrated by his initial exhortation to the younger women to "love their husbands" (v. 4). Any marriage relationship that is conceived and maintained only on the basis of each member adhering to certain prescribed legal requirements is probably doomed from the beginning. In considering the New Testament teaching on marriage, especially in Paul's letters, the emphasis appears to be on the maintenance of a mutual or reciprocal commitment of the husband and the wife to an exclusive, intimate, loving, and caring partnership. When these prescribed biblical attitudes between husband and wife prevail, there will be little (if any) need for resorting to God's intended order for establishing authority within the home.

That Paul has given more attention to the young women and has been more specific in his exhortations suggests that the behavior of this group was creating more problems for the Cretan church than perhaps the behavior of other groups designated in 2:2-10. This observation is also suggested by the "so that" (*hina*) clause that concludes this section on the young women. It expresses that the purpose of these specific exhortations is "so that no one will malign the word of God." The Greek term rendered "malign" in the NIV is literally "to be blasphemed" (*blasphēmētai*). It is possible that in the preaching of the gospel, with all of its implications for Christian freedom (variously interpreted) and equality in Christ, the God-given order of authority within marriage and the home life was becoming confused and compromised. This possible deterioration of scriptural (OT) as well as cultural norms with regard to the home may have further encouraged strong hostility among the false teachers to the gospel message, i.e., "the word of God." Any deviation in normal domestic order or behavior among Christian families (based upon their newfound freedom in Christ) probably resulted in charges of *blasphemy* against a message encouraging or allowing changes in familial relationships. The use of such strong religiously oriented language suggests that this charge emanated from opponents (i.e., Judaizers, the circumcision). Therefore Paul directly and specifically called for a change in behavior that is in keeping with God's natural order as seen in the Scriptures and the cultural norms relating to marriage and family life.[16] H. Währisch's comments are appropriate for Christian behavior at any time, in any place. He states: "Christians for their part must take care that they do not, by their own conduct, give cause for blasphemy against God or against His word (1 Tim 6:1; Titus 2:5). Indeed, the behaviour of Christ's disciples (even towards each other) should contribute to the glory of the Father (Matt 5:16)."[17]

(5) Exhortations for Younger Men (2:6-8)

[6]Similarly, encourage the young men to be self-controlled. [7]In everything set them an example by doing what is good. In your teaching show integrity, seriousness [8]and soundness of speech that cannot be condemned, so that those who oppose you may be ashamed because they have nothing bad to say about us.

2:6 Paul's exhortation for the younger men was to be conveyed both by Titus's words and personal example: "Similarly, encourage the young men to be self-controlled." Titus's words to the younger men encouraged (exhorted, imperative mood) them to achieve self-control. This concept of self-control, self-mastery, sensibleness, from the Greek word group *sōphrōn*, is now directly applied to the younger men (cf. vv. 2,4-5). Paul's obvious concern that the Cretan believers demonstrate the characteristics associated with the Greek word group *sophron* (self-control, sound-mindedness, sensible behavior) might suggest that the Cretan believers had been wrongly influenced by aberrant forms of Christianity. Such influences may have included, but not be limited to, false teaching that gave a distorted understanding of Christian freedom or perhaps promoted displays of *spirituality* that emphasized outward manifestations of the Holy Spirit (which may have appeared totally irrational to nonbelievers). These influences would indeed be detrimental to Christian behavior, which should be characterized as sensible, rational, and self-controlled.[18]

---

[16]A. Padgett, "The Pauline Rationale for Submission: Biblical Feminism and the *hina* Clauses of Titus 2:1-10," *EvQ* 59 (1987): 39-52, argues that Paul's teaching on marital submission by the wife to her husband was culturally conditioned and only taught by Paul to accommodate the gospel message to accepted marital traditions of his day in order not to offend pagans who were being evangelized. Padgett concludes that on the basis of Paul's affirmation of the equality of the sexes (Gal 3:28) his teaching on marital subjection need not be applicable to Christians today since it was obviously culturally motivated. While providing stimulating ideas and insights, Padgett's failure to adequately explore Paul's teaching in Eph 5:21-24; Col 3:18; and 1 Tim 2:11-15. (as well as 1 Pet 3:1-6) raises questions with regard to some of his conclusions.

[17]H. Währisch, NIDNTT 3:343.

[18]The only other occurrences of σώφρονας in Paul are in Rom 12:3 and 2 Cor 5:13. The Rom 12:3 usage occurs in a play on words. The 2 Cor 5:13 usage occurs within the context of

2:7 Grammatically, the prepositional phrase "in everything" (*peri panta*) may be translated with either "to be self-controlled" in v. 6 or "set them an example" in v. 7. However, it appears preferable to render this phrase with "to be self-controlled" in v. 6. This broadens the range of the self-control that is required and does not reduce the full force of the emphatic term "yourself" (*seauton*) in v. 7, which is definitely joined to "set them an example."[19] Curiously, the NIV does not translate the reflexive pronoun "yourself" (*seauton*). However, Paul used it to emphasize the necessity of Titus's personal role in teaching the young men by example.[20] The common expression "More is caught than taught" aptly sums up the power of teaching by personal example. That Paul directed Titus to be an example to the young men strongly suggests that Titus himself was a young man. Titus was to be a role model with regard to good works, in contrast to the false teachers (cf. 1:16).

Titus's example was to extend beyond his normal, daily conduct. Specifically, he was to demonstrate the art of effectively communicating the true gospel message. In content his teaching (literally *the* teaching) had to show integrity (lit. "not corrupt"). Paul's combination of these terms in this phrase suggests the idea of "sound doctrine" so familiar to the Pastorals. In style his teaching was to demonstrate "seriousness" (*semnotēta*). The presentation of the message was to be characterized by dignity and inspire respect in the hearers.[21]

2:8 It is unlikely that the phrase "soundness of speech" (*logon hygiē*) refers in this context to "sound doctrine."[22] Rather, "sound speech" (*logon hygiē*) may refer to a healthy, persuasive, well-thought-out, and attractively delivered presentation of the Christian gospel, characterized

---

Paul's defense against his opponents that he was "out of his mind," "beside himself" (author's translation). Whereas his opponents charged that he was ἐξέστημεν, Paul contrasted this charge by claiming that he and his helpers were "in our right mind" (σωφρόνουμεν). M. A. G. Haykin ("The Fading Vision? The Spirit and Freedom in the Pastoral Epistles," *EQ* 57 [1985]: 305) observes: "Nonetheless, there is indirect evidence that the Pastoral Epistles were written to refute a movement, whose doctrine and conduct were characterized by enthusiastic excesses. For instance, the great emphasis upon self-control in the Pastoral Epistles would seem to indicate such a state of affairs.

[19] Kelly, *Pastoral Epistles*, 242; Fee, *1, 2 Timothy, Titus*, 188; Dibelius and Conzelmann, *Pastoral Epistles*, 141.

[20] Paul's emphasis on teaching by example is evident; cf. 1 Cor 11:1; 1 Tim 4:12; 1 Thess 1:7; 2 Thess 3:9; Phil 3:17.

[21] W. Foerster, TDNT 7:195.

[22] Interpretations that suggest that λόγον ὑγιῆ means *sound doctrine* appear to place unwarranted emphasis on the adjective ὑγιῆ, especially associating it with its usage with διδασκαλία. The context here, however, with ἐν τῇ διδασκαλίᾳ ἀφθορίαν occurring so closely to, yet independently of, λογον ὑγιη indicated that the latter phrase does not refer to "sound doctrine" (meaning the expression to Christian teaching as a "body" of instruction, whether oral or written).

as "speech that cannot be condemned." Paul obviously recognized that the medium plays an important part in the effectiveness or successful communication of the message.

Paul concluded this exhortation to the "young men" by way of Titus's example by stating its purpose: "So that those who oppose you may be ashamed because they have nothing bad to say about us." Because the phrase translated "those who oppose you" is singular in the Greek text (i.e., the one in opposition, the opponent), speculations regarding the identity of this opponent are varied. These speculations have ranged from Satan (as an individual) to a personal representative of some group of opponents. Paul's desire that the opponents "may be ashamed because they have nothing bad to say about us" does not imply that he thinks the communication of the gospel can be so good that it will be unchallenged or uncriticized. Paul's own experience as a teacher or preacher of the gospel demonstrated that this would not be the case. Rather, his concern was that no legitimate challenge or criticism be offered. Of course, criticisms will be made; yet hostile critics will ultimately be "ashamed" (*entrapē*) in the sense of publicly suffering loss of respect as it becomes apparent that their criticisms are groundless. Interestingly, Paul included himself by stating "they have nothing bad to say about *us*" (author's emphasis). Titus was thus reminded that his teaching, both by word and example, would reflect not only on himself but on Paul as well, since he functioned on Crete under the apostle's authority and as his personal representative.

(6) Exhortations for Slaves (2:9-10)

⁹Teach slaves to be subject to their masters in everything, to try to please them, not to talk back to them, ¹⁰and not to steal from them, but to show that they can be fully trusted, so that in every way they will make the teaching about God our Savior attractive.

2:9 Paul concluded his exhortations to various groups within the Cretan church by addressing the Christian slaves. The socioeconomic institution of slavery was extremely widespread in both Greek and Roman society. Slavery was protected by civil law. The military conquests of Rome produced many prisoners of war who were subsequently sold as slaves. Unlike the American institution of slavery in the eighteenth and nineteenth centuries, slavery in the ancient world was not racially restricted, nor did it apply primarily to uneducated or socially deprived persons. Many slaves were well-educated, skilled individuals and therefore contributed greatly to the social and economic fabric of society. The condition of the slave's life may have ranged from holding a position of trust and relative comfort to being treated in a most cruel and heinous manner. At any rate, slaves were the material possessions of their masters, who exercised complete authority over their activities and destinies.[23]

Other New Testament instruction for Christian slaves is found in Eph 6:5-8; Col 3:22-25; 1 Tim 6:1-2; and 1 Pet 2:18-25. Paul's Letter to Philemon concerning the restoration of his runaway slave, Onesimus, newly converted by Paul, is pertinent to the New Testament attitude toward slavery. New Testament writers encouraged the Christian slaves to serve their masters obediently, whether or not the master was a Christian.

Although the New Testament appears to accept slavery as part of the socioeconomic fabric of its time and does not openly condemn it, it does *not* sanction slavery as a God-ordained institution. The New Testament does display a much different attitude to slavery from what was common at that time. The Christian gospel offered slaves, as well as freemen, the freedom from sin and its power that all men and women need. Converted slaves were brought into the fellowship of the church as sharing equally in God's grace as demonstrated in the New Testament "household rules."[24] These "Household Rules" indicate that Christian masters have certain responsibilities for their slaves (cf. Eph 6:9; Col 4:1). The abolition of cultural, social, and sexual distinctions "in Christ Jesus" stated by Paul in Gal 3:28 and practiced in the churches contained the seed that would finally abolish the institution of slavery. Instead of overtly attacking this unjust yet widespread institution protected by civil authority, the gospel would slowly destroy slavery by its power to change individual lives and attitudes.[25]

Paul directed Titus: "Teach slaves to be subject to their masters in everything." The verb rendered "teach" in the NIV is supplied from the term *parakalei* (lit. "exhort") in v. 6. In a certain sense, it may appear unnecessary that slaves would be exhorted "to be subject to their masters in everything" since they were actually the property of the master and had no other practical option. However, this particular exhortation to slaves (cf. 1 Tim 6:1-2; Col 3:22-25; Eph 6:5-8; 1 Pet 2:18-25) may

---

[23]For a concise survey of slavery in the ancient world, see Longenecker, *NT Social Ethics for Today*, 48-51.

[24]Slaves are included in the "Household Rules" in Col 3:22-25; Eph 6:5-8; and 1 Pet 2:18-25.

[25]Longenecker (*NT Social Ethics for Today*, 59-60) observes: "Rather than engaging in a head-on confrontation with slavery, Paul sought to elevate the quality of personal relationships within the existing structures of society. His insistence on mutual acceptance among Christians, while disparaged by some, was in reality an explosive concept which ultimately could have its full impact only in the abolition of the institution of slavery, for it calls on believers of whatever social status to relate to one another in a manner that transcends the merely legal and the conventional norms."

reflect an actual or potential problem among Christian slaves in light of their newfound "freedom" in Christ as compared with their forced servitude.[26] Or Paul may simply have been encouraging Christian slaves to make the best of their social position and relationship to their masters by voluntarily "subjecting themselves" (*hypotassesthai*, middle voice) rather than serving with a reluctant and obstinate attitude. Christian slaves were "to be subject to their [*own*] masters" (author's translation) even as the young women were "to be subject to their *own* husbands" (author's translation, cf. 2:5). Their subjection was strictly on the basis of an order within a specific context or relationship and not on the basis of any innate inferiority.

The phrase "in everything" (*en pasin*) may be grammatically connected with either *hypotassesthai*, meaning *to be subject in all things* or *all respects* or with *euarestous*, meaning *pleasing in all things* or *all respects*. Although either rendering is acceptable and neither rendering will significantly alter Paul's intended meaning, some commentators emphasized that "to be subject . . . in everything" necessarily excluded demands that were contrary to God's laws (cf. Acts 5:29).[27] With the exception of this verse, the term "well-pleasing" (*euarestous*) is employed in the New Testament only with reference to a person's being well-pleasing or acceptable to God.[28] Obviously, it suggests a high standard for pleasing earthly, human masters.

Paul mentioned two specific negative forms of behavior that may have been universally common among slaves but that the Christian slave should avoid. They should not talk back. Contradicting and arguing with their masters would be neither acceptable nor well-pleasing, resulting in relationships characterized by aggravation and tension.

2:10 Christian slaves also were not to "steal" from their masters. Many slaves probably had ample opportunity to engage in petty theft to the detriment of their masters. Christians were not to be engaged in such activity. Christian slaves were not only exhorted to avoid such behavior but were "to show that they can be fully trusted."

The strong adversative "but" (*alla*) indicates Paul's emphatic rejection of this negative behavior and his enthusiastic encouragement to the positive characteristic of complete trustworthiness. The purpose of such behavior among Christian slaves is stated in the final *hina* clause of this

---

[26]The political and social ramifications of Christian slaves behaving inappropriately would be far-reaching. Barrett, *Pastoral Epistles*, 136, correctly notes: "Christian slaves constituted a special danger to the good repute of the Church. Their Christian freedom could if wrongly expressed lead to the opinion that they and their brethren were social revolutionaries."

[27]Lock, *Pastoral Epistles*, 142.

[28]Cf. Rom 12:1-2; 14:18; 2 Cor 5:9; Eph 5:10; Phil 4:18; Col 3:20; Heb 13:21.

section: "So that in every way they will make the teaching about God our Savior attractive." In v. 5 Paul's stated purpose in encouraging specific behavior among the young women suggests avoiding a negative consequence: "So that no one will malign the word of God." Here in v. 10 the prescribed behavior for Christian slaves was designed to produce a positive consequence. In both v. 5 and v. 10 the gospel message, whether termed "the word of God" or "the teaching about God our Savior," will be judged by the behavior of Christians. Especially noteworthy is the fact that the exemplary behavior of those at the lowest level of society (i.e., slaves) has the effect of "making attractive" (*kosmosin*, "adorning") the gospel. Surely the gospel's transforming power in the lives of those who had every reason to be bitter would stand out clearer and brighter than in those who lived in freedom and dignity unknown to slaves.

It is unfortunate that many teachers or preachers have applied Paul's teaching on slavery in his epistles to the employer/employee relationship in modern economies. Such applications dilute the tremendous power of the gospel as seen within the dark and unjust institution of slavery. The focus of Paul's teaching with regard to Christian slaves must not be missed. Against the bleak hopelessness of this system of bondage, the Christian slave's devotion to the gospel and resulting godly attitudes and actions serve to make attractive in an unparalleled way the ultimate freedom that is only realized in Christ.

Summary. Paul's specific exhortations to the various groups within the Cretan church in 2:1-10 reveal two foundational aspects of Christian behavior. First, his repeated use of the term "self-control" throughout this entire passage is applicable to all groups. This indicates the need for Christians to live sensibly and reasonably within a fragmented world characterized by chaos and confusion.

Second, the literary structure of this section of the epistle is marked by his repeated use of the Greek conjunction "so that" (*hina*) in vv. 4,5, 8,10. This clearly demonstrates the missionary aspects of everyday Christian behavior within a hostile and lost world. The effect of individual Christian behavior on unbelievers cannot be underestimated. Inevitably, unbelievers judge the gospel message by the lives of those who embrace it. As we live and identify ourselves as Christians, we can make the gospel message attractive and credible by our godly attitudes and behavior. However, if we are perceived as unloving and hypocritical, we provide unbelievers with good reason to be skeptical about the power of the gospel. Paul's exhortations, both to these Cretan groups and to Christians of every age, should alert us to the tremendous importance of being in reality what we profess in word. T. Taylor's comment in 1619 expresses this principle to all believers: "Profession without practice strikes not only the person professing, but also the Word of God which he professes, by giving occasion to the profane to blaspheme and scoff at God's holy religion (Rom 2:24)."[29]

2. The Theological Basis for Christian Behavior (2:11-15)

[11] For the grace of God that brings salvation has appeared to all men. [12] It teaches us to say "No" to ungodliness and worldly passions, and to live self-controlled, upright and godly lives in this present age, [13] while we wait for the blessed hope—the glorious appearing of our great God and Savior, Jesus Christ, [14] who gave himself for us to redeem us from all wickedness and to purify for himself a people that are his very own, eager to do what is good.

[15] These, then, are the things you should teach. Encourage and rebuke with all authority. Do not let anyone despise you.

Simply defined, theology is *the study of God:* who he is and what he does. For many Christians theology is somewhat mysterious; it suggests ideas and concepts that are deep, profound, and often confusing. While it is true that some aspects of theology are difficult, if not impossible, for the finite human mind to understand, it is equally true that much of theology can be easily understood. The doctrines that comprise theology basically consist of statements about God's character and work in human history. The purpose of theological study should be to increase our knowledge of God. However, the ultimate goal of increasing our knowledge of God should be Christian lives characterized by growth in obedience to God's revealed will.

For this reason Paul clearly connected the practical, behavioral exhortations in 2:2-10 with the profound theological statements of 2:11-15. As noted previously, Paul's *specific* behavioral exhortations are clearly referred to as "what is *in accord with* sound doctrine" (2:1, author's emphasis). In 2:11-14 Paul offered "sound doctrine" per se. His use of the conjunction "for" (*gar*) indicates the logical connection between the previous practical/behavioral exhortations and his forthcoming theological statements, which constitute the second outstanding theological affirmation of this epistle (cf. 1:1-4). Both the grammatical structure and the vocabulary of vv. 11-14 suggest the possibility that Paul incorporated material from early Christian confessions, creeds, prayers, or hymns.[30]

2:11 Paul asserted, "For the grace of God that brings salvation has appeared to all men." The New Testament concept of "the grace of God" is his beneficial activity on behalf of humans (both corporately and individually). God's grace toward us is based solely on his love and our total inability to meet God's standards. God's grace is a gift we do not deserve

---

[29]T. Taylor, *Exposition of Titus* (Minneapolis: Klock & Klock, reprint 1980), 276.

[30]A. T. Hanson, *Pastoral Letters*, 115.

and cannot earn. Without God's grace, there can be no salvation since grace is foundational to salvation (Eph 2:4-9). The NIV renders the adjective *sōtērios*, "that brings salvation," as modifying "the grace of God," with which it agrees in case, number, and gender (cf. also KJV). However, *sōtērios* may be understood as modifying "all men" (*pasin anthropois*), thus rendering "that brings salvation to all men" (cf. RSV, NASB).[31] Either translation is acceptable, though perhaps the arguments for the latter rendering are slightly more convincing. Neither rendering implies universalism (i.e., that all people are saved). Rather, the point is that salvation is universally offered to all without exception.

God's grace "has appeared" (*epephanē*). This verb occurs in Luke 1:79 (metaphorically) with regard to Jesus' birth and in Acts 27:20 (literally) with regard to the appearance of the sun and stars. The only other occurrences of this verb are in Titus 2:11 and 3:4, where it clearly refers to the manifestation of God's salvation. Paul may have intended this highly suggestive term to illustrate the dawning of the light of God's gospel upon a dark and lost world (cf. Eph 5:8; Col 1:13). Or he may have chosen this term as a contrast to its common usage with reference to the "divine appearances" of the Roman emperors.[32] In either case, Paul stated that God's salvation (characterized by his grace) "appeared" at a given time in history (note the aorist tense) for "all men" indiscriminately (e.g., Jew and Gentile, slave and free). "The grace of God" was revealed and personified in Jesus Christ. This appearing was not limited to his birth but refers to his entire life including his death, resurrection, and exaltation, which accomplished the salvation now offered to "all men."

Paul did not limit the operation of God's grace toward Christians to justification in the restricted, legal sense of the conversion experience.[33] Rather, throughout his letters Paul indicated that God's grace continues to operate in the sanctification process of the Christian's life. God's grace is active and powerful. It sustains in time of need (2 Cor 12:9), it provides strength (1 Cor 15:10; 2 Tim 2:1), it produces thanksgiving and glory to God (2 Cor 4:15), it affects our conversations (Col 4:6), and it enables believers to live holy and godly lives (2 Cor 1:12).

---

[31] E. K. Simpson, *The Pastoral Epistles* (Grand Rapids: Eerdmans, 1954), 107, argues that σωτηριος followed by a dative case is a classical idiom meaning *bringing salvation to*. It is also noteworthy that the full meaning of the intransitive verb form ἐπεφανέω ("appeared") is achieved without taking πᾶσιν ἀνθρώποις ("all men") as an indirect object.

[32] C. F. D. Moule, "The Influence of Circumstances on the Use of Christological Terms," *JTS*, n.s. 10 (1959): 262.

[33] Any suggestion that the use of the term "grace" outside the context of justification or salvation indicates non-Pauline authorship of Titus reveals a failure to grasp the multifaceted nature of God's grace presented by Paul throughout his epistles. Cf. Dibelius and Conzelmann, *Pastoral Epistles*, 145.

2:12 The continual operation of God's grace in the lives of Christians is one of Paul's strongest aspirations for the churches, as evidenced by his epistolary salutations and concluding benedictions. Therefore it is not unusual for Paul to have stated that God's grace "teaches us" (*paideuousa hēmas*, present participle, continuous action). The Greek verb *paideuō* commonly means *to instruct, educate*; however, its biblical usage may contain the nuance of *discipline* or *chastisement*. Education in Christian behavior is seldom a painless process since it involves the correction of human behavior which by nature stands in opposition to God. Both the negative and positive aspects of this Christian education are stated next in general terms.

Stated negatively, God's grace "teaches us to say 'No' to ungodliness and worldly passions." There must be a conscious, willful repudiation of thoughts, words, and actions that are opposed to true godliness.

There must also be a renunciation of desires for things, pleasures, and values derived from this present, worldly system which is hostile to God (cf. Eph 6:12; 1 John 2:16). As has been correctly observed, "The true learning of heaven must begin with the *un*learning and laying *off* of all which stands in the way of the development of the new man."[34]

Stated positively, the grace of God teaches us "to live self-controlled, upright and godly lives in this present age." The use of the adverb *sōphronos* from the Greek word group *sōphrōn* (meaning *self-controlled, sensible, sober-minded*) recalls the familiar application of this characteristic in the exhortations to the various groups in 2:2-10. The adverb rendered "upright" denotes conduct that cannot be condemned. The adverb rendered "godly lives" denotes lives that are pleasing to God. It remains uncertain whether these three adverbs should be understood as being so distinct in meaning that they are intentionally employed to refer specifically to the Christian's relationship to himself ("self-controlled"), to others ("upright"), and to God ("godly").

In stating the positive characteristics of Christian living, Paul concluded with the phrase "in this present age." This additional thought suggests that such Christian living must be demonstrated in an evil world that is hostile to God (Gal 1:4; Eph 6:10-12). Furthermore, the mention of "this present age" presupposes another, future age for which the Christian believer hopes with assurance and perseverance. This future age, characterized by eternal life (1:2), has been inaugurated in the work of Christ during his incarnation. At his second coming the future age will be fully realized by every Christian believer.

2:13 While in "this present age," Paul stated that Christians "wait for the blessed hope—the glorious appearing of our great God and Savior,

---

[34]Van Oosterzee, *Titus*, 16.

Jesus Christ." This combination of waiting and hoping for complete and realized redemption, both from one's sinful nature and this present evil world, is more fully expressed by Paul in Rom 8:18-25 (cf. also Phil 3:20-21). The NIV correctly interprets the "and" (*kai*) in this phrase, "the blessed hope and appearing" (*tēn makarian elpida kai epiphaneian*), as an epexegetical *kai*, thus defining "the blessed hope" as being "the glorious appearing." This particular phrase, "the glorious appearing of our great God and Savior, Jesus Christ," has been the subject of much discussion and debate throughout centuries of biblical scholarship.[35] Although the discussions have involved several grammatical questions, only two are significant.

The first question involves whether the genitive noun "glory," *doxēs*, should be rendered adjectivally as "glorious appearing" (NIV, KJV) or be strictly translated as a noun, thus "the appearing of the glory" (RSV, NASB). Grammatically, this latter rendering is more natural and therefore slightly preferred. It also preserves the parallelism between the "appearing of the *grace of God*" (author's translation) in 2:11 and the "appearing of the *glory of the great God*" in this phrase. Jesus' own teaching emphasized that his second coming will be accompanied by a display of divine "glory" (cf. Matt 16:27; Mark 8:38; Luke 9:26).

The second and more significant grammatical question is whether the terms God (*theou*) and Savior (*sōtēros*) refer to *one* person or *two* persons. Since both terms are governed by one definite article, the most grammatically natural meaning is that they refer to *one* person.[36] The full import of this rendering becomes apparent as "Jesus Christ" is used appositionally to "our great God and Savior." This text, therefore, directly applies the title "God" (*theos*) to Jesus Christ. For this reason this text has been so studied and debated. The basic arguments against the acceptance of this text as directly applying the title "God" (*theos*) to Jesus are as follows:

1. Theologically, the New Testament writers generally avoid referring to Jesus as *theos*.

2. Grammatically, it is possible to translate the words of this text to render *theou* and *sōtēros* as two persons, notwithstanding the use of only one definite article.[37]

---

[35]For the most thorough treatment of this phrase, see M. J. Harris, "Titus 2:13 and the Deity of Christ," *Pauline Studies: Essays Presented to Professor F. F. Bruce on His 70th Birthday*, ed. D. Hagner and M. J. Harris (Grand Rapids: Eerdmans, 1980), 262-77.

[36]The translation of the NIV, RSV, NASB, NEB, and the KJV all support this meaning.

[37]G. B. Winer (*A Grammar of the Idiom of the New Testament*, 7th ed. [Andover: Draper: 1881], 130) argues: "The Article is omitted before σωτῆρος because the word is made definite by the Genitive ἡμῶν, and the apposition *precedes* the proper name: *of the great God and of our Saviour Jesus Christ.*" Interestingly, however, Winer admits that he presents

3. Literarily, the Pastoral Epistles often refer to God and Jesus within the same context, obviously referring to two distinct persons.

The basic arguments supporting the acceptance of this text as directly applying the title of "God" (*theos*) to Jesus are as follows:

1. Theologically, while the New Testament writers rarely applied the title *theos* to Jesus, it is virtually certain that John 20:28; Rom 9:5; Heb 1:8; and 2 Pet 1:1 directly refer to Jesus as *Theos*.[38]

2. Grammatically, although the syntax of the phrase may yield several possibilities for meaning, the more natural rendering takes *theou* and *sōterōs* as one person, in apposition to Jesus Christ.[39]

3. Literarily, the references to God and Jesus as distinct persons within the same contexts in the Pastorals do not necessarily exclude the title *theos* from being applied to Jesus in another context in the Pastorals. Also the referent of the term "appearing" (*epiphaneia*), which occurs four times in the Pastorals (1 Tim 6:14; 2 Tim 1:10; 4:1,8) and elsewhere only in 2 Thess 2:8, is always Jesus. The use of the adjective "great" (*megalou*) with God is reminiscent of Old Testament references to God's greatness (e.g., Deut 10:17; Pss 48:1; 86:10; Isa 12:6; Jer 32:18; Dan 2:45; 9:4). In the following verse (2:14), Paul expressly alluded to Old Testament works of God in redeeming Israel (see comments below) and attributed these works to Jesus' work of redemption. This demonstrates his Christological application of Old Testament ideas and concepts of God to Jesus. It is reasonable to assume that Paul could apply an Old Testament descriptive term of God to Jesus as easily as Old Testament terminology concerning God's work. The unusual phrase "the great God," found only here in the New Testament, is best accounted for as a Christological application of an Old Testament description of God. Paul may have employed this specific phrase as a contrast to known descriptions of pagan gods of that day (cf. Acts 19:28).

4. Historically, the term "god and savior" was commonly combined in pagan religions of that time in reference to a single divine figure. In this

---

this argument because "doctrinal convictions, deduced from Paul's teaching, that this apostle could not have called Christ *the great God*, induced me to show that there is no grammatical obstacle to taking σωτ. . . . Χριστου by itself as a second object" (130, n. 2). Cf. M. Zerwick, *Biblical Greek* (Rome: Pontifical Biblical Institute, 1963), 60, para. 185.

[38] For discussion of this New Testament Christological question, see R. E. Brown, "Does the New Testament Call Jesus God?" *Theological Studies* 26 (1965): 545-73; O. Cullmann, *The Christology of the New Testament*, rev. ed. (Philadelphia: Westminster, 1963), 306-14; and R. N. Longenecker, *The Christology of Early Jewish Christianity*, SBT 17, 2nd Series (Naperville: Allenson, 1970), 136-41.

[39] The position is supported by A. T. Robertson, *A Grammar of the Greek New Testament in the Light of Historical Research* (New York: Hodder & Stoughton, 1914), 786; C. F. D. Moule, *An Idiom Book of New Testament Greek*, 2nd ed. (Cambridge: University Press, 1959), 109-10; N. Turner, *Grammatical Insights into the New Testament* (Edinburgh: T & T Clark, 1965), 15-16.

historical context it is reasonable to assume they would be understood as referring to a single figure.[40]

Although the arguments in support of this phrase applying *theos* to Jesus Christ are convincing, it should be noted that the deity of Jesus Christ is not determined by whether he is specifically referred to as "God" in the New Testament. The fact of his deity is established by his supernatural birth; his sinless life; his fulfillment of Old Testament messianic prophecy; his demonstrated authority over nature, disease, demons, and death; his claim upon the attributes and prerogatives of God, including forgiving sins and judging sinners; and his resurrection from the dead and his heavenly exaltation.

The importance of the deity of Jesus Christ, as claimed by Jesus himself and the apostles, cannot be ignored. The ultimate significance of this claim for every person is vividly expressed in C. S. Lewis's often-quoted statement:

> "I am ready to accept Jesus as a great moral teacher, but I don't accept His claim to be God." That is the one thing we must not say. A man who was merely a man and said the sort of things Jesus said would not be a great moral teacher. He would either be a lunatic—on a level with the man who says he is a poached egg—or else he would be the Devil of Hell. You must make your choice. Either this man was, and is, the Son of God: or else a madman or something worse. You can shut Him up for a fool, you can spit at Him and kill Him as a demon, or you can fall at His feet and call Him Lord and God. But let us not come with any patronizing nonsense about His being a great human teacher. He has not left that open to us. He did not intend to.[41]

2:14 Having referred to Jesus Christ as our Savior in v. 13, Paul now described him as the one "who gave himself for us to redeem us from all wickedness and to purify for himself a people that are his very own, eager to do what is good." The main components of this statement echo many of the themes Jesus himself taught concerning his own death, especially those found in the ransom saying of Mark 10:45. The voluntary nature of his death is emphasized by the words "gave himself" (*edōken heauton*).[42] The fact that his death was for the benefit of sinners is contained in the words "for us" (*hyper hēmōn*). Whereas *hyper* may technically signify *on*

---

[40]Dibelius and Conzelmann, *Pastoral Epistles*, 102-3, especially noting the comments on "God, the Savior" (Θεὸς σωτήρ). On the implication for this term, Harris ("Titus 2:13 and the Deity of Christ," 263) writes, "Moreover, given the widespread use of the phrase Θεὸς καὶ σωτήρ in the first-century cultic terminology . . . it seems unnatural to separate σωτῆρος from Θεοῦ."

[41]C. S. Lewis, *Mere Christianity* (New York: Macmillan, 1960), 56.

[42]Mark 10:45, "The Son of Man [came] . . . *to give* [δοῦναι] His life." See also John 10:11,17-18. Cf. Paul's use in Gal 1:4.

behalf of, the parallelism of this phrase to that in Mark 10:45, which uses *anti* meaning *in place of*, certainly suggests the substitutionary nature of Jesus' self-sacrifice.[43] Paul stated that the purpose of Jesus' self-sacrifice is twofold: redemption and purification.

Redemption is expressed in terms of ransom (cf. 1 Tim 2:6). Verbally, this echoes Mark 10:45 and closely parallels Ps 130:8, "He himself will redeem Israel . . . from all their sins" (Ps 129:8 in LXX, *lytrōsetai . . . ek pasōn tōn anomiōn auton*). This ransom payment delivers humanity "from all wickedness." This phrase suggests deliverance from both the power of sin (cf. Rom 6:17-18,22) and the penalty of sin (cf. Rom 6:23; 8:1).

Purification is the second purpose stated for Christ's redeeming self-sacrifice. He "gave himself for us . . . to purify for himself a people that are his very own." The term rendered "purify" (*katharisē, to cleanse*) echoes Ezek 37:23 (LXX) and suggests the cleansing by the "blood of the covenant" which was central to Old Testament religion (Exod 24:6-8) as well as the "blood of the *new* covenant" (Luke 22:20) shed by Jesus Christ for redemption and cleansing (Heb 9:12-14; 1 John 1:7). Just as redemption and cleansing made Israel a "treasured possession" (*laos periousios*, Exod 19:5, LXX), so by his sacrifice Christ purchased those for whom he died with the result that they are "a people that are his very own" (*laon periousion*). Finally, Christ's own people will be characterized as "eager to do what is good." Paul's use of the noun "eager" (*zēlōtēn*) suggests the intensity with which Christians should pursue "doing what is good." What Paul had in mind when he referred to "do[ing] what is good" may be understood from his other writings (cf. Rom 12:9-21; 1 Cor 13; Gal 5:13-26; Eph 4:1-3,25-32; Phil 2:1-15; Col 3:8-17).

It is in this last phrase, "do[ing] what is good," that the relationship between theology and the practical aspects of Christian living is evident. Good theological teaching is indispensable in supplying both the *why* (the motivation) and the *how* (the enablement) of practical Christian living, as well as defining the *what* (the good works) of expected behavior. We must understand the profound truth that God, in his grace, offers salvation to all through the voluntary self-sacrifice of his Son, Jesus Christ. We must see that salvation delivers us from the power and penalty of our sin and therefore cleanses us and reconciles us to God, making us his treasured possession. It is this theological teaching that provides the *why* of living so as to please him, i.e., "do[ing] what is good." Even an elementary understanding of the character and nature of God and his work in history on our behalf strongly motivates us to please him by our lives. This "eager" response to who God is and what he has done for us is infinitely

---

[43]On the meaning of ὑπέρ as expressing substitution in certain contexts, see E. K. Simpson, 110-12.

higher than the "ought to" or "better not" mentality of "works salvation." The *how* of practical Christian living is suggested in knowing that this saving grace of God (2:11) is also the educating grace of God (2:12). Again, God's grace is powerfully active in the sanctification process of learning and doing what is good. Even the *what* of practical Christian living can only be fully understood in the context of who God is and what he has done. The life of Jesus most fully demonstrates this theology (John 14:9-12; 15:1-15; cf. Luke 10:25-37) and provides a pattern for attitude and behavior that is truly "good." As we begin to think theologically and embrace these doctrines in obedience, we will begin to experience the *why*, *how*, and *what* of daily living that is pleasing to God.

2:15 The NIV rendering of v. 15 represents the meaning of the Greek text, but it fails to convey the terseness or toughness Paul intended. "These [things]" (*tauta*), placed at the beginning of this sentence for emphasis, may refer to all of Paul's instructions to Titus from 1:10ff. His repetition of the verb "rebuke" (*elegche* in this verse, which he also used in 1:13, suggests that the specific content of Paul's instructions in 1:10-16 be included in "these [things]." Next, Paul used the imperative mood of the verbs in urging Titus to speak (*lalei*), exhort (*parakalei*), and finally rebuke (*elegche*) with regard to his instructions. There appears to be a progression of intensity in Paul's choice of verbs, perhaps appropriate to the receptivity of the hearers. The addition of the phrase "with all authority" (*meta pasēs epitagēs*) is a noteworthy addition to "rebuke" since Paul is the only New Testament writer to use this particular term for authority (*epitagēs*). Paul's final personal comment to Titus in this section, "Do not let anyone despise you," is similar to his encouragement to Timothy (1 Tim 4:12) yet with the obvious omission of youth in the case of Titus. Perhaps Titus was somewhat older than Timothy, yet he was included with the "young men" but definitely was not an "older man" (cf. 2:7). Although Paul commanded Titus to speak, exhort, and rebuke, he also commanded him, "Do not let anyone despise you." Titus's behavior in acting as Paul's apostolic representative had to be above contempt and beyond reproach. In his duty to command and demand certain behavior among the Christians on Crete, Titus needed personal respect.

Summary. The highest and purest motivation for Christian behavior is not based on what we can do for God but rather upon what God has done for us and yet will do. The false teachers on Crete assumed that their religious works earned them God's favor. But Paul taught that only as we grasp the full theological significance of God's grace can we eagerly do what is pleasing to him. Paul also reminded believers that they are *waiting* with *hope* and that as they attempt through God's grace "to do what is good," Jesus Christ will ultimately bring forth his rule of righteousness at his second coming.

───── **IV. CHRISTIAN BEHAVIORAL STANDARDS (3:1-11)** ─────

1. The Need for Christian Behavioral Standards (3:1-2)

Paul then took up the matter of standards for Christian conduct with regard to pagan society in general. Whereas his exhortations in 2:1-10 appear to relate more directly to Christian behavior among believers and the impact that such behavior would have on the nonbeliever, Paul then addressed the direct relationship the Cretan Christians were to have with the pagan world.

(1) Respect for Governmental Authorities (3:1)

¹Remind the people to be subject to rulers and authorities, to be obedient, to be ready to do whatever is good,

3:1 Paul's instruction to Titus is expressed with the present tense and imperative mood of the verb "remind" and means *keep reminding them.* The choice of this term "remind" suggests that Paul may already have taught the Cretans concerning their obligations and standards of behavior within a pagan culture. Although his instructions begin by referring specifically to civil authorities (v. 1), this quickly evolves to include "all men" in general. The statement in 3:1-2 constitutes one complete sentence containing a list of behavioral expectations that are delineated grammatically by the use of verbal infinitives (usually expressed in English with "to," e.g., "to be subject," "to be obedient").

Paul said, "Remind the people to be subject to rulers and authorities." The Greek terms for "rulers and authorities" (*archais* and *exousiais*) refer in this context to the secular, governmental authorities (cf. Luke 12:11). However, elsewhere in the New Testament, the meaning is expanded to include spiritual, supernatural powers (e.g., Eph 6:12). The instruction that Christians "be subject to" (*hypotassesthai*) the civil government indicates

that such authorities are part of God's overall order for human society.[1]
Christians are not exempt from reasonable and appropriate obligations
toward the governmental authorities (Rom 13:1-7; 1 Pet 2:13-17).[2] Paul's
apparent concern for the Christian's attitude toward the state may reflect the
possibility that some Christians wrongly interpreted their allegiance to
Christ as being contrary to any allegiance to the state. A proper Christian
attitude toward the state requires the Christians "to be obedient"
(*peitharchein*).[3] It is not likely that the Roman state was promoting
emperor worship at this time; otherwise Paul surely would not have added
this requirement.[4] Biblical teaching is clear that blind, unquestioning obedience to the state in opposition to God's law is not required (cf. Acts 5:29).
Yet not only are Christians "to be subject" (in attitude) and "to be obedient" (in actions), but they are also "to be ready to do whatever is good."
Literally, Christians are "to be ready for [or to do] every good work" (*pros
pan ergon agathon etoimous einai*). This extends the Christian's responsibilities from a mere passive posture (obeying laws) to an active, positive
involvement in society. This idea is a practical outworking of Jesus' teaching concerning being "the salt of the earth . . . and the light of the world
. . . that they may see your good deeds and praise your Father in heaven"
(Matt 5:13-16).[5]

(2) Respect for All (3:2)

**[2]to slander no one, to be peaceable and considerate, and to show true
humility toward all men.**

3:2 In v. 2 there is an obvious shift in the object of the verb forms
from civil authorities to the people in a secular society in general. The
objects are stated as "no one" and "all men." Christians are "to slander no
one." The Greek term for "slander" is *blasphēmein*, from which the
English term "to blaspheme" is derived. Essentially, blasphemy is the
verbal expression of evil and malicious thoughts directed toward a person
who is held in contempt. Whereas the Scriptures speak of the absolute

---

[1]Cf. Ps 22:28; Prov 8:15-16; Dan 2:20-21,37; 5:21.

[2]Cf. Rom 13:1-7. See the excellent treatment of this subject by C. E. B. Cranfield, "The
Christian's Political Responsibility According to the New Testament," *SJT* 15 (1962): 176-
92, also contained in his book *The Bible and Christian Life* (Edinburgh: T & T Clark, 1985),
48-68.

[3]The addition of πειθαρχεῖν following ὑποτάσσεσθαι supports the argument that "to be
subject to" does not necessarily contain the idea of obedience. Cf. the discussion on Titus 2:5.

[4]C. K. Barrett, *The Pastoral Epistles* (Oxford: Clarendon, 1963), 139.

[5]In Titus "good work" is rendered ἔργον ἀγαθὸν (1:16; 3:1), and "good works" is rendered καλῶν ἔργων (2:7,14; 3:8,14). Except for the difference in number (singular and plural) there appears to be no intended distinction between the adjectives καλός and ἀγαθός.

seriousness of blasphemy toward deity, specifically toward God the Father, Jesus Christ, and the Holy Spirit, it equally recognizes and condemns blasphemy toward celestial beings and humans (Lev 24:15-16; Matt 12:31; Luke 22:65; Acts 23:4-5; 1 Pet 4:14; Jude 8). Christians should be careful not to speak evil of or verbally abuse others, who are created in God's own image and the object of his saving grace (Jas 3:9).

Christians are "to be peaceable," not contentious or quarrelsome. Christians are "to be considerate" (gentle, kind, forebearing). They should be willing to defer to others, although it may require them to relinquish some of their own rights. And finally, Christians are "to show true humility toward all men." The Greek term rendered "true humility" in the NIV is *prautēta* (*meekness*). Grammatically, this final characteristic appears to constitute a summary phrase. This is supported by the use of the term "true humility" (*prautēta*), whose definition embraces some aspect of each of the verbal infinitives preceding it in this context (i.e., "in subjection," "obedient," "ready to do good works," "speaking no evil," "peaceable," and "considerate" [author's translations]). This rich New Testament term is used descriptively of Jesus (Matt 11:29; 21:5; 2 Cor 10:1), included as a "fruit of the Spirit" (Gal 5:23), and is repeatedly encouraged as a desirable personal Christian quality (1 Cor 4:21; Gal 6:1; Eph 4:2; Col 3:12; 1 Tim 6:11; Jas 3:13; 1 Pet 3:4,15). Paul used the combination of *prautētos* and *epieikeias* ("meekness" and "gentleness") in a compound phrase to describe Christ in 2 Cor 10:1. His use of these two terms together within Titus 3:2 may indicate his expectation that the same attitude and behavior exhibited by Jesus be the standard for the Christian's relationship toward "rulers and authorities" and toward "all men."

2. The Theological Basis for Proper Behavior (3:3-8)

[3] At one time we too were foolish, disobedient, deceived and enslaved by all kinds of passions and pleasures. We lived in malice and envy, being hated and hating one another. [4] But when the kindness and love of God our Savior appeared, [5] he saved us, not because of righteous things we had done, but because of his mercy. He saved us through the washing of rebirth and renewal by the Holy Spirit, [6] whom he poured out on us generously through Jesus Christ our Savior, [7] so that, having been justified by his grace, we might become heirs having the hope of eternal life. [8] This is a trustworthy saying. And I want you to stress these things, so that those who have trusted in God may be careful to devote themselves to doing what is good. These things are excellent and profitable for everyone.

3:3 Paul then described the degenerate condition of the pagan society in which Christians had to live. Interestingly, his comments focus on the human condition within the society. Humankind's innate sinful nature and the intensity with which it can manifest itself determines the degradation of all human society. Identifying himself and all Christians with sinful and degenerate humanity, Paul emphatically asserted, "At one time we too were foolish, disobedient, deceived and enslaved by all kinds of passions and pleasures." The use of "for" (KJV, *gar*) in the Greek text establishes the logical connection between the statements in 3:1-2 and 3:3-8. Christians, though at one time degenerate and lost, were objects of God's kindness and love, which resulted in their salvation. Christians are to demonstrate this same kindness and love to lost individuals and society, making Christianity attractive and resulting in the salvation of others (cf. 2:10).

The verb "were," placed at the beginning of this sentence, emphatically contrasts the Christian's *former degenerate condition* ("at one time," *pote*), which is described in v. 3, with the *present regenerate condition* ("but when," *hote de*), which is described in vv. 4-7. Paul set forth the unregenerate human condition with eight descriptive characteristics. He stated that "we too were foolish," i.e., unintelligent, senseless. Our minds did not grasp self-evident truths about God. We were "disobedient" to God and his will for our lives. We were "deceived," misled, perhaps by Satan (cf. 2 Cor 4:4). We were "enslaved by all kinds of passions and pleasures." In Rom 6:6-23, Paul expressly characterized sin in terms of bondage. "Malice" refers to wickedness, perhaps characterized by "ill-will" to others. "Envy" denotes a continual dissatisfaction with one's own position, possessions, or power as compared to that of another. And finally, Paul concluded that we were "being hated" and "hating one another." These terms, both passive and active, represent the logical results of self-centered, sinful humanity. There is nothing contained in this description of the depraved human condition that could be characterized as un-Pauline (cf. Rom 1:18-32). On the contrary, in comparison to other biblical portrayals of the human condition, it is a rather mild expression. Speaking of man's sinful condition, Jer 17:9 (RSV) succinctly sums up the matter: "The heart is deceitful above all things and desperately corrupt; who can understand it?"

3:4 This expression of humanity's depraved condition marks the beginning of the third outstanding theological statement in this brief letter (cf. 1:1-4; 2:11-15). Having initiated a contrast at the beginning of v. 3 with the words "At one time we too were," Paul completed it in vv. 4-7, beginning with the words "But when." In the Greek text vv. 4-7 form one sentence that eloquently summarizes God's work in humanity's salvation.[6]

---

[6]Most recent commentators suggest that vv. 4-7 contain some early Christian traditions which are woven into its structure, although there is little agreement about the *nature* of this early material. Some examples are D. Guthrie, *The Pastoral Epistles* (Grand Rapids: Eerdmans, 1957),

Paul's beginning phrase, "But when the kindness and love of God our Savior appeared," closely parallels 2:11. Both describe the manifestation of God's saving grace as having "appeared" (see comments on 2:11). Whereas 2:11 states that "the grace of God appeared," in 3:4 Paul stated that "the kindness and love of God appeared." The term for kindness, *chrēstotēs*, is unique to Paul in the New Testament. The "divine orientation" of this term is noted in its usual application to God (Rom 2:4; 11:22; Eph 2:7; Col 3:12), its designation as a "fruit of the Spirit" (Gal 5:22), and the fact that Paul expressly stated that man does not naturally possess this attribute (Rom 3:12; Ps 13:3 [LXX]). God's "kindness" includes his generosity and goodness, especially toward humanity and for humanity's benefit (cf. Rom 2:4). The term rendered "love" is *philanthrōpia*, from which the English word "philanthropy' is derived. It specifically denotes God's "love for mankind." The combination of such infinite "kindness" and "love for mankind" facilitates our understanding of "the grace of God . . . that brings salvation to all men" (2:11).[7] The purpose of the manifestation of God's kindness and love was to bring salvation; therefore God is referred to as "our Savior" (see comments on 1:3).

3:5 Paul's assertion, "he saved us," in v. 5 constitutes the main verb in this lengthy sentence (vv. 4-7). It is the fact of God's saving action in Jesus Christ that is amplified and explained by each additional clause and phrase. Paul left absolutely no doubt concerning the basis of human salvation. His explanation is presented in the form of a contrast that is indicated by the use of the strong adversative "but," *alla*. The contrast is between humankind's attempts to achieve salvation through their own effort and salvation as a result of God's mercy. Paul stated: "He saved us, not because of righteous things we had done, *but* because of his mercy" (author's emphasis). The use of the negative "not" (*ouk*) at the beginning of the clause serves to heighten the contrast indicated by the adversative "but" (*alla*), as does the explicit use of the personal pronouns "we" ("we had done") and "his" ("his mercy"). The phrase rendered "because of

---

204, "hymn"; J. N. D. Kelly, *A Commentary on the Pastoral Epistles* (Peabody, Mass.: Hendrickson, 1960), 254, "hymn or liturgical piece connected with baptism"; A. T. Hanson, *The Pastoral Letters* (Cambridge: University Press, 1966), 120, "an extract from a baptismal liturgy." G. D. Fee (*1 and 2 Timothy, Titus* [Peabody, Mass.: Hendrickson, 1988], 203) states: "However, despite the exalted nature of its prose, it altogether lacks the poetic elements of a hymn. More likely this is an early creedal formulation that presents Pauline soteriology (the doctrine of salvation) in a highly condensed form."

[7] The compound usage of ἡ χρηστότης καὶ ἡ φιλάνθρωπία is not uncommon in Hellenistic Greek; cf. *BAGD*, 866; *TDNT* 9, 107-12, 489-91. Understood as a compound and therefore as a single concept in this context (note the singular verb form ἐπεφάνη), Paul may have employed this compound as corresponding to and defining the concept of "the grace of God" (2:11). In this sense the terms offer a more concentrated understanding of the abstract notion of "the grace of God" by indicating God's "attitudes" in bestowing his grace.

righteous things" (*ek ergōv tōn en dikaiosynē*) appears to be equivalent to Paul's more familiar phrase "works of the law" (*ek ergōn nomou*). Neither "the works of the law" (a phrase more specifically applicable to Jews) nor "righteous things we had done" (perhaps a more generally applicable phrase encompassing good moral behavior) will achieve humankind's salvation. Paul could not be more clear in addressing the matter of the basis of salvation: People cannot save themselves! Salvation depends solely and completely on God's grace, displayed in "his mercy," revealed and achieved by his Son, Jesus Christ, and applied to humankind by the Holy Spirit.

The biblical fact that people cannot earn salvation strikes at the very heart of human pride and thus denies people the opportunity of exalting themselves. It is a reflection of this pride that popular conceptions of attaining salvation revolve around "keeping the law," "doing more good deeds than bad deeds," or living up to some (usually undefined) "moral standard."

Theologically, the purpose of the Old Testament law is *not* to show how humans could save themselves. Rather, the purpose of the law is to show humans that they *cannot* save themselves and that their only hope for salvation is in the gracious promise of God (Gal 3:10-27). Humanity's sinful acts are the result of a sinful nature. Salvation cannot be attained by suppressing sinful acts, by doing more righteous acts than sinful acts, or by living a better life in comparison to others. Salvation can only be attained by effectively dealing with humanity's sinful nature. This requires a new birth (John 3:3-8), a transference from being in Adam to being in Christ (Rom 5:12-19; 1 Cor 15:21-22), a new creation (2 Cor 5:17; Gal 6:15). These metaphors for salvation indicate the radical change in heart that can be accomplished by God alone. This strong, clear, and precise statement in Titus 3:5 concerning the basis of salvation reflects a determined effort by Paul to eliminate any confusion in the minds of the Cretan Christians regarding the role of good works in the Christian life. Thus far in this letter, Paul had emphasized the necessity for good works among Christians and toward the pagan world as a demonstration of the true gospel (cf. 1:16; 2:7,14; 3:1,8,14). Good works are the result, not the cause, of the saving, transforming power of God's grace in one's life. Theologically, they have no saving, transforming power. C. H. Spurgeon rightly states: "Works of righteousness are the fruit of salvation, and the root must come before the fruit. The Lord saves His people out of clear, unmixed, undiluted mercy and grace, and for no other reason."[8]

Paul proceeded, "He saved us through the washing of rebirth and renewal by the Holy Spirit." For the sake of clarity, the NIV repeats the

---

[8]C. H. Spurgeon, *The Treasury of the Bible*, vol. 7 (Grand Rapids: Baker, reprint, 1988), 905.

main verb, he "saved" us, although it appears only once in the Greek text. Scholarly discussion on this phrase is plentiful because of a grammatical ambiguity in its compound construction and the precise meaning of the term "washing" (*loutrou*).

The grammatical question centers on the omission of the preposition "through" (*dia*) before the second phrase, "renewal by the Holy Spirit." This omission clearly indicates that the phrase "through the washing of rebirth and renewal by the Holy Spirit" refers to a single event rather than referring to two distinct events. If "through" (*dia*) were used before "renewal," thus rendering "through the washing of rebirth and *through* renewal of the Holy Spirit," it would describe two events instead of one. Simply stated, the text indicates that "washing" is an activity of the Holy Spirit and that this washing involves "rebirth" (*palingenesias*) and "renewal" (*anakainōseōs*). The Greek term for "rebirth" denotes "a new creation" (cf. Matt 19:28), and Paul used this analogy with reference to salvation (2 Cor 5:17). The Greek term for "renewal" refers to an internal change, which in this context may suggest a process begun within the believer from the moment of conversion.[9]

The second question that has sparked scholarly discussion is whether the term "washing" (*loutrou*) refers to the external ordinance of water baptism or to an internal, spiritual baptism.[10] Most commentators who understand this washing as a reference to water baptism (e.g., Huther, Fairbairn, Locke, Kelly, Dibelius and Conzelmann, Barrett) do not suggest that rebirth is based upon participation in water baptism.[11] Any suggestion

---

[9]Because of the omission of διά before ἀνακαινώσεως, this text cannot be used to support an argument that the NT teaches a "baptism in the Spirit" at some time subsequent to the conversion experience. See J. D. G. Dunn, *Baptism in the Holy Spirit*, SBT 15, 2nd series (Naperville, Ill.: Allenson, 1970), 165-67.

[10]This term "washing" (λουτροῦ) is only found again in Eph 5:26 in the context of Paul's analogy of husbands and wives to Christ and the church. Paul described Christ as cleansing the church "by the *washing* of water with the word." Commentators admit the difficulty of this phrase yet generally agree that "washing" (λουτροῦ) is a reference to water baptism. However, G. B. Carid (*Paul's Letters from Prison* [Oxford: University Press, 1976], 89) raises significant questions about accepting this common interpretation. He states: "The phrase *the washing of water with the word* sounds like an allusion to baptism, but it can hardly be intended as a simple reference to the sacrament and the accompanying word spoken over or by the convert. For here it is not individual Christians but the whole church that is cleansed and consecrated. Language reminiscent of baptism is being used to describe something more comprehensive and universal." Cf. also Dunn's discussion of this passage, *Baptism in the Holy Spirit*, 162-65.

[11]However, the comment by E. F. Scott, 176, demonstrates the problem of taking this phrase out of context and thus interpreting "washing" as having a magical effect. He states: "The writer of the Pastorals seems to think of baptism as efficacious by itself. Out of His mercy God has granted us this mysterious rite through which the Spirit works for our renewal. . . . The writer of the Pastorals conceives of the mercy of God as acting immediately

of salvation being attained through the ordinance of baptism is absolutely contrary to Paul's previous statement regarding the futility of works of righteousness as the basis of salvation. Interpreting "washing" as referring to water baptism raises further questions concerning the activity of the Holy Spirit in this external ordinance. The New Testament often describes a close association between Christian conversion, the giving of the Holy Spirit, and the act of water baptism. However, there does not appear to be a set, prescribed New Testament pattern nor a clear definition of interrelationship, especially in Acts.[12] The complicated relationship between water baptism and the Holy Spirit's role in it will remain a theological mystery. Those commentators agreeing that this "washing" is equivalent to water baptism vary in their explanations of how the Holy Spirit relates to the "washing of rebirth and renewal" in this passage.

An alternative interpretation is that the "washing" refers to an internal, spiritual cleansing as denoted by the terms contained in the phrase "rebirth and renewal by the Holy Spirit." If this phrase indicates that it is the Holy Spirit who does the "washing," then the "rebirth and renewal" must be an internal, spiritual cleansing. Therefore, "washing" cannot refer to the external ordinance of water baptism.[13] If washing alludes to baptism in this text, then it is to "Spirit baptism" at conversion and not "water baptism." The amount of scholarly wrestling with this text indicates that there is no simple resolution to these questions. While neither interpretation is without difficulties, the latter alternative is preferred as less problematic.

3:6 Concerning the Holy Spirit, Paul continued, "Whom he poured out on us generously through Jesus Christ our Savior." It is noteworthy that each Person of the Trinity is referred to in this passage and particularly in this text: *God* poured out the *Holy Spirit* through *Jesus Christ*. The verb "poured out" (*execheen*) echoes the description of the coming of the Holy Spirit at Pentecost (cf. Acts 2:17,33 [Joel 2:28]). The additional words "on us" (*eph hēmas*) indicate that the pouring out of the Holy

---

through the sacred rite. In other words, the Church is now on its way towards a magical estimate of baptism, and this is evidenced by the use of what appear to be fixed ritual terms."

[12] Dunn, *Baptism in the Holy Spirit*, 90, observes: "There are few problems so puzzling in NT theology as that posed by Acts in its treatment of conversion-initiation. The relation between the gift of the Spirit and water-baptism is particularly confusing—sometimes sharply contrasted (1:5; 11:16), sometimes quite unconnected (2:4; 8:1f.; 18:25), sometimes in natural sequence (2:28; 19:5f.), sometimes the other way about (9:17[?]; 10:44-48)." Cf. J. Polhill, *Acts*, NAC (Nashville: Broadman, 1992), 217-18.

[13] This position is best stated by D. E. Hiebert, *Titus*, EBC vol. 11, ed. F. E. Gaebelein (Grand Rapids: Zondervan, 1978), 445. Also cf. Fee, 204-5, who concludes "that washing probably alludes to baptism but is in fact a metaphor for spiritual cleansing and not a synonym for baptism itself, the emphasis in the entire phrase being on the cleansing, regenerative work of the Holy Spirit.

Spirit is not limited to the historic event at Pentecost but rather is shared by all believers. The descriptive term "generously" suggests that God's pouring out of the Holy Spirit is totally sufficient for the needs of every believer. This provides a contrast with the limited personal role of the Holy Spirit demonstrated in the Old Testament (2 Cor 3:2-6). This generous outpouring of the Holy Spirit is the direct result of the work of "Jesus Christ, our Savior" (cf. John 14:16-17, 26; 16:7-13; Acts 2:33).

3:7 Having referred to "Jesus Christ, our Savior," Paul restated the basis of our salvation with a clause introduced by "so that" (*hina*). The phrase "having been justified by his grace" recalls the main verb of the entire sentence, "he saved us" (v. 5).[14] The use of the term "justified" expresses a favorite Pauline expression for salvation (Rom 3:24; 5:1,9; 1 Cor 6:11; Gal 2:16-17; 3:24). The expression "by his grace" refers to "God's grace," which is the basis of Christian salvation (cf. 2:11; 3:4). The force of the term rendered "so that" (*hina*) is applied to the final phrase, which truly expresses the goal, purpose, or result of our salvation: so "that . . . we might become heirs having the hope of eternal life." New Testament salvation is often expressed in the familial terms of "children" (e.g., John 1:12; Rom 8:16) and "sonship" (Rom 8:14; Gal 4:6; Heb 2:10). The logical extension from "son" to "heir" can be seen throughout the New Testament (cf. Rom 8:17; Gal 4:6-7; Eph 3:6; Heb 6:17-20; Jas 2:5).

The soteriological and eschatological aspects of Christians' being "heirs" is readily apparent in this final phrase. Paul asserted that "he saved us" (v. 5) "so that . . . we might become heirs" (v. 7). Christian salvation results in adoption into God's family, which in turn makes believers "heirs." This is the soteriological aspect. The eschatological aspect of Christians' being "heirs" is understood in the fact that all believers still await their final *future* redemption and the full realization of eternal life. What has been promised by God in Christ to his heirs has not yet been experienced in the fullest measure (Rom 8:23-25). In becoming "heirs" (through salvation), Christians become possessors of a guaranteed future referred to as "the hope of eternal life" (see comments on 1:2).

This outstanding theological statement in 3:3-7 encompasses the gospel in a nutshell. Beginning with humankind's lost condition, Paul summarized the elements of salvation from the perspective of God's work. Each

---

[14]J. R. W. Stott, *The Cross of Christ* (Downers Grove: InterVarsity, 1986), 188. Commenting on Titus 3:5-7, Stott has observed: "Indeed, the great affirmation 'he saved us' is broken down into its component parts, which are 'the washing of rebirth and renewal by the Holy Spirit' on the one hand and being justified by His grace on the other. The justifying work of the Son and the regenerating work of the Spirit cannot be separated. It is for this reason that good works of love follow justification and new birth as their necessary evidence. For salvation, which is never 'by works,' is always 'unto works.'"

Person of the Trinity is presented as working together to achieve human-kind's salvation. Paul left no doubt that salvation is truly God's own work.

3:8 Paul concluded by stating, "This is a trustworthy saying" (*pistos ho logos*). These three Greek words, used in all three Pastoral Epistles (1 Tim 1:15; 3:1; 4:9; 2 Tim 2:11; Titus 3:8) serve to emphasize either what is to be said or what has been said and may indicate Paul's intentional use of creedal, catechetical, hymnic, or liturgical material.[15] Whether this "trustworthy saying" includes all or part of vv. 4-7 is uncertain. However, in the absence of convincing arguments to the contrary and because of the cogent summary of the gospel contained therein, vv. 4-7 probably constitute this "trustworthy saying."

Having made a strong theological statement in vv. 3-7, Paul exhorted Titus, "And I want you to stress these things." Probably, Paul did not intend to limit "these things" to vv. 3-7 but included his instructions from 3:1. Paul desired that Titus "stress [speak confidently of, be insistent on] these things." His similar directive to Titus in 2:15 suggests some sense of urgency as well as the possibility that Titus may have needed encouragement to act and speak firmly and confidently. Paul stated his purpose in directing Titus to "stress these things." It was "so that those who have trusted in God may be careful to devote themselves to doing what is good." Once again Paul connected theological understanding with Christian behavior described as good works (*kalōn ergōn*). Those who have trusted in God (cf. God as "Savior," 1:3; 2:10; 3:4) are "to be careful" (in the sense of "paying close attention") "to devote themselves" to "good works."[16] In so doing, they will be like the One in whom they have trusted. Paul observed, "These things are excellent and profitable for everyone." Good works constitute "these things." Such intrinsically good works will surely be "profitable" or useful to "everyone" (lit. "men," in the sense of *society* in general).

3. Final Warning Concerning False Teaching and Division (3:9-11)

⁹But avoid foolish controversies and genealogies and arguments and quarrels about the law, because these are unprofitable and useless. ¹⁰Warn a divisive person once, and then warn him a second time. After that, have nothing to do with him. ¹¹You may be sure that such a man is warped and sinful; he is self-condemned.

3:9 Having offered an eloquent theological summary of the gospel and its inherent motivation to profitable good works, Paul again warned

---

[15]For a thorough study of this formula and the Pastoral sayings it refers to, see G. W. Knight III, *The Faithful Sayings in the Pastoral Letters* (Grand Rapids: Baker, 1979).

[16]In this context the term προΐστασθαι should not be rendered "engage in honourable occupations" as NEB. See Barrett, 144; B. Reicke, TDNT 6:703.

Titus concerning the "unprofitable" works of the false teachers. The adversative conjunction "but" (*de*) marks the contrast between correct theological teaching and its "profitable" results and false teaching and its "unprofitable" results. Paul's warning to "avoid foolish controversies and genealogies and arguments and quarrels about the law, because they are unprofitable and useless" recalls Paul's previous instructions to Titus in 1:10-11,13-16.

Some differences appear in Paul's instructions to Titus concerning dealing with false teachers in 1:10-16 and those instructions described in 3:9-11.[17] In the first chapter Titus was exhorted to "rebuke them sharply," with the purpose of correcting and restoring them to "sound doctrine." This heresy of the Judaizers clearly threatened the very heart of the gospel, the true nature of salvation itself. However, in this present warning Titus was to "avoid" divisive discussions or debates. He was to have nothing to do with them if restoration failed after a second warning. Although the issues described appear to be more peripheral and esoteric in 3:9, they certainly suggest a Jewish perspective and mind-set. Whether Paul's description of these issues in 3:9-11 is a direct amplification of the false teaching in 1:10-16 is uncertain. Even if these errors are less significant in terms of diluting the central issue of salvation, Paul recognized the long-range damage and division within the church resulting from such controversies. He specifically instructed Titus on a procedure for handling such matters, making it clear that such behavior would not be tolerated. Paul evidently prescribed different action for different problems (cf. 2 Tim 2:24-26).

The verbal similarities with 1 Tim 1:4 (genealogies), 1 Tim 6:4 (controversies and quarrels), 2 Tim 2:16 (avoid), and 2 Tim 2:23 (foolish and stupid arguments) all occur in the context of dealing with false teaching. This suggests that similar, if not identical, false doctrines were common during this period. The reference to "the law" (i.e., the Mosaic law) establishes the Jewish nature of the false teaching (see comments on 1:10,14-16). These "foolish" matters concerning the minutia of the Mosaic law and its Jewish interpretations were divisive (producing "arguments and quarrels") and were "unprofitable" and "useless" ("worthless," author's translation). P. Fairbairn best describes the false teaching as "utterly wanting in the practical element which so remarkably characterizes the true doctrine of the gospel."[18]

3:10 Concerning those persons who promote false teaching, Paul commanded that Titus "warn a divisive person once, and then warn him a

---

[17]See perceptive comments by J. Quinn, *The Letter to Titus*, AB 35 (New York: Doubleday, 1990), 244.

[18]P. Fairbairn, *Commentary on the Pastoral Epistles* (1874; reprint, Grand Rapids: Zondervan, 1956), 301.

second time. After that, have nothing to do with him." Paul described a false teacher as a "divisive person" (*hairetikon*). The terms *heresy* and *heretic* are derived from this Greek word. Although this adjective appears only here in the New Testament, the noun form *hairesis* refers to sects within Judaism (Acts 5:17; 15:5; 24:5,14; 28:22) and factions or parties within the church (1 Cor 11:19). Paul even included "factions" as one of "the deeds of the flesh" (Gal 5:20). While Paul stood squarely against false teaching (1:13; 2:15), his use of the term "divisive" indicates the destructive nature of those promoting error among believers (cf. 1:11). Divisions within the church result in believers who are confused, frustrated, angry, and hurt. They become ineffective in ministering to one another and to a lost world in desperate need of the gospel of Jesus Christ and the "good works" characteristic of genuine Christians. Reminiscent of Jesus' teaching (Matt 18:15-17), Paul required personal confrontation characterized by patience (i.e., two warnings).[19] If this failed, Paul allowed no hesitation in "having nothing to do with him" (lit. "reject" him). Hiebert aptly sums up the reasonableness of this rejection by stating, "Further efforts would not be a good stewardship of his time and energies and would give the offender an undeserved sense of importance."[20]

3:11 Paul concluded, "You may be sure that such a man is warped and sinful; he is self-condemned." Because the "factious man" refused to change, Titus could "be sure" (lit. "knowing," *eidos*) of three things concerning this person: First, he was "warped." This term renders the verb *ekstrephō*, used here in the perfect tense, passive mood. Literally, it means *he has been* (perfect passive) *and remains off the track*. Second, he was "sinful," literally "he continues to sin" (*hamartanei*, present tense). And finally, because he willfully continued in his sin, "he is self-condemned." Paul's use of the rare term "self-condemned" (*autokatakritos*) suggests that having refused correction, the factious person actually participates in his own condemnation since he is without excuse.

Summary. The significance of refuting false teaching in this letter is indicated by Paul's direct attack on factious men at the beginning of the letter (1:10ff.) and now at its conclusion (3:9-11). His outstanding theological statements (1:1-4; 2:11-15; 3:3-7) provide the "sound doctrine" that motivates believers to "good works" and makes the gospel "attractive" to a lost world. In contrast, the false teachers with their erroneous teaching motivate their followers to works that in essence "deny" a true knowledge of God (1:16) and destroy the doctrinal unity of the church.

---

[19]Cf. W. Lock, *The Pastoral Epistles*, ICC (Edinburgh: T & T Clark, 1924), 157, on Jewish practice of warning offensive teachers.

[20]Hiebert, *Titus*, 448.

When the church cannot agree on the essentials of Christianity and is characterized by conflict and divisions, it is displeasing to God and ineffective to a lost world.

─────────────── SECTION OUTLINE ───────────────

V. PERSONAL DIRECTIONS AND CLOSING SALUTATIONS (3:12-15)

─────────── **V. PERSONAL DIRECTIONS AND CLOSING** ───────────
SALUTATIONS (3:12-15)

[12] As soon as I send Artemas or Tychicus to you, do your best to come to me at Nicopolis, because I have decided to winter there. [13] Do everything you can to help Zenas the lawyer and Apollos on their way and see that they have everything they need. [14] Our people must learn to devote themselves to doing what is good, in order that they may provide for daily necessities and not live unproductive lives.

[15] Everyone with me sends you greetings. Greet those who love us in the faith.

Grace be with you all.

3:12 In accordance with his usual custom, Paul ended this letter with some personal directions, comments, and greetings. He first indicated future plans concerning both Titus and himself, stating: "As soon as I send Artemas or Tychicus to you, do your best to come to me at Nicopolis, because I have decided to winter there." Although Paul was still undecided about whether to send Artemas or Tychicus to Titus in Crete, he was planning for Titus to join him in Nicopolis for the winter months. This is the only reference to Artemas in the New Testament. It is likely that Tychicus referred to Paul's traveling companion (Acts 20:4), "dear brother and faithful servant in the Lord" (cf. Eph 6:21; Col 4:7), and his personal representative to churches (2 Tim 4:12). Either Artemas or Tychicus would be sent to Titus (*pros se*) presumably for the purpose of taking his place in Crete. Upon his replacement's arrival, Titus was directed to "do your best [i.e., "make every effort," NASB] to come to me at Nicopolis." Although Nicopolis ("city of victory") was not an uncommon city name in the ancient world, Paul probably referred to the Nicopolis in Epirus located on the Ambraciot Gulf of the Adriatic Sea. The geographical location of this Nicopolis fits well as a place to "winter" and would be a natural starting point for Titus's subsequent trip to Dalmatia (2 Tim. 4:10). Paul himself had not yet reached Nicopolis as indicated by his use of "there" (*ekei*). His assertion "I have decided to winter there" reveals that he was a free man, not imprisoned as he wrote. Concerning Paul's intention to winter in Nicopolis, Barrett observes: "It would be natural for Paul to confine his longer journeys to the summer, and to use the winter to consolidate work in an important centre; but it must be admitted that we have no definite evidence to prove that this was his regular practice, and 2 Cor 11:25f. suggests that he took risks."[1]

3:13 If Zenas and Apollos were presently on Crete (as seems likely), they probably delivered this letter to Titus. This is the only reference to Zenas in the New Testament; however, the additional description "the lawyer" reveals a common Pauline literary trait (cf. "Luke, the doctor," Col 4:14; also Rom 16:23; 2 Tim 4:14). The term "lawyer" (*nomikon*) in this context indicates that Zenas was either an expert in Jewish law (e.g., Matt 22:35; Luke 7:30) or perhaps a Roman civil jurist. Undoubtedly, Apollos was the converted Alexandrian Jew known from Acts 18–19 and 1 Corinthians. Paul instructed Titus, "Do everything you can to help Zenas the lawyer and Apollos on their way." Using the same Greek verb *propempō* ("help send forward," author's translation), this appeal for Christian aid along the journey is found in Acts 15:3; 21:5; Rom 15:24; 1 Cor 16:6,11; 2 Cor 1:16; and 3 John 6. Titus was also to "see that they have everything they need." Supplying the needs of those who traveled from their homes to proclaim the gospel was a reasonable and evidently honored expectation among Christians. Even though Paul specifically placed the obligation to help Zenas and Apollos upon Titus ("do everything *you* can to help," author's emphasis), his example of this good work should be a lesson to other Cretan Christians.

3:14 Paul continued, "Our people must learn to devote themselves to doing what is good, in order that they may provide for daily necessities and not live unproductive lives." In v. 14 the Greek phrase rendered "doing what is good" ("doing good works," *kalōn ergōn proistasthai*) is identical to Paul's insistence in v. 8 that Christians "be careful to devote themselves to doing *what is good*" (i.e., *kalōn ergōn proistasthai*). This particular opportunity to help Zenas and Apollos would be a concrete example of at least one kind of good work. The final phrase in this sentence, "in order that they may provide for daily necessities and not live unproductive lives," applies to their assisting others with pressing needs. "Unproductive" is literally "unfruitful."

3:15 Paul frequently extended greetings from himself and those Christians with him to recipients of his letters, "Everyone with me sends you greetings" (cf. 1 Cor 16:19-21; 2 Cor 13:12; Phil 4:22; 2 Tim 4:21). His concluding greeting, "Greet those who love us in the faith," may suggest Paul's deliberate exclusion of those persons who resisted his apostolic teaching (i.e., those who obviously do *not* love us in the faith). The phrase "in the faith" is literally "in faith" (*en pistei*). It may mean *in the faith*, thus referring to a common belief, or it may simply mean *faithfully*.

---

[1]C. K. Barrett, *The Pastoral Epistles* (Oxford: Clarendon, 1963), 147.

The closing benediction, "Grace be with you all," is a prayer for God's grace to be realized in each believer's life. The use of the plural "you" in the phrase "you all" suggests that although this letter was designated for Titus (1:4), Paul expected it to be shared with the entire Cretan church.

Selected Subject Index[1]

---

[1]Indexes were prepared by Lanese Dockery.

Person Index

Scripture Index